# LITERATURE FROM THE IRISH LITERARY REVIVAL

## An Anthology

Edited by

## Vernon L. Ingraham

UNIVERSITY
PRESS OF
AMERICA

Copyright © 1982 by

**University Press of America, Inc.**

P.O. Box 19101, Washington, D.C. 20036

ISBN (Perfect): 0-8191-2080-4
ISBN    (Cloth): 0-8191-2079-0

Library of Congress Catalog Card Number: 81-40528

Acknowledgements: Thanks are gratefully offered to the following publishers and proprietors of copyright for permission to reprint material included in this volume:

The Devin-Adair Company for "The Ploughing of the Leaca," from The Wager and Other Stories, by Daniel Corkery, copyright 1950 by the Devin-Adair Co., renewed 1978. For "The Tent," from The Stories of Liam O'Flaherty, by Liam O'Flaherty, copyright 1956 by the Devin-Adair Co. For four poems from Collected Poems of Gogarty, by Oliver St. John Gogarty: "To the Maids Not to Walk in the Wind," "Ringsend," "Death May Be Very Gentle," and "Golden Stockings," copyright 1954 by Oliver St. John Gogarty.

The Macmillan Publishing Co., Inc. for "The Threepenny Piece" by James Stephens from Here Are Ladies, copyright 1913 by Macmillan Publishing Co., Inc., renewed 1941 by James Stephens. For "A Glass of Beer," "Nora Criona," and "O'Bruadair," by James Stephens, copyright 1912, 1918 by Macmillan Publishing Co., Inc., renewed 1940, 1946 by James Stephens. For "Cathleen ni Houlihan," copyright 1934, 1952 by Macmillan Publishing Co., Inc. For "No Second Troy," "September 1913," "The Magi," "The Fisherman," "Two Songs of a Fool," "Easter 1916," "The Second Coming," "Sailing to Byzantium,". "Two Songs from a Play," "Byzantium," "After Long Silence," "Crazy Jane Talks with the Bishop," "Crazy Jane on the Mountain," "I Am of Ireland," "Lapis Lazuli," "The Circus Animals' Desertion," and "Under Ben Bulben," reprinted with permission of Macmillan Publishing Co., Inc. from Collected Poems by William Butler Yeats, copyright 1912, 1916, 1919, 1924, 1928, 1933 by Bertha Georgie Yeats. Copyright 1940 by Georgie Yeats, renewed 1968 by Bertha Georgie Yeats, Michael Butler Yeats and Anne Yeats. For "The Stolen Child," "The Lake Isle of Innisfree," "To Ireland in the Coming Times," "The Host of the Air," "The Song of Wandering Aengus," and "Adam's Curse," reprinted from Collected Poems of William Butler Yeats (New York: Macmillan, 1956). For "To the Four Courts, Please," reprinted from Collected Poems by James Stephens (New York: Macmillan, 1954).

A D Peters and Co., Ltd. Writers' Agents for "Prayer for the Speedy End of Three Great Misfortunes," and "A Grey Eye Weeping," from The Fountain of Magic by Frank O'Connor, reprinted by permission of A D Peters and Co., Ltd.

Russell and Volkening, Inc. for "Carrowmore," "The Nuts of Knowledge," "A New Theme," "In Connemara,"

"Tragedy," "Momentary," and "Exiles," from The Collected
Poems of "AE" by George Russell, reprinted by permission
of Russell and Volkening as agents for the author, copyright 1913 by George Russell.

A. B. Rye, for self and Co-Trustees, for "A Dublin Ballad," by Sir Arnold Bax, written under the name of
Dermot O'Byrne.

Simon Campbell, executor for Joseph Campbell, for
"Chesspieces," and "Ad Limina," by Joseph Campbell.

Mrs. Frances Sommerville for Dr. Michael Solomons, copyright holder, for "The Others," "Nelson Street," "A
Piper," and "The Land War," by Seumas O'Sullivan.

Curtis Brown, Ltd. for "Fugue," by Sean O'Faolain, from
The Finest Short Stories of Sean O'Faolain, pub. by
Little, Brown and Company, May 9, 1951, copyright 1951
by Sean O'Faolain; copyright renewed. Reprinted by
permission of Curtis Brown, Ltd.

St. Martin's Press, Inc. for The Plough and the Stars
by Sean O'Casey; St. Martin's Press, Inc.; Macmillan
and Co., Ltd.

Colin Smythe Limited, Publishers, for "Spreading the
News," by Lady Augusta Gregory, by permission of Colin
Smythe, Ltd., and the Lady Gregory Estate.

Random House, Inc. for "The Passing of the Shee," and
"Beg-Innish," by John Millington Synge, from The Complete Works of John M. Synge, and "Riders to the Sea,"
by John Millington Synge, from The Complete Works of
John M. Synge, copyright 1909 and renewed 1937 by Edward Synge and Francis Edmund Stephens. Reprinted by
permission of Random House, Inc.

Viking Penquin, Inc. for "Tilly," "She Weeps Over
Rahoon," and "Ecce Puer," by James Joyce, from The
Portable James Joyce, copyright 1946, 1947, renewed
1974, 1975 by The Viking Press, Inc.. Reprinted by
permission of Viking Penquin, Inc.. Also, "Ivy Day in
the Committee Room," and "The Dead," from Dubliners by
James Joyce. Copyright 1967 by The Estate of James
Joyce. Reprinted by permission of Viking Penquin, Inc.

It would be remiss on my part to omit indebtedness to
the following: Mrs. Jean Morgan for a cheerful attention to the typing of the manuscript; Betsey Converse
and Mary Gillard, for help in proof-reading; Jeanne

Aber, in charge of the Irish collection at Boston College, and staff at Bapst Library at Boston College for their assistance in my research; and, my good friend Earl Dias who kindly scrutinized the Introduction.

N. B. Arduous attempts to locate the copyright owners of works by Padraic Colum, and F. R. Higgins, have proved unsuccessful. Inclusion of the poems by the foregoing authors in no way implies any desire to violate any rights, or avoid payment of permission fees.

Dedicated to
the enduring memory
of
my mother,
my father,
and
my brother

# Table of Contents

# INTRODUCTION

It is impossible to deal with literature from the Irish Literary Revival (1889-1932) without some knowledge of the intricate skeins that make up the political and cultural fabric of those years. Any literate person is aware that Ireland's history has been a troubled one for centuries. The first conquest of Ireland by England, under Henry II in 1171, was only the beginning of a series of agonies that were to beset Ireland to the present day. The issue of Irish subjugation by the English is an inflammatory one, and it is altogether too easy to treat an extremely complicated situation simplistically.

Between 1171 and the late 1600s the English were in a constant struggle to control the whole of Ireland. They would buy the loyalty of Irish chiefs, or enter into conflict to gain ground. On occasion they held the entire island, while at other times they controlled only part of it. By the 1700s the English believed they had finally gained supremacy. There had been a period of religious persecution which was heightened in 1603, when Charles Blount, lord deputy of Ireland, moved Irish Catholics from northern Ulster province and replaced them with Scottish Presbyterians. It is from this time that northern Ireland became a Protestant stronghold. The campaign of Oliver Cromwell in 1649 involved a massive slaughtering of Irish Catholics, to be followed by Cromwell's policy of "confiscation and plantation," which brought to the island the Protestant English landlord. Later in the century, under the reign of William and Mary, more land was seized and given to Scottish and English Protestants. Now, beyond the physical ravages of war, and the religious persecution, was to be added financial hardship, because those Irish Catholics who were allowed to remain on the land and cultivate it had to pay exorbitant rents for the privilege, while their landlords often resided in England.

Although it is true that there clearly existed a class given preferential treatment, it is also true that problems ensued which embittered this "privileged" class. Crippling restrictions on Irish trade, the source of much of their income, moved many of those who profited from their religious and cultural background to find themselves increasingly in opposition to the crown. Eventually, resistance movements struggled into being, and a history of divisiveness characterized by internecine warfare took place. The first movement

which might claim our attention was that under the
leadership of Theobald Wolfe Tone (1763-1798), a young
Protestant lawyer from Dublin. This movement, known as
the Society of United Irishmen, had as its objectives:
parliamentary and agrarian reform; representation of
both Protestants and Catholics to the national parliament; Catholic relief from discriminatory law; and the
abolition of compulsory tithes to the church. Parliament declared the Society illegal, and it was forced to
move underground, with the result that it became a mili-
tant organization. The peasantry caught the temper of
the Society and engaged in armed uprisings, whereupon
the English instituted the Insurrection Act (1796),
which brought about severe repression. Tone was captured in 1798, and in that year he committed suicide.
What threatened to become a national uprising was
brought to a speedy end.

In 1801, the English Parliament passed the Act of
Union, formally making Ireland a part of the United
Kingdom. There was immediate demand for repeal, and a
movement headed by Daniel O'Connell (1775-1847) was especially vigorous for a brief period. English pressure
finally succeeded, and O'Connell backed down--although
Ireland was never to accept the notion of union. An
earlier movement, the Catholic Association, also under
the leadership of O'Connell, had been responsible for
the English Parliament enacting a bill for Catholic
emancipation which was a major step in the attempt to
abolish religious discrimination, although restrictive
property-qualification laws for voting in Ireland were
passed at the same time.

Ireland's economic difficulties were not lessen-
ing, and the Irish land question eventually became an
issue in England. Prime Minister Gladstone (1809-1898)
recognized the injustice of the land system and was
instrumental in bringing about some relief through
legislation enacted in 1870; but it fell far short of
remedying the evils that existed.

From this condition of national crisis there
evolved a number of nationalist movements. Doubtless,
the best known of these was headed by the Fenian brotherhood, founded simultaneously in America, by Irish im-
migrants, and in Dublin in 1858. The name of the brotherhood derived from the heroic warriors of ancient Ireland who were known as the Fianna. The brotherhood was
responsible for several violent, but abortive, uprisings. After an unsuccessful rebellion in 1868, the
brotherhood dissolved. It is the fervor of this group

xi

which inspired an influential secret society known as the Irish Republican Brotherhood to persist up into the early part of the twentieth century; and, so imaginatively captivating was the source of the name, that all future Irish nationalists were to be called Fenians.

Entwined with these movements was a political party known as the Irish Home Rule Party, which envisioned a moderate form of Irish independence. In the late 1870s Charles Stewart Parnell, a Protestant landowner and aristocrat, assumed leadership of the party. Parnell was an amazingly charismatic and able politician who so captured the devotion of the people that they soon looked to him as a messianic figure. Further attempts by Gladstone to rectify injustices of the past came too late. The Irish now wanted complete political independence. Parnell had been imprisoned in 1881, and Gladstone realized that he would have to work with Parnell if further violence was to be avoided. Gladstone was effective in getting Parnell released from prison after Parnell had promised to help pacify Ireland. Gladstone, in return, assured Parnell he would assist him in obtaining home rule for Ireland. But, violent outbreaks of terrorism persisted, and Gladstone's home-rule bill of 1886 was defeated.

Between a coercive act passed by Parliament in 1892 and a divorce suit scandal involving Parnell as correspondent, which resulted in his political ruin and subsequent untimely death in 1891, Ireland found itself leaderless and hopelessly divided. For a while, the Irish cause was profoundly weakened in the political field.

Early in the 1890s, a new kind of movement evolved. It was dedicated to the safeguarding of Ireland's national identity. An integral part of this movement was the Gaelic League, which was founded in 1893 and was led by an Anglo-Irish Protestant named Douglas Hyde (1860-1949). The Gaelic League promoted Irish as the national language and sought to educate the citizenry in Ireland's early culture, its ancient legends, and Celtic mythology. Although there was no political motivation to this movement, it could not help but abet the strivings of nationalism.

Simultaneous with the activity of the Gaelic League there arose an insistent clamor from the working people of Ireland who had felt oppressed by their employers for a long period of time. James Larkin (1876-1947) organized the Irish Transport and General Workers'

Union in 1908. His influence was so strongly felt that the employers retaliated by forming the Federated Employers of Dublin as a means to breaking strike action. In October, 1913, the Irish Citizen Army, a paramilitary branch of Larkin's union, was formed to protect workers from assault by the police. This group was to play an important role in the years ahead.

In 1893, Gladstone's second home-rule bill was defeated. Nationalist fervor was again on the increase. The Irish Citizen Army reorganized after the 1913 strike-lockout and saw that its commitment to the working class was tied to independence from England, without which their socialistic goals could not be achieved. In this same year was formed another paramilitary organization, the Irish Volunteers. Some of the notable figures associated with this group were Sir Roger Casement (1864-1916), the poet Padraic Pearse (1879-1916), and Eamon de Valera (1882-1975). One further nationalist group, previously mentioned, was the long-established secret Irish Republican Brotherhood, which had its origins in the nineteenth-century Fenian movement.

One of the most dramatic incidents in modern Irish history took place through an unlikely alliance of the three aforementioned organizations when they concurred in their belief that England had to be made aware, once and for all, of the Irish demand for independence. The Easter Rebellion of 1916 was a virtually suicidal uprising, but it did constitute a turning point in Irish-English relations. On this fateful day, without arms which had been expected from Germany, and confusion within their own ranks, a body of some 1,500 zealots marched out to take the English garrison in Dublin. The English were taken off guard, and it initially appeared as if the rebels might succeed. They occupied some important buildings in the center of Dublin and raised the flag of the republic over the General Post Office. Padraic Pearse appeared and read a proclamation of independence. But the general public, characteristic of their behavior in the past, failed to respond, and the English soon gained control of the situation. It was, in short, a debacle. The fervor of a few had led to a slaughter, but they had made their hatred of the English manifest. Fifteen of the rebel leaders were executed under drumhead courts-martial. The summary manner of the deaths created a wave of revulsion among people who had, up to this time, been fairly unmoved. The need to deal with Irish independence became obvious. Eamon de Valera and the remaining leaders were released in a general amnesty.

As a result of the Rebellion, a group which had first appeared early during the cultural revival, Sinn Fein ("we ourselves"), became a powerful force in Ireland. Arthur Griffith (1872-1922), its leader, had as his goal Irish economic independence as a corollary to the Gaelic League's desire for cultural autonomy. In the general election of 1918, the Sinn Fein easily won a majority of the Irish seats in Parliament. Capitalizing on their strength, they refused to be seated and formed an independent parliament of Ireland with Eamon de Valera as president. Parliament outlawed what they conceived of as an illegal body, but this did not intimidate the rebels. The Sinn Fein employed covert attacks on the Royal Irish Constabulary, and England's response was to attempt to destroy the upstart government. Troops were sent to the island, amongst which were the so-called Black and Tans, named after their uniforms which were half-army and half-police. This body became known for their savage raids throughout Ireland. The Irish Republican Army arose from the dispersed members of earlier paramilitary units to combat this new menace.

The Anglo-Irish War (1919-1921) awakened the general populace of England to the severity of the situation, and Parliament was finally moved to dealing with the independent parliament of Ireland. A meeting took place between the leaders of the two bodies. In 1920 the English Parliament had passed an act that gave limited self-government to a divided Ireland. The southern section of Ireland, consisting of twenty-six counties, and the northern six counties of the province of Ulster were each to form parliaments subservient to the English Parliament. That act only intensified the existing problems. A meeting between the leaders of the two parliaments, mentioned before, in July 1921, led to a treaty which created further difficulties. The northern counties became officially known as Northern Ireland and retained allegiance to England. The southern counties became the Irish Free State, its status being that of a dominion within the Commonwealth. A major division sprang into being between those who advocated an Irish Republic composed of all of Ireland and the Free Staters who supported the division. Irishman fought against Irishman, and the country was once again plunged into pitiful disarray until de Valera and the Irish Republican Army saw the hopelessness of their cause and conceded to the Free Staters by recognizing that the only sane course was to accept a constitutional approach to government. Eamon de Valera broke with the Sinn Fein and formed his own party,

Fianna Fail, and, by 1932 his party was in power and would retain power for the following sixteen years. In 1937, de Valera became prime minister, and the Irish Free State prepared a new constitution establishing itself as Eire, a sovereign nation. Eventually, all ties with England were broken in 1949, when Eire became the fully independent Republic of Ireland. But, as is too-well-known, the tortured history was not to cease, for violence continues to the present day in Northern Ireland.

. . .

Take the foregoing as a catalytic agent for artistry, and it is almost inevitable that a phenomenon such as the Irish Literary Revival should arise out of the fractious tensions of that tragic history. Yeats and Joyce tower; Olympian figures, they stride amidst the powerful forces surrounding them, working their magic out of the turmoil that encompassed them. One Protestant, the other Catholic, they rise above the mundane through the power of true art. With these giants in their presence, the wonder is that so many of their contemporaries were able to command the deserved acclaim which they achieved. The human condition has historically been one of unrest. However much we long for serenity, the truth is that greatness is often born of anguish.

In 1889, William Butler Yeats' collection of long poems in The Wanderings of Oisin and Other Poems heralded the advent of a period second to none in the history of modern literature. Interestingly enough, it is neither poetry, for which Yeats is best known, nor the novel, for which Joyce is best known, but rather the genre of drama which was most influential in the cultural movement that must be associated with the avowed desire of the Gaelic League. The Irish Literary Theatre was a society formed in 1899 by Yeats and Lady Augusta Gregory. It was reorganized as the National Theatre Society, and, later, in 1904, it became the Abbey Theatre. Yeats was a major contributor, writing several nationalistic verse dramas and the prose drama Cathleen ni Houlihan. Lady Gregory endeavored to capture the rhythms of peasant speech, and John Millington Synge also turned his gifts to a recreation of folk patterns that existed--most notably the stark lives lived by the inhabitants of the Aran Islands (off the west coast of Ireland). Other names associated with the early theatrical movement were those of Edward Martyn and George Moore.

W.G. Fay and his brother, Frank, were important
additions when they joined the Irish Literary Theatre
in 1902. The brothers were extremely successful in
developing an accomplished acting company through their
coaching. So rapidly did the degree of acting ability
rise that by 1903 the company, now called the Irish
National Theatre Society, performed abroad, appearing
with success at Queen's Gate Hall, South Kensington.

It was in 1903 that John Millington Synge, whom
many critics consider the leading dramatic genius of
the society, joined the organization. Synge had been
encouraged by Yeats to go to the Aran Islands and im-
merse himself in the unspoiled ambience of a people
close to the soil, whose language and lives were almost
elemental. A work of Synge's entitled In the Shadow
of the Glen was produced in 1903. Without intending to
be abrasive, he nevertheless managed to create works
that offended the sensibilities of vast numbers of the
audience. The rioting which took place when The Play-
boy of the Western World was first presented is sufficient evidence.

So widespread was the reputation of the company
that they received considerable international attention,
and, in 1904, they appeared at the London Royalty Theatre, where Synge's tragic work, Riders to the Sea,
was immediately recognized as a masterpiece of theater.
It is in this year that an English benefactress, Miss
A.E.F. Horniman, lent her support to the company,
having been impressed by the South Kensington perfor-
mance of the year before. Although the only member of
the group with whom she could seemingly get on was
Yeats, she nevertheless generously purchased the lease
of the old Mechanics' Institute on Abbey Street in
Dublin, thereby providing a home for the company. The
world famous Abbey Theatre developed from this gift.
The theatre opened on December 7, 1904, with the pre-
sentation of Yeats' Cathleen ni Houlihan and On Baile's
Strand, Synge's In the Shadow of the Glen and Lady
Gregory's Spreading the News. The following year the
dramatic organization became known as the Irish National
Theatre Society, Ltd.

During the revolutionary years (1916-1923), the
group did not fare well, though Sean O'Casey joined
them at that time. The theatrical company had weath-
ered much adversity, and, in 1926, when rioting greeted
O'Casey's The Plough and the Stars, it was taken in
stride with the kind of hauteur worthy of an established
institution. Yeats delivered a scathing address to the

unruly audience. After 1939, the theatre suffered a
decline, and on the night of July 17, 1951, the famous
Abbey Theatre was destroyed by fire.

Though it is true that drama lay at the center of
the Irish Literary Revival, other genres were impres-
sively represented in that rich period. The short
story has always flourished in Irish literature, and
this era was to be no exception. The stories contained
in this volume attest to the mastery of those who made
significant contributions.

The novel may be seen as the weakest offering,
with the exception of the works by James Joyce. Some
of the names that should be noted in the area of the
novel are: George Moore, James Stephens, Seumas
O'Kelly, Liam O'Flaherty, Daniel Figgis, and Joseph
O'Neill.

As other novelists suffered from the presence of
Joyce, so did other poets suffer from the presence of
Yeats. Those unfamiliar with the age covered by this
work may be pleasantly surprised by the competency of
such poets as Joseph Campbell, Seumas O'Sullivan,
Thomas MacDonagh, and F. R. Higgins. More familiar
names in the area of poetry are: A.E. (George Russell),
Oliver St. John Gogarty, and Padraic Colum.

Any collection of work of this nature is subject
to criticism. Individual bias is almost bound to creep
in. There has been an attempt to be faithful to the
times; to present the multi-faceted configuration of a
period and a people caught in a seeming web of destiny
that is not easy to unravel. There will be those who
feel that the wit, so often taken for granted as en-
demic to the Irish, is not sufficiently present. The
wit is there, but it is undercut by the tragedies that
abounded and the deliberate singling out for honor, by
the key spokesmen of the Irish Literary Revival, of
those figures of the past--Cuchulain, who slew his only
son, in ignorance, and Deirdre of the Sorrows.

Vernon L. Ingraham
(Lower Waterford, Vt., 1981)

# THE PLOUGHING OF THE LEACA

## by Daniel Corkery

With which shall I begin--man or place? Perhaps I
had better first tell of the man; of him the incident
left so withered that no sooner had I laid eyes on him
than I said: Here is one whose blood at some terrible
moment of his life stood still, stood still and never
afterwards regained its quiet, old-time ebb-and-flow.
A word or two then about the place--a sculped-out
shell in the Kerry mountains, an evil-looking place,
green-glaring like a sea when a storm has passed. To
connect man and place together, even as they worked
one with the other to bring the tragedy about, ought
not then to be so difficult.

I had gone into those desolate treeless hills
searching after the traces of an old-time Gaelic family that once were lords of them. But in this moun-
tainy glen I forgot my purpose almost as soon as I entered it.

In that round-ended valley--they call such a valley
a coom--there was but one farmhouse, and Considine was
the name of the householder--Shawn Considine, the man
whose features were white with despair; his haggard
appearance reminded me of what one so often sees in
war-ravaged Munster--a ruined castle-wall hanging out
above the woods, a grey spectre. He made me welcome,
speaking slowly, as if he was not used to such ameni-
ties. At once I began to explain my quest. I soon
stumbled; I felt that his thoughts were far away. I
started again. A daughter of his looked at me--Nora
was her name--looked at me with meaning; I could not
read her look aright. Haphazardly I went through old
family names and recalled old-world incidents; but
with no more success. He then made to speak; I could
catch only broken phrases, repeated again and again.
"In the presence of God." "In the Kingdom of God."
"All gone for ever." "Let them rest in peace"--(I
translate from the Irish). Others, too, there were of
which I could make nothing. Suddenly I went silent.
His eyes had begun to change. They were not becoming
fiery or angry--that would have emboldened me, I would
have blown on his anger; a little passion, even an
outburst of bitter temper would have troubled me but
little if in its sudden revelation I came on some new
fact or even a new name in the broken story of that

1

ruined family. But no; not fiery but cold and terror-
stricken were his eyes becoming. Fear was rising in
them like dank water. I withdrew my gaze, and his
daughter ventured on speech:

"If you speak of the cattle, noble person, or of
the land, or of the new laws, my father will converse
with you; but he is dark about what happened long
ago." Her eyes were even more earnest than her
tongue--they implored the pity of silence.

So much for the man. A word now about the place
where his large but neglected farmhouse stood against
a bluff of rock. To enter that evil-looking green-
mountained glen was like entering the jaws of some
slimy, cold-blooded animal. You felt yourself leaving
the sun, you shrunk together, you hunched yourself as
if to bear an ugly pressure. In the far-back part of
it was what is called in the Irish language a leaca--
a slope of land, a lift of land, a bracket of land
jutting out from the side of a mountain. This leaca,
which the daughter explained was called Leaca-na-
Naomh--the Leaca of the Saints--was very remarkable.
It shone like a gem. It held the sunshine as a field
holds its crop of golden wheat. On three sides it was
pedestalled by the sheerest rock. On the fourth side
it curved up to join the parent mountain-flank. Huge
and high it was, yet height and size took some time to
estimate, for there were mountains all around it.
When you had been looking at it for some time you said
aloud: "That leaca is high!" When you had stared for
a longer time you said: "That leaca is immensely
high--and huge!" Still the most remarkable thing
about it was the way it held the sunshine. When all
the valley had gone into the gloom of twilight--and
this happened in the early afternoon--the leaca was
still at midday. When the valley was dark with night
and the lamps had been long alight in the farmhouse,
the leaca had still the red gleam of sunset on it. It
hung above the misty valley like a velarium--as they
used to call that awning-cloth which hung above the
emperor's seat in the amphitheatre.

"What is it called, do you say?" I asked again.

"Leaca-na-Naomh," she replied.

"Saints used to live on it?"

"The Hermits," she answered, and sighed deeply.

2

Her trouble told me that that leaca had to do with
the fear that was burrowing like a mole in her father's heart. I would test it. Soon afterwards the
old man came by, his eyes on the ground, his lips
moving.

"That leaca," I said, "what do you call it?"

He looked up with a startled expression. He was
very white; he couldn't abide my steady gaze.

"Nora," he cried, raising his voice suddenly and
angrily, "cas isteach iad, cas isteach iad!"[1] He almost roared at the gentle girl.

"Turn in--what?" I said, roughly, "the cattle are
in long ago."

"'Tis right they should," he answered, leaving me.

Yes, this leaca and this man had between them
moulded out a tragedy, as between two hands.

Though the sun had gone still I sat staring at it.
It was far off, but whatever light remained in the sky
had gathered to it. I was wondering at its clear def-
inition among all the vague and misty mountain-shapes
when a voice, quivering with age, high and untuneful,
addressed me:

"'Twould be right for you to see it when there's
snow on it."

"Ah!"

"'Tis blinding!" The voice had changed so much as
his inner vision strengthened that I gazed up quickly
at him. He was a very old man, somewhat fairy-like in
appearance, but he had the eyes of a boy! These eyes
told me he was one who had lived imaginatively. Therefore I almost gripped him lest he should escape; from
him would I learn of Leaca-na-Naomh. Shall I speak of
him as a vassal of the house, or as a tatter of the
family, or as a spall of the rough landscape? He was
native to all three. His homespun was patched with
patches as large and as straight-cut as those you'd
see on a fisherman's sail. He was, clothes and all,

1. Trans. "turn them inside, turn them inside!"

3

the same colour as the aged lichen of the rocks; but his eyes were as fresh as dew.

Gripping him, as I have said, I searched his face, as one searches a poem for a hidden meaning.

"When did it happen, this dreadful thing?" I said.

He was taken off his guard. I could imagine, I could almost feel his mind struggling, summoning up an energy sufficient to express his idea of how as well as when the thing happened. At last he spoke deliberately.

"When the master,"--I knew he meant the house-holder--"was at his best, his swiftest and strongest in health, in riches, in force and spirit." He hammered every word.

"Ah!" I said; and I noticed the night had begun to thicken, fitly I thought, for my mind was already making mad leaps into the darkness of conjecture. He began to speak a more simple language:

"In those days he was without burden or ailment-- unless maybe every little biteen of land between the rocks that he had not as yet brought under the plough was a burden. This, that, yonder, all those fine fields that have gone back again into heather and furze, it was he made them. There's sweat in them! But while he bent over them in the little dark days of November, dropping his sweat, he would raise up his eyes and fix them on the leaca. That would be worth all of them, and worth more than double all of them if it was brought under the plough."

"And why not?" I said.

"Plough the bed of the saints?"

"I had forgotten."

"You are not a Gael of the Gaels maybe?"

"I had forgotten; continue; it grows chilly."

"He had a serving-man; he was a fool; they were common in the country then; they had not been as yet herded into asylums. He was a fool; but a true Gael. That he never forgot; except once."

4

"Continue."

"He had also a sire horse, Griosach he called him, he was so strong, so high and princely."

"A plough horse?"

"He had never been harnessed. He was the master's pride and boast. The people gathered on the hillsides when he rode him to Mass. You looked at the master; you looked at the horse; the horse knew the hillsides were looking at him. He made music with his hoofs, he kept his eyes to himself, he was so proud."

"What of the fool?"

"Have I spoken of the fool?"

"Yes, a true Gael."

"'Tis true, that word. He was as strong as Griosach. He was what no one else was: he was a match for Griosach. The master petted the horse. The horse petted the master. Both of them knew they went well together. But Griosach the sire horse feared Liam Ruadh the fool; and Liam Ruadh the fool feared Griosach the sire horse. For neither had as yet found out that he was stronger than the other. They would play together like two strong boys, equally matched in strength and daring. They would wrestle and throw each other. Then they would leave off; and begin again when they had recovered their breath."

"Yes," I said, "the master, the horse Griosach, the fool Liam--now, the Leaca, the Leaca."

"I have brought in the leaca. It will come in again, now! The master was one day standing at a gap for a long time; there was no one near him. Liam Ruadh came near him. 'It is not lucky to be so silent as that,' he said. The master raised his head and answered:

"'The Leaca for wheat.'

"The fool nearly fell down in a sprawling heap. No one had ever heard of anything like that.

"'No,' he said like a child.

5

"'The Leaca for wheat,' the master said again, as
if there was someone inside him speaking.

"The fool was getting hot and angry.

"'The Leaca for prayer!' he said.

"'The Leaca for wheat,' said the master, a third
time.

"When the fool heard him he gathered himself up and
roared--a loud 'O-oh!' it went around the hills like
sudden thunder; in the little breath he had left he
said: 'The Leaca for prayer!'

"The master went away from him; who could tell what
might have happened?

"The next day the fool was washing a sheep's dis-
eased foot--he had the struggling animal held firm
when the master slipped behind him and whispered in
his ear:

"'The Leaca for wheat.'

"Before the fool could free the animal the master
was gone. He was a wild, swift man that day. He
laughed. It was that self-same night he went into the
shed where Liam slept and stood a moment looking at
the large face of the fool working in his dreams. He
watched him like that a minute. Then he flashed the
lantern quite close into the fool's eyes so as to daz-
zle him, and he cried out harshly,'The Leaca for
wheat,' making his voice appear far off, like a trum-
pet-call, and before the fool could understand where
he was, or whether he was asleep or awake, the light
was gone and the master was gone.

"Day after day the master put the same thought into
the fool's ear. And Liam was becoming sullen and
dark. Then one night long after we were all in our
sleep we heard a wild crash. The fool had gone to the
master's room. He found the door bolted. He put his
shoulder to it. The door went in about the room, and
the arch above it fell in pieces around the fool's
head--all in the still night.

"'Who's there? What is it?' cried the master,
starting up in his bed.

6

"'Griosach for the plough!' said the fool.

"No one could think of Griosach being hitched to a plough. The master gave him no answer. He lay down in his bed and covered his face. The fool went back to his straw. Whenever the master now said 'The Leaca for wheat' the fool would answer 'Griosach for the plough.'

"The tree turns the wind aside, yet the wind at last twists the tree. Like wind and tree, master and fool played against each other, until at last they each of them had spent their force.

"'I will take Griosach and Niamh and plough the leaca,' said the fool; it was a hard November day.

"'As you wish,' said the master. Many a storm finishes with a little sob of wind. Their voices were now like a little wind.

"The next night a pair of smiths were brought into the coom all the way from Aunascawl. The day after that the mountains were ringing with their blows as the ploughing-gear was overhauled. Without rest or laughter or chatter the work went on, for Liam was at their shoulders, and he hardly gave them time to wipe their sweaty hair. One began to sing: ''Tis my grief on Monday now,' but Liam struck him one blow and stretched him. He returned to his work quiet enough after that. We saw the fool's anger rising. We made way for him; and he was going back and forth the whole day long; in the evening his mouth began to froth and his tongue to blab. We drew away from him; wondering what he was thinking of. The master himself began to grow timid; he hadn't a word in him; but he kept looking up at us from under his brow as if he feared we would turn against him. Sure we wouldn't; wasn't he our master--even what he did?

"When the smiths had mounted their horses that night to return to Aunascawl one of them stooped down to the master's ear and whispered: 'Watch him, he's in a fever.'

"'Who?'

"'The fool.' That was a true word.

"Some of us rode down with the smiths to the mouth

7

of the pass, and as we did so snow began to fall silently and thickly. We were glad; we thought it might put back the dreadful business of the ploughing. When we returned towards the house we were talking. But a boy checked us.

"'Whisht!' he said.

"We listened. We crept beneath the thatch of the stables. Within we heard the fool talking to the horses. We knew he was putting his arms around their necks. When he came out, he was quiet and happy-looking. We crouched aside to let him pass. Then we told the master.

"'Go to your beds,' he said, coldly enough.

"We played no cards that night; we sang no songs; we thought it too long until we were in our dark beds. The last thing we thought of was the snow falling, falling, falling on Leaca-na-Naomh and on all the mountains. There was not a stir or a sigh in the house. Everyone feared to hear his own bed creak. And at last we slept.

"What awoke me? I could hear voices whispering. There was fright in them. Before I could distinguish one word from another I felt my neck creeping. I shook myself. I leaped up. I looked out. The light was blinding. The moon was shining on the slopes of new snow. There was none falling now; a light, thin wind was blowing out of the lovely stars.

"Beneath my window I saw five persons standing in a little group, all clutching one another like people standing in a flooded river. They were very still; they would not move even when they whispered. As I wondered to see them so fearfully clutching one another a voice spoke in my room:

"' For God's sake, Stephen, get ready and come down.'

"'Man, what's the matter with ye?'

"'For God's sake come down.'

"'Tell me, tell me!'

"'How can I? Come down!'

8

"I tried to be calm; I went out and made for that little group, putting my hand against my eyes, the new snow was so blinding.

"'Where is the master?' I said.

"'There!' They did not seem to care whether or not I looked at the master.

"He was a little apart; he was clutching a jut of rock as if the land was slipping from his feet. His cowardice made me afraid. I was hard put to control my breath.

"'What are ye, are ye all staring at?' I said.

"'Leaca-na-----'--the voice seemed to come from over a mile away, yet it was the man beside me had spoken.

"I looked. The leaca was a dazzling blaze, it was true, but I had often before seen it as bright and wonderful. I was puzzled.

"'Is it the leaca, ye're all staring--' I began; but several of them silently lifted up a hand and pointed towards it. I could have stared at them instead; whether or not it was the white moonlight that was on them, they looked like men half-frozen, too chilled to speak. But I looked where those outstretched hands silently bade me. Then I, too, was struck dumb and became one of that icy group, for I saw a little white cloud moving across the Leaca, a feathery cloud, and from the heart of it there came every now and then a little flash of fire, a spark. Sometimes, too, the little cloud would grow thin, as if it were scattering away, at which times it was a moving shadow we saw. As I blinked at it I felt my hand groping about to catch something, to catch someone, to make sure of myself; for the appearance of everything, the whiteness, the stillness, and then that moving cloud whiter than everything else, whiter than anything in the world, and so like an angel's wing moving along the leaca, frightened me until I felt like fainting away. To make things worse, straight from the little cloud came down a whisper, a long, thin, clear, silvery cry: 'Griosach! Ho-o-o-oh! Ho-o-o-oh!' a ploughing cry. We did not move; we kept our silence: everyone knew that that cry was going through everyone else as through himself, a stroke of coldness. Then I understood why the master was

9

hanging on to a rock; he must have heard the cry before anyone else. It was terrible, made so thin and
silvery by the distance; and yet it was a cry of joy--
the fool had conquered Griosach!

"I do not know what wild thoughts had begun to come
into my head when one man in the group gasped out
'Now!' and then another, and yet another. Their
voices were breath, not sound. Then they all said
'Ah!' and I understood the fear that had moved their
tongues. I saw the little cloud pause a moment on the
edge of the leaca, almost hang over the edge, and then
begin to draw back. The fool had turned his team on
the verge and was now ploughing up against the hill.

"'O-o-h,' said the master, in the first moment of
relief; it was more like a cry of agony. He looked
round at us with ghastly eyes; and our eyeballs turned
towards his, just as cold and fixed. Again, that silvery cry floated down to us 'Griosach! Ho-o-o-oh!'
And again the stroke of coldness passed through every
one of us. The cry began to come more frequently,
more triumphantly, for now again the little cloud was
ploughing down the slope, and its pace had quickened.
It was making once more for that edge beneath which
was a sheer fall of hundreds of feet.

"Behind us, suddenly, from the direction of the
thatched stables came a loud and high whinny--a call
to a mate. It was so unexpected, and we were all so
rapt up in what was before our eyes, that it shook us,
making us spring from one another. I was the first to
recover.

"'My God,' I said, 'that's Niamh, that's Niamh!'

"The whinny came again; it was Niamh surely.

"'What is he ploughing with, then? What has he
with Griosach?'

"A man came running from the stables; he was trying
to cry out: he could hardly be heard:

"'Griosach and Lugh! Griosach and Lugh!'

"Lugh was another sire horse; and the two sires
would eat each other; they always had ill-will for
each other. The master was staring at us.

"''Tisn't Lugh?' he said, with a gurgle in his

10

voice.

"No one could answer him. We were thinking if the
mare's cry reached the sires their anger would blaze
up and no one could hold them; but why should Liam
have yoked such a team?

"'Hush! hush!' said a woman's voice.

"We at once heard a new cry; it came down from the
leaca:

"'Griosach, Back! Back!' It was almost inaudible,
but we could feel the swiftness and terror in it.
'Back! Back!' came down again. 'Back, Griosach,back!'

"'They're fighting, they're fighting--the sires!'
one of our horse-boys yelled out--the first sound
above a breath that had come from any of us, for he
was fonder of Lugh than of the favorite Griosach, and
had forgotten everything else. And we saw that the
little cloud was almost at a stand-still; yet that it
was disturbed; sparks were flying from it; and we
heard little clanking sounds, very faint, coming from
it. They might mean great leaps and rearings.

"Suddenly we saw the master spring from that rock
to which he had been clinging as limp as a leaf in
autumn, spring from it with great life and roar up
towards the leaca:

"'Liam! Liam! Liam Ruadh!' He turned to us,'Shout,
boys, and break his fever,' he cried, 'Shout, shout!'

"We were glad of that.

"'Liam! Liam! Liam Ruadh!' we roared.

"'My God! My God!' we heard as we finished. It was
the master's voice; he then fell down. At once we
raised our voices again; it would keep us from seeing
or hearing what was happening on the leaca.

"'Liam! Liam! Liam Ruadh!'

"There was wild confusion.

"'Liam! Liam! Liam! Ruadh! Ruadh! Ruadh! the mountains were singing back to us, making the confusion
worse. We were twisted about--one man staring at the
ground, one at the rock in front of his face, another

11

at the sky high over the leaca, and one had his hand
stretched out like a sign-post on a hilltop, I remember him best; none of us were looking at the leaca itself. But we were listening and listening, and at
last they died, the echoes, and there was a cold silence, cold, cold. Then we heard old Diarmuid's pas-
sionless voice begin to pray:

"'Abhaile ar an sioruidheacht go raibh a anam.' 'At
home in Eternity may his soul--'. We turned round,
one by one, without speaking a word, and stared at the
leaca. It was bare! The little cloud was still in
the air--a white dust ascending. Along the leaca we
saw two thin shadowy lines--they looked as if they had
been drawn in very watery ink on its dazzling surface.
Of horses, plough, and fool there wasn't a trace.
They had gone over the edge while we roared.

"Noble person, as they went over I'm sure Liam
Ruadh had one fist at Lugh's bridle, and the other at
Griosach's, and that he was swinging high in the air
between them. Our roaring didn't break his fever, say
that it didn't, noble person? But don't question the
master about it. I have told you all!"

"I will leave this place tonight," I said.

"It is late, noble person."

"I will leave it now, bring me my horse."

That is why I made no further inquiries in that
valley as to the fate of that old Gaelic family that
were once lords of those hills. I gave up the quest.
Sometimes a thought comes to me that Liam Ruadh might
have been the last of an immemorial line, no scion of
which, if God had left him his senses, would have
ploughed the Leaca of the Saints, no, not even if it
were to save him from begging at fairs and in public
houses.

THE THREEPENNY-PIECE

by James Stephens


When Brien O'Brien died, people said that it did
not matter very much, because he would have died young
in any case. He would have been hanged, or his head
would have been split in two halves with a hatchet, or
he would have tumbled down the cliff when he was drunk
and been smashed into jelly. Something like that was
due to him, and everybody likes to see a man get what
he deserves to get.

But, as ethical writs cease to run when a man is
dead, the neighbours did not stay away from his wake.
They came, and they said many mitigating things across
the body with the bandaged jaws and the sly grin, and
they reminded each other of this and that queer thing
which he had done, for his memory was crusted over
with stories of wild laughable things, and other
things which were wild but not laughable.

Meanwhile, he was dead, and one was at liberty to
be a trifle sorry for him. Further, he belonged to
the O'Brien nation, a stock to whom reverence was due.
A stock not easily forgotten. The historic memory
could reconstruct forgotten glories of station and
battle, of terrible villainy and terrible saintliness,
the pitiful, valorous, slow descent to the degradation
which was not yet wholly victorious. A great stock!
The O'Neills remembered it. The O'Tools and the Mac-
Sweeneys had stories by the hundred of love and hate.
The Burkes and the Geraldines and the new strangers
had memories also.

His family was left in the poorest way, but they
were used to that, for he had kept them as poor as he
left them, or found them, for that matter. They had
shaken hands with Charity so often that they no longer
disliked the sallow-faced lady, and, so, certain small
gifts made by the neighbours were accepted, not very
thankfully, but very readily. These gifts were almost
always in kind. A few eggs. A bag of potatoes. A
handful of meal. A couple of twists of tea--such
like.

One of the visitors, however, moved by an extraordinary dejection, slipped a silver threepenny-piece
into the hand of Brien's little daughter Sheila, aged

four years, and later on she did not like to ask for
it back again.

Little Sheila had been well trained by her father.
She knew exactly what should be done with money, and
so, when nobody was looking, she tip-toed to the coffin and slipped the threepenny-piece into Brien's hand.
That hand had never refused money when it was alive,
it did not reject it either when it was dead.

They buried him the next day.

He was called up for judgment the day after, and
made his appearance with a miscellaneous crowd of
wretches, and there he again received what was due to
him. He was removed protesting and struggling to the
place decreed.

"Down," said Rhadamanthus,[1] pointing with his great
hand, and down he went.

In the struggle he dropped the threepenny-piece,
but he was so bustled and heated that he did not observe his loss. He went down, far down, out of sight,
out of remembrance, to a howling, black gulf with
others of his unseen kind.

A young seraph, named Cuchulain,[2] chancing to pass
that way shortly afterwards, saw the threepenny-piece
peeping brightly from the rocks, and he picked it up.

He looked at it in astonishment. He turned it over
and over, this way and that way. Examined it at the
stretch of his arm, and peered minutely at it from two
inches' distance--

"I have never in my life seen anything so beautifully wrought," said he, and, having stowed it in his
pouch along with some other trinkets, he strolled
homewards again through the massy gates.

It was not long before Brien discovered his loss,

1. Rhadamanthus was the son of Zeus and Europa. Renowned for his justice on earth, the gods made him
   one of the judges of Hades.
2. Cuchulain was an Irish legendary hero of Ulster, of
   exceeding strength and remarkable beauty. He is
   the central figure of the Ulster legends.

and, suddenly, through the black region, his voice
went mounting and brawling.

"I have been robbed," he yelled. "I have been robbed in heaven!"

Having begun to yell he did not stop. Sometimes he
was simply angry and made a noise. Sometimes he became sarcastic and would send his query swirling up-
wards--

"Who stole the threepenny-bit?" he roared. He addressed the surrounding black space--

"Who stole the last threepenny-bit of a poor man?"

Again and again his voice pealed upwards. The
pains of his habitation lost all their sting for him.
His mind had nourishment and the heat within him van-
quished the fumes without. He had a grievance, a
righteous cause, he was buoyed and strengthened, nothing could silence him. They tried ingenious devices,
all kinds of complicated things, but he paid no heed,
and the tormentors were in despair.

"I hate these sinners from the kingdom of Kerry,"
said the Chief Tormentor, and he sat moodily down on
his own circular saw; and that worried him also, for
•he was clad only in a loin cloth.

"I hate the entire Clan of the Gael," said he;"why
cannot they send them somewhere else?" and then he
started practising again on Brien.

It was no use. Brien's query still blared upwards
like the sound of the great trump itself. It wakened
and rung the rocky caverns, screamed through fissure
and funnel, and was battered and slung from pinnacle
to crag and up again. Worse! his companions in doom
became interested and took up the cry, until at last
the uproar became so appalling that the Master himself
could not stand it.

"I have not had a wink of sleep for three nights,"
said that harassed one, and he sent a special embassy
to the powers.

Rhadamanthus was astonished when they arrived. His
elbow was leaning on his vast knee, and his heavy head
rested on a hand that was acres long, acres wide.

15

"What is all this about?" said he.

"The Master cannot go to sleep," said the spokesman of the embassy, and he grinned as he said it, for it sounded queer even to himself.

"It is not necessary that he should sleep," said Rhadamanthus. "I have never slept since time began, and I will never sleep until time is over. But the complaint is curious. What has troubled your master?"

"Hell is turned upside down and inside out," said the fiend. "The tormentors are weeping like little children. The principalities[3] are squatting on their hunkers doing nothing. The orders[4] are running here and there fighting each other. The styles[5] are leaning against walls shrugging their shoulders, and the damned are shouting and laughing and have become callous to torment."

"It is not my business," said the judge.

"The sinners demand justice," said the spokesman.

"They've got it," said Rhadamanthus, "let them stew in it."

"They refuse to stew," replied the spokesman, wringing his hands.

Rhadamanthus sat up.

"It is an axiom in law," said he, "that however complicated an event may be, there can never be more than one person at the extreme bottom of it. Who is the person?"

"It is one Brien of the O'Brien nation, late of the kingdom of Kerry. A bad one! He got the maximum punishment a week ago."

3. In medieval angelology, one of the nine orders of angels, which has been variously reckoned as the seventh, fifth, or fourth.
4. According to medieval angelology, any of the nine grades of angels; also, any similar class of beings.
5. In medieval angelology one of the lower grades of angels in the nine orders.

For the first time in his life Rhadamanthus was
disturbed. He scratched his head, and it was the
first time he had ever done that either.

"You say he got the maximum," said Rhadamanthus,
"then it's a fix! I have damned him for ever, and
better or worse than that cannot be done. It is none
of my business," said he angrily, and he had the depu-
tation removed by force.

But that did not ease the trouble. The contagion
spread until ten million billions of voices were
chanting in unison, and uncountable multitudes were
listening between their pangs.

"Who stole the threepenny-bit? Who stole the
threepenny-bit?"

That was still their cry. Heaven rang with it as
well as hell. Space was filled with that rhythmic
tumult. Chaos and empty Nox[6] had a new discord added
to their elemental throes. Another memorial was
drafted below, showing that unless the missing coin
was restored to its owner hell would have to close its
doors. There was a veiled menace in the memorial
also, for Clause 6 hinted that if hell was allowed to
go by the board heaven might find itself in some jeop-
ardy thereafter.

The document was dispatched and considered. In
consequence a proclamation was sent through all the
wards of Paradise, calling on whatever person, archangel, seraph, cherub, or acolyte had found a threepenny-piece since mid-day of the tenth of August then
instant, that the same person, archangel, seraph,
cherub, or acolyte, should deliver the said threepenny-piece to Rhadamanthus at his Court, and should
receive in return a free pardon and a receipt.

The coin was not delivered.

That young seraph, Cuchulain, walked about like a
person who was strange to himself. He was not tormented: he was angry. He frowned, he cogitated and
fumed. He drew one golden curl through his fingers
until it was lank and drooping; save the end only,
that was still a ripple of gold. He put the end in

6. A goddess, night personified. She was the daughter
   of Chaos.

17

his mouth and strode moodily chewing it. And every
day his feet turned in the same direction--down the
long entrance boulevard, through the mighty gates,
along the strip of carved slabs, to that piled wilderness where Rhadamanthus sat monumentally.

Here delicately he went, sometimes with a hand outstretched to help his foothold, standing for a space
to think ere he jumped to a further rock, balancing
himself for a moment ere he leaped again. So he would
come to stand and stare gloomily upon the judge.

He would salute gravely, as was meet, and say, "God
bless the work"; but Rhadamanthus never replied, save
by a nod, for he was very busy.

Yet the judge did observe him, and would sometimes
heave ponderous lids to where he stood, and so, for a
few seconds, they regarded each other in an interval
of that unceasing business.

Sometimes for a minute or two the young seraph Cuchulain would look from the judge to the judged as
they crouched back or strained forward, the good and
the bad all in the same tremble of fear, all unknowing
which way their doom might lead. They did not look at
each other. They looked at the judge high on his ebon
throne, and they could not look away from him. There
were those who knew, guessed clearly their doom;
abashed and flaccid they sat, quaking. There were
some who were uncertain--rabbit-eyed these, not less
quaking than the others, biting at their knuckles as
they peeped upwards. There were those hopeful, yet
searching fearfully backwards in the wilderness of
memory, chasing and weighing their sins; and these
last, even when their bliss was sealed and their steps
set on an easy path, went faltering, not daring to
look around again, their ears strained to catch a--
"Halt, miscreant! this other is your way!"

So, day by day, he went to stand near the judge;
and one day Rhadamanthus, looking on him more intently,
lifted his great hand and pointed--

"Go you among those to be judged," said he.

For Rhadamanthus knew. It was his business to look
deep into the heart and the mind, to fish for secrets
in the pools of being.

And the young seraph Cuchulain, still rolling his

18

golden curl between his lips, went obediently forward and set down his nodding plumes between two who whimpered and stared and quaked.

When his turn came, Rhadamanthus eyed him intently for a long time--

"Well!" said Rhadamanthus.

The young seraph Cuchulain blew the curl of gold away from his mouth--

"Findings are keepings," said he loudly, and he closed his mouth and stared very impertinently at the judge.

"It is to be given up," said the judge.

"Let them come and take it from me," said the seraph Cuchulain. And suddenly (for these things are at the will of spirits) around his head the lightnings span, and his hands were on the necks of thunders.

For the second time in his life Rhadamanthus was disturbed, again he scratched his head--

"It's a fix," said he moodily. But in a moment he called to those whose duty it was--

"Take him to this side," he roared.

And they advanced. But the seraph Cuchulain swung to meet them, and his golden hair blazed and shrieked; and the thunders rolled at his feet, and about him a bright network that hissed and stung--and those who advanced turned haltingly backwards and ran screaming.

"It's a fix," said Rhadamanthus; and for a little time he stared menacingly at the seraph Cuchulain.

But only for a little time. Suddenly he put his hands on the rests of his throne and heaved upwards his terrific bulk. Never before had Rhadamanthus stood from his ordained chair. He strode mightily forward and in an instant had quelled that rebel. The thunders and lightnings were but moonbeams and dew on that stony carcass. He seized the seraph Cuchulain, lifted him to his breast as one lifts a sparrow, and tramped back with him--

"Fetch me that other," said he, sternly, and he sat

19

down.

Those whose duty it was sped swiftly downwards to
find Brien of the O'Brien nation; and while they were
gone, all in vain the seraph Cuchulain crushed flamy
barbs against that bosom of doom. Now, indeed, his
golden locks were drooping and his plumes were broken
and tossed; but his fierce eye still glared courageously against the nipple of Rhadamanthus.

Soon they brought Brien. He was a sight of woe--
howling, naked as a tree in winter, black as a tarred
wall, carved and gashed, tattered in all but his
throat, wherewith, until one's ears rebelled, he
bawled his one demand.

But the sudden light struck him to a wondering silence, and the sight of the judge holding the seraph
Cuchulain like a limp flower to his breast held him
gaping--

"Bring him here," said Rhadamanthus.

And they brought him to the steps of the throne--

"You have lost a medal!" said Rhadamanthus. "This
one has it."

Brien looked straitly at the seraph Cuchulain.

Rhadamanthus stood again, whirled his arm in an
enormous arc, jerked, and let go, and the seraph Cuchulain went swirling through space like a slung
stone--

"Go after him, Kerryman," said Rhadamanthus, stooping; and he seized Brien by the leg, whirled him wide
and out and far; dizzy, dizzy as a swooping comet, and
down, and down, and down.

Rhadamanthus seated himself. He motioned with his
hand--

"Next," said he, coldly.


Down went the seraph Cuchulain, swirling in wide
tumbles, scarcely visible for quickness. Sometimes,
with outstretched hands, he was a cross that dropped
plumb. Anon, head urgently downwards, he dived

steeply. Again, like a living hoop, head and heels together, he spun giddily. Blind, deaf, dumb, breathless, mindless; and behind him Brien of the O'Brien
nation came pelting and whizzing.

What of that journey! Who could give it words? Of
the suns that appeared and disappeared like winking
eyes. Comets that shone for an instant, went black
and vanished. Moons that came, and stood, and were
gone. And around all, including all, boundless space,
boundless silence; the black, unmoving void--the deep,
unending quietude, through which they fell with Saturn
and Orion, and mildly-smiling Venus, and the fair,
stark-naked moon and the decent earth wreathed in
pearl and blue. From afar she appeared, the quiet one
all lonely in the void. As sudden as a fair face in a
crowded street. Beautiful as the sound of falling
waters. Beautiful as the sound of music in a silence.
Like a white sail on a windy sea. Like a green tree
in a solitary place. Chaste and wonderful she was.
Flying afar. Flying aloft like a joyous bird when the
morning breaks on the darkness and he shrills sweet
tidings. She soared and sang. Gently she sang to
timid pipes and flutes of tender straw and murmuring,
distant strings. A song that grew and swelled,
gathering to a multitudinous, deep-thundered harmony,
until the over-burdened ear failed before the appalling uproar of her ecstasy, and denounced her. No
longer a star! No longer a bird! A plumed and horned
fury! Gigantic, gigantic, leaping and shrieking tem-
pestuously, spouting whirlwinds of lightning, tearing
gluttonously along her path, avid, rampant, howling
with rage and terror she leaped, dreadfully she leaped
and flew. . . .

Enough! They hit the earth--they were not smashed,
there was that virtue in them. They hit the ground
just outside the village of Donnybrook where the back
road runs to the hills; and scarcely had they bumped
twice when Brien of the O'Brien nation had the seraph
Cuchulain by the throat--

"My threepenny-bit," he roared, with one fist up--

But the seraph Cuchulain only laughed--

"That!" said he. "Look at me, man. Your little
medal dropped far beyond the rings of Saturn."

And Brien stood back looking at him--He was as

21

naked as Brien was.  He was as naked as a stone, or an eel, or a pot, or a new-born babe.  He was very naked.

So Brien of the O'Brien nation strode across the path and sat down by the side of a hedge--

"The first man that passes this way," said he, "will give me his clothes, or I'll strangle him."

The seraph Cuchulain walked over to him--

"I will take the clothes of the second man that passes," said he, and he sat down.

THE WEAVER'S GRAVE

A Story of Old Men

by Seumas O'Kelly


Mortimer Hehir, the weaver, had died and they had come in search of his grave to Cloon na Morav, the Meadow of the Dead. Meehaul Lynskey, the nail-maker, was first across the stile. There was excitement in his face. His long warped body moved in a shuffle over the ground. Following him came Cahir Bowes, the stonebreaker, who was so beaten down from the hips forward, that his back was horizontal as the back of an animal. His right hand held a stick which propped him up in front, his left hand clutched his coat behind, just above the small of the back. By these devices he kept himself from toppling head over heels as he walked. Mother earth was the brow of Cahir Bowes by magnetic force, and Cahir Bowes was resisting her fatal kiss to the last. And just now there was animation in the face he raised from its customary contemplation of the ground. Both old men had the air of those who had been unexpectedly let loose. For a long time they had lurked somewhere in the shadows of life, the world having no business for them, and now, suddenly, they had been remembered and called forth to perform an office which nobody else on earth could perform. The excitement in their faces as they crossed over the stile into Cloon na Morav expressed a vehemence in their belated usefulness. Hot on their heels came two dark, handsome, stoutly built men, alike even to the cord that tied their corduroy trousers under their knees, and, being grave-diggers, they carried flashing spades. Last of all, and after a little delay, a firm white hand was laid on the stile, a dark figure followed, the figure of a woman whose palely sad face was picturesquely, almost dramatically, framed in a black shawl which hung from the crown of the head. She was the widow of Mortimer Hehir, the weaver, and she followed the others into Cloon na Morav, the Meadow of the Dead.

To glance at Cloon na Morav as you went by on the hilly road, was to get an impression of a very old burial-ground; to pause on the road and look at Cloon na Morav was to become conscious of its quiet situation, of winds singing down from the hills in a chant for the dead; to walk over to the wall and look at the

23

mounds inside was to provoke quotations from Gray's
'Elegy'; to make the sign of the Cross, lean over the
wall, observe the gloomy lichened background of the
wall opposite, and mark the things that seemed to
stray about, like yellow snakes in the grass, was to
think of Hamlet moralizing at the graveside of Ophelia, and hear him establish the identity of Yorrick.
To get over the stile and stumble about inside, was to
forget all these things and to know Cloon na Morav for
itself. Who could tell the age of Cloon na Morav?
The mind could only swoon away into mythology, paddle
about in the dotage of paganism, the toothless infancy.
of Christianity. How many generations, how many septs,
how many clans, how many families, how many people,
had gone into Cloon na Morav? The mind could only
take wing on the romances of mathematics. The ground
was billowy, grotesque. Several partially suppressed
insurrections--a great thirsting, worming, pushing
and shouldering under the sod--had given it character.
A long tough growth of grass wired it from end to end.
Nature, by this effort, endeavouring to control the
strivings of the more daring of the insurgents of
Cloon na Morav. No path here; no plan or map or reg-
ister existed; if there ever had been one or the other
it had been lost. Invasions and wars and famines and
feuds had swept the ground and left it. All claims to
interment had been based on powerful traditional
rights. These rights had years ago come to an end--
all save in a few outstanding cases, the rounding up
of a spent generation. The overflow from Cloon na
Morav had already set a new cemetery on its legs a
mile away, a cemetery in which limestone headstones
and Celtic crosses were springing up like mushrooms,
advertising the triviality of a civilization of men
and women, who, according to their own epitaphs, had
done exactly the two things they could not very well
avoid doing: they had all, their obituary notices
said, been born and they had all died. Obscure quotations from Scripture were sometimes added by way of
apology. There was an almost unanimous expression of
forgiveness to the Lord for what had happened to the
deceased. None of this lack of humour in Cloon na
Morav. Its monuments were comparatively few, and such
of them as it had not swallowed were well within the
general atmosphere. No obituary notice in the place
was complete; all were either wholly or partially
eaten up by the teeth of time. The monuments that had
made a stout battle for existence were pathetic in
their futility. The vanity of the fashionable of dim
ages made one weep. Who on earth could have brought

in the white marble slab to Cloon na Morav? It had
grown green with shame. Perhaps the lettering, once
readable upon it, had been conscientiously picked out
in gold. The shrieking winds and the fierce rains of
the hills alone could tell. Plain heavy stones, their
shoulders rounded with a chisel, presumably to give
them some off-handed resemblance to humanity, now
swooned at fantastic angles from their settings, as if
the people to whose memory they had been dedicated had
shouldered them away as an impertinence. Other slabs
lay in fragments on the ground, filling the mind with
thoughts of Moses descending from Mount Sinai and,
waxing angry at sight of his followers dancing about
false gods, casting the stone tables containing the
Commandments to the ground, breaking them in pieces--
the most tragic destruction of a first edition that
the world has known. Still other heavy square dark
slabs, surely creatures of a pagan imagination, were
laid flat down on numerous short legs, looking sometimes like representations of monstrous black cockroaches, and again like tables at which the guests of
Cloon na Morav might sit down, goblin-like, in the
moon-light, when nobody was looking. Most of the legs
had given way and the tables lay overturned, as if
there had been a quarrel at cards the night before.
Those that had kept their legs exhibited great cracks
or fissures across their backs, like slabs of dark ice
breaking up. Over by the wall, draped in its pattern
of dark green lichen, certain families of dim ages had
made an effort to keep up the traditions of the Eastern sepulchres. They had showed an aristocratic re-
luctance to take to the common clay in Cloon na Morav.
They had built low casket-shaped houses against the
gloomy wall, putting an enormously heavy iron door
with ponderous iron rings--like the rings on a pier by
the sea--at one end, a tremendous lock--one wondered
what Goliath kept the key--finally cementing the whole
thing up and surrounding it with spiked iron railings.
In these contraptions very aristocratic families locked up their dead as if they were dangerous wild animals. But these ancient vanities only heightened the
general democracy of the ground. To prove a traditional right to a place in its community was to have
the bond of your pedigree sealed. The act of burial
in Cloon na Morav was in itself an epitaph. And it
was amazing to think that there were two people still
over the sod who had such a right--one Mortimer Hehir,
the weaver, just passed away, the other Malachi
Roohan, a cooper, still breathing. When these two
survivors of a great generation got tucked under the

sward of Cloon na Morav its terrific history would,
for all practical purposes, have ended.

## II

Meehaul Lynskey, the nailer, hitched forward his
bony shoulders and cast his eyes over the ground--eyes
that were small and sharp, but unaccustomed to range
over wide spaces. The width and the wealth of Cloon
na Morav were baffling to him. He had spent his long
life on the look-out for one small object so that he
might hit it. The colour that he loved was the golden
glowing end of a stick of burning iron; wherever he
saw that he seized it in a small sconce at the end of
a long handle, wrenched it off by a twitch of the
wrist, hit it with a flat hammer several deft taps,
dropped it into a vessel of water, out of which it
came a cool and perfect nail. To do this thing several hundred times six days in the week, and pull the
chain of a bellows at short intervals, Meehaul Lynskey
had developed an extraordinary dexterity of sight and
touch, a swiftness of business that no mortal man
could exceed, and so long as he had been pitted against
nail-makers of flesh and blood he had more than held
his own;he had, indeed, even put up a tremendous but
an unequal struggle against the competition of nail-
making machinery. Accustomed as he was to concentrate
on a single, glowing, definite object, the complexity
and disorder of Cloon na Morav unnerved him. But he
was not going to betray any of these professional de-
fects to Cahir Bowes, the stone-breaker. He had been
sent there as an ambassador by the caretaker of Cloon
na Morav, picked out for his great age, his local
knowledge, and his good character, and it was his
business to point out to the twin grave-diggers, sons
of the caretaker, the weaver's grave, so that it might
be opened to receive him. Meehaul Lynskey had a
knowledge of the place, and was quite certain as to a
great number of grave sites, while the caretaker,
being an official without records, had a profound ignorance of the whole place.

Cahir Bowes followed the drifting figure of the
nail-maker over the ground, his face hitched up between his shoulders, his eyes keen and grey, glint-
like as the mountains of stones he had in his day
broken up as road material. Cahir, no less than
Meehaul, had his knowledge of Cloon na Morav and some
of his own people were buried here. His sharp, clear
eyes took in the various mounds with the eye of a

26

prospector. He, too, had been sent there as an ambassador, and as between himself and Meehaul Lynskey he did not think there could be any two opinions; his knowledge was superior to the knowledge of the nailer. Whenever Cahir Bowes met a loose stone on the grass, quite instinctively he turned it over with his stick, his sharp old eyes judging its grain with a professional swiftness, then cracking at it with his stick. If the stick were a hammer the stone, attacked on its most vulnerable spot, would fall to pieces like glass. In stones Cahir Bowes saw not sermons but seams. Even the headstones he tapped significantly with the ferrule of his stick, for Cahir Bowes had an artist's passion for his art, though his art was far from creative. He was one of the great destroyers, the reducers, the makers of chaos, a powerful and remorseless critic of the Stone Age.

The two old men wandered about Cloon na Morav, in no hurry whatever to get through with their business. After all they had been a long time pensioned off, forgotten, neglected,by the world. The renewed sensation of usefulness was precious to them. They knew that when this business was over they were not likely to be in request for anything in this world again. They were ready to oblige the world, but the world would have to allow them their own time. The world, made up of the two grave-diggers and the widow of the weaver, gathered all this without any vocal proclamation. Slowly, mechanically as it were, they followed the two ancients about Cloon na Morav. And the two ancients wandered about with the labour of age and the hearts of children. They separated, wandered about silently as if they were picking up old acquaintances, stumbling upon forgotten things, gathering up the threads of days that were over, reviving their memories, and then drew together, beginning to talk slowly, almost casually, and all their talk was of the dead, of the people who lay in the ground about them. They warmed to it, airing their knowledge, calling up names and complications of family relationships, telling stories, reviving all virtues, whispering at past vices, past vices that did not sound like vices at all, for the long years are great mitigators and run in splendid harness with the coyest of all the virtues, Charity. The whispered scandals of Cloon na Morav were seen by the twin grave-diggers and the widow of the weaver through such a haze of antiquity that they were no longer scandals but romances. The rake and the drab, seen a good way down the avenue,

27

merely look picturesque. The grave-diggers rested
their spades in the ground, leaning on the handles in
exactly the same graveyard pose, and the pale widow
stood in the background, silent, apart, patient, and,
like all dark, tragic-looking women, a little mysterious.

The stone-breaker pointed with his quivering stick
at the graves of the people whom he spoke about. Every
time he raised that forward support one instinctively
looked, anxious and fearful, to see if the clutch were
secure on the small of the back. Cahir Bowes had the
sort of shape that made one eternally fearful for his
equilibrium. The nailer, who, like his friend the
stone-breaker, wheezed a good deal, made short, sharp
gestures, and always with the right hand; the fingers
were hooked in such a way, and he shot out the arm in
such a manner, that they gave the illusion that he
held a hammer and that it was struck out over a very
hot fire. Every time Meehaul Lynskey made this gesture one expected to see sparks flying.

'Where are we to bury the weaver?' one of the grave-
diggers asked at last.

Both old men laboured around to see where the interruption, the impertinence, had come from. They
looked from one twin to the other, with gravity, indeed anxiety, for they were not sure which was which,
or if there was not some illusion in the resemblance,
some trick of youth to baffle age.

'Where are we to bury the weaver?' the other twin
repeated, and the strained look on the old men's faces
deepened. They were trying to fix in their minds
which of the twins had interrupted first and which
last. The eyes of Meehaul Lynskey fixed on one twin
with the instinct of his trade, while Cahir Bowes
ranged both and eventually wandered to the figure of
the widow in the background, silently accusing her of
impatience in a matter which it would be indelicate
for her to show haste.

'We can't stay here for ever,' said the first twin.

It was the twin upon whom Meehaul Lynskey had fastened his small eyes, and, sure of his man this time,
Meehaul Lynskey hit him.

'There's many a better man than you,' said Meehaul

28

Lynskey, 'that will stay here for ever.' He swept
Cloon na Morav with the hooked fingers.

'Them that stays in Cloon na Morav for ever,' said
Cahir Bowes with a wheezing energy, 'have nothing to
be ashamed of--nothing to be ashamed of. Remember
that,young fellow.'

Meechaul Lynskey did not seem to like the inter-
vention, the help, of Cahir Bowes. It was a sort of
implication that he had not--he, mind you,--had not
hit the nail properly on the head.

'Well, where are we to bury him, anyway?' said the
twin, hoping to profit by the chagrin of the nailer--
the nailer who, by implication, had failed to nail.

'You'll bury him,' said Meehaul Lynskey, 'where all
belonging to him is buried.'

'We come,' said the other twin, 'with some sort of
intention of that kind.' He drawled out the words, in
imitation of the old men. The skin relaxed on his
handsome dark face and then bunched in puckers of humour about the eyes; Meehaul Lynskey's gaze, wandering
for once, went to the handsome dark face of the other
twin and the skin relaxed and then bunched in puckers
of humour about his eyes, so that Meehaul Lynskey had
an unnerving sensation that these young grave-diggers
were purposely confusing him.

'You'll bury him,' he began with some vehemence,
and was amazed to again find Cahir Bowes taking the
words out of his mouth, snatching the hammer out of
his hand, so to speak.

'----where you're told to bury him,' Cahir Bowes
finished for him.

Meehaul Lynskey was so hurt that his long slanting
figure moved away down the graveyard, then stopped
suddenly. He had determined to do a dreadful thing.
He had determined to do a thing that was worse than
kicking a crutch from under a cripple's shoulder; that
was like stealing the holy water out of a room where a
man lay dying. He had determined to ruin the last
day's amusement on this earth for Cahir Bowes and himself by prematurely and basely disclosing the weaver's
grave!

29

'Here,' called back Meehaul Lynskey, 'is the weaver's grave, and here you will bury him.'

All moved down to the spot, Cahir Bowes going with extraordinary spirit, the ferrule of his terrible stick cracking on the stones he met on the way.

'Between these two mounds,' said Meehaul Lynskey, and already the twins raised their twin spades in a sinister movement, like swords of lancers flashing at a drill.

'Between these two mounds,' said Meehaul Lynskey 'is the grave of Mortimer Hehir.'

'Hold on!' cried Cahir Bowes. He was so eager, so excited, that he struck one of the grave-diggers a whack of his stick on the back. Both grave-diggers swung about to him as if both had been hurt by the one blow.

'Easy there,' said the first twin.

'Easy there,' said the second twin.

'Easy yourselves,' cried Cahir Bowes. He wheeled about his now quivering face on Meehaul Lynskey.

'What is it you're saying about the spot between the mounds?' he demanded.

'I'm saying,' said Meehaul Lynskey vehemently,'that it's the weaver's grave.'

'What weaver?' asked Cahir Bowes.

'Mortimer Hehir,' replied Meehaul Lynskey. 'There's no other weaver in it.'

'Was Julia Rafferty a weaver?'

'What Julia Rafferty?'

'The midwife, God rest her.'

'How could she be a weaver if she was a midwife?'

'Not a one of me knows. But I'll tell you what I do know and know rightly: that it's Julia Rafferty is in that place and no weaver at all.'

30

'Amn't I telling you it's the weaver's grave?'

'And amn't I telling you it's not?'

'That I may be as dead as my father but the weaver was buried there.'

'A bone of a weaver was never sunk in it as long as weavers was weavers. Full of Raffertys it is.'

'Alive with weavers it is.'

'Heavenlyful Father, was the like ever heard: to say that a grave was alive with dead weavers.'

'It's full of them--full as a tick.'

'And the clean grave that Mortimer Hehir was never done boasting about--dry and sweet and deep and no way bulging at all. Did you see the burial of his father ever?'

'I did, in troth, see the burial of his father--forty year ago if it's a day.'

'Forty year ago--it's fifty-one year come the sixteenth of May. It's well I remember it and it's well I have occasion to remember it, for it was the day after that again that myself ran away to join the soldiers, my aunt hot foot after me, she to be buying me out the week after, I a high-spirited fellow morebetoken.'

'Leave the soldiers out of it and leave your aunt out of it and stick to the weaver's grave. Here in this place was the last weaver buried, and I'll tell you what's more. In a straight line with it is the grave of ----'

'A straight line, indeed! Who but yourself, Meehaul Lynskey, ever heard of a straight line in Cloon na Morav? No such thing was ever wanted or ever allowed in it.'

'In a straight direct line, measured with a rule---'

'Measured with crooked, stumbling feet, maybe feet half reeling in drink.'

'Can't you listen to me now?'

31

'I was always a bad warrant to listen to anything
except sense. Yourself ought to be the last man in
the world to talk about straight lines, you with the
sight scattered in your head, with the divil of sparks
flying under your eyes.'

'Don't mind me sparks now, nor me sight neither,
for in a straight measured line with the weaver's
grave was the grave of the Cassidys.'

'What Cassidys?'

'The Cassidys that herded for the O'Sheas.'

'Which O'Sheas?'

'O'Shea Ruadh of Cappakelly. Don't you know any
one at all, or is it gone entirely your memory is?'

'Cappakelly <u>inagh</u>![1] And who cares a whistle about
O'Shea Ruadh, he or his seed, breed and generations?
It's a rotten lot of landgrabbers they were.'

'Me hand to you on that. Striving ever they were
to put their red paws on this bit of grass and that
perch of meadow.'

'Hungry in themselves even for the cutaway bog.'

'And Mortimer Hehir a decent weaver, respecting
every man's wool.'

'His forehead pallid with honesty over the yard and
the loom.'

'If a bit broad-spoken when he came to the door for
a smoke of the pipe.'

'Well, there won't be a mouthful of clay between
himself and O'Shea Ruadh now.'

'In the end what did O'Shea Ruadh get after all his
striving?'

'I'll tell you that. He got what land suits a
blind fiddler.'

1. A satirical expression of dissent or disbelief.

'Enough to pad the crown of the head and tap the
sole of the foot! Now you're talking.'

'And the devil a word out of him now no more than
any one else in Cloon na Morav.'

'It's easy talking to us all about land when we're
packed up in our timber boxes.'

'As the weaver was when he got sprinkled with the
holy water in that place.'

'As Julia Rafferty was when they read the prayers
over her in that place, she a fine buxom, cheerful
woman in her day, with great skill in her business.'

'Skill or no skill, I'm telling you she's not there,
wherever she is.'

'I suppose you want me to take her up in my arms
and show her to you?'

'Well then, indeed, Cahir, I do not. 'Tisn't a
very handsome pair you would make at all, you not able
to stand much more hardship than Julia herself.'

From this there developed a slow, laboured, aged
dispute between the two authorities. They moved from
grave to grave, pitting memory against memory, story
against story, knocking down reminiscence with reminiscence, arguing in a powerful intimate obscurity
that no outsider could hope to follow, blasting knowledge with knowledge, until the whole place seemed
strewn with the corpses of their arguments. The two
grave-diggers followed them about in a grim silence;
impatience in their movements, their glances; the
widow keeping track of the grand tour with a miserable
feeling, a feeling, as site after site was rejected,
that the tremendous exclusiveness of Cloon na Morav
would altogether push her dead man, the weaver, out of
his privilege. The dispute ended, like all epics,
where it began. Nothing was established, nothing settled. But the two old men were quite exhausted,
Meehaul Lynskey sitting down on the back of one of the
monstrous cockroaches, Cahir Bowes leaning against a
tombstone that was half-submerged, its end up like the
stern of a derelict at sea. Here they sat glaring at
each other like a pair of grim vultures.

The two grave-diggers grew restive. Their business

33

had to be done. The weaver would have to be buried.
Time pressed. They held a consultation apart. It
broke up after a brief exchange of views, a little
laughter.

'Meehaul Lynskey is right,' said one of the twins.

Meehaul Lynskey's face lit up. Cahir Bowes looked
as if he had been slapped on the cheeks. He moved out
from his tombstone.

'Meehaul Lynskey is right,' repeated the other
twin. They had decided to break up the dispute by
taking sides. They raised their spades and moved to
the site which Meehaul had urged upon them.

'Don't touch that place,' Cahir Bowes cried,raising
his stick. He was measuring the back of the grave-
digger again when the man spun round upon him, menace
in his handsome dark face.

'Touch me with that stick,' he cried, 'and I'll---'

Some movement in the background, some agitation in
the widow's shawl, caused the grave-digger's menace to
dissolve, the words to die in his mouth, a swift flush
mounting the man's face like a flash. It was as if
she had cried out, 'Ah, don't touch the poor old,
cranky fellow! you might hurt him.' And it was as if
the grave-digger had cried back: 'He has annoyed me
greatly, but I don't intend to hurt him. And since
you say so with your eyes I won't even threaten him.'

Under pressure of the half threat, Cahir Bowes
shuffled back a little way, striking an attitude of
feeble dignity, leaning out on his stick while the
grave-diggers got to work.

'It's the weaver's grave, surely,' said Meehaul
Lynskey.

'If it is,' said Cahir Bowes, 'remember his father
was buried down seven feet. You gave into that this
morning.'

'There was no giving in about it,' said Meehaul
Lynskey. 'We all know that one of the wonders of
Cloon na Morav was the burial of the last weaver seven
feet, he having left it as an injunction on his family. The world knows he went down the seven feet.'

34

'And remember this,' said Cahir Bowes, 'that Julia
Rafferty was buried no seven feet. If she is down
three feet it's as much as she went.'

Sure enough, the grave-diggers had not dug down
more than three feet of ground when one of the spades
struck hollowly on unhealthy timber. The sound was
unmistakable and ominous. There was silence for a moment. Then Cahir Bowes made a sudden short spurt up a
mound beside him, as if he were some sort of mechanical animal wound up, his horizontal back quivering.
On the mound he made a superhuman effort to straighten
himself. He got his ears and his blunt nose into a
considerable elevation. He had not been so upright
for twenty years. And raising his weird countenance,
he broke into a cackle that was certainly meant to be
a crow. He glared at Meehaul Lynskey, his emotion so
great that his eyes swam in a watery triumph.

Meehaul Lynskey had his eyes, as was his custom,
upon one thing, and that thing was the grave, and especially the spot on the grave where the spade had
struck the coffin. He looked stunned and fearful.
His eyes slowly withdrew their gimlet-like scrutiny
from the spot, and sought the triumphant crowing figure of Cahir Bowes on the mound.

Meehaul Lynskey looked as if he would like to say
something, but no words came. Instead he ambled away,
retired from the battle, and standing apart, rubbed
one leg against the other, above the back of the
ankles, like some great insect. His hooked fingers at
the same time stroked the bridge of his nose. He was
beaten.

'I suppose it's not the weaver's grave,' said one
of the grave-diggers. Both of them looked at Cahir
Bowes.

'Well, you know it's not,' said the stonebreaker.
'It's Julia Rafferty you struck. She helped many a one
into the world in her day, and it's poor recompense to
her to say she can't be at rest when she left it.' He
turned to the remote figure of Meehaul Lynskey and
cried: 'Ah-ha, well you may rub your ignorant legs.
And I'm hoping Julia will forgive you this day's ugly
work.'

In silence, quickly, with reverence, the twins
scooped back the clay over the spot. The widow looked

35

on with the same quiet, patient, mysterious silence.
One of the grave-diggers turned on Cahir Bowes.

'I suppose you know where the weaver's grave is?'
he asked.

Cahir Bowes looked at him with an ancient tartness,
then said:

'You suppose!'

'Of course, you know where it is.'

Cahir Bowes looked as if he knew where the gates of
heaven were and that he might--or might not--enlighten
an ignorant world. It all depended! His eyes wandered knowingly out over the meadows beyond the graveyard. He said:

'I do know where the weaver's grave is.'

'We'll be very much obliged to you if you show it
to us.'

'Very much obliged,' endorsed the other twin.

The stonebreaker, thus flattered, led the way to a
new site, one nearer to the wall, where were the pla-
giarisms of the Eastern sepulchres. Cahir Bowes made
little journeys about, measuring so many steps from
one place to another, mumbling strange and unintelligible information to himself, going through an extraordinary geometrical emotion, striking the ground
hard taps with his stick.

'Glory be to the Lord,' cried Meehaul Lynskey, 'he's
like the man they had driving the water for the well
in the quarry field, he whacking the ground with his
magic hazel wand.'

Cahir Bowes made no reply. He was too absorbed in
his own emotion. A little steam was beginning to as-
cend from his brow. He was moving about the ground
like some grotesque spider weaving an invisible web.

'I suppose now,' said Meehaul Lynskey, addressing
the marble monument, 'that as soon as Cahir hits the
right spot one of the weavers will turn about below.
Or maybe he expects one of them to whistle up at him
out of the ground. That's it; devil a other! When

36

we hear the whistle we'll all know for certain where to bury the weaver.'

Cahir Bowes was contracting his movements, so that he was now circling about the one spot, like a dog going to lie down.

Meehaul Lynskey drew a little closer, watching eagerly, his grim yellow face, seared with yellow marks from the fires of his workshop, tightened up in a sceptical pucker. His half-muttered words were bitter with an aged sarcasm. He cried:

'Say nothing; he'll get it yet, will the man of knowledge, the know-all, Cahir Bowes! Give him time. Give him until this day twelve month. Look at that for a right-about-turn on the left heel. Isn't the nimbleness of that young fellow a treat to see? Are they whistling to you from below, Cahir? Is it dancing to the weaver's music you are? That's it, devil a other.'

Cahir Bowes was mapping out a space on the grass with his stick. Gradually it took, more or less, the outline of a grave site. He took off his hat and mopped his steaming brow with a red handkerchief, saying:

'There's the weaver's grave.'

'God in Heaven,' cried Meehaul Lynskey, 'will you look at what he calls the weaver's grave? I'll say nothing at all. I'll hold my tongue. I'll shut up. Not one word will I say about Alick Finlay, the mildest man that ever lived, a man full of religion, never at the end of his prayers! But, sure, it's the saints of God that get the worst of it in this world, and if Alick escaped during life, faith he's in for it now, with the pirates and the body-snatchers of Cloon na Morav on top of him.'

A corncrake began to sing in the near-by meadow, and his rasping notes sounded like a queer accompaniment to the words of Meehaul Lynskey. The grave-diggers, who had gone to work on the Cahir Bowes site, laughed a little, one of them looking for a moment at Meehaul Lynskey, saying:

'Listen to that damned old corncrake in the meadow! I'd like to put a sod in his mouth.'

37

The man's eye went to the widow. She showed no emotion one way or the other, and the grave-digger got back to his work. Meehaul Lynskey, however, wore the cap. He said:

'To be sure! I'm to sing dumb. I'm not to have a word out of me at all. Others can rattle away as they like in this place, as if they owned it. The ancient good old stock is to be nowhere and the scruff of the hills let rampage as they will. That's it, devil a other. Castles falling and dunghills rising! Well, God be with the good old times and the good old mannerly people that used to be in it, and God be with Alick Finlay, the holiest----'

A sod of earth came through the air from the direction of the grave, and skimming Meehaul Lynskey's head, dropped somewhere behind. The corncrake stopped his notes in the meadow, and Meehaul Lynskey stood statuesque in a mute protest, and silence reigned in the place while the clay sang up in a swinging rhythm from the grave.

Cahir Bowes, watching the operations with intensity, said:

'It was nearly going astray on me.'

Meehaul Lynskey gave a little snort. He asked:

'What was?'

'The weaver's grave.'

'Remember this: the last weaver is down seven feet. And remember this: Alick Finlay is down less than Julia Rafferty.'

He had no sooner spoken when a fearful thing happened. Suddenly out of the soft cutting of the earth a spade sounded harsh on tinware, there was a crash, less harsh, but painfully distinct, as if rotten boards were falling together, then a distinct subsidence of the earth. The work stopped at once. A moment's fearful silence followed. It was broken by a short, dry laugh from Meehaul Lynskey. He said:

'God be merciful to us all! That's the latter end of Alick Finlay.'

The two grave-diggers looked at each other. The

38

shawl of the widow in the background was agitated. One
twin said to the other:

'This can't be the weaver's grave.'

The other agreed. They all turned their eyes upon
Cahir Bowes. He was hanging forward in a pained
strain, his head quaking, his fingers twitching on his
stick. Meehaul Lynskey turned to the marble monument
and said with venom:

'If I was guilty I'd go down on my knees and beg
God's pardon. If I didn't I'd know the ghost of Alick
Finlay, saint as he was, would leap upon me and guzzle
me--for what right would I have to set anybody at him
with driving spades when he was long years in his
grave?'

Cahir Bowes took no notice. He was looking at the
ground, searching about, and slowly, painfully, began
his web-spinning again. The grave-diggers covered in
the ground without a word. Cahir Bowes appeared to
get lost in some fearful maze of his own making. A
little whimper broke from him now and again. The
steam from his brow thickened in the air, and eventually he settled down on the end of a headstone, having
got the worst of it. Meehaul Lynskey sat on another
stone facing him, and they glared, sinister and grotesque, at each other.

'Cahir Bowes,' said Meehaul Lynskey, 'I'll tell you
what you are, and then you can tell me what I am.'

'Have it whatever way you like,' said Cahir Bowes.
'What is it that I am?'

'You're a gentleman, a grand oul' stonebreaking
gentleman. That's what you are, devil a other!'

The wrinkles on the withered face of Cahir Bowes
contracted, his eyes stared across at Meehaul Lynskey,
and two yellow teeth showed between his lips. He
wheezed:

'And do you know what you are?'

'I don't.'

'You're a nailer, that's what you are, a damned
nailer.'

39

They glared at each other in a quaking, grim silence.

And it was at this moment of collapse, of deadlock, that the widow spoke for the first time. At the first sound of her voice one of the twins perked his head, his eyes going to her face. She said in a tone as quiet as her whole behaviour:

'Maybe I ought to go up to the Tunnel Road and ask Malachi Roohan where the grave is.'

They had all forgotten the oldest man of them all, Malachi Roohan. He would be the last mortal man to enter Cloon na Morav. He had been the great friend of Mortimer Hehir, the weaver, in the days that were over, and the whole world knew that Mortimer Hehir's knowledge of Cloon na Morav was perfect. Maybe Malachi Roohan would have learned a great deal from him. And Malachi Roohan, the cooper, was so long bed-ridden that those who remembered him at all thought of him as a man who had died a long time ago.

'There's nothing else for it,' said one of the twins, leaving down his spade, and immediately the other twin laid his spade beside it.

The two ancients on the headstones said nothing. Not even they could raise a voice against the possibilities of Malachi Roohan, the cooper. By their terrible aged silence they gave consent, and the widow turned to walk out of Cloon na Morav. One of the grave-diggers took out his pipe. The eyes of the other followed the widow, he hesitated, then walked after her. She became conscious of the man's step behind her as she got upon the stile, and turned her palely sad face upon him. He stood awkwardly, his eyes wandering, then said:

'Ask Malachi Roohan where the grave is, the exact place.'

It was to do this the widow was leaving Cloon na Morav; she had just announced that she was going to ask Malachi Roohan where the grave was. Yet the man's tone was that of one who was giving her extraordinarily acute advice. There was a little half-embarrassed note of confidence in his tone. In a dim way the widow thought that, maybe, he had accompanied her to the stile in a little awkward impulse of sympathy. Men

40

were very curious in their ways sometimes. The widow
was a very well-mannered woman, and she tried to look
as if she had received a very valuable direction. She
said:

'I will. I'll put that question to Malachi Roohan.'

And then she passed out over the stile.

### III

The widow went up the road, and beyond it struck the
first of the houses of the near-by town. She passed
through faded streets in her quiet gait, moderately
grief-stricken at the death of her weaver. She had
been his fourth wife, and the widowhoods of fourth
wives have not the rich abandon, the great emotional
cataclysm, of first, or even second, widowhoods. It
is a little chastened in its poignancy. The widow had
a nice feeling that it would be out of place to give
way to any of the characteristic manifestations of normal widowhood. She shrank from drawing attention to
the fact that she had been a fourth wife. People's
memories become so extraordinarily acute to family history in times of death! The widow did not care to come
in as a sort of dramatic surprise in the gossip of the
people about the weaver's life. She had heard snatches
of such gossip at the wake the night before. She was
beginning to understand why people love wakes and the
intimate personalities of wakehouses. People listen
to, remember, and believe what they hear at wakes. It
is more precious to them than anything they ever hear
in school, church, or playhouse. It is hardly because
they get certain entertainment at the wake. It is more
because the wake is a grand review of family ghosts.
There one hears all the stories, the little flattering
touches, the little unflattering bitternesses, the traditions, the astonishing records, of the clans. The
woman with a memory speaking to the company from a
chair beside a laid-out corpse carries more authority
than the bishop allocuting from his chair. The wake is
realism. The widow had heard a great deal at the wake
about the clan of the weavers, and noted, without expressing any emotion, that she had come into the story
not like other women, for anything personal to her own
womanhood--for beauty, or high spirit, or temper, or
faithfulness, or unfaithfulness--but simply because she
was a fourth wife, a kind of curiosity, the back-wash
of Mortimer Hehir's romances. The widow felt a remote
sense of injustice in all this. She had said to

41

herself that widows who had been fourth wives deserved
more sympathy than widows who had been first wives,
for the simple reason that fourth widows had never
been, and could never be, first wives! The thought
confused her a little, and she did not pursue it, instinctively feeling that if she did accept the conventional view of her condition she would only crys-
tallize her widowhood into a grievance that nobody
would try to understand, and which would, accordingly,
be merely useless. And what was the good of it, anyhow? The widow smoothed her dark hair on each side of
her head under her shawl.

She had no bitter and no sweet memories of the
weaver. There was nothing that was even vivid in
their marriage. She had no complaints to make of Mortimer Hehir. He had not come to her in any fiery love
impulse. It was the marriage of an old man with a
woman years younger. She had recognized him as an old
man from first to last, a man who had already been
thrice through a wedded experience, and her tempera-
ment, naturally calm, had met his half-stormy, half-
petulant character, without suffering any sort of
shock. The weaver had tried to keep up to the illusion of a perennial youth by dyeing his hair, and
marrying one wife as soon as possible after another.
The fourth wife had come to him late in life. She had
a placid understanding that she was a mere flattery to
the weaver's truculent egoism.

These thoughts, in some shape or other, occupied,
without agitating, the mind of the widow as she passed,
a dark shadowy figure through streets that were clam-
orous in their quietudes, painful in their lack of all
the purposes for which streets have ever been created.
Her only emotion was one which she knew to be quite
creditable to her situation: a sincere desire to see
the weaver buried in the grave to which the respectability of his family and the claims of his ancient
house fully and fairly entitled him. The proceedings
in Cloon na Morav had been painful, even tragical, to
the widow. The weavers had always been great authorities and zealous guardians of the ancient burial place.
This function had been traditional and voluntary with
them. This was especially true of the last of them,
Mortimer Hehir. He had been the greatest of all authorities on the burial places of the local clans. His
knowledge was scientific. He had been the grand sa-
vant of Cloon na Morav. He had policed the place.
Nay, he had been its tyrant. He had over and over

42

again prevented terrible mistakes, complications that
would have appalled those concerned if they were not
beyond all such concerns.  The widow of the weaver had
often thought that in his day Mortimer Hehir had made
his solicitation for the place a passion, unreasonable,
almost violent.  They said that all this had sprung
from a fear that had come to him in his early youth
that through some blunder an alien, an inferior, even
an enemy, might come to find his way into the family
burial place of the weavers.  This fear had made him
what he was.  And in his later years his pride in the
family burial place became a worship.  His trade had
gone down, and his pride had gone up.  The burial
ground in Cloon na Morav was the grand proof of his
aristocracy.  That was the coat-of-arms, the estate,
the mark of high breeding, in the weavers.  And now
the man who had minded everybody's grave had not been
able to mind his own.  The widow thought that it was
one of those injustices which blacken the reputation
of the whole earth.  She had felt, indeed, that she
had been herself slack not to have learned long ago
the lie of this precious grave from the weaver himself; and that he himself had been slack in not properly instructing her.  But that was the way in this
miserable world!  In his passion for classifying the
rights of others, the weaver had obscured his own.  In
his long and entirely successful battle in keeping
alien corpses out of his own aristocratic pit he had
made his own corpse alien to every pit in the place.
The living high priest was the dead pariah of Cloon na
Morav.  Nobody could now tell except, perhaps, Malachi
Roohan, the precise spot which he had defended against
the blunders and confusions of the entire community, a
dead-forgetting, indifferent, slack lot!

    The widow tried to recall all she had ever heard
the weaver say about his grave, in the hope of getting
some clue, something that might be better than the
scandalous scatter-brained efforts of Meehaul Lynskey
and Cahir Bowes.  She remembered various detached
things that the weaver, a talkative man, had said
about his grave.  Fifty years ago since that grave had
been last opened, and it had then been opened to receive the remains of his father.  It had been thirty
years previous to that since it had taken in his father, that is, the newly dead weaver's father's father.
The weavers were a long-lived lot, and there were not
many males of them; one son was as much as any one of
them begot to pass to the succession of the loom; if
there were daughters they scattered, and their graves

43

were continents apart. The three wives of the late
weaver were buried in the new cemetery. The widow
remembered that the weaver seldom spoke of them, and
took no interest in their resting place. His heart
was in Cloon na Morav and the sweet, dry, deep, aristocratic bed he had there in reserve for himself. But
all his talk had been generalization. He had never,
that the widow could recall, said anything about the
site, about the signs and measurements by which it
could be identified. No doubt, it had been well known
to many people, but they had all died. The weaver had
never realized what their slipping away might mean to
himself. The position of the grave was so intimate to
his own mind that it never occurred to him that it
could be obscure to the minds of others. Mortimer
Hehir had passed away like some learned and solitary
astronomer who had discovered a new star, hugging its
beauty, its exclusiveness, its possession to his
heart, secretly rejoicing how its name would travel
with his own through heavenly space for all time--and
forgetting to mark its place among the known stars
grouped upon his charts. Meehaul Lynskey and Cahir
Bowes might now be two seasoned astronomers of venal
knowledge looking for the star which the weaver, in
his love for it, had let slip upon the mighty complexity of the skies.

The thing that is clearest to the mind of a man is
often the thing that is most opaque to the intelli-
gence of his bosom companion. A saint may walk the
earth in the simple belief that all the world beholds
his glowing halo; but all the world does not; if it
did the saint would be stoned. And Mortimer Hehir had
been as innocently proud of his grave as a saint might
be ecstatic of his halo. He believed that when the
time came he would get a royal funeral--a funeral fit-
ting to the last of the line of great Cloon na Morav
weavers. Instead of that they had no more idea of
where to bury him than if he had been a wild tinker of
the roads.

The widow, thinking of these things in her own
mind, was about to sigh when, behind a window pane,
she heard the sudden bubble of a roller canary's song.
She had reached, half absent-mindedly, the home of
Malachi Roohan, the cooper.

IV

The widow of the weaver approached the door of

44

Malachi Roohan's house with an apologetic step, pawing
the threshold a little in the manner of peasant women--
a mannerism picked up from shy animals--before she
stooped her head and made her entrance.

Malachi Roohan's daughter withdrew from the fire a
face which reflected the passionate soul of a cook.
The face cooled as the widow disclosed her business.

'I wouldn't put it a-past my father to have knowledge of the grave,' said the daughter of the house,
adding, 'The Lord a mercy on the weaver.'

She led the widow into the presence of the cooper.

The room was small and low and stuffy, indifferent-
ly served with light by an unopenable window. There
was the smell of old age, of decay, in the room. It
brought almost a sense of faintness to the widow. She
had the feeling that God had made her to move in the
ways of old men--passionate, cantankerous, egoistic
old men, old men for whom she was always doing something, always remembering things, from missing buttons
to lost graves.

Her eyes sought the bed of Malachi Roohan with an
unemotional, quietly sceptical gaze. But she did not
see anything of the cooper. The daughter leaned over
the bed, listened attentively, and then very deftly
turned down the clothes, revealing the bust of Malachi
Roohan. The widow saw a weird face, not in the least
pale or lined, but ruddy, with a mahogany bald head, a
head upon which the leathery skin--for there did not
seem any flesh--hardly concealed the stark outlines of
the skull. From the chin there strayed a grey beard,
the most shaken and whipped-looking beard that the
widow had ever seen; it was, in truth, a very miracle
of a beard, for one wondered how it had come there,
and having come there, how it continued to hang on,
for there did not seem anything to which it could
claim natural allegiance. The widow was as much astonished at this beard as if she saw a plant growing
in a pot without soil. Through its gaps she could see
the leather of the skin, the bones of a neck, which
was indeed a neck. Over this head and shoulders the
cooper's daughter bent and shouted into a crumpled
ear. A little spasm of life stirred in the mummy. A
low, mumbling sound came from the bed. The widow was
already beginning to feel that, perhaps, she had done
wrong in remembering that the cooper was still extant.

45

But what else could she have done?  If the weaver was
buried in a wrong grave she did not believe that his
soul would ever rest in peace.  And what could be more
dreadful than a soul wandering on the howling winds of
the earth?  The weaver would grieve, even in heaven,
for his grave, grieve, maybe, as bitterly as a saint
might grieve who had lost his halo.  He was a passionate old man, such an old man as would have a turbulent
spirit.  He would surely----.  The widow stifled the
thoughts that flashed into her mind.  She was no more
superstitious than the rest of us, but----.  These
vague and terrible fears, and her moderately decent
sorrow, were alike banished from her mind by what followed.  The mummy on the bed came to life.  And, what
was more, he did it himself.  His daughter looked on
with the air of one whose sensibilities had become
blunted by a long familiarity with the various stages
of his resurrections.  The widow gathered that the
daughter had been well drilled; she had been taught
how to keep her place.  She did not tender the slightest help to her father as he drew himself together on
the bed.  He turned over on his side, then on his
back, and stealthily began to insinuate his shoulder
blades on the pillow, pushing up his weird head to the
streak of light from the little window.  The widow
had been so long accustomed to assist the aged that
she made some involuntary movement of succour.  Some
half-seen gesture by the daughter, a sudden lifting of
the eyelids on the face of the patient, disclosing a
pair of blue eyes, gave the widow instinctive pause.
She remained where she was, aloof like the daughter of
the house.  And as she caught the blue of Malachi
Roohan's eyes it broke upon the widow that here in the
essence of the cooper there lived a spirit of extraordinary independence.  Here, surely, was a man who had
been accustomed to look out for himself, who resented
the attentions, even in these days of his flickering
consciousness.  Up he wormed his shoulder blades, his
mahogany skull, his leathery skin, his sensational
eyes, his miraculous beard, to the light and to the
full view of the visitor.  At a certain stage of the
resurrection--when the cooper had drawn two long,
stringy arms from under the clothes--his daughter made
a drilled movement forward, seeking something in the
bed.  The widow saw her discover the end of a rope,
and this she placed in the hands of her indomitable
father.  The other end of the rope was fastened to the
iron rail at the foot of the bed.  The sinews of the
patient's hands clutched the rope, and slowly, wonder-
fully, magically, as it seemed to the widow, the

46

cooper raised himself to a sitting posture in the bed.
There was dead silence in the room except for the laboured breathing of the performer. The eyes of the
widow blinked. Yes, there was that ghost of a man
hoisting himself up from the dead on a length of rope
reversing the usual procedure. By that length of rope
did the cooper hang on to life, and the effort of life.
It represented his connection with the world, the
world which had forgotten him, which marched past his
window outside without knowing the stupendous thing
that went on in his room. There he was, sitting up in
the bed, restored to view by his own unaided efforts,
holding his grip on life to the last. It cost him
something to do it, but he did it. It would take him
longer and longer every day to grip along that length
of rope; he would fail ell by ell, sinking back to the
last helplessness on his rope, descending into eternity as a vessel is lowered on a rope into a dark,
deep well. But there he was now, still able for his
work, unbeholding to all, self-dependent and alive,
looking a little vaguely with his blue eyes at the
widow of the weaver. His daughter swiftly and quietly
propped pillows at his back, and she did it with the
air of one who was allowed a special privilege.

'Nan!' called the old man to his daughter.

The widow, cool-tempered as she was, almost jumped
on her feet. The voice was amazingly powerful. It
was like a shout, filling the little room with vibra-
tions. For four things did the widow ever after remember Malachi Roohan--for his rope, his blue eyes,
his powerful voice, and his magic beard. They were
thrown on the background of his skeleton in powerful
relief.

'Yes, Father,' his daughter replied, shouting into
his ear. He was apparently very deaf. This infirmity
came upon the widow with a shock. The cooper was full
of physical surprises.

'Who's this one?' the cooper shouted, looking at
the widow. He had the belief that he was delivering
an aside.

'Mrs. Hehir.'

'Mrs. Hehir--what Hehir would she be?'

'The weaver's wife.'

47

'The weaver?  Is it Mortimer Hehir?'

'Yes, Father.'

'In troth I know her.  She's Delia Morrissey, that
married the weaver; Delia Morrissey that he followed
to Munster, a raving lunatic with the dint of love.'

A hot wave of embarrassment swept the widow.  For a
moment she thought the mind of the cooper was wandering.  Then she remembered that the maiden name of the
weaver's first wife was, indeed, Delia Morrissey.  She
had heard it, by chance, once or twice.

'Isn't it Delia Morrissey herself we have in it?'
the old man asked.

The widow whispered to the daughter:

'Leave it so.'

She shrank from a difficult discussion with the
spectre on the bed on the family history of the weaver.
A sense of shame came to her that she could be the
wife to a contemporary of this astonishing old man
holding on to the life rope.

'I'm out!' shouted Malachi Roohan, his blue eyes
lighting suddenly.  'Delia Morrissey died.  She was
one day eating her dinner and a bone stuck in her
throat.  The weaver clapped her on the back, but it
was all to no good.  She choked to death before his
eyes on the floor.  I remember that.  And the weaver
himself near died of grief after.  But he married
secondly.  Who's this he married secondly, Nan?'

Nan did not know.  She turned to the widow for en-
lightenment.  The widow moistened her lips.  She had
to concentrate her thoughts on a subject which, for
her own peace of mind, she had habitually avoided.  She
hated genealogy.  She said a little nervously:

'Sara MacCabe.'

The cooper's daughter shouted the name into his ear.

'So you're Sally MacCabe, from Looscaun, the one
Mortimer took off the blacksmith?  Well, well, that
was a great business surely, the pair of them hot-
tempered men, and your own beauty going to their heads

48

like strong drink.'

He looked at the widow, a half-sceptical, half-admiring expression flickering across the leathery face. It was such a look as he might have given to Dergorvilla of Leinster,[2] Deirdre of Uladh,[3] or Helen of Troy.[4]

The widow was not the notorious Sara MacCabe from Looscaun; that lady had been the second wife of the weaver. It was said they had led a stormy life, made up of passionate quarrels and partings, and still more passionate reconciliations. Sara MacCabe from Looscaun not having quite forgotten or wholly neglected the blacksmith after her marriage to the weaver. But the widow again only whispered to the cooper's daughter:

'Leave it so.'

'What way is Mortimer keeping?' asked the old man.

'He's dead,' replied the daughter.

The fingers of the old man quivered on the rope.

'Dead? Mortimer Hehir dead?' he cried. 'What in the name of God happened to him?'

Nan did not know what happened to him. She knew that the widow would not mind, so, without waiting for a prompt, she replied:

'A weakness came over him, a sudden weakness.'

'To think of a man being whipped off all of a

2. Misspelled. Dervorgilla is associated with two different legends -- 1. As the wife of O'Rourke of Breany who eloped with MacMurrough of Leinster, thereby precipitating the Norman invasion; 2. As a woman who was famous for her piety. It is doubtless the former legend that is applicable here.
3. A beautiful heroine of Irish legend from the Ulster cycle. It was prophesied at her birth that she would bring great misfortunes; hence, "Deirdre of the Sorrows."
4. The beautiful wife of Menelaus, abducted by Paris, son of Priam who was King of Troy. Helen's abduction was responsible for the Trojan war.

49

sudden like that!' cried the cooper. 'When that's the way it was with Mortimer Hehir what one of us can be sure at all? Nan, none of us is sure! To think of the weaver, with his heart as strong as a bull, going off in a little weakness! It's the treacherous world we live in, the treacherous world, surely. Never another yard of tweed will he put up on his old loom! Morty, Morty, you were a good companion, a great warrant to walk the hills, whistling the tunes, pleasant in your conversation and as broad-spoken as the Bible.'

'Did you know the weaver well, Father?' the daughter asked.

'Who better?' he replied, 'Who drank more pints with him than what myself did? And indeed it's to his wake I'd be setting out, and it's under his coffin my shoulder would be going, if I wasn't confined to my rope.'

He bowed his head for a few moments. The two women exchanged a quick, sympathetic glance.

The breathing of the old man was the breathing of one who slept. The head sank lower.

The widow said:

'You ought to make him lie down. He's tired.'

The daughter made some movement of dissent; she was afraid to interfere. Maybe the cooper could be very violent if roused. After a time he raised his head again. He looked in a new mood. He was fresher, more wide-awake. His beard hung in wisps to the bedclothes.

'Ask him about the grave,' the widow said.

The daughter hesitated a moment, and in that moment the cooper looked up as if he had heard, or partially heard. He said:

'If you wait a minute now I'll tell you what the weaver was.' He stared for some seconds at the little window.

'Oh, we'll wait,' said the daughter, and turning to the widow, added, 'won't we, Mrs. Hehir?'

'Indeed we will wait,' said the widow.

'The weaver,' said the old man suddenly, 'was a

dream.'

He turned his head to the women to see how they had
taken it.

'Maybe,' said the daughter, with a little touch of
laughter, 'maybe Mrs. Hehir would not give in to that.'

The widow moved her hands uneasily under her shawl.
She stared a little fearfully at the cooper. His blue
eyes were clear as lake water over white sand.

'Whether she gives in to it, or whether she doesn't
give in to it,' said Malachi Roohan, 'it's a dream
Mortimer Hehir was. And his looms, and his shuttles,
and his warping bars, and his bonnin, and the threads
that he put upon the shifting racks, were all a dream.
And the only thing he ever wove upon his loom was a
dream.'

The old man smacked his lips, his hard gums whacking. His daughter looked at him with her head a little
to one side.

'And what's more,' said the cooper, 'every woman
that ever came into his head, and every wife he married
was a dream. I'm telling you that, Nan, and I'm telling it to you of the weaver. His life was a dream,
and his death is a dream. And his widow there is a
dream. And all the world is a dream. Do you hear me,
Nan, this world is all a dream.'

'I hear you very well, Father,' the daughter sang
in a piercing voice.

The cooper raised his head with a jerk, and his
beard swept forward, giving him an appearance of vivid
energy. He spoke in a voice like a trumpet blast:

'And I'm a dream!'

He turned his blue eyes on the widow. An unnerving
sensation came to her. The cooper was the most dreadful old man she had ever seen, and what he was saying
sounded the most terrible thing she had ever listened
to. He cried:

'The idiot laughing in the street, the king looking
at his crown, the woman turning her head to the sound
of a man's step, the bells ringing in the belfry, the

51

man walking his land, the weaver at his loom, the cooper handling his barrel, the Pope stooping for his red slippers--they're all a dream. And I'll tell you why they're a dream: because this world was meant to be a dream.'

'Father,' said the daughter, 'you're talking too much. You'll over-reach yourself.'

The old man gave himself a little pull on the rope. It was his gesture of energy, a demonstration of the fine fettle he was in. He said:

'You're saying that because you don't understand me.'

'I understand you very well.'

'You only think you do. Listen to me now, Nan. I want you to do something for me. You won't refuse me?'

'I will not refuse you, Father; you know very well I won't.'

'You're a good daughter to me, surely, Nan. And do what I tell you now. Shut close your eyes. Shut them fast and tight. No fluttering of the lids now.'

'Very well, Father.'

The daughter closed her eyes, throwing up her face in the attitude of one blind. The widow was conscious of the woman's strong, rough features, something good-natured in the line of the large mouth. The old man watched the face of his daughter with excitement. He asked:

'What is it that you see now, Nan?'

'Nothing at all, Father.'

'In troth you do. Keep them closed tight and you'll see it.'

'I see nothing only----'

'Only what? Why don't you say it?'

'Only darkness, Father.'

'And isn't that something to see? Isn't it easier
52

to see darkness than to see light?  Now, Nan, look into the darkness.'

'I'm looking, Father.'

'And think of something--anything at all--the stool before the kitchen fire outside.'

'I'm thinking of it.'

'And do you remember it?'

'I do well.'

'And when you remember it what do you want to do-- sit on it, maybe?'

'No, Father.'

'And why wouldn't you want to sit on it?'

'Because--because I'd like to see it first, to make sure.'

The old man gave a little crow of delight.  He cried:

'There it is!  You want to make sure that it is there, although you remember it well.  And that is the way with everything in this world.  People close their eyes and they are not sure of anything.  They want to see it again before they believe.  There is Nan, now, and she does not believe in the stool before the fire, the little stool she's looking at all her life, that her mother used to seat her on before the fire when she was a small child.  She closes her eyes, and it is gone!  And listen to me now, Nan--if you had a man of your own and you closed your eyes you wouldn't be too sure he was the man you remembered, and you'd want to open your eyes and look at him to make sure he was the man you knew before the lids dropped on your eyes. And if you had children about you and you turned your back and closed your eyes and tried to remember them you'd want to look at them to make sure.  You'd be no more sure of them than you are now of the stool in the kitchen.  One flash of the eyelids and everything in this world is gone.'

'I'm telling you, Father, you're talking too much.'

'I'm not talking half enough.  Aren't we all uneasy

53

about the world, the things in the world that we can
only believe in while we're looking at them? From one
season of our life to another haven't we a kind of belief that some time we'll waken up and find everything
different? Didn't you ever feel that, Nan? Didn't
you think things would change, that the world would be
a new place altogether, and that all that was going on
around us was only a business that was doing us out of
something else? We put up with it while the little
hankering is nibbling at the butt of our hearts for
the something else! All the men there be who believe
that some day The Thing will happen, that they'll turn
round the corner and waken up in the new great Street!'

'And sure,' said the daughter, 'maybe they are
right, and maybe they will waken up.'

The old man's body was shaken with a queer spasm of
laughter. It began under the clothes on the bed,
worked up his trunk, ran along his stringy arms, out
into the rope, and the iron foot of the bed rattled. A
look of extraordinarily malicious humour lit up the
vivid face of the cooper. The widow beheld him with
fascination, a growing sense of alarm. He might say
anything. He might do anything. He might begin to
sing some fearful song. He might leap out of bed.

'Nan,' he said, 'do you believe you'll swing round
the corner and waken up?'

'Well,' said Nan, hesitating a little, 'I do.'

The cooper gave a sort of peacock crow again. He
cried:

'Och! Nan Roohan believes she'll waken up! Waken
up from what? From a sleep and from a dream, from
this world! Well, if you believe that, Nan Roohan, it
shows you know what's what. You know what the thing
around you, called the world, is. And it's only
dreamers who can hope to waken up--do you hear me, Nan;
it's only dreamers who can hope to waken up.'

'I hear you,' said Nan.

'The world is only a dream, and a dream is nothing
at all! We all want to waken up out of the great
nothingness of this world.'

'And,please God, we will,' said Nan.

'You can tell all the world from me,' said the
cooper, 'that we won't.'

'And why won't we, Father?'

'Because,' said the old man, 'we ourselves are the
dream. When we're over the dream is over with us.
That's why.'

'Father,' said the daughter, her head again a little
to one side, 'you know a great deal.'

'I know enough,' said the cooper shortly.

'And maybe you could tell us something about the
weaver's grave. Mrs. Hehir wants to know.'

'And amn't I after telling you all about the
weaver's grave? Amn't I telling you it is all a
dream?'

'You never said that, Father. Indeed you never
did.'

'I said everything in this world is a dream, and
the weaver's grave is in this world, below in Cloon na
Morav.'

'Where in Cloon na Morav? What part of it, Father?
That is what Mrs. Hehir wants to know. Can you tell
her?'

'I can tell her,' said Malachi Roohan. 'I was at
his father's burial. I remember it above all burials,
because that was the day the handsome girl, Honor
Costello, fell over a grave and fainted. The sweat
broke out on young Donohoe when he saw Honor Costello
tumbling over the grave. Not a marry would he marry
her after that, and he sworn to it by the kiss of her
lips. "I'll marry no woman that fell on a grave," says
Donohoe. "She'd maybe have a child by me with turned-
in eyes or a twisted limb." So he married a farmer's
daughter, and the same morning Honor Costello married
a cattle drover. Very well, then. Donohoe's wife had
no child at all. She was a barren woman. Do you hear
me, Nan? A barren woman she was. And such childer as
Honor Costello had by the drover! Yellow hair they
had, heavy as seaweed, the skin of them clear as the
wind, and limbs as clean as a whistle! It was said
the drover was of the blood of the Danes, and it broke
out in Honor Costello's family!'

55

'Maybe,' said the daughter, 'they were Vikings.'

'What are you saying?' cried the old man testily.
'Ain't I telling you it's Danes they were. Did any
one ever hear a greater miracle?'

'No one ever did,' said the daughter, and both
women clicked their tongues to express sympathetic wonder at the tale.

'And I'll tell you what saved Honor Costello,' said
the cooper. 'When she fell in Cloon na Morav she
turned her cloak inside out.'

'What about the weaver's grave, Father? Mrs. Hehir
wants to know.'

The old man looked at the widow; his blue eyes
searched her face and her figure; the expression of
satirical admiration flashed over his features. The
nostrils of the nose twitched. He said:

'So that's the end of the story! Sally MacCabe,
the blacksmith's favourite, wants to know where she'll
sink the weaver out of sight! Great battles were
fought in Looscaun over Sally MacCabe! The weaver
thought his heart would burst, and the blacksmith
damned his soul for the sake of Sally MacCabe's idle
hours.'

'Father,' said the daughter of the house, 'let the
dead rest.'

'Ay,' said Malachi Roohan, 'let the foolish dead
rest. The dream of Looscaun is over. And now the
pale woman is looking for the black weaver's grave.
Well, good luck to her!'

The cooper was taken with another spasm of grotesque
laughter. The only difference was that this time it
began by the rattling of the rail of the bed, travelled
along the rope, down his stringy arms dying out somewhere in his legs in the bed. He smacked his lips, a
peculiar harsh sound, as if there was not much meat to
it.

'Do I know where Mortimer Hehir's grave is?' he said
ruminatingly. 'Do I know where me rope is?'

'Where is it, then?' his daughter asked. Her
patience was great.

'I'll tell you that,' said the cooper.  'It's under the elm tree of Cloon na Morav.  That's where it is surely.  There was never a weaver yet that did not find rest under the elm tree of Cloon na Morav.  There they all went as surely as the buds came on the branches.  Let Sally MacCabe put poor Morty there; let her give him a tear or two in memory of the days that his heart was ready to burst for her, and believe you me no ghost will ever haunt her.  No dead man ever yet came back to look upon a woman!'

A furtive sigh escaped the widow.  With her handkerchief she wiped a little perspiration from both sides of her nose.  The old man wagged his head sympathetically.  He thought she was the long dead Sally MacCabe lamenting the weaver!  The widow's emotion arose from relief that the mystery of the grave had at last been cleared up.  Yet her dealings with old men had taught her caution.  Quite suddenly the memory of the handsome dark face of the grave-digger who had followed her to the stile came back to her.  She remembered that he said something about 'the exact position of the grave.' The widow prompted yet another question:

'What position under the elm tree?'

The old man listened to the question; a strained look came into his face.

'Position of what?' he asked.

'Of the grave.'

'Of what grave?'

'The weaver's grave.'

Another spasm seized the old frame, but this time it came from no aged merriment.  It gripped his skeleton and shook it.  It was as if some invisible powerful hand had suddenly taken him by the back of the neck and shaken him.  His knuckles rattled on the rope.  They had an appalling sound.  A horrible feeling came to the widow that the cooper would fall to pieces like a bag of bones.  He turned his face to his daughter.  Great tears had welled into the blue eyes, giving them an appearance of childish petulance, then of acute suffering.

'What are you talking to me of graves for?' he asked, and the powerful voice broke.  'Why will you be

57

tormenting me like this?  It's not going to die I am,
is it?  Is it going to die I am, Nan?'

The daughter bent over him as she might bend over a
child.  She said:

'Indeed, there's great fear of you.  Lie down and
rest yourself.  Fatigued out and out you are.'

The grip slowly slackened on the rope.  He sank
back, quite helpless, a little whimper breaking from
him.  The daughter stooped lower, reaching for a pillow
that had fallen in by the wall.  A sudden sharp snarl
sounded from the bed, and it dropped from her hand.

'Don't touch me!' the cooper cried.  The voice was
again restored, powerful in its command.  And to the
amazement of the widow she saw him again grip along
the rope and rise in the bed.

'Amn't I tired telling you not to touch me?' he
cried.  'Have I any business talking to you at all?
Is it gone my authority is in this house?'

He glared at his daughter, his eyes red with anger,
like a dog crouching in his kennel, and the daughter
stepped back, a wry smile on her large mouth.  The
widow stepped back with her, and for a moment he held
the women with their backs to the wall by his angry
red eyes.  Another growl and the cooper sank back inch
by inch on the rope.  In all her experience of old men
the widow had never seen anything like this old man;
his resurrections and his collapse.  When he was quite
down the daughter gingerly put the clothes over his
shoulders and then beckoned the widow out of the room.

The widow left the house of Malachi Roohan, the
cooper, with the feeling that she had discovered the
grave of an old man by almost killing another.

V

The widow walked along the streets, outwardly calm,
inwardly confused.  Her first thought was 'the day is
going on me!'  There were many things still to be done
at home; she remembered the weaver lying there, quiet
at last, the candles lighting about him, the brown
habit over him, a crucifix in his hands--everything as
it should be.  It seemed ages to the widow since he
had really fallen ill.  He was very exacting and
peevish all that time.  His death agony had been

58

protracted, almost melodramatically violent. A few
times the widow had nearly run out of the house,
leaving the weaver to fight the death battle alone.
But her common sense, her good nerves, and her religious convictions had stood to her, and when she put
the pennies on the weaver's eyes she was glad she had
done her duty to the last. She was glad now that she
had taken the search for the grave out of the hands of
Meehaul Lynskey and Cahir Bowes; Malachi Roohan had
been a sight, and she would never forget him, but he
had known what nobody else knew. The widow, as she
ascended a little upward sweep of the road to Cloon na
Morav, noted that the sky beyond it was more vivid, a
red band of light having struck across the grey-blue,
just on the horizon. Up against this red background
was the dark outline of landscape, and especially
Cloon na Morav. She kept her eyes upon it as she drew
nearer. Objects that were vague on the landscape began to bulk up with more distinction.

She noted the back wall of Cloon na Morav, its green
lichen more vivid under the red patch of the skyline.
And presently, above the green wall, black against the
vivid sky, she saw elevated the bulk of one of the
black cockroaches. On it were perched two drab figures, so grotesque, so still, that they seemed part of
the thing itself. One figure was sloping out from the
end of the tombstone so curiously that for a moment
the widow thought it was a man who had reached down
from the table to see what was under it. At the other
end of the table was a slender warped figure, and as
the widow gazed upon it she saw a sign of animation.
The head and face, bleak in their outlines, were raised
up in a gesture of despair. The face was turned flush
against the sky, so much so that the widow's eyes instinctively sought the sky too. Above the slash of
red, in the west, was a single star, flashing so
briskly and so freshly that it might have never shone
before. For all the widow knew, it might have been a
young star frolicking in the heavens with all the joy
of youth. Was that, she wondered, at what the old
man, Meehaul Lynskey, was gazing. He was very, very
old, and the star was very, very young! Was there
some protest in the gesture of the head he raised to
that thing in the sky; was there some mockery in the
sparkle of the thing of the sky for the face of the
man? Why should a star be always young, a man aged so
soon? Should not a man be greater than a star? Was
it this Meehaul Lynskey was thinking? The widow could
not say, but something in the thing awed her. She had

the sensation of one who surprises a man in some act
that lifts him above the commonplaces of existence.
It was as if Meehaul Lynskey were discovered prostrate
before some altar, in the throes of a religious agony.
Old men were, the widow felt, very, very strange, and
she did not know that she would ever understand them.
As she looked at the bleak head of Meehaul Lynskey up
against the vivid patch of the sky, she wondered if
there could really be something in that head which
would make him as great as a star, immortal as a star?
Suddenly Meehaul Lynskey made a movement. The widow
saw it quite distinctly. She saw the arm raised, the
hand go out, with its crooked fingers, in one, two,
three quick short taps in the direction of the star.
The widow stood to watch, and the gesture was so familiar, so homely, so personal, that it was quite un-
derstandable to her. She knew then that Meehaul
Lynskey was not thinking of any great things at all.
He was only a nailer! And seeing the Evening Star
sparkle in the sky he had only thought of his workshop,
of the bellows, the irons, the fire, the sparks, and
the glowing iron which might be made into a nail while
it was hot! He had in imagination seized a hammer and
made a blow across interstellar space at Venus! All
the beauty and youth of the star frolicking on the pale
sky above the slash of vivid redness had only suggested
to him the making of yet another nail! If Meehaul
Lynskey could push up his scarred yellow face among the
stars of the sky he would only see in them the sparks
of his little smithy.

Cahir Bowes was, the widow thought, looking down at
the earth, from the other end of the tombstone, to see
if there were any hard things there which he could
smash up. The old men had their backs turned upon
each other. Very likely they had had another discussion since, which ended in this attitude of mutual
contempt. The widow was conscious again of the un-
reasonableness of old men, but not much resentful of
it. She was too long accustomed to them to have any
great sense of revolt. Her emotion, if it could be
called an emotion, was a settled, dull toleration of
all their little bigotries.

She put her hand on the stile for the second time
that day, and again raised her palely sad face over
the graveyard of Cloon na Morav. As she did so she
had the most extraordinary experience of the whole
day's sensations. It was such a sensation as gave her
at once a wonderful sense of the reality and the un-
reality of life. She paused on the stile, and had a

60

clear insight into something that had up to this moment
been obscure. And no sooner had the thing become definite and clear than a sense of the wonder of life came
to her. It was all very like the dream Malachi Roohan
had talked about.

In the pale grass, under the vivid colours of the
sky, the two grave-diggers were lying on their backs,
staring silently up at the heavens. The widow looked
at them as she paused on the stile. Her thoughts of
these men had been indifferent, subconscious up to
this instant. They were handsome young men. Perhaps
if there had been only one of them the widow would have
been, more attentive. The dark handsomeness did not
seem the same thing when repeated. Their beauty, if
one could call it beauty, had been collective, the
beauty of flowers, of dark, velvety pansies, the distinctive marks of one faithfully duplicated on the
other. The good looks of one had, to the mind of the
widow, somehow nullified the good looks of the other.
There was too much borrowing of Peter to pay Paul in
their well-favoured features. The first grave-digger
spoiled the illusion of individuality in the second
grave-digger. The widow had not thought so, but she
would have agreed if anybody whispered to her that a
good-looking man who wanted to win favour with a woman
should never have so complete a twin brother. It would
be possible for a woman to part tenderly with a man,
and, if she met his image and likeness around the corner, knock him down. There is nothing more powerful,
but nothing more delicate in life than the valves of
individuality. To create the impression that humanity
was a thing which could be turned out like a coinage
would be to ruin the whole illusion of life. The twin
grave-diggers had created some sort of such impression,
vague, and not very insistent, in the mind of the
widow, and it had made her lose any special interest
in them. Now, however, as she hesitated on the stile,
all this was swept from her mind at a stroke. The
most subtle and powerful of all things, personality,
sprang silently from the twins and made them, to the
mind of the widow, things as far apart as the poles.
The two men lay at length, and exactly the same length
and bulk, in the long, grey grass. But, as the widow
looked upon them, one twin seemed conscious of her
presence, while the other continued his absorption in
the heavens above. The supreme twin turned his head,
and his soft, velvety brown eyes met the eyes of the
widow. There was welcome in the man's eyes. The
widow read that welcome as plainly as if he had spoken
his thoughts. The next moment he had sprung to his

61

feet, smiling. He took a few steps forward, then,
self-conscious, pulled up. If he had only jumped up
and smiled the widow would have understood. But those
few eager steps forward and then that stock stillness!
The other twin rose reluctantly, and as he did so the
widow was conscious of even physical differences in the
brothers. The eyes were not the same. No such velvety
soft lights were in the eyes of the second one. He was
more sheepish. He was more phlegmatic. He was only a
plagiarism of the original man! The widow wondered how
she had not seen all this before. The resemblance between the twins was only skin deep. The two old men,
at the moment the second twin rose, detached themselves
slowly, almost painfully, from their tombstone, and all
moved forward to meet the widow. The widow, collecting
her thoughts, piloted her skirts modestly about her
legs as she got down from the narrow stonework of the
stile and stumbled into the contrariness of Cloon na
Morav. A wild sense of satisfaction swept her that she
had come back the bearer of useful information.

'Well,' said Meehaul Lynskey, 'did you see Malachi
Roohan?' The widow looked at his scorched, sceptical,
yellow face, and said:

'I did.'

'Had he any word for us?'

'He had. He remembers the place of the weaver's
grave.' The widow looked a little vaguely about Cloon
na Morav.

'What does he say?'

'He says it's under the elm tree.'

There was silence. The stonebreaker swung about on
his legs, his head making a semi-circular movement over
the ground, and his sharp eyes were turned upward, as
if he were searching the heavens for an elm tree. The
nailer dropped his underjaw and stared tensely across
the ground, blankly, patiently, like a fisherman on the
edge of the shore gazing over an empty sea. The grave-
digger turned his head away shyly, like a boy, as if he
did not want to see the confusion of the widow; the man
was full of the most delicate mannerisms. The other
grave-digger settled into a stolid attitude, then the
skin bunched up about his brown eyes in puckers of
humour. A miserable feeling swept the widow. She had

62

the feeling that she stood on the verge of some collapse.

'Under the elm tree,' mumbled the stonebreaker.

'That's what he said,' added the widow.  'Under the
elm tree of Cloon na Morav.'

'Well,' said Cahir Bowes, 'when you find the elm
tree you'll find the grave.'

The widow did not know what an elm tree was.  Nothing had ever happened in life as she knew it to render
any special knowledge of trees profitable, and therefore desirable.  Trees were good; they made nice firing
when chopped up; timber, and all that was fashioned out
of timber, came from trees.  This knowledge the widow
had accepted as she had accepted all the other remote
phenomena of the world into which she had been born.
But that trees should have distinctive names, that they
should have family relationships, seemed to the mind of
the widow only an unnecessary complication of the af-
fairs of the universe.  What good was it?  She could
understand calling fruit trees fruit trees and all
other kinds simply trees.  But that one should be an
elm and another an ash, that there should be name after
name, species after species, giving them peculiarities
and personalities, was one of the things that the widow
did not like.  And at this moment, when the elm tree of
Malachi Roohan had raised a fresh problem in Cloon na
Morav, the likeness of old men to old trees--their
crankiness, their complexity, their angles, their very
barks, bulges, gnarled twistiness, and kinks--was very
close, and brought a sense of oppression to the sorely-
tried brain of the widow.

'Under the elm tree,' repeated Meehaul Lynskey.
'The elm tree of Cloon na Morav.'  He broke into an
aged cackle of a laugh.  'If I was any good at all at
making a rhyme I'd make one about that elm tree, devil
a other but I would.'

The widow looked around Cloon na Morav, and her
eyes, for the first time in her life, were consciously
searching for trees.  If there were numerous trees
there she could understand how easy it might be for
Malachi Roohan to make a mistake.  He might have mis-
taken some other sort of tree for an elm--the widow
felt that there must be plenty of other trees very like
an elm.  In fact, she reasoned that other trees, do
their best, could not help looking like an elm.  There

63

must be thousands and millions of people like herself
in the world who pass through life in the belief that
a certain kind of tree was an elm when, in reality, it
may be an ash or an oak or a chestnut or a beech, or
even a poplar, a birch, or a yew.  Malachi Roohan was
never likely to allow anybody to amend his knowledge
of an elm tree.  He would let go his rope in the belief
that there was an elm tree in Cloon na Morav, and that
under it was the weaver's grave--that is, if Malachi
Roohan had not, in some ghastly aged kink, invented the
thing.  The widow, not sharply, but still with an ap-
preciation of the thing, grasped that a dispute about
trees would be the very sort of dispute in which
Meehaul Lynskey and Cahir Bowes would, like the very
old men that they were, have revelled.  Under the impulse of the message she had brought from the cooper
they would have launched out into another powerful
struggle from tree to tree in Cloon na Morav; they
would again have strewn the place with the corpses of
slain arguments, and in the net result they would not
have been able to establish anything either about elm
trees or about the weaver's grave.  The slow, sad gaze
of the widow for trees in Cloon na Morav brought to her,
in these circumstances, both pain and relief.  It was a
relief that Meehaul Lynskey and Cahir Bowes could not
challenge each other to a battle of trees; it was a
pain that the tree of Malachi Roohan was nowhere in
sight.  The widow could see for herself that there was
not any sort of a tree in Cloon na Morav.  The ground
was enclosed upon three sides by walls, on the fourth
by a hedge of quicks.5  Not even old men could trans-
form a hedge into an elm tree.  Neither could they make
the few struggling briars clinging about the railings
of the sepulchres into anything except briars.  The elm
tree of Malachi Roohan was now non-existent.  Nobody
would ever know whether it had or had not ever existed.
The widow would as soon give the soul of the weaver to
the howling winds of the world as go back and interview
the cooper again on the subject.

'Old Malachi Roohan,' said Cahir Bowes with tolerant
decision, 'is doting.'

'The nearest elm tree I know,' said Meehaul Lynskey,
'is half a mile away.'

'The one above at Carragh?' questioned Cahir Bowes.


5. Equals quickset, whitethorn or other shrubs of which
   hedges are made.

64

'Aye, beside the mill.'

No more was to be said. The riddle of the weaver's grave was still the riddle of the weaver's grave. Cloon na Morav kept its secret. But, nevertheless, the weaver would have to be buried. He could not be housed indefinitely. Taking courage from all the harrowing aspects of the deadlock, Meehaul Lynskey went back, plump and courageously to his original allegiance.

'The grave of the weaver is there,' he said, and he struck out his hooked fingers in the direction of the disturbance of the sod which the grave-diggers had made under pressure of his earlier enthusiasm.

Cahir Bowes turned on him with a withering, quavering glance.

'Aren't you afraid that God would strike you where you stand?' he demanded.

'I'm not--not a bit afraid,' said Meehaul Lynskey. 'It's the weaver's grave.'

'You say that,' cried Cahir Bowes, 'after what we all saw and what we all heard?'

'I do,' said Meehaul Lynskey, stoutly. He wiped his lips with the palm of his hand, and launched out into one of his arguments, as usual, packed with particulars.

'I saw the weaver's father lowered in that place. And I'll tell you, what's more, it was Father Owen MacCarthy that read over him, he a young red-haired curate in this place at the time, long before ever he became parish priest of Benelog. There was I, standing in this exact spot, a young man, too, with a light moustache, holding me hat in me hand, and there one side of me--maybe five yards from the marble stone of the Keernahans--was Patsy Curtin that drank himself to death after, and on the other side of me was Honor Costello, that fell on the grave and married the cattle drover, a big, loose-shouldered Dane.'

Patiently, half absent-mindedly, listening to the renewal of the dispute, the widow remembered the words of Malachi Roohan, and his story of Honor Costello, who fell on the grave over fifty years ago. What memories these old men had! How unreliable they were, and yet flashing out astounding corroborations of each other.

Maybe there was something in what Meehaul Lynskey was
saying. Maybe--but the widow checked her thoughts.
What was the use of it all? This grave could not be
the weaver's grave; it had been grimly demonstrated to
them all that it was full of stout coffins. The widow,
with a gesture of agitation, smoothed her hair down the
gentle slope of her head under the shawl. As she did
so her eyes caught the eyes of the grave-digger; he was
looking at her! He withdrew his eyes at once, and began to twitch the ends of his dark moustache with his
fingers.

'If,' said Cahir Bowes, 'this be the grave of the
weaver, what's Julia Rafferty doing in it? Answer me
that, Meehaul Lynskey.'

'I don't know what's she doing in it, and what's
more, I don't care. And believe you my word, many a
queer thing happened in Cloon na Morav that had no
right to happen in it. Julia Rafferty, maybe, isn't
the only one that is where she had no right to be.'

'Maybe she isn't,' said Cahir Bowes, 'but it's there
she is, anyhow, and I'm thinking it's there she's
likely to stay.'

'If she's in the weaver's grave,' cried Meehaul
Lynskey, 'what I say is, out with her!'

'Very well, then, Meehaul Lynskey. Let you yourself
be the powerful man to deal with Julia Rafferty. But
remember this, and remember it's my word, that touch
one bone in this place and you touch all.'

'No fear at all have I to right a wrong. I'm no
backslider when it comes to justice, and justice I'll
see done among the living and the dead.'

'Go ahead, then, me hearty fellow. If Julia herself
is in the wrong place somebody else must be in her own
place, and you'll be following one rightment with
another wrongment until in the end you'll go mad with
the tangle of dead men's wrongs. That's the end that's
in store for you, Meehaul Lynskey.'

Meehaul Lynskey spat on his fist and struck out with
the hooked fingers. His blood was up.

'That I may be as dead as my father!' he began in a
traditional oath, and at that Cahir Bowes gave a little
cry and raised his stick with a battle flourish. They

66

went up and down the dips of the ground, rising and
falling on the waves of their anger, and the widow
stood where she was, miserable and downhearted, her
feet growing stone cold from the chilly dampness of the
ground. The twin, who did not now count, took out his
pipe and lit it, looking at the old men with a stolid
gaze. The twin who now counted walked uneasily away,
bit an end off a chunk of tobacco, and came to stand in
the ground in a line with the widow, looking on with
her several feet away; but again the widow was conscious of the man's growing sympathy.

'They're a nice pair of boyos, them two old lads,'
he remarked to the widow. He turned his head to her.
He was very handsome.

'Do you think they will find it?' she asked. Her
voice was a little nervous, and the man shifted on his
feet, nervously responsive.

'It's hard to say,' he said. 'You'd never know what
to think. Two old lads, the like of them, do be very
tricky.'

'God grant they'll get it,' said the widow.

'God grant,' said the grave-digger.

But they didn't. They only got exhausted as before,
wheezing and coughing, and glaring at each other as
they sat down on two mounds.

The grave-digger turned to the widow.

She was aware of the nice warmth of his brown eyes.

'Are you waking the weaver again tonight?' he asked.

'I am,' said the widow.

'Well, maybe some person--some old man or woman from
the country--may turn up and be able to tell where the
grave is. You could make inquiries.'

'Yes,' said the widow, but without any enthusiasm,
'I could make inquiries.'

The grave-digger hesitated for a moment, and said
more sympathetically, 'We could all, maybe, make inquiries.' There was a softer personal note, a note of
adventure, in the voice.

67

The widow turned her head to the man and smiled at him quite frankly.

'I'm beholding to you,' she said and then added with a little wounded sigh, 'Everyone is very good to me.'

The grave-digger twirled the ends of his moustache.

Cahir Bowes, who had heard, rose from his mount and said briskly, 'I'll agree to leave it at that.' His air was that of one who had made an extraordinary personal sacrifice. What he was really thinking was that he would have another great day of it with Meehaul Lynskey in Cloon na Morav tomorrow. He'd show that oul' fellow, Lynskey, what stuff Boweses were made of.

'And I'm not against it,' said Meehaul Lynskey. He took the tone of one who was never to be outdone in magnanimity. He was also thinking of another day of effort tomorrow, a day that would, please God, show the Boweses what the Lynskeys were like.

With that the party came straggling out of Cloon na Morav, the two old men first, the widow next, the grave-diggers waiting to put on their coats and light their pipes.

There was a little upward slope on the road to the town, and as the two old men took it the widow thought they looked very spent after their day. She wondered if Cahir Bowes would ever be able for that hill. She would give him a glass of whiskey at home, if there was any left in the bottle. Of the two, and as limp and slack as his body looked, Meehaul Lynskey appeared the better able for the hill. They walked together, that is to say, abreast, but they kept almost the width of the road between each other, as if this gulf expressed the breach of friendship between them on the head of the dispute about the weaver's grave. They had been making liars of each other all day, and they would, please God, make liars of each other all day tomorrow. The widow, understanding the meaning of this hostility, had a faint sense of amusement at the contrariness of old men. How could she tell what was passing in the head which Cahir Bowes hung, like a fuchsia drop, over the road? How could she know of the strange rise and fall of the thoughts, the little frets, the tempers, the faint humours, which chased each other there? Nobody--not even Cahir Bowes himself--could account for them. All the widow knew was that Cahir Bowes stood suddenly on the road. Something had happened in his

68

brain, some old memory cell long dormant had become
nascent, had a stir, a pulse, a flicker of warmth, of
activity, and swiftly as a flash of lightning in the
sky, a glow of lucidity lit up his memory. It was as
if a searchlight had suddenly flooded the dark corners
of his brain. The immediate physical effect on Cahir
Bowes was to cause him to stand stark still on the
road, Meehaul Lynskey going ahead without him. The
widow saw Cahir Bowes pivot on his heels, his head, at
the end of the horizontal body, swinging round like the
movement of a hand on a runaway clock. Instead of
pointing up the hill homeward the head pointed down the
hill and back to Cloon na Morav. There followed the
most extraordinary movements--shufflings, gyrations--
that the widow had ever seen. Cahir Bowes wanted to
run like mad away down the road. That was plain. And
Cahir Bowes believed that he was running like mad away
down the road. That was also evident. But what he
actually did was to make little jumps on his feet, his
stick rattling the ground in front, and each jump did
not bring him an inch of ground. He would have gone
more rapidly in his normal shuffle. His efforts were
like a terrible parody on the springs of a kangaroo.
And Cahir Bowes, in a voice that was now more a scream
than a cackle, was calling out unintelligible things.
The widow, looking at him, paused in wonder, then over
her face there came a relaxation, a colour, her eyes
warmed, her expression lost its settled pensiveness,
and all her body was shaken with uncontrollable
laughter. Cahir Bowes passed her on the road in his
fantastic leaps, his abortive buck-jumps, screaming
and cracking his stick on the ground, his left hand
still gripped tightly on the small of his back behind,
a powerful brake on the small of his back.

Meehaul Lynskey turned back and his face was shaken
with an aged emotion as he looked after the stone-
breaker. Then he removed his hat and blessed himself.

'The cross of Christ between us and harm,' he exclaimed. 'Old Cahir Bowes has gone off his head at
last. I thought there was something up with him all
day. It was easily known there was something ugly
working in his mind.'

The widow controlled her laughter and checked herself, making the sign of the Cross on her forehead,
too. She said:

'God forgive me for laughing and the weaver with the
habit but fresh upon him.'

69

The grave-digger who counted was coming out somewhat
eagerly over the stile, but Cahir Bowes, flourishing
his stick, beat him back again and then himself re-
entered Cloon na Morav. He stumbled over the grass,
now rising on a mound, now disappearing altogether in
a dip of the ground, travelling in a giddy course like
a hooker in a storm; again, for a long time, he remained submerged, showing, however, the eternal stick,
his periscope, his indication to the world that he was
about his business. In a level piece of ground, marked
by stones with large mottled white marks upon them, he
settled and cried out to all, and calling God to wit-
ness, that this surely was the weaver's grave. There
was scepticism, hesitation, on the part of the grave-
diggers, but after some parley, and because Cahir Bowes
was so passionate, vehement, crying and shouting, drib-
bling water from the mouth, showing his yellow teeth,
pouring sweat on his forehead, quivering on his legs,
they began to dig carefully in the spot. The widow, at
this, re-arranged the shawl on her head and entered
Cloon na Morav, conscious, as she shuffled over the
stile, that a pair of warm brown eyes were, for a moment, upon her movements and then withdrawn. She stood
a little way back from the digging and awaited the result with a slightly more accelerated beating of the
heart. The twins looked as if they were ready to
strike something unexpected at any moment, digging
carefully, and Cahir Bowes hung over the place, cackling and crowing, urging the men to swifter work. The
earth sang up out of the ground, dark and rich in colour, gleaming like gold, in the deepening twilight in
the place. Two feet, three feet, four feet of earth
came up, the spades pushing through the earth in regular and powerful pushes, and still the coast was clear.
Cahir Bowes trembled with excitement on his stick.
Five feet of a pit yawned in the ancient ground. The
spade work ceased. One of the grave-diggers looked up
at Cahir Bowes and said:

'You hit the weaver's grave this time right enough.
Not another grave in the place could be as free as
this.'

The widow sighed a quick little sigh and looked at
the face of the other grave-digger, hesitated, then
allowed a remote smile of thankfulness to flit across
her palely sad face. The eyes of the man wandered away
over the darkening spaces of Cloon na Morav.

'I got the weaver's grave surely,' cried Cahir
Bowes, his old face full of a weird animation. If he

70

had found the Philosopher's Stone[6] he would only have
broken it. But to find the weaver's grave was an ac-
complishment that would help him into a wisdom before
which all his world would bow. He looked around triumphantly and said:

'Where is Meehaul Lynskey now; what will the people
be saying at all about his attack on Julia Rafferty's
grave? Julia will haunt him, and I'd sooner have any
one at all haunting me than the ghost of Julia Rafferty. Where is Meehaul Lynskey now? Is it ashamed to
show his liary face he is? And what talk had Malachi
Roohan about an elm tree? Elm tree, indeed! If it's
trees that is troubling him now let him climb up one of
them and hang himself from it with his rope! Where is
that old fellow, Meehaul Lynskey, and his rotten head?
Where is he, I say? Let him come in here now to Cloon
na Morav until I be showing him the weaver's grave,
five feet down and not a rib or a knuckle in it, as
clean and beautiful as the weaver ever wished it. Come
in here, Meehaul Lynskey, until I hear the lies panting
again in your yellow throat.'

He went in his extraordinary movement over the
ground, making for the stile all the while talking.

Meehaul Lynskey had crouched behind the wall outside
when Cahir Bowes led the diggers to the new site, his
old face twisted in an attentive, almost agonizing
emotion. He stood peeping over the wall, saying to
himself:

'Whisht, will you! Don't mind that old madman. He
hasn't it at all. I'm telling you he hasn't it.
Whisht, will you! Let him dig away. They'll hit something in a minute. They'll level him when they find
out. His brain has turned. Whisht, now, will you, and
I'll have that rambling old lunatic, Cahir Bowes, in a
minute. I'll leap in on him. I'll charge him before
the world. I'll show him up. I'll take the gab out of
him. I'll lacerate him. I'll lambaste him. Whisht,
will you!'

But as the digging went on and the terrible cries of
triumph arose inside Meehaul Lynskey's knees knocked
together. His head bent level to the wall, yellow and

6. In alchemy, believed to be a substance capable of
   transmuting baser metals into gold and also of re-
   storing youth to the aged.

71

grimacing, nerves twitching across it, a little yellow
froth gathering at the corners of the mouth.  When
Cahir Bowes came beating for the stile Meehaul Lynskey
rubbed one leg with the other, a little below the calf,
and cried brokenly to himself:

'God in Heaven, he has it!  He has the weaver's
grave.'

He turned about and slunk along in the shadow of the
wall up the hill, panting and broken.  By the time
Cahir Bowes had reached the stile Meehaul Lynskey's
figure was shadowily dipping down over the crest of the
road.  A sharp cry from Cahir Bowes caused him to
shrink out of sight like a dog at whom a weapon had
been thrown.

The eyes of the grave-digger who did not now count
followed the figure of Cahir Bowes as he moved to the
stile.  He laughed a little in amusement, then wiped
his brow.  He came up out of the grave.  He turned to
the widow and said:

'We're down five feet.  Isn't that enough in which
to sink the weaver in?  Are you satisfied?'

The man spoke to her without any pretense at fine
feeling.  He addressed her as a fourth wife should be
addressed.  The widow was conscious but unresentful of
the man's manner.  She regarded him calmly and without
any resentment.  On her part there was no resentment
either, no hypocrisy, no make-believe.  Her unemotional
eyes followed his action as he stuck his spade into the
loose mould on the ground.  A cry from Cahir Bowes dis-
tracted the man, he laughed again, and before the widow
could make a reply he said:

'Old Cahir is great value.  Come down until we hear
him handling the nailer.'

He walked away down over the ground.

The widow was left alone with the other grave-
digger.  He drew himself up out of the pit with a sinu-
ous movement of the body which the widow noted.  He
stood without a word beside the pile of heaving clay
and looked across at the widow.  She looked back at
him and suddenly the silence became full of unspoken
words, of flying, ringing emotions.  The widow could
see the dark green wall, above it the band of still
deepening red, above that the still more pallid grey

72

sky, and directly over the man's head the gay frolicking of the fresh star in the sky.  Cloon na Morav was
flooded with a deep, vague light.  The widow scented
the fresh wind about her, the cool fragrance of the
earth, and yet a warmth that was strangely beautiful.
The light of the man's dark eyes were visible in the
shadow which hid his face.  The pile of earth beside
him was like a vague shape of miniature bronze mountains.  He stood with a stillness which was tense and
dramatic.  The widow thought that the world was
strange, the sky extraordinary, the man's head against
the red sky a wonder, a poem, above it the sparkle of
the great young star.  The widow knew that they would
be left together like this for one minute, a minute
which would be as a flash and as eternity.  And she
knew now that sooner or later this man would come to
her and that she would welcome him.  Below at the stile
the voice of Cahir Bowes was cackling in its aged
notes.  Beyond this the stillness was the stillness of
heaven and earth.  Suddenly a sense of faintness came
to the widow.  The whole place swooned before her eyes.
Never was this world so strange, so like the dream that
Malachi Roohan had talked about.  A movement in the
figure of the man beside the heap of bronze had come to
her as a warning, a fear, and a delight.  She moved
herself a little in response, made a step backward. The
next instant she saw the figure of the man spring
across the open black mouth of the weaver's grave to
her.

A faint sound escaped her and then his breath was
hot on her face, his mouth on her lips.

Half a minute later Cahir Bowes came shuffling back,
followed by the twin.

'I'll bone him yet,' said Cahir Bowes.  'Never you
fear I'll make that old nailer face me.  I'll show him
up at the weaver's wake tonight!'

The twin laughed behind him.  He shook his head at
his brother, who was standing a pace away from the
widow.  He said:

'Five feet.'

He looked into the grave and then looked at the
widow, saying:

'Are you satisfied?'

73

There was silence for a second or two, and when she spoke the widow's voice was low but fresh, like the voice of a young girl.  She said:

'I'm satisfied.'

THE TENT

by Liam O'Flaherty


A sudden squall struck the tent. White glittering
hailstones struck the shabby canvas with a wild noise.
The tent shook and swayed slightly forward, dangling
its tattered flaps. The pole creaked as it strained.
A rent appeared near the top of the pole like a silver
seam in the canvas. Water immediately trickled through
the seam, making a dark blob.

A tinker and his two wives were sitting on a heap of
straw in the tent, looking out through the entrance at
the wild moor that stretched in front of it, with a
snowcapped mountain peak rising like the tip of a cone
over the ridge of the moor about two miles away. The
three of them were smoking cigarettes in silence. It
was evening, and they had pitched their tent for the
night in a gravel pit on the side of the mountain road,
crossing from one glen to another. Their donkey was
tethered to the cart beside the tent.

When the squall came the tinker sat up with a start
and looked at the pole. He stared at the seam in the
canvas for several moments and then he nudged the two
women and pointed upwards with a jerk of his nose. The
women looked but nobody spoke. After a minute or so
the tinker sighed and struggled to his feet.

"I'll throw a few sacks over the top," he said.

He picked up two brown sacks from the heap of blan-
kets and clothes that were drying beside the brazier
in the entrance and went out. The women never spoke,
but kept on smoking.

The tinker kicked the donkey out of his way. The
beast had stuck his hindquarters into the entrance of
the tent as far as possible, in order to get the heat
from the wood burning in the brazier. The donkey
shrank away sideways still chewing a wisp of the hay
which the tinker had stolen from a haggard[1] the other
side of the mountain. The tinker scrambled up the
bank against which the tent was pitched. The bank was
covered with rank grass into which yesterday's snow had
melted in muddy cakes.

1. A barnyard enclosure

The top of the tent was only about eighteen inches
above the bank.  Beyond the bank there was a narrow
rough road, with a thick copse of pine trees on the far
side, within the wired fence of a demesne, but the
force of the squall was so great that it swept through
the trees and struck the top of the tent as violently
as if it were standing exposed on the open moor.  The
tinker had to lean against the wind to prevent himself
being carried away.  He looked into the wind with wide-
open nostrils.

"It can't last," he said, throwing the two sacks
over the tent, where there was a rent in the canvas.
He then took a big needle from his jacket and put a few
stitches in them.

He was about to jump down from the bank when somebody hailed him from the road.  He looked up and saw a
man approaching, with his head thrust forward against
the wind.  The tinker scowled and shrugged his shoulders.  He waited until the man came up to him.

The stranger was a tall, sturdily built man, with a
long face and firm jaws and great sombre dark eyes, a
fighter's face.  When he reached the tinker he stood
erect with his feet together and his hands by his sides
like a soldier.  He was fairly well dressed, his face
was clean and well shaved, and his hands were clean.
There was a blue figure of something or other tattooed
on the back of his right hand.  He looked at the
tinker frankly with his sombre dark eyes.  Neither
spoke for several moments.

"Good evening," the stranger said.

The tinker nodded without speaking.  He was looking
the stranger up and down, as if he were slightly afraid
of this big, sturdy man, who was almost like a policeman or a soldier or somebody in authority.  He looked
at the man's boots especially.  In spite of the muck
of the roads, the melted snow and the hailstones, they
were still fairly clean, and looked as if they were
constantly polished.

"Travellin'?" he said at length.

"Eh," said the stranger, almost aggressively.  "Oh!
Yes, I'm lookin' for somewhere to shelter for the
night."

The stranger glanced at the tent slowly and then

76

looked back to the tinker again.

"Goin' far?" said the tinker.

"Don't know," said the stranger angrily. Then he almost shouted: "I have no bloody place to go to . . . only the bloody roads."

"All right, brother," said the tinker, "come on."

He nodded towards the tent and jumped down into the pit. The stranger followed him, stepping carefully down to avoid soiling his clothes.

When he entered the tent after the tinker and saw the women he immediately took off his cap and said: "Good evening." The two women took their cigarettes from their mouths, smiled and nodded their heads.

The stranger looked about him cautiously and then sat down on a box to the side of the door near the brazier. He put his hands to the blaze and rubbed them. Almost immediately a slight steam rose from his clothes. The tinker handed him a cigarette, murmuring: "Smoke?"

The stranger accepted the cigarette, lit it, and then looked at them. None of them were looking at him, so he sized them up carefully, looking at each suspiciously with his sombre dark eyes. The tinker was sitting on a box opposite him, leaning languidly backwards from his hips, a slim, tall, graceful man, with a beautiful head poised gracefully on a brown neck, and great black lashes falling down over his half-closed eyes, just like a woman. A womanish-looking fellow, with that sensuous grace in the languid pose of his body which is found only among aristocrats and people who belong to a very small workless class, cut off from the mass of society yet living at their expense. A young fellow with proud, contemptuous, closed lips and an arrogant expression in his slightly expanded nostrils. A silent fellow, blowing out cigarette smoke through his nostrils and gazing dreamily into the blaze of the wood fire. The two women were just like him in texture, both of them slatterns, dirty and unkempt, but with the same proud, arrogant, contemptuous look in their beautiful brown faces. One was dark-haired and black-eyed. She had rather a hard expression in her face and seemed very alert. The other woman was golden-haired, with a very small head and finely developed jaw, that stuck out level with her forehead. She

77

was surpassingly beautiful, in spite of her ragged
clothes and the foul condition of her hair, which was
piled on her tiny skull in knotted heaps, uncombed.
The perfect symmetry and delicacy of her limbs, her
bust and her long throat that had tiny freckles in the
white skin, made the stranger feel afraid of her, of
her beauty and her presence in the tent.

"Tinkers," he said to himself.  "Awful bloody
people."

Then he turned to the tinker.

"Got any grub in the place. . . eh. . . mate?" he
said brusquely, his thick lips rapping out every word
firmly, like one accustomed to command inferiors.  He
hesitated before he added the word "mate," obviously
disinclined to put himself on a level of human inter-
course with the tinker.

The tinker nodded and turned to the dark-haired
woman.

"Might as well have supper now, Kitty," he said
softly.

The dark-haired woman rose immediately, and taking
a blackened can that was full of water, she put it on
the brazier.  The stranger watched her.  Then he addressed the tinker again.

"This is a hell of a way to be, eh?" he said. "Stuck
out on a mountain.  Thought I'd make Roundwood to-
night.  How many miles is it from here?"

"Ten," said the tinker.

"Good God!" said the stranger.

Then he laughed and, putting his hand in his breast
pocket, he pulled out a half-pint bottle of whiskey.

"This is all I got left," he said, looking at the
bottle.

The tinker immediately opened his eyes wide when he
saw the bottle.  The golden-haired woman sat up and
looked at the stranger eagerly, opening her brown eyes
wide and rolling her tongue in her cheek.  The dark-
haired woman, rummaging in a box, also turned around to
look.  The stranger winked an eye and smiled.

"Always welcome," he said. "Eh? My curse on it, anyway. Anybody got a corkscrew?"

The tinker took a knife from his pocket, pulled out a corkscrew from its side and handed it to the man. The man opened the bottle.

"Here," he said, handing the bottle to the tinker. "Pass it round. I suppose the women'll have a drop."

The tinker took the bottle and whispered to the dark-haired woman. She began to pass him mugs from the box.

"Funny thing," said the stranger, "when a man is broke and hungry, he can get whiskey but he can't get grub. Met a man this morning in Dublin and he knew bloody well I was broke, but instead of asking me to have a meal, or giving me some money, he gave me that. I had it with me all along the road and I never opened it."

He threw the end of his cigarette out the entrance.

"Been drinkin' for three weeks, curse it," he said.

"Are ye belongin' to these parts?" murmured the tinker, pouring out the whiskey into the tin mugs.

"What's that?" said the man, again speaking angrily, as if he resented the question. Then he added: "No. Never been here in me life before. Question of goin' into the workhouse or takin' to the roads. Got a job in Dublin yesterday. The men downed tools when they found I wasn't a member of the union. Thanks. Here's luck."

"Good health, sir," the women said.

The tinker nodded his head only, as he put his own mug to his lips and tasted it. The stranger drained his at a gulp.

"Ha," he said. "Drink up, girls. It's good stuff."

He winked at them. They smiled and sipped their whiskey.

"My name is Carney," said the stranger to the tinker. "What do they call you?"

79

"Byrne," said the tinker.   "Joe Byrne."

"Hm!  Byrne," said Carney.   "Wicklow's full o'
Byrnes.  Tinker, I suppose?"

"Yes," murmured the tinker, blowing a cloud of cigarette smoke through his puckered lips.  Carney shrugged
his shoulders.

"Might as well," he said.  "One thing is as good as
another.  Look at me.  Sergeant-major in the army two
months ago.  Now I'm tramping the roads.  That's
boiling."

The dark-haired woman took the can off the fire.
The other woman tossed off the remains of her whiskey
and got to her feet to help with the meal.  Carney
shifted his box back farther out of the way and watched
the golden-haired woman eagerly.  When she moved about,
her figure was so tall that she had to stoop low in
order to avoid the roof of the tent.  She must have
been six feet in height, and she wore high-heeled shoes
which made her look taller.

"There is a woman for ye," thought Carney.  "Must be
a gentleman's daughter.  Lots o' these shots out of a
gun in the county Wicklow.  Half the population is il-
legitimate.  Awful bloody people, these tinkers.  I
suppose the two of them belong to this Joe.  More like
a woman than a man.  Suppose he never did a stroke of
work in his life."

There was cold rabbit for supper, with tea and  .
bread and butter.  It was excellent tea, and it tasted
all the sweeter on account of the storm outside which
was still raging.  Sitting around the brazier they
could see the hailstones driving through a grey mist,
sweeping the bleak black moor and the cone-shaped peak
of the mountain in the distance, with a whirling cloud
of snow around it.  The sky was rent here and there
with a blue patch, showing through the blackness.

They ate the meal in silence.  Then the women
cleared it away.  They didn't wash the mugs or plates,
but put everything away, probably until morning.  They
sat down again after drawing out the straw, bed-shape,
and putting the clothes on it that had been drying near
the brazier.  They all seemed to be in a good humour
now with the whiskey and the food.  Even the tinker's
face had grown soft, and he kept puckering up his lips
in a smile.  He passed around cigarettes.

80

"Might as well finish that bottle," said Carney. "Bother the mugs. We can drink outa the neck."

"Tastes sweeter that way," said the golden-haired woman, laughing thickly, as if she were slightly drunk. At the same time she looked at Carney with her lips open.

Carney winked at her. The tinker noticed the wink and the girl's smile. His face clouded and he closed his lips very tightly. Carney took a deep draught and passed him the bottle. The tinker nodded his head, took the bottle and put it to his lips.

"I'll have a stretch," said Carney. "I'm done in. Twenty miles since morning. Eh?"

He threw himself down on the clothes beside the yellow-haired woman. She smiled and looked at the tinker. The tinker paused with the bottle to his lips and looked at her through almost closed eyes savagely. He took the bottle from his lips and bared his white teeth. The golden-headed woman shrugged her shoulders and pouted. The dark-haired woman laughed aloud, stretched back with one arm under her head and the other stretched out towards the tinker.

"Sht," she whistled through her teeth. "Pass it along, Joe."

He handed her the bottle slowly, and as he gave it to her she clutched his hand and tried to pull him to her. But he tore his hand away, got up and walked out of the tent rapidly.

Carney had noticed nothing of this. He was lying close to the woman by his side. He could feel the softness of her beautiful body and the slight undulation of her soft side as she breathed. He became overpowered with desire for her and closed his eyes, as if to shut out the consciousness of the world and of the other people in the tent. Reaching down he seized her hand and pressed it. She answered the pressure. At the same time she turned to her companion and whispered:

"Where's he gone?"

"I dunno. Rag out."

"What about?"

81

"Phst."

"Give us a drop."

"Here ye are."

Carney heard the whispering, but he took no notice
of it.  He heard the golden-headed one drinking and
then drawing a deep breath.

"Finished," she said, throwing the bottle to the
floor.  Then she laughed softly.

"I'm going out to see where he's gone," whispered
the dark-haired one.  She rose and passed out of the
tent.  Carney immediately turned around and tried to
embrace the woman by his side.  But she bared her teeth
in a savage grin and pinioned his arms with a single
movement.

"Didn't think I was strong," she said, putting her
face close to his and grinning at him.

He looked at her seriously, surprised and still more
excited.

"What ye goin' to do in Roundwood?" she said.

"Lookin' for a job," he muttered thickly.

She smiled and rolled her tongue in her cheek.

"Stay here," she said.

He licked his lip and winked his right eye.  "With
you?"

She nodded.

"What about him?" he said, nodding towards the door.

She laughed silently.  "Are ye afraid of Joe?"

He did not reply, but, making a sudden movement, he
seized her around the body and pressed her to him.  She
did not resist, but began to laugh, and bared her teeth
as she laughed.  He tried to kiss her mouth, but she
threw back her head and he kissed her cheek several
times.

Then suddenly there was a hissing noise at the door.

Carney sat up with a start. The tinker was standing in
the entrance, stooping low, with his mouth open and his
jaw twisted to the right, his two hands hanging loosely
by his sides, with the fingers twitching. The dark-
haired woman was standing behind him, peering over his
shoulder. She was smiling.

Carney got to his feet, took a pace forward, and
squared himself. He did not speak. The golden-headed
woman uttered a loud peal of laughter, and, stretching
out her arms, she lay flat on the bed, giggling.

"Come out here," hissed the tinker.

He stepped back. Carney shouted and rushed at him,
jumping the brazier. The tinker stepped aside and
struck Carney a terrible blow in the jaw as he passed
him. Carney staggered against the bank and fell in a
heap. The tinker jumped on him like a cat, striking
him with his hands and feet all together. Carney
roared; "Let me up, let me up. Fair play." But the
tinker kept on beating him until at last he lay motion-
less at the bottom of the pit.

"Ha," said the tinker.

Then he picked up the prone body, as lightly as if
it were an empty sack, and threw it to the top of the
bank.

"Be off, you--," he hissed.

Carney struggled to his feet on the top of the bank
and looked at the three of them. They were all standing now in front of the tent, the two women grinning,
the tinker scowling. Then he staggered on to the road,
with his hands to his head.

"Good-bye dearie," cried the golden-headed one.

Then she screamed. Carney looked behind and saw the
tinker carrying her into the tent in his arms.

"God Almighty!" cried Carney, crossing himself.

Then he trudged away fearfully through the storm
towards Roundwood.

"God Almighty!" he cried at every two yards. "God
Almighty!"

83

FUGUE

by Sean O'Faolain


The clouds lifted slowly from the ridge of the
mountains and the dawn rim appeared. As I stooped low
to peer over the frame of the little attic window I
whispered to Rory that it was pitch dark; and indeed it
was far darker than the night before when we had had
the full moon in the sky. Rory leaned up on one elbow
in bed, and asked me if I could hear anything from beyond the river.

The damp of dawn was everywhere. It softened the
lime gable of the outhouse beneath me, it hung over the
sodden hay in the barn and, like the fog and mist last
night under the blazing moon, it floated over the rum-
bling river to my right. I could imagine the flow
taking strange courses in its flood, swishing in this
neither dawn nor day nor dark through all the alders
and the reeds and the rushes and, doubtless, covering
the steppingstones that we hoped would give us an escape to the mountains beyond.

So I whispered to Rory that I could only hear the
water falling in the weirs, and tumbling out of his bed
he called a curse from Christ on the whore of a river
that was holding us here to be plugged by the Tans[1] for
a pair of Irish bitches.

As I peered, standing in bare feet on the timber
floor, I recalled last night with a shudder. We were
retreating from Inchigeela by the back roads and we two
had lost ourselves in the barren and rocky place they
call the Rough, a difficult place by day and almost im-
passable by night. We had tramped up and down and up
and down until I felt my eyes closing as I stumbled
along, and scarcely had the energy to push back my bandolier when it came sliding around my elbows. Rory, a
country fellow, seemed tireless, but my shirt clung to
my back with cold sweat. The fog lay like a white
quilt under the moon, covering the countryside, and
black shadows miles long and miles wide stretched
across the land. Up and down we went, the fog growing
thicker as we stumbled into boggy valleys, our feet


1. The Black and Tans, so-called because their uniforms
   were half English khaki and half Royal Irish Constabulary black, were temporary policemen.

85

squelching in the sodden turf, and fear hovering round
our hearts. Earlier in the evening before the night
fell, I had heard a noise before us in the lag, and had
clicked a bullet in my rifle breech and fallen flat,
but Rory swore at me and asked me in amazement if I
meant to fight them. After that I had no guts for anything but to get away from the danger of an encounter,
to get across the river and the main road before the
dawn, and up to the higher mountain on Ballyvourney
beyond. So we trudged on and every natural night sound
terrified us, a bird's cry, a barking dog with his
double note, bark-bark, and then silence, bark-bark,
and like that now and again the whole night long from
one mountainside or another. People say the most lonely thing of all is the bark of a dog at night, but to
us the most lonely sight was the odd twinkle of a
light, miles away, one dot of light and all the rest of
the land in darkness, except for the moon in the sky.
The little light meant friends, a fireside, words of
advice, comfort--but for us only the squelching and the
trudging that seemed never to end, and maybe a bullet
in the head before morning.

Once only we rested when Rory lost all patience and
flung caution to the wind to light a cigarette in the
hollow of his palms. I stretched out on the sodden
moss--God, how restful it would be to sleep there for
an hour or two--and tried to keep awake by watching the
coming of the red glow in his palm every time Rory drew
in a fresh puff. The moon was a few nights from full
roundness, and I thought it looked like a jolly wench
laughing at us both, and the missing segment like a
bonnety tam cocked on the side of her fat head. The
devil would look after his own, Rory was saying, blast
them, two again' twenty, we couldn't fight them. Rory
pulled me up and we went on, and I cursed Rory for not
knowing the lay of his own countryside and he cursed me
for a city snot that had no business out here in the
mountains. Then we heard the cattle plunging in the
boggy hollow beneath us, and we plunged ahead ourselves
down a sharp descent where the river must have cut its
way centuries ago: down we went sliding and running
until the heavenly sight of trees broke against the sky
and the dark mass of a house against them. Rory knew
it for Dan Jamesy's house and we hammered with our
rifle butts on the door, anxious only for sleep, and
food, and the sight of friends. From an upper window
she called to us and Rory spoke his name. Used to this
sort of thing, and pitying us, she came down, bare-
footed, her black hair around her, a black cloak on her
shoulders not altogether drawn over her pale breast, a

86

candle blown madly by the wind slanting in her hand.

Rory had dressed himself while I peered out at the
wall of mountain before me, and slinging his equipment
over one shoulder he went down to eat something before
we faced the river and the road--both half a mile away
now. I followed him in a moment and found the old woman of the house and a little boy seated on the settle,
his eyes wide with interest, hers full of uneasiness at
our being in her house, a danger to her sons and husband. The young woman who had opened the door the
night before stood like a statue before the wide fireplace, her bright arm bare to the elbow, and--curious
gesture--her hand on the crown of her head as if to
keep in position the hair brushed and close-combed
around her skull like a black velvet cap shining in the
firelight. She smiled at me as I entered, but I was
too anxious to smile back. Rory asked her many questions about the encircling troops, and she replied,
looking down at his ruddy earnest face, that some lor-
ries had passed by an hour ago, and when he asked about
the river she said that it had risen over the stones
and could not be crossed. She stooped down to reach
the teapot, keeping one hand on her hip as she poured
the tea: before the hour was out I recollected how she
looked at me while she poured me out a cupful, and at
the recollection I felt just as when I saw, the night
before, an odd, twinkling window light heading a deserted valley full of moonlight and mist. Stooping
again, she replaced the pot and went to sit on the
other side of the little boy, and laying one hand on
his knee spoke to him.

"That fir Tom brought last night has no fire in it."

"'Tis a bad fire, God bless it."

"Get a good log, now, Jamesy, will you? Will you?"
The little fellow looked at us only, and said, "I
will," but he did not stir. The old woman broke in
irritably:

"Wisha, Jamesy couldn't."

"Indeed, Jamesy is a great man, isn't he, Jamesy?
Imagine Jamesy not to be able to carry a baulk[2] of fir!
Will you, Jamesy?"

2. A log.

87

But Jamesy sat with dangling legs watching us eat
and she rose and with easy steps went out: the old
woman stirred the wood fire; one of the sons handled
my revolver with dull curiosity, and another fumbled in
a rope loft over Rory's head and replied that another
lorry was gone by. We prepared for the river and the
road, on our guard, not so afraid as when the night was
all around. I went to the door to see if it rained,
and stood looking into the dark archway of the stables
and at the dark hollows under the thatch--nowhere else
could I see the soft, silent fall. As I looked at the
dark archway she appeared in it with an armful of logs
and raised her head towards me and smiled once again,
and then she approached, pulling her blue apron over
her head to protect her from the rain. Her smile tortured me. Then Rory and the old man of the house came
out and went towards the stables, arguing about a horse
to carry us over the flood, and I followed them, and we
came at last to where the river was tearing madly over
the drowned stones.

As I sat behind the old fellow on his white mare,
clasping him firmly about the waist, and trying to keep
my eyes from the swirling water that tore the gravel
from the unsteady hoofs, I saw from the corners of my
eyes the drops that splashed up and flashed in the sun
as they fell again on the prancing knees and the brown
water. I saw at the identical moment the young woman
in the blowing wind of the night, and her looks at me
twice, thrice that morning. I longed for an end to
this vagabond life, longed for I dared not think what;
but there was in it the scent and light of flowers and
the scent of woman and her caresses. She had looked at
me as if we had between us some secret love: not one
woman in ten thousand will look so at one man in as
many thousand, perhaps not one in all his life, never
more than one I would have said a day ago, and now one
such had looked at my eyes and I thought at once of the
evening glow of the city streets when the sun has gone
behind the tallest houses, when the end of the day is
near, and the canyon-alleys are suffused with dusk and
slow-moving lights: when men waken from the sleep of
day and returning in upon themselves think of love, and
the darkness where love is, and wander out from the
city to the dark fields.

Rory had forgotten that he must not look down and he
fell sidewise on the horse's back, and when he reached
the opposite bank he began talking of his foolishness
and never ceased reverting to it the whole day. He
looked down, you see, he looked down into the flood, he

88

forgot, man, he looked down, and, by God, if he hadn't
looked, but he looked into the water, he knew he
shouldn't--wasn't it I myself was telling you not to
look at the flood, but whatever happened I looked down.
And, cripes! When I did . . . To have peace for my own
thoughts I told him that he had but little talk the
night before; but he did not heed my jibes, and chat-
tered on, glad of the morning and reckless about the
last mile between us and the foothills. He was a little bellied fellow, his mouth like a crack across a
potato, his cap distended by a cane hoop just like a
plate on the top of his head. He had pinned a colored
miniature of the Virgin to the front of his queer cap,
and when in the mood, his talk bubbled from him in anything but a virginal flow. How he had sworn at me yesterday when he sighted the enemy troops, and I could
not see at all the tiny khaki figures below us on the
lower slopes!

"Do you see them?" he had cried with equal stress on
each word after the manner of his dialect. "Christ,
can't you see them?" he had shouted in rage, saying it
as if it were spelled in two syllables, Chi-rist.
"Will you look at them, Christ, will you look at them
when I tell you?"

I used to wonder at his affection for me in spite of
such failures. In better mood now he jabbered on while
we made our way up against the sprung wind and a hilly
place. At last we heard the incessant knocking of a
threshing engine on the bald summit in front of us, and
we made our way to it. Up here the wind was a storm,
and it blew the chaff about the sky like yellow snow
blown before the wind. First the blue slate roof, then
the white walls of the house, the yellow stack of corn,
the stone-wall fences of the fields, and at last the
little black engine jumping like a kettle on the hob,
while all the time the men swung their arms to and fro
in labor: soon we were among them, telling one group
after another of the night's and day's adventures.
Rory gabbled between every pant after his climb, telling about the horse and how I could not see the little
gray figures when they came around us the evening before. From where we stood, the Rough looked like a
flat plain and the distant mountains like hunchbacks in
a row. I watched the whole country change with the
shadows of the flying clouds, listening to the engine,
with its disyllabic knocking, ceaseless since morning,
and the wind's cry, and Rory shouting above it all.

"There was the bloody mare in the middle of the

river, I'm not in the habit of horses, you know, a man
that was used to horses wouldn't mind, but I wasn't in
the habit of them and I never was, and what did I do
and the bloody mare there in the middle of the river,
what did I do, what did I do? The thing I did! What
should I do, I ask you, but look down at the flood, so
look down at the flood I did. I looked down and only
for the lad got a grip of me I was down, Cripes, I
was. I was! If I would only not look down at the
flood, you see, but I looked down, and by Christ!"

Here Rory began to shake in his excitement, too
moved to be articulate.

The chaff was always driving away before the wind,
and now and again someone would look up and around at
the sky and say to the man whose stack was being
threshed in this communal fashion of the mountains:

"Maybe it will hold dry."

The other would look up and around and say:

"Maybe it will. It might then. It's a strong
wind."

Then they would set to work again, piking and toss-
ing the broken sheaves and we moved down at last to the
road.

The road twisted eastward behind the rocks, and
nothing but the tops of the telegraph poles showed
where it ran after that. It was bare and empty, so we
ran for it, crossed it, and in another moment Rory was
crying that a lorry was coming around the bend. Hearts
leaping, we doubled our pace and fell upon our bellies
in the moss, squirming around like legless things to
face the road. In a moment more the shots began to
whine away over our heads, and I saw two awkward figures firing at us as they ran: I fired wildly in reply until my bolt jammed, and then rolled away into a
hollow that by the fortunes of war lay behind me:
thereupon I ran through the rocky place, through the
bracken and the bog, more madly than ever in my life
before, and raced for such a lengthy spell that when at
last I fell helpless upon the ground my breath pumped
in and out painfully and my heart beat against my side
like a thing trying to leave my body. I heard the
shots still ringing and the bullets whining high up in
the air, flying no doubt in a great parabola so that I
fancied I heard them thud when spent into the soft

earth, their curve completed.

When at last they ceased and our hearts returned to
a normal beat we had come to a little low-flung wood of
birch and rowan, the silver bark peeling black stripes
horizontally from the birch, the red berries of the
rowan wind-blown on its delicate branches. Gray rocks
covered the interstices of the trees and the sun fell
sometimes on the rock to warm the cold color: a stream
twisted through the rough ground and its sound was soft
and bass, and up on a sudden promontory silhouetted
against the sky was a single figure who was working in
a series of vigorous thrusts on a spade. We remained
in the little wood for many hours, listening to the
bass viol of the falling water, to the wind pulling at
the larchtops and shaking the tender rowan, and sometimes listening with attention to the drumming of a
lorry as it passed in and out of earshot in the near
distance.

Excited by danger, and by the beauty of this calm
place, the falling stream beside me, the trees moving
all around, I began to think again of the young woman
in the black cloak who had become aware that I too
lived just as much as anyone she had hitherto known at
church or fair. I saw her always as she had come to us
in the night, her black cloak hanging heavily against
her skin as she led us to the quiet kitchen and the
dead embers on the hearth. Surely life had a less
miser purpose in this encounter than in the thousands
of thousands of meetings when men cross and recross in
towns and country places? Time and again they had appeared barren and futile, but rather than believe them
fruitless, rather than feel as a spool revolving in a
shuttle, I had lived instead in the unrest of a chess-
man fingered by a hesitant player. Now sloth of mind,
as sometimes before, drew down my heart to the beauty
of this life, and in this little birdless wood I began
to dream. When the stream had carved itself a majesty,
passing barges and lights on the barges would ride the
brown smoke of the evening air, each crossing the
scurrying wake of waves from swifter hulls to disappear
slowly through the dusk while men sat on each deck and
smoked in content with life, and recalled all the dead
among my acquaintances who have suffered too willingly
the futility of life. There is an owl in the Celtic
fable who had seen each rowan as a seed upon a tree,
and its length seven times fallen to the earth and
seven times over raised in leaf; it had seen the men
whose bones were washed from these boulders when the
rain was rounding them to pebbles from seven hundred

times their height this dropping evening; it had seen
the men for whom the promontory above me was a bottom-
less valley and the hollow place where Rory and I sat
was a high mountain before the Flood. Such an owl
called out of the dusk at me and its cry filled me with
age and the peace that comes when we feel the wheels of
the passing years turn so slowly it is almost complete
rest. I dozed as I lay--life stopped for me while my
eyes swayed and fell.

But Rory, his mind whirling, sang of passionate
life. He sang the song of the old Newgate murderer,
the song found scrawled upon his Newgate cell after
they hanged him and buried him. How eerie to see him
ghosting like this in Ireland, his disjointed spine
rattling. Rory, not aware that before the night had
fallen death would have got him, too--his body plugged
full of English lead--sang cheerily:

> My name is Samuel Hall, Samuel Hall,
> My name is Samuel Hall, Samuel Hall,
> My name is Samuel Hall,
> And I've only got one ball,
> Here's my curse upon you all,
> > God damn your eyes!

> I killed a man 'tis said, so 'tis said,
> I killed a man 'tis said, so 'tis said,
> I hit him on the head,
> With a bloody lump of lead,
> And I laid the bugger dead,
> > God damn your eyes!

I did not heed the words, but the sense, entering my
mind, broke my dream. Looking up I saw the west grow
cold and saffron as if the threshers of the morn, re-
duplicated in valley after valley, had blown a storm of
corn sheaves against the falling cape of night. A
score of birds fulfilling their ancient ritual flew
homeward in formation: as they passed into the blazing
sun I dropped my eyes again to the stream, but while I
had turned away it had changed to silver against the
dark stones. Dusk was dropping upon us secretly and we
must move on to some house where we could sit before
the flames and doze before a chimney wall browned with
soot and invading rain and sleep quietly while the
night passed by.

We tramped ahead, keeping to the back roads still,
but quite without fear now that we were so many miles
from the enemy, and at last, high up among the hills,

walking in the reaches of the wind, we came to the little roadside house that was shop and post office in
one, and we sat there wearily by the fire.

The land was cold and windswept here, and the few
elms that stood outside, landmark for many miles
around, were torn by the wind like the clouds in the
sky. Rory was to stay here for the night, but I had to
move farther on, so I sat by the fire waiting impatiently for the cart that was to carry me part of the
last few miles to supper and bed. At the end of the
kitchen the old carter was whispering across the little
counter with the woman of the house; the young daughter
of the house stood beside them lighting an oil lamp
that hung from a beam overhead. Presently the two gray
pates were lit from above. The glow fell on the un-
painted counter, plain as when its planks first arrived
from the town of Macroom twenty miles away and were
flung on the kitchen floor for the admiration of the
little fat woman with her little fat baby. The glow
fell on the soiled and mutilated bank notes, on the
silver and copper coins, on the blue sugar bags and the
dun surfaces of the remainder of Saturday night's gro-
ceries. I waited while they talked in a secretive
whisper, perhaps over the account, perhaps about their
old-wives' gossip of the countryside. Perhaps they
were wishing us wandering guerrillas farther on and
wishing the fighting at an end lest their houses be
burned over their heads. Outside in the windy night
the old horse was tethered to an elm, its head bent low
and its eyes heavy with sleep like a Buddha's. I sat
by the fire and raked in the ashes with the muzzle of
my rifle.

I felt it would rain heavily tonight though the wind
was getting stronger, and once again I thought of the
girl in the black cloak; but already she had slipped
many miles into the things of the past, and in another
day she would have slipped wholly from my mind not to
be recalled unless in some odd place at some odd time
when I would wonder about our strange encounter, and in
sentimental mood wonder if she ever asked a comrade
where I had gone, saying that I was a nice boy, perhaps
more than that. She had been at such a door as this in
her mother's arms. She would stand there again in one,
two, three years' time bidding farewell to the very
last mocking couple of her bridal party, and, looking
at the sky with her young husband, see the coming of
the rain and lock and latch the door upon it, and returning to the dying fire would hear the first drops
fall on the warm core, and the rising howl strip

93

the elms; he would draw her toward him and she, feeling
her youth passed forever, would weep softly and secretly in the dark and then smile for her first ungirdling.
What lovely weavings the old Weaver thinks of, as if
all will not fray away in the end and moths rise from
the eyes of his dears. Even storms crumble at the end
in dust.

I heard Rory chant some passage from a hedge-school
memory, and turning I saw the young girl of the house
watching him, ready for a burst of laughter at the end.

"This," chanted Rory, "is a man, the beauty of whose
eloquence and the wisdom of whose conversation are
balanced only by the impeccability of his character and
the noble qualities of the mind wherewith God has en-
dowed him, for it is abundantly clear to me," continued
the emperor in a graver tone, "that wherever the original refulgence of the human mind is neither adumbrated
in its infancey nor adulterated in its maturity, the
unique powers of the will of man must inevitably produce in every individual, no matter in what clime he
has been born, nor under what star he has first seen
the light of day, if only he be true to what is right
and turn from what is wrong, the genius of an Alex-
ander, the oratory of a Cicero, the wisdom of a Solo-
mom, or the sublime skill of a Leonardo da Vinci, as
the case may befall."

The little bellied fellow finished with a breathless
rush, and turning to the girl clapped his hands and
clapped her hands with his in applause at his own per-
formance.

I found that this child was to accompany me a little
way on the road. We snuggled into the back of the cart
and sat shouting our farewells as it jolted away from
the two yellow squares of light and from the figures
crowding the open door. Then as we entered the spacious dark, silence fell on us three. I stretched back
on the floor of the cart listening to the braggart
storm. I felt young and willful under its breath; I
loved to hear its impotent whine: off behind the ridge
of mountain through which a pass had been cut maybe
five centuries ago by roadmakers rotted in the grave
there came the great spreading light of the moon. We
were following the direction of the racing clouds, flying beyond us in the sky. My eyes were beginning to
close with the rough swaying of the cart when suddenly
the child clasping my hand said:

"Are you afraid of the pookas?[3]  I am!"

And fell upon my breast and laid her head by mine
and I put an arm around her and we lay so, jolting
along under the stars and the driving fleeces overhead.
Presently I left them, and the old cart was soon out of
earshot.

Jogging on through the dark, my thoughts wandered at
will, I pictured the bed where I would sleep.  I had
slept in so many hundreds that it might be any size or
shape, but I chose from my set of images one bed most
suitable to the stormy night.  It was the marriage bed
of the peasants, made of plain wood, closed on back,
side and top, and only the front left open, and that
sometimes covered by a curtain on a string.  It was
like a beehive with a flat crown and sloping roofs,
shallow at head and foot, so that a man could stand in
comfort only in the middle of the bed.  The storm might
howl for all I cared, the rain might drench the
stooks[4] and fill the yards with pools of dung; the windows might rattle--I would sleep the night through and
wake to find the skies clearing in the morning.  I was
hungry for food and sleep, and in this bed I would lie
for a while thinking over the day's happenings, trying
to find a scheme for things in the true dreamer's way,
a scheme into which everyone would fit as by nature,
the woman of the cloak, the little girl, myself, the
dead husband, the carter, the crowds that meet and re-
meet, as it seemed aimlessly, blindly--and all these
would jumble in my mind and quaint combinations occur
and confuse me, and my reasoning fall under the sway of
interweaving images and sleep come secretly with her
hood.

At last the bright square of window light slid into
view, quartered by the crucifix framework, and I found
the causeway to the door and groped my way to it after
the window vanished in its own recess.  I played blind-
man's buff with the door and at last with outstretched
hands I stumbled against it and grasped the latch.  Fire
flames, a settle, and maybe a white cloth and something
to eat other than dry bread and tea with goat's milk.
I lifted the latch and looked in:  a young woman stood

3. A kind of fairy:  a mischievous and often malignant
   goblin that usually appears in the form of a horse,
   but sometimes as a bull, a buck-goat, etc.
4. Shocks of corn, usually containing twelve sheaves.

95

with her back to me stiffened in a posture of surprise
as when I first fumbled at the door, but, relaxing and
turning when I spoke, touched her soft hair and bade
me enter:  it was the young woman of the morning.

"Is there e'er a wake here?" I asked, seeing the
lone kitchen, my voice trembling as I spoke.

"Devil a wake then!"  She was smiling at me again.

"Ye're very quiet then," I said, looking around at
the clean-swept kitchen, and then at her skin like a
boy's under its first white down.

"'Tis quiet, wisha," she answered, making way for me
as I moved to the settle.  I asked if there would be
room for the night, and she said there would be and
welcome.

"And a bit to eat for a hungry man?"

"Surely, if you don't mind waiting for just a moment
or two."

I wanted to ask how she came before me to the hither
side of the country twelve long miles away from last
night's hostel.  I flung aside my bandolier and rain-
coat; I laid my rifle and pack and belt in a corner.
She went to the end of the kitchen and I heard the
splash of water and the paddling of hands, and when she
returned to me by the fire, wiping her fingers, they
were rosy when the apron fell.  She half knelt before
the fire to blow it with a hand bellows, and as she
worked her body formed a single curve, one breast on
one knee, and her arms circling the knee while she
worked lustily at the bellows.  I could see the little
wrinkles at each corner of her lips--laughter wrinkles,
maybe?

"Are the old people in bed?" I asked.

"Yes."  Her voice trembled, I thought.

"And the rest?  Where's the rest from you?"

"There's nobody else.  Tom, my brother, is on the
run in Kerry."

I leaned back on the settle and the flames crackled
into life.

"Well, you must be very lonely here all alone."

"I have got used to it," she answered, patting her hair with the fingers of her hands: how soft it looked! Then she stood up and began to spread a white cloth on the white table, and then to lay a milk jug, a cup and saucer, a sugar basin, a pot of jam.

"Do you live here?"

"Yes."

"But you're not always as desolate as this--surely?"

"Desolate, just as you say; this is a lonely district, you know."

"Well, it's not so bad at all now," said I. "I shouldn't mind if I lived here--the mountains and the valleys . . ."

She halted in her step and faced me: the little mouth was gathered into a hard white button of flesh.

"You would soon tire of these mountains! The city, though, that's where I'd like to live. There's company there, and sport and educated people, and a chance to live whatever life you choose!"

She had put two eggs into a little black pot of boiling water, and the water bubbled and leaped around them with a hissing. A blast of wind came down the chimney and drove a cloud of fire smoke into the kitchen. We sat silent and presently went to the table and she poured me red tea to drink and I cut the brown loaf and plastered it with butter and jam, and ate greedily. She sat before the fire, and I asked her why she did not like the district, but she only looked at me and said nothing. I asked again, pleading that I wished to know, really and truly. She answered:

"Because this farm is bare and high. The land is poor. And this downland has a northern aspect."

A heavy drop of rain fell on the fire--the storm was howling. I saw the sea of discontent and unrest that these words were born of, saw the drizzling rain and no sun shining on it, saw her looks steal round her to this farm and to that and back from them to her own home. Another gust of wind blew the smoke around her and she turned away from it and clasped my knee to prevent herself from falling from the low stool.

"You'll be choked," said I, and her eyebrows stirred and she smiled at me. I laid my palm on her hand and thought of the whole livelong day I had spent, the rick that must be threshed before the wind fell, the carter jogging through the wet night, the sea of darkness outside the door. How many days could I live without a complete revolt! I spoke earnestly.

"It's a cruel country to have to live in."

She spoke kindly to me then.

"I think you are honest," she said.

"Do you think that?"

"I think you are honest. Really honest," she said again.

Looking at her soft eyes, and at her soft hair, my eyes wandered down to the first shadows of her breasts: she caught my glance and looked down at her warm bosom and then at me and she smiled. As I moved to her I saw the little broken corner of her tooth; I had no word to say; so I sat beside her before the leaping flames and put my arms around her and felt in the cup of my hollow palm the firm casque of her breast. Smiling at me as a sick woman might smile upon a doctor who brought her ease from pain she slipped my hand beneath her blouse to where I felt the warmth of her skin and her warm protruding nipple, and I leaned to her for a kiss.

A rush of feet came to the door and the little girl from the roadside house flung it wide with a cry to me to run, to run; Rory was shot dead; they were coming west for me! I bundled up my equipment, ran in a flash through the open door into the dark night, and raced on and on—stumbling and falling and going I cared not where but away from headlamp lights flashing to the north. When I fell into a panting walk I was like a man who has been listening to music the livelong day and after it his mind is full of strange chords, and ill-recollected they torture him with a sense of something lost. On my bare head the rain fell heavily and aslant, now and again it was blown into my face by the wind, and the clouds totally blotted out the moon. Full of terror for such a death as I knew Rory's was I filled every house with armed men, fierce men to whom killing was a little thing and torture but little

more, and my imagination and the stories I had heard
drove me blindly on through the sodden night.  I
trudged a way through the pathless bogs and tore
through briery dikes:  all that night I found no shelter from the lashing rain and I met not a single tree
in leaf:  long after midnight I saw a little glinting
window leap suddenly out of the dark about a mile away,
and as I thrust away from it, away to safety, into the
rain, the memory of its light tortured me as the memory
of cool winds must torture the damned of hell.  At last
I came on a lonely ruin on the mountain, three walls,
and I lay on the lee side of it while the rain dripped
on me from the remnants of its eaves.

When I awoke, a dim radiance lit the falling haze,
but whether it was the dawn or the sinking moon or any
hour past three or before three I could not say.  No
sound was to be heard:  no living thing moved:  no bird
stirred the wet air:  the falling haze made no sound.
I rose chattering and trembling, and my feet plashed
through the wet earth and the drowned grass, and when
I halted there was quiet.  I crossed a little stone
wall and one of the stones fell with a mighty sound.
I might have been the last human creature to crawl to
the last summit of the world, waiting until the Deluge
and the fortieth night of rain would strain him upwards
on his toes while the water licked his stretched neck.
Yet everywhere they slept sound abed, my dark woman
curling her warm body beneath the bedclothes, the
warmer for the wet fall without, thinking if she turned
and heard the dripping eaves--that the winter was at
last come.

> Cold till doom!
> The storm has spread.
> A river is each furrow on the slope,
> Each ford is a full pool.
>
> Each lake is a great tidal sea,
> Each pool is a great lake,
> Horses cannot cross the ford,
> Nor two feet.
>
> The fish of Ireland are wandering,
> There is no strand upon which the waves
>     do not pound.
> Not a town is in the land,
> Not a bell, not a crane's whining cry.

The wolves in the wood of Cuan cannot rest,
They cannot sleep in their lair:
Even the little wren cannot shelter
In her tiny nest on the side of Lon.

Keen wind and cold ice
Have burst upon the little world of birds.
The blackbird cannot shelter its side
In the wood of Cuan.

Cozy was our pot upon the nook,
In the crazy hut on the slope of Lon:
The snow has crushed the wood,
And toilsome is the climb to Ben-bo.

The ancient bird of Glenn Rye
Is grieved by the cold wind:
Her misery and her pain are great,
The ice will get into her throat.

From flock and from down to rise
Were folly for thee! Take it to heart.
Ice heaped on every ford,
Wherefore I say "cold till doom."

Down below me in the valley I heard an early cart;
the morning wind, light and bitter, sang occasionally
in the key of the flooded streams. The dawn moved
along the rim of the mountains and as I went down the
hill I felt the new day come up around me and life
begin once more its ancient, ceaseless gyre.[5]

5. A circular motion; a spiral form.

# IVY DAY IN THE COMMITTEE ROOM

by James Joyce


Old Jack raked the cinders together with a piece of
cardboard and spread them judiciously over the whiten-
ing dome of coals.  When the dome was thinly covered
his face lapsed into darkness but, as he set himself to
fan the fire again, his crouching shadow ascended the
opposite wall and his face slowly re-emerged into
light.  It was an old man's face, very bony and hairy.
The moist blue eyes blinked at the fire and the moist
mouth fell open at times, munching once or twice mechanically when it closed.  When the cinders had caught
he laid the piece of cardboard against the wall, sighed
and said:

"That's better now, Mr. O'Connor."

Mr. O'Connor, a grey-haired young man, whose face
was disfigured by many blotches and pimples, had just
brought the tobacco for a cigarette into a shapely cyl-
inder but when spoken to he undid his handiwork medita-
tively.  Then he began to roll the tobacco again medi-
tatively and after a moment's thought decided to lick
the paper.

"Did Mr. Tierney say when he'd be back?" he asked in
a husky falsetto.

"He didn't say."

Mr. O'Connor put his cigarette into his mouth and
began to search his pockets.  He took out a pack of
thin pasteboard cards.

"I'll get you a match," said the old man.

"Never mind, this'll do," said Mr. O'Connor.

He selected one of the cards and read what was
printed on it:
              MUNICIPAL ELECTIONS

              ———

              Royal Exchange Ward

              ———

Mr. Richard J. Tierney, P.L.G., respectfully solicits
  the favour of your vote and influence at the coming

election in the Royal Exchange Ward.

———

Mr. O'Connor had been engaged by Tierney's agent to canvass one part of the ward but, as the weather was inclement and his boots let in the wet, he spent a great part of the day sitting by the fire in the Committee Room in Wicklow Street with Jack, the old caretaker. They had been sitting thus since the short day had grown dark. It was the sixth of October, dismal and cold out of doors.

Mr. O'Connor tore a strip off the card and, lighting it, lit his cigarette. As he did so the flame lit up a leaf of dark glossy ivy in the lapel of his coat. The old man watched him attentively and then, taking up the piece of cardboard again, began to fan the fire slowly while his companion smoked.

"Ah, yes," he said, continuing, "it's hard to know what way to bring up children. Now who'd think he'd turn out like that! I sent him to the Christian Brothers and I done what I could for him, and there he goes boosing about. I tried to make him someway decent."

He replaced the cardboard wearily.

"Only I'm an old man now I'd change his tune for him. I'd take the stick to his back and beat him while I could stand over him—as I done many a time before. The mother, you know, she cocks him up with this and that. . . ."

"That's what ruins children," said Mr. O'Connor.

"To be sure it is," said the old man. "And little thanks you get for it, only impudence. He takes th'upper hand of me whenever he sees I've a sup taken. What's the world coming to when sons speaks that way to their fathers?"

"What age is he?" said Mr. O'Connor.

"Nineteen," said the old man.

"Why don't you put him to something?"

"Sure, amn't I never done at the drunken bowsy ever since he left school? 'I won't keep you,' I says. 'You must get a job for yourself.' But, sure, it's worse whenever he gets a job; he drinks it all."

102

Mr. O'Connor shook his head in sympathy, and the old man fell silent, gazing into the fire. Someone opened the door of the room and called out:

"Hello! Is this a Freemason's[1] meeting?"

"Who's that?" said the old man.

"What are you doing in the dark?" asked a voice.

"Is that you, Hynes?" asked Mr. O'Connor.

"Yes. What are you doing in the dark?" said Mr. Hynes, advancing into the light of the fire.

He was a tall, slender young man with a light brown moustache. Imminent little drops of rain hung at the brim of his hat and the collar of his jacket-coat was turned up.

"Well, Mat," he said to Mr. O'Connor, "how goes it?"

Mr. O'Connor shook his head. The old man left the hearth, and after stumbling about the room returned with two candlesticks which he thrust one after the other into the fire and carried to the table. A denuded room came into view and the fire lost all its cheerful colour. The walls of the room were bare except for a copy of an election address. In the middle of the room was a small table on which papers were heaped.

Mr. Hynes leaned against the mantelpiece and asked:

"Has he paid you yet?"

"Not yet," said Mr. O'Connor. "I hope to God he'll not leave us in the lurch to-night."

Mr. Hynes laughed.

"O, he'll pay you. Never fear," he said.

"I hope he'll look smart about it if he means business," said Mr. O'Connor.

1. A member of a widespread and celebrated secret society (called more fully Free and Accepted Masons), consisting of persons who are united for fraternal purposes.

103

"What do you think, Jack?" said Mr. Hynes satirically to the old man.

The old man returned to his seat by the fire, saying:

"It isn't but he has it, anyway. Not like the other tinker."

"What other tinker?" said Mr. Hynes.

"Colgan," said the old man scornfully.

"It is because Colgan's a working-man you say that? What's the difference between a good honest bricklayer and a publican²--eh? Hasn't the working-man as good a right to be in the Corporation as anyone else--ay, and a better right than those shoneens that are always hat in hand before any fellow with a handle to his name? Isn't that so, Mat?" said Mr. Hynes, addressing Mr. O'Connor.

"I think you're right," said Mr. O'Connor.

"One man is a plain honest man with no hunker-sliding about him. He goes in to represent the labour classes. This fellow you're working for only wants to get some job or other."

"Of course, the working-classes should be represented," said the old man.

"The working-man," said Mr. Hynes, "gets all kicks and no halfpence. But it's labour produces everything. The working-man is not looking for fat jobs for his sons and nephews and cousins. The working-man is not going to drag the honour of Dublin in the mud to please a German monarch."

"How's that?" said the old man.

"Don't you know they want to present an address of welcome to Edward Rex if he comes here next year? What do we want kowtowing to a foreign king?"

2. The keeper of a public house--i.e. especially any house where intoxicating liquors are sold by retail to be consumed on the premises, whether affording lodging and meals or not.

104

"Our man won't vote for the address,"said Mr. O'Connor. "He goes in on the Nationalist ticket."

"Won't he?" said Mr. Hynes. "Wait till you see whether he will or not. I know him. Is it Tricky Dicky Tierney?"

"By God! perhaps you're right, Joe," said Mr.O'Connor. "Anyway, I wish he'd turn up with the spondulics."3

The three men fell silent. The old man began to rake more cinders together. Mr. Hynes took off his hat, shook it and then turned down the collar of his coat, displaying, as he did so, an ivy leaf in the lapel.

"If this man was alive," he said, pointing to the leaf, "we'd have no talk of an address of welcome."

"That's true," said Mr. O'Connor.

"Musha, God be with them times!" said the old man. "There was some life in it then."

The room was silent again. Then a bustling little man with a snuffling nose and very cold ears pushed in the door. He walked over quickly to the fire, rubbing his hands as if he intended to produce a spark from them.

"No money, boys," he said.

"Sit down here, Mr. Henchy," said the old man, offering him his chair.

"O, don't stir, Jack, don't stir," said Mr. Henchy.

He nodded curtly to Mr. Hynes and sat down on the chair which the old man vacated.

"Did you serve Aungier Street?" he asked Mr. O'Connor.

"Yes," said Mr. O'Connor, beginning to search his pockets for memoranda.

"Did you call on Grimes?"

3. Money.

"I did."

"Well? How does he stand?"

"He wouldn't promise. He said: 'I won't tell anyone
what way I'm going to vote.' But I think he'll be all
right."

"Why so?"

"He asked me who the nominators were; and I told
him. I mentioned Father Burke's name. I think it'll
be all right."

Mr. Henchy began to snuffle and to rub his hands
over the fire at a terrific speed. Then he said:

"For the love of God, Jack, bring us a bit of coal.
There must be some left."

The old man went out of the room.

"It's no go," said Mr. Henchy, shaking his head.
"I asked the little shoeboy, but he said: 'O, now, Mr.
Henchy, when I see the work going on properly I won't
forget you, you may be sure.' Mean little tinker!
'Usha, how could he be anything else?"

"What did I tell you, Mat?" said Mr. Hynes. "Tricky
Dicky Tierney."

"O, he's as tricky as they make 'em," said Mr.
Henchy. "He hasn't got those little pigs' eyes for
nothing. Blast his soul! Couldn't he pay up like a
man instead of: 'O, now, Mr. Henchy, I must speak to
Mr. Fanning. . . . I've spent a lot of money'? Mean
little schoolboy of hell! I suppose he forgets the
time his little old father kept the hand-me-down shop
in Mary's Lane."

"But is that a fact?" asked Mr. O'Connor.

"God, yes," said Mr. Henchy. "Did you never hear
that? And the men used to go in on Sunday morning
before the houses were open to buy a waistcoat or a
trousers—moya! But Tricky Dicky's little old father
always had a tricky little black bottle up in a corner.
Do you mind now? That's that. That's where he first
saw the light."

The old man returned with a few lumps of coal which

106

he placed here and there on the fire.

"That's a nice how-do-you-do," said Mr. O'Connor. "How does he expect us to work for him if he won't stump up?"

"I can't help it," said Mr. Henchy. "I expect to find the bailiffs in the hall when I go home."

Mr. Hynes laughed and, shoving himself away from the mantelpiece with the aid of his shoulders, made ready to leave.

"It'll be all right when King Eddie comes," he said. "Well, boys, I'm off for the present. See you later. 'Bye, 'bye."

He went out of the room slowly. Neither Mr. Henchy nor the old man said anything, but, just as the door was closing, Mr. O'Connor, who had been staring moodily into the fire, called out suddenly:

"'Bye, Joe."

Mr. Henchy waited a few moments and then nodded in the direction of the door.

"Tell me," he said across the fire, "what brings our friend in here? What does he want?"

"'Usha, poor Joe!" said Mr. O'Connor, throwing the end of his cigarette into the fire, "he's hard up, like the rest of us."

Mr. Henchy snuffled vigorously and spat so copiously that he nearly put out the fire, which uttered a hissing protest.

"To tell you my private and candid opinion," he said, "I think he's a man from the other camp. He's a spy of Colgan's, if you ask me. Just go round and try and find out how they're getting on. They won't suspect you. Do you twig[4]?"

"Ah, poor Joe is a decent skin," said Mr. O'Connor.

"His father was a decent, respectable man," Mr. Henchy admitted. "Poor old Larry Hynes! Many a good

_____

4. Meaning; to understand, or catch the point.

turn he did in his day! But I'm greatly afraid our
friend is not nineteen carat. Damn it, I can understand a fellow being hard up, but what I can't understand is a fellow sponging. Couldn't he have some
spark of manhood about him?"

"He doesn't get a warm welcome from me when he
comes," said the old man. "Let him work for his own
side and not come spying around here."

"I don't know," said Mr. O'Connor dubiously, as he
took out cigarette-papers and tobacco. "I think Joe
Hynes is a straight man. He's a clever chap, too, with
the pen. Do you remember that thing he wrote . . . ?"

"Some of these hillsiders[5] and fenians[6] are a bit
too clever if you ask me," said Mr. Henchy. "Do you
know what my private and candid opinion is about some
of those little jokers? I believe half of them are in
the pay of the Castle."

"There's no knowing," said the old man.

"O, but I know it for a fact," said Mr. Henchy.
"They're Castle hacks. . . . I don't say Hynes. . . .
No, damn it, I think he's a stroke above that. . . .
But there's a certain little nobleman with a cock-eye--
you know the patriot I'm alluding to?"

Mr. O'Connor nodded.

"There's a lineal descendant of Major Sirr for you
if you like! O, the heart's blood of a patriot! That's
a fellow now that'd sell his country for fourpence--ay
--and go down on his bended knees and thank the Almighty Christ he had a country to sell."

There was a knock at the door.

"Come in!" said Mr. Henchy.


5. Irish rebels.
6. Members of the Fenian Brotherhood, a secret organization, founded in New York in 1856 and in the following year extended to Ireland where it was known
   as the Irish Republican Brotherhood, consisting
   mainly of Irishmen, and men of Irish birth or ances-
   try, having for its aim the overthrow of English
   rule in Ireland.

A person resembling a poor clergyman or a poor actor appeared in the doorway. His black clothes were tightly buttoned on his short body and it was impossible to say whether he wore a clergyman's collar or a layman's, because the collar of his shabby frock-coat, the uncovered buttons of which reflected the candlelight, was turned up about his neck. He wore a round hat of hard black felt. His face, shining with raindrops, had the appearance of damp yellow cheese save where two rosy spots indicated the cheekbones. He opened his very long mouth suddenly to express disappointment and at the same time opened wide his very bright blue eyes to express pleasure and surprise.

"O Father Keon!" said Mr. Henchy, jumping up from his chair. "Is that you? Come in!"

"O, no, no, no!" said Father Keon quickly, pursing his lips as if he were addressing a child.

"Won't you come in and sit down?"

"No, no, no!" said Father Keon, speaking in a discreet, indulgent, velvety voice. "Don't let me disturb you now! I'm just looking for Mr. Fanning. . . ."

"He's round at the Black Eagle," said Mr. Henchy. "But won't you come in and sit down a minute?"

"No, no, thank you. It was just a little business matter," said Father Keon. "Thank you, indeed."

He retreated from the doorway and Mr. Henchy, seizing one of the candlesticks, went to the door to light him downstairs.

"O, don't trouble, I beg!"

"No, but the stairs is so dark."

"No, no, I can see. . . . Thank you, indeed."

"Are you right now?"

"All right, thanks. . . . Thanks."

Mr. Henchy returned with the candlestick and put it on the table. He sat down again at the fire. There was silence for a few moments.

"Tell me, John," said Mr. O'Connor, lighting his

cigarette with another pasteboard card.

"Hm?"

"What he is exactly?"

"Ask me an easier one," said Mr. Henchy.

"Fanning and himself seem to me very thick.  They're
often in Kavanagh's together.  Is he a priest at all?"

"'Mmmyes, I believe so. . . .  I think he's what you
call a black sheep.  We haven't many of them, thank
God! but we have a few. . . .  He's an unfortunate man
of some kind. . . ."

"And how does he knock it out?" asked Mr. O'Connor.

"That's another mystery."

"Is he attached to any chapel or church or institution or----"

"No," said Mr. Henchy, "I think he's travelling on
his own account. . . .  God forgive me," he added, "I
thought he was the dozen of stout."

"Is there any chance of a drink itself?" asked Mr.
O'Connor.

"I'm dry too," said the old man.

"I asked that little shoeboy three times," said Mr.
Henchy, "would he send up a dozen of stout.  I asked
him again now, but he was leaning on the counter in his
shirt-sleeves having a deep goster⁷ with Alderman
Cowley."

"Why didn't you remind him?" said Mr. O'Connor.

"Well, I couldn't go over while he was talking to
Alderman Cowley.  I just waited till I caught his eye,
and said:  'About that little matter I was speaking to
you about. . . .'  'That'll be all right, Mr. H.,' he
said.  Yerra, sure the little hop-o'-my-thumb has forgotten all about it."

"There's some deal on in that quarter," said Mr.

7. Gossipy talk.

110

O'Connor thoughtfully. "I saw the three of them hard at it yesterday at Suffolk Street corner."

"I think I know the little game they're at," said Mr. Henchy. "You must owe the City Fathers money nowadays if you want to be made Lord Mayor. Then they'll make you Lord Mayor. By God! I'm thinking seriously of becoming a City Father myself. What do you think? Would I do for the job?"

Mr. O'Connor laughed.

"So far as owing money goes. . . ."

"Driving out of the Mansion House," said Mr. Henchy, "in all my vermin, with Jack here standing up behind me in a powdered wig--eh?"

"And make me your private secretary, John."

"Yes. And I'll make Father Keon my private chaplain. We'll have a family party."

"Faith, Mr. Henchy," said the old man, "you'd keep up better style than some of them. I was talking one day to old Keegan, the porter. 'And how do you like your new master, Pat?' says I to him. 'You haven't much entertaining now,' says I. 'Entertaining!' says he. 'He'd live on the smell of an oil-rag.' And do you know what he told me? Now, I declare to God I didn't believe him."

"What?" said Mr. Henchy and Mr. O'Connor.

"He told me: 'What do you think of a Lord Mayor of Dublin sending out for a pound of chops for his dinner? How's that for high living?' says he. 'Wisha! wisha,' says I. 'A pound of chops,' says he, 'coming into the Mansion House.' 'Wisha!' says I, 'what kind of people is going at all now?'"

At this point there was a knock at the door, and a boy put in his head.

"What is it?" said the old man.

"From the <u>Black Eagle</u>," said the boy, walking in sideways and depositing a basket on the floor with a noise of shaken bottles.

The old man helped the boy to transfer the bottles

from the basket to the table and counted the full
tally.  After the transfer the boy put his basket on
his arm and asked:

"Any bottles?"

"What bottles?" said the old man.

"Won't you let us drink them first?" said Mr. Henchy.

"I was told to ask for bottles."

"Come back to-morrow," said the old man.

"Here, boy!" said Mr. Henchy, "will you run over to
O'Farrell's and ask him to lend us a corkscrew--for Mr.
Henchy, say.  Tell him we won't keep it a minute.
Leave the basket there."

The boy went out and Mr. Henchy began to rub his
hands cheerfully, saying:

"Ah, well, he's not so bad after all.  He's as good
as his word, anyhow."

"There's no tumblers," said the old man.

"O, don't let that trouble you, Jack," said Mr.
Henchy.  "Many's the good man before now drank out of
the bottle."

"Anyway, it's better than nothing," said Mr. O'Connor.

"He's not a bad sort," said Mr. Henchy, "only Fanning has such a loan of him.  He means well, you know,
in his own tinpot way."

The boy came back with the corkscrew.  The old man
opened three bottles and was handing back the corkscrew
when Mr. Henchy said to the boy:

"Would you like a drink, boy?"

"If you please, sir," said the boy.

The old man opened another bottle grudgingly, and
handed it to the boy.

"What age are you?" he asked.

112

"Seventeen," said the boy.

As the old man said nothing further, the boy took the bottle, said: "Here's my best respects, sir, to Mr. Henchy," drank the contents, put the bottle back on the table and wiped his mouth with his sleeve. Then he took up the corkscrew and went out of the door sideways, muttering some form of salutation.

"That's the way it begins," said the old man.

"The thin edge of the wedge," said Mr. Henchy.

The old man distributed the three bottles which he had opened and the men drank from them simultaneously. After having drank each placed his bottle on the mantelpiece within hand's reach and drew in a long breath of satisfaction.

"Well, I did a good day's work to-day," said Mr. Henchy, after a pause.

"That so, John?"

"Yes. I got him one or two sure things in Dawson Street, Crofton and myself. Between ourselves, you know, Crofton (he's a decent chap, of course), but he's not worth a damn as a canvasser. He hasn't a word to throw to a dog. He stands and looks at the people while I do the talking."

Here two men entered the room. One of them was a very fat man, whose blue serge clothes seemed to be in danger of falling from his sloping figure. He had a big face which resembled a young ox's face in expression, staring blue eyes and a grizzled moustache. The other man, who was much younger and frailer, had a thin, clean-shaven face. He wore a very high double collar and a wide-brimmed bowler hat.

"Hello, Crofton!" said Mr. Henchy to the fat man. "Talk of the devil . . ."

"Where did the boose come from?" asked the young man. "Did the cow calve?"

"O, of course, Lyons spots the drink first thing!" said Mr. O'Connor, laughing.

"Is that the way you chaps canvass," said Mr. Lyons, "and Crofton and I out in the cold and rain looking for

113

votes?"

"Why, blast your soul," said Mr. Henchy, "I'd get
more votes in five minutes than you two'd get in a
week."

"Open two bottles of stout, Jack," said Mr. O'Connor.

"How can I?" said the old man, "when there's no
corkscrew?"

"Wait now, wait now!" said Mr. Henchy, getting up
quickly. "Did you ever see this little trick?"

He took two bottles from the table and, carrying
them to the fire, put them on the hob. Then he sat
down again by the fire and took another drink from his
bottle. Mr. Lyons sat on the edge of the table, pushed
his hat towards the nape of his neck and began to swing
his legs.

"Which is my bottle?" he asked.

"This, lad," said Mr. Henchy.

Mr. Crofton sat down on a box and looked fixedly at
the other bottle on the hob. He was silent for two
reasons. The first reason, sufficient in itself, was
that he had nothing to say; the second reason was that
he considered his companions beneath him. He had been
a canvasser for Wilkins, the Conservative, but when the
Conservatives had withdrawn their man and, choosing the
lesser of two evils, given their support to the Nationalist candidate, he had been engaged to work for Mr.
Tierney.

In a few minutes an apologetic "Pok!" was heard as
the cork flew out of Mr. Lyons' bottle. Mr. Lyons
jumped off the table, went to the fire, took his bottle
and carried it back to the table.

"I was just telling them, Crofton," said Mr. Henchy,
"that we got a good few votes to-day."

"Who did you get?" asked Mr. Lyons.

"Well, I got Parkes for one, and I got Atkinson for
two, and I got Ward of Dawson Street. Fine old chap he
is, too--regular old toff, old Conservative! 'But
isn't your candidate a Nationalist?' said he. 'He's a

114

respectable man,' said I. 'He's in favour of whatever
will benefit this country. He's a big ratepayer,' I
said. 'He has extensive house property in the city and
three places of business and isn't it to his own advantage to keep down the rates? He's a prominent and
respected citizen,' said I, 'and a Poor Law Guardian,
and he doesn't belong to any party, good, bad, or indifferent.' That's the way to talk to 'em."

"And what about the address to the King?" said Mr.
Lyons, after drinking and smacking his lips.

"Listen to me," said Mr. Henchy. "What we want in
this country, as I said to old Ward, is capital. The
King's coming here will mean an influx of money into
this country. The citizens of Dublin will benefit by
it. Look at all the factories down by the quays there,
idle! Look at all the money there is in the country,
if we only worked the old industries, the mills, the
shipbuilding yards and factories. It's capital we
want."

"But look here, John," said Mr. O'Connor. "Why
should we welcome the King of England? Didn't Parnell
himself . . ."

"Parnell," said Mr. Henchy, "is dead. Now, here's
the way I look at it. Here's this chap come to the
throne after his old mother keeping him out of it till
the man was grey. He's a man of the world, and he
means well by us. He's a jolly fine decent fellow, if
you ask me, and no damn nonsense about him. He just
says to himself: 'The old one never went to see these
wild Irish. By Christ, I'll go myself and see what
they're like.' And are we going to insult the man when
he comes over here on a friendly visit? Eh? Isn't
that right, Crofton?"

Mr. Crofton nodded his head.

"But after all now," said Mr. Lyons argumentatively,
"King Edward's life, you know, is not the very . . ."

"Let bygones be bygones," said Mr. Henchy. I admire
the man personally. He's just an ordinary knockabout
like you and me. He's fond of his glass of grog and
he's a bit of a rake, perhaps, and he's a good sports-
man. Damn it, can't we Irish play fair?"

"That's all very fine," said Mr. Lyons. "But look
at the case of Parnell now."

115

"In the name of God," said Mr. Henchy, "where's the analogy between the two cases?"

"What I mean," said Mr. Lyons, "is we have our ideals. Why, now, would we welcome a man like that? Do you think now after what he did Parnell was a fit man to lead us? And why, then, would we do it for Edward the Seventh?"

"This is Parnell's anniversary," said Mr. O'Connor, "and don't let us stir up any bad blood. We all respect him now that he's dead and gone--even the Conservatives," he added, turning to Mr. Crofton.

Pok! The tardy cork flew out of Mr. Crofton's bottle. Mr. Crofton got up from his box and went to the fire. As he returned with his capture he said in a deep voice:

"Our side of the house respects him, because he was a gentleman."

"Right you are, Crofton!" said Mr. Henchy fiercely. "He was the only man that could keep that bag of cats in order. 'Down, ye dogs! Lie down, ye curs!' That's the way he treated them. Come in Joe! Come in!" he called out, catching sight of Mr. Hynes in the doorway.

Mr. Hynes came in slowly.

"Open another bottle of stout, Jack," said Mr. Henchy. "O, I forgot there's no corkscrew. Here, show me one here and I'll put it at the fire."

The old man handed him another bottle and he placed it on the hob.

"Sit down, Joe," said Mr. O'Connor, "we're just talking about the Chief."

"Ay, ay!" said Mr. Henchy.

Mr. Hynes sat on the side of the table near Mr. Lyons but said nothing.

"There's one of them, anyhow," said Mr. Henchy, "that didn't renege him. By God, I'll say for you, Joe! No, by God, you stuck to him like a man!"

"O, Joe," said Mr. O'Connor suddenly. "Give us that thing you wrote--do you remember? Have you got it on

116

you?"

"O, ay!" said Mr. Henchy. "Give us that. Did you ever hear that, Crofton? Listen to this now: splendid thing."

"Go on," said Mr. O'Connor. "Fire away, Joe."

Mr. Hynes did not seem to remember at once the piece to which they were alluding, but, after reflecting a while, he said:

"O, that thing is it. . . . Sure that's old now."

"Out with it, man!" said Mr. O'Connor.

"'Sh, 'sh," said Mr. Henchy. "Now, Joe!"

Mr. Hynes hesitated a little longer. Then amid the silence he took off his hat, laid it on the table and stood up. He seemed to be rehearsing the piece in his mind. After a rather long pause he announced:

THE DEATH OF PARNELL

6th October, 1891

He cleared his throat once or twice and then began to recite:

He is dead. Our Uncrowned King is dead.
O, Erin, mourn with grief and woe
For he lies dead whom the fell gang
Of modern hypocrites laid low.

He lies slain by the coward hounds
He raised to glory from the mire;
And Erin's hopes and Erin's dreams
Perish upon her monarch's pyre.

In palace, cabin or in cot
The Irish heart where'er it be
Is bowed with woe--for he is gone
Who would have wrought her destiny.

He would have had his Erin famed,
The green flag gloriously unfurled,
Her statesmen, bards and warriors raised
Before the nations of the World.

117

He dreamed (alas, 'twas but a dream!)
  Of Liberty: but as he strove
To clutch that idol, treachery
  Sundered him from the thing he loved.

Shame on the coward, caitiff hands
  That smote their Lord or with a kiss
Betrayed him to the rabble-rout
  Of fawning priests--no friends of his.

May everlasting shame consume
  The memory of those who tried
To befoul and smear the exalted name
  Of one who spurned them in his pride.

He fell as fall the mighty ones,
  Nobly undaunted to the last,
And death has now united him
  With Erin's heroes of the past.

No sound of strife disturb his sleep!
  Calmly he rests: no human pain
Or high ambition spurs him now
  The peaks of glory to attain.

They had their way: they laid him low,
  But Erin, list, his spirit may
Rise, like the Phoenix from the flames,
  When breaks the dawning of the day,

The day that brings us Freedom's reign.
  And on that day may Erin well
Pledge in the cup she lifts to Joy
  One grief--the memory of Parnell.

Mr. Hynes sat down again on the table. When he had
finished his recitation there was a silence and then a
burst of clapping: even Mr. Lyons clapped. The applause continued for a little time. When it had ceased
all the auditors drank from their bottles in silence.

Pok! The cork flew out of Mr. Hynes' bottle, but
Mr. Hynes remained sitting flushed and bare-headed on
the table. He did not seem to have heard the invita-
tion.

"Good man, Joe!" said Mr. O'Connor, taking out his
cigarette papers and pouch the better to hide his
emotion.

"What do you think of that, Crofton?" cried Mr.

Henchy. "Isn't that fine? What?"

Mr. Crofton said that it was a very fine piece of writing.

THE DEAD

by James Joyce


Lily, the caretaker's daughter, was literally run
off her feet. Hardly had she brought one gentleman
into the little pantry behind the office on the ground
floor and helped him off with his overcoat than the
wheezy hall-door bell clanged again and she had to
scamper along the bare hallway to let in another guest.
It was well for her she had not to attend to the ladies
also. But Miss Kate and Miss Julia had thought of that
and had converted the bathroom upstairs into a ladies'
dressing-room. Miss Kate and Miss Julia were there,
gossiping and laughing and fussing, walking after each
other to the head of the stairs, peering down over the
banisters and calling down to Lily to ask her who had
come.

It was always a great affair, the Misses Morkan's
annual dance. Everybody who knew them came to it, members of the family, old friends of the family, the members of Julia's choir, any of Kate's pupils that were
grown up enough, and even some of Mary Jane's pupils
too. Never once had it fallen flat. For years and
years it had gone off in splendid style, as long as
anyone could remember; ever since Kate and Julia, after
the death of their brother Pat, had left the house in
Stoney Batter and taken Mary Jane, their only niece, to
live with them in the dark, gaunt house on Usher's
Island, the upper part of which they had rented from
Mr. Fulham, the corn-factor on the ground floor. That
was a good thirty years ago if it was a day. Mary
Jane, who was then a little girl in short clothes, was
now the main prop of the household, for she had the
organ in Haddington Road. She had been through the
Academy and gave a pupils' concert every year in the
upper room of the Antient Concert Rooms. Many of her
pupils belonged to the better-class families on the
Kingstown and Dalkey line. Old as they were, her aunts
also did their share. Julia, though she was quite
grey, was still the leading soprano in Adam and Eve's,
and Kate, being too feeble to go about much, gave music
lessons to beginners on the old square piano in the
back room. Lily, the caretaker's daughter, did house-
maid's work for them. Though their life waa modest,
they believed in eating well; the best of everything:
diamond-bone sirloins, three-shilling tea and the best
bottled stout. But Lily seldom made a mistake in the
orders, so that she got on well with her three

121

mistresses. They were fussy, that was all. But the
only thing they would not stand was back answers.

Of course, they had good reason to be fussy on such
a night. And then it was long after ten o'clock and
yet there was no sign of Gabriel and his wife. Besides
they were dreadfully afraid that Freddy Malins might
turn up screwed. They would not wish for worlds that
any of Mary Jane's pupils should see him under the influence; and when he was like that it was sometimes
very hard to manage him. Freddy Malins always came
late, but they wondered what could be keeping Gabriel:
and that was what brought them every two minutes to the
banisters to ask Lily had Gabriel or Freddy come.

"O, Mr. Conroy," said Lily to Gabriel when she
opened the door for him, "Miss Kate and Miss Julia
thought you were never coming. Good-night, Mrs. Conroy."

"I'll engage they did," said Gabriel, "but they forget that my wife here takes three mortal hours to dress
herself."

He stood on the mat, scraping the snow from his
goloshes, while Lily led his wife to the foot of the
stairs and called out:

"Miss Kate, here's Mrs. Conroy."

Kate and Julia came toddling down the dark stairs at
once. Both of them kissed Gabriel's wife, said she
must be perished alive, and asked was Gabriel with her.

"Here I am as right as the mail, Aunt Kate! Go on
up. I'll follow," called out Gabriel from the dark.

He continued scraping his feet vigorously while the
three women went upstairs, laughing, to the ladies'
dressing-room. A light fringe of snow lay like a cape
on the shoulders of his overcoat and like toecaps on
the toes of his goloshes; and, as the buttons of his
overcoat slipped with a squeaking noise through the
snow-stiffened frieze, a cold, fragrant air from out-
of-doors escaped from crevices and folds.

"Is it snowing again, Mr. Conroy?" asked Lily.

She had preceded him into the pantry to help him off
with his overcoat. Gabriel smiled at the three syllables she had given his surname and glanced at her.

She was a slim, growing girl, pale in complexion and with hay-coloured hair. The gas in the pantry made her look still paler. Gabriel had known her when she was a child and used to sit on the lowest step nursing a rag doll.

"Yes, Lily," he answered, "and I think we're in for a night of it."

He looked at the pantry ceiling, which was shaking with the stamping and shuffling of feet on the floor above, listened for a moment to the piano and then glanced at the girl, who was folding his overcoat carefully at the end of a shelf.

"Tell me, Lily," he said in a friendly tone, "do you still go to school?"

"O no, sir," she answered. "I'm done schooling this year and more."

"O, then," said Gabriel gaily, "I suppose we'll be going to your wedding one of these fine days with your young man, eh?"

The girl glanced back at him over her shoulder and said with great bitterness:

"The men that is now is only all palaver and what they can get out of you."

Gabriel coloured, as if he felt he had made a mistake and, without looking at her, kicked off his goloshes and flicked actively with his muffler at his patent-leather shoes.

He was a stout, tallish young man. The high colour of his cheeks pushed upwards even to his forehead, where it scattered itself in a few formless patches of pale red; and on his hairless face there scintillated restlessly the polished lenses and the bright gilt rims of the glasses which screened his delicate and restless eyes. His glossy black hair was parted in the middle and brushed in a long curve behind his ears where it curled slightly beneath the groove left by his hat.

When he had flicked lustre into his shoes he stood up and pulled his waistcoat down more tightly on his plump body. Then he took a coin rapidly from his pocket.

123

"O Lily," he said, thrusting it into her hands, "it's Christmas-time, isn't it? Just . . . here's a little. . . ."

He walked rapidly towards the door.

"O no, sir!" cried the girl, following him. "Really, sir, I wouldn't take it."

"Christmas-time! Christmas-time!" said Gabriel, almost trotting to the stairs and waving his hand to her in deprecation.

The girl, seeing that he had gained the stairs, called out after him:

"Well, thank you, sir."

He waited outside the drawing-room door until the waltz should finish, listening to the skirts that swept against it and to the shuffling of feet. He was still discomposed by the girl's bitter and sudden retort. It had cast a gloom over him which he tried to dispel by arranging his cuffs and the bows of his tie. He then took from his waistcoat pocket a little paper and glanced at the headings he had made for his speech. He was undecided about the lines from Robert Browning, for he feared they would be above the heads of his hearers. Some quotation that they would recognise from Shakespeare or from the Melodies would be better. The indelicate clacking of the men's heels and the shuffling of their soles reminded him that their grade of culture differed from his. He would only make himself ridiculous by quoting poetry to them which they could not understand. They would think that he was airing his superior education. He would fail with them just as he had failed with the girl in the pantry. He had taken up a wrong tone. His whole speech was a mistake from first to last, an utter failure.

Just then his aunts and his wife came out of the ladies' dressing-room. His aunts were two small, plainly dressed old women. Aunt Julia was an inch or so the taller. Her hair, drawn low over the tops of her ears, was grey; and grey also, with darker shadows, was her large flaccid face. Though she was stout in build and stood erect, her slow eyes and parted lips gave her the appearance of a woman who did not know where she was or where she was going. Aunt Kate was more vivacious. Her face, healthier than her sister's, was all puckers and creases, like a shrivelled red apple, and her hair, braided in the same old-fashioned way, had not lost its ripe nut colour.

They both kissed Gabriel frankly. He was their favourite nephew, the son of their dead elder sister, Ellen, who had married T. J. Conroy of the Port and Docks.

"Gretta tells me you're not going to take a cab back to Monkstown to-night, Gabriel," said Aunt Kate.

"No," said Gabriel, turning to his wife, "we had quite enough of that last year, hadn't we? Don't you remember, Aunt Kate, what a cold Gretta got out of it? Cab windows rattling all the way, and the east wind blowing in after we passed Merrion. Very jolly it was. Gretta caught a dreadful cold."

Aunt Kate frowned severely and nodded her head at every word.

"Quite right, Gabriel, quite right," she said. "You can't be too careful."

"But as for Gretta there," said Gabriel, "she'd walk home in the snow if she were let."

Mrs. Conroy laughed.

"Don't mind him, Aunt Kate," she said. "He's really an awful bother, what with green shades for Tom's eyes at night and making him do the dumb-bells, and forcing Eva to eat the stirabout.[1] The poor child! And she simply hates the sight of it! . . . O, but you'll never guess what he makes me wear now!"

She broke out into a peal of laughter and glanced at her husband, whose admiring and happy eyes had been wandering from her dress to her face and hair. The two aunts laughed heartily, too, for Gabriel's solicitude was a standing joke with them.

"Goloshes!" said Mrs. Conroy. "That's the latest. Whenever it's wet underfoot I must put on my goloshes. To-night even, he wanted me to put them on, but I wouldn't. The next thing he'll buy me will be a diving suit."

1. A porridge of oatmeal or cornmeal boiled in water or milk and stirred.

125

Gabriel laughed nervously and patted his tie reassuringly, while Aunt Kate nearly doubled herself, so heartily did she enjoy the joke. The smile soon faded from Aunt Julia's face and her mirthless eyes were directed towards her nephew's face. After a pause she asked:

"And what are goloshes, Gabriel?"

"Goloshes, Julia!" exclaimed her sister. "Goodness me, don't you know what goloshes are? You wear them over your . . . over your boots, Gretta, isn't it?"

"Yes," said Mrs. Conroy. "Guttapercha[2] things. We both have a pair now. Gabriel says everyone wears them on the continent."

"O, on the continent," murmured Aunt Julia, nodding her head slowly.

Gabriel knitted his brows and said, as if he were slightly angered:

"It's nothing very wonderful, but Gretta thinks it very funny because she says the word reminds her of Christy Minstrels."

"But tell me, Gabriel," said Aunt Kate, with brisk tact. "Of course, you've seen about the room. Gretta was saying . . ."

"O, the room is all right," replied Gabriel. "I've taken one in the Gresham."

"To be sure," said Aunt Kate, "by far the best thing to do. And the children, Gretta, you're not anxious about them?"

"O, for one night," said Mrs. Conroy. "Besides, Bessie will look after them."

"To be sure," said Aunt Kate again. "What a comfort it is to have a girl like that; one you can depend on! There's that Lily, I'm sure I don't know what has come over her lately. She's not the girl she was at all."

2. A substance resembling rubber but containing more resin from the latex of several Malaysian trees. It is nearly white to brown, hard and rather elastic, softens on heating, and can be vulcanized.

Gabriel was about to ask his aunt some questions on this point, but she broke off suddenly to gaze after her sister, who had wandered down the stairs and was craning her neck over the banisters.

"Now, I ask you," she said almost testily, "where is Julia going? Julia! Julia! Where are you going?"

Julia, who had gone half way down one flight, came back and announced blandly:

"Here's Freddy."

At the same moment a clapping of hands and a final flourish of the pianist told that the waltz had ended. The drawing-room door was opened from within and some couples came out. Aunt Kate drew Gabriel aside hurriedly and whispered into his ear:

"Slip down, Gabriel, like a good fellow and see if he's all right, and don't let him up if he's screwed. I'm sure he's screwed. I'm sure he is."

Gabriel went to the stairs and listened over the banisters. He could hear two persons talking in the pantry. Then he recognised Freddy Malins' laugh. He went down the stairs noisily.

"It's such a relief," said Aunt Kate to Mrs. Conroy, "that Gabriel is here. I always feel easier in my mind when he's here. . . . Julia, there's Miss Daly and Miss Power will take some refreshment. Thanks for your beautiful waltz, Miss Daly. It made lovely time."

A tall wizen-faced man, with a stiff grizzled moustache and swarthy skin, who was passing out with his partner, said:

"And may we have some refreshment, too, Miss Morkan?"

"Julia," said Aunt Kate summarily, "and here's Mr. Browne and Miss Furlong. Take them in, Julia, with Miss Daly and Miss Power."

"I'm the man for the ladies," said Mr. Browne, pursing his lips until his moustache bristled and smiling in all his wrinkles. "You know, Miss Morkan, the reason they are so fond of me is----"

He did not finish his sentence, but, seeing that

127

Aunt Kate was out of earshot, at once led the three
young ladies into the back room. The middle of the
room was occupied by two square tables placed end to
end, and on these Aunt Julia and the caretaker were
straightening and smoothing a large cloth. On the
sideboard were arrayed dishes and plates and glasses
and bundles of knives and forks and spoons. The top of
the closed square piano served also as a sideboard for
viands and sweets. At a smaller sideboard in one corner two young men were standing, drinking hop-bitters.

Mr. Browne led his charges thither and invited them
all, in jest, to some ladies' punch, hot, strong and
sweet. As they said they never took anything strong,
he opened three bottles of lemonade for them. Then he
asked one of the young men to move aside, and, taking
hold of the decanter, filled out for himself a goodly
measure of whisky. The young men eyed him respectfully while he took a trial sip.

"God help me," he said smiling, "it's the doctor's
orders."

His wizened face broke into a broader smile, and the
three young ladies laughed in musical echo to his
pleasantry, swaying their bodies to and fro, with nervous jerks of their shoulders. The boldest said:

"O, now, Mr. Browne, I'm sure the doctor never or-
dered anything of the kind."

Mr. Browne took another sip of his whisky and said,
with sidling mimicry:

"Well, you see, I'm like the famous Mrs. Cassidy,
who is reported to have said: 'Now, Mary Grimes, if I
don't take it, make me take it, for I feel I want it.'"

His hot face had leaned forward a little too confi-
dentially and he had assumed a very low Dublin accent
so that the young ladies, with one instinct, received
his speech in silence. Miss Furlong, who was one of
Mary Jane's pupils, asked Miss Daly what was the name
of the pretty waltz she had played; and Mr. Browne,
seeing that he was ignored, turned promptly to the two
young men who were more appreciative.

A red-faced young woman, dressed in pansy, came into
the room, excitedly clapping her hands and crying:

"Quadrilles! Quadrilles!"

128

Close on her heels came Aunt Kate, crying:

"Two gentlemen and three ladies, Mary Jane!"

"O, here's Mr. Bergin and Mr. Kerrigan," said Mary
Jane. "Mr. Kerrigan, will you take Miss Power? Miss
Furlong, may I get you a partner, Mr. Bergin. O,
that'll just do now."

"Three ladies, Mary Jane," said Aunt Kate.

The two young gentlemen asked the ladies if they
might have the pleasure, and Mary Jane turned to Miss
Daly.

"O, Miss Daly, you're really awfully good, after
playing for the last two dances, but really we're so
short of ladies to-night."

"I don't mind in the least, Miss Morkan."

"But I've a nice partner for you, Mr. Bartell
D'Arcy, the tenor. I'll get him to sing later on.  All
Dublin is raving about him."

"Lovely voice, lovely voice!" said Aunt Kate.

As the piano had twice begun the prelude to the
first figure Mary Jane led her recruits quickly from
the room. They had hardly gone when Aunt Julia wandered slowly into the room, looking behind her at something.

"What is the matter, Julia?" asked Aunt Kate anxiously. "Who is it?"

Julia, who was carrying in a column of table-
napkins, turned to her sister and said, simply, as if
the question had surprised her:

"It's only Freddy, Kate, and Gabriel with him."

In fact right behind her Gabriel could be seen pi-
loting Freddy Malins across the landing. The latter,
a young man of about forty, was of Gabriel's size and
build, with very round shoulders. His face was fleshy
and pallid, touched with colour only at the thick hanging lobes of his ears and at the wide wings of his
nose. He had coarse features, a blunt nose, a convex
and receding brow, tumid and protruded lips. His
heavy-lidded eyes and the disorder of his scanty hair

129

made him look sleepy. He was laughing heartily in a
high key at a story which he had been telling Gabriel
on the stairs and at the same time rubbing the knuckles
of his left fist backwards and forwards into his left
eye.

"Good-evening, Freddy," said Aunt Julia.

Freddy Malins bade the Misses Morkan good-evening in
what seemed an offhand fashion by reason of the habitu-
al catch in his voice and then, seeing that Mr. Browne
was grinning at him from the sideboard, crossed the
room on rather shaky legs and began to repeat in an
undertone the story he had just told to Gabriel.

"He's not so bad, is he?" said Aunt Kate to Gabriel.

Gabriel's brows were dark but he raised them quickly
and answered:

"O, no, hardly noticeable."

"Now, isn't he a terrible fellow!" she said. "And
his poor mother made him take the pledge on New Year's
Eve. But come on, Gabriel, into the drawing-room."

Before leaving the room with Gabriel she signalled
to Mr. Browne by frowning and shaking her forefinger in
warning to and fro. Mr. Browne nodded in answer and,
when she had gone, said to Freddy Malins:

"Now, then, Teddy, I'm going to fill you out with a
good glass of lemonade just to buck you up."

Freddy Malins, who was nearing the climax of his
story, waved the offer aside impatiently but Mr.Browne,
having first called Freddy Malins' attention to a disarray in his dress, filled out and handed him a full
glass of lemonade. Freddy Malins' left hand accepted
the glass mechanically, his right hand being engaged in
the mechanical readjustment of his dress. Mr. Browne,
whose face was once more wrinkling with mirth, poured
out for himself a glass of whisky while Freddy Malins
exploded, before he had well reached the climax of his
story, in a kink of high-pitched bronchitic laughter
and, setting down his untasted and overflowing glass,
began to rub the knuckles of his left fist backwards
and forwards into his left eye, repeating words of his
last phrase as well as his fit of laughter would allow
him.
            .   .   .   .   .   .   .   .   .   .   .

130

Gabriel could not listen while Mary Jane was playing her Academy piece, full of runs and difficult passages, to the hushed drawing-room. He liked music but the piece she was playing had no melody for him and he doubted whether it had any melody for the other listeners, though they had begged Mary Jane to play something. Four young men, who had come from the refreshment-room to stand in the doorway at the sound of the piano, had gone away quietly in couples after a few minutes. The only persons who seemed to follow the music were Mary Jane herself, her hands racing along the key-board or lifted from it at the pauses like those of a priestess in momentary imprecation, and Aunt Kate standing at her elbow to turn the page.

Gabriel's eyes, irritated by the floor, which glittered with beeswax under the heavy chandelier, wandered to the wall above the piano. A picture of the balcony scene in <u>Romeo and Juliet</u> hung there and beside it was a picture of the two murdered princes in the Tower which Aunt Julia had worked in red, blue and brown wools when she was a girl. Probably in the school they had gone to as girls that kind of work had been taught for one year. His mother had worked for him as a birthday present a waistcoat of purple tabinet,[3] with little foxes' heads upon it, lined with brown satin and having round mulberry buttons. It was strange that his mother had had no musical talent though Aunt Kate used to call her the brains carrier of the Morkan family. Both she and Julia had always seemed a little proud of their serious and matronly sister. Her photograph stood before the pierglass.[4] She held an open book on her knees and was pointing out something in it to Constantine who, dressed in a man-o'-war suit, lay at her feet. It was she who had chosen the names of her sons for she was very sensible of the dignity of family life. Thanks to her, Constantine was now senior curate in Balbriggan and, thanks to her, Gabriel himself had taken his degree in the Royal University. A shadow passed over his face as he remembered her sullen opposition to his marriage. Some slighting phrases she had used still rankled in his memory; she had once spoken of Gretta as being country cute and that was not true of Gretta at all. It was Gretta who had nursed her

3. A kind of poplin, often with a watered surface, made chiefly in Ireland.
4. A large high mirror, as, originally, a narrow one designed to occupy the pier or wall space between windows.

during all her last long illness in their home at
Monkstown.

He knew that Mary Jane must be near the end of her
piece for she was playing again the opening melody with
runs of scales after every bar and while he waited for
the end the resentment died down in his heart. The
piece ended with a trill of octaves in the treble and a
final deep octave in the bass. Great applause greeted
Mary Jane as, blushing and rolling up her music nervously, she escaped from the room. The most vigorous
clapping came from the four young men in the doorway
who had gone away to the refreshment-room at the beginning of the piece but had come back when the piano had
stopped.

Lancers were arranged. Gabriel found himself part-
nered with Miss Ivors. She was a frank-mannered talkative young lady, with a freckled face and prominent
brown eyes. She did not wear a low-cut bodice and the
large brooch which was fixed in the front of her collar
bore on it an Irish device and motto.

When they had taken their places she said abruptly:

"I have a crow to pluck with you."

"With me?" said Gabriel.

She nodded her head gravely.

"What is it?" asked Gabriel, smiling at her solemn
manner.

"Who is G. C.?" answered Miss Ivors, turning her
eyes upon him.

Gabriel coloured and was about to knit his brows, as
if he did not understand, when she said bluntly:

"O, innocent Amy! I have found out that you write
for The Daily Express. Now, aren't you ashamed of
yourself?"

"Why should I be ashamed of myself?" asked Gabriel,
blinking his eyes and trying to smile.

"Well, I'm ashamed of you," said Miss Ivors
frankly. "To say you'd write for a paper like that. I

didn't think you were a West Briton."5

A look of perplexity appeared on Gabriel's face. It was true that he wrote a literary column every Wednesday in The Daily Express, for which he was paid fifteen shillings. But that did not make him a West Briton surely. The books he received for review were almost more welcome than the paltry cheque. He loved to feel the covers and turn over the pages of newly printed books. Nearly every day when his teaching in the college was ended he used to wander down the quays to the second-hand booksellers, to Hickey's on Bachelor's Walk, to Webb's or Massey's on Aston's Quay, or to O'Clohissey's in the by-street. He did not know how to meet her charge. He wanted to say that literature was above politics. But they were friends of many years' standing and their careers had been parallel, first at the University and then as teachers: he could not risk a grandiose phrase with her. He continued blinking his eyes and trying to smile and murmured lamely that he saw nothing political in writing reviews of books.

When their turn to cross had come he was still perplexed and inattentive. Miss Ivors promptly took his hand in a warm grasp and said in a soft friendly tone:

"Of course, I was only joking. Come, we cross now."

When they were together again she spoke of the University question6 and Gabriel felt more at ease. A friend of hers had shown her his review of Browning's poems. That was how she had found out the secret: but she liked the review immensely. Then she said suddenly:

5. The implication is that Gabriel is neither truly British nor Irish.
6. Robert Peel, British prime minister, thought to divert Irish preoccupation with Home Rule to the area of higher education. The plan was to found a Queen's University to be located in Dublin, which was to be carefully controlled by Dublin Castle. Patterned on the University of London, Queen's University would be an examining institution, not a teaching institution. Also, the University would be secular in structure. Through the bishops, the people of Ireland repudiated Peel's suggested gift, and the British government took this as further evidence of Irish stubbornness and ingratitude.

"O, Mr. Conroy, will you come for an excursion to the Aran Isles this summer? We're going to stay there a whole month. It will be splendid out in the Atlantic. You ought to come. Mr. Clancy is coming, and Mr. Kilkelly and Kathleen Kearney. It would be splendid for Gretta too if she'd come. She's from Connacht, isn't she?"

"Her people are," said Gabriel shortly.

"But you will come, won't you?" said Miss Ivors, laying her warm hand eagerly on his arm.

"The fact is," said Gabriel, "I have just arranged to go----"

"Go where?" asked Miss Ivors.

"Well, you know, every year I go for a cycling tour with some fellows and so----"

"But where?" asked Miss Ivors.

"Well, we usually go to France or Belgium or perhaps Germany," said Gabriel awkwardly.

"And why do you go to France and Belgium," said Miss Ivors, "instead of visiting your own land?"

"Well," said Gabriel, "it's partly to keep in touch with the languages and partly for a change."

"And haven't you your own language to keep in touch with--Irish?" asked Miss Ivors.

"Well," said Gabriel, "if it comes to that, you know, Irish is not my language."

Their neighbours had turned to listen to the cross-examination. Gabriel glanced right and left nervously and tried to keep his good humour under the ordeal which was making a blush invade his forehead.

"And haven't you your own land to visit," continued Miss Ivors, "that you know nothing of, your own people, and your own country?"

"O, to tell you the truth," retorted Gabriel suddenly, "I'm sick of my own country, sick of it!"

"Why?" asked Miss Ivors.

Gabriel did not answer for his retort had heated him.

"Why?" repeated Miss Ivors.

They had to go visiting together and, as he had not answered her, Miss Ivors said warmly:

"Of course, you've no answer."

Gabriel tried to cover his agitation by taking part in the dance with great energy. He avoided her eyes for he had seen a sour expression on her face. But when they met in the long chain he was surprised to feel his hand firmly pressed. She looked at him from under her brows for a moment quizzically until he smiled. Then, just as the chain was about to start again, she stood on tiptoe and whispered into his ear:

"West Briton!"

When the lancers were over Gabriel went away to a remote corner of the room where Freddy Malins' mother was sitting. She was a stout feeble old woman with white hair. Her voice had a catch in it like her son's and she stuttered slightly. She had been told that Freddy had come and that he was nearly all right. Gabriel asked her whether she had had a good crossing. She lived with her married daughter in Glasgow and came to Dublin on a visit once a year. She answered placidly that she had had a beautiful crossing and that the captain had been most attentive to her. She spoke also of the beautiful house her daughter kept in Glasgow, and of all the friends they had there. While her tongue rambled on Gabriel tried to banish from his mind all memory of the unpleasant incident with Miss Ivors. Of course the girl or woman, or whatever she was, was an enthusiast but there was a time for all things. Perhaps he ought not to have answered her like that. But she had no right to call him a West Briton before people, even in joke. She had tried to make him ridiculous before people, heckling him and staring at him with her rabbit's eyes.

He saw his wife making her way towards him through the waltzing couples. When she reached him she said into his ear:

"Gabriel, Aunt Kate wants to know won't you carve the goose as usual. Miss Daly will carve the ham and I'll do the pudding."

135

"All right," said Gabriel.

"She's sending in the younger ones first as soon as this waltz is over so that we'll have the table to ourselves."

"Were you dancing?" asked Gabriel.

"Of course I was. Didn't you see me? What row had you with Molly Ivors?"

"No row. Why? Did she say so?"

"Something like that. I'm trying to get that Mr. D'Arcy to sing. He's full of conceit, I think."

"There was no row," said Gabriel moodily, "only she wanted me to go for a trip to the west of Ireland and I said I wouldn't."

His wife clasped her hands excitedly and gave a little jump.

"O, do go, Gabriel," she cried. "I'd love to see Galway again."

"You can go if you like," said Gabriel coldly.

She looked at him for a moment, then turned to Mrs. Malins and said:

"There's a nice husband for you, Mrs. Malins."

While she was threading her way back across the room Mrs. Malins, without adverting to the interruption, went on to tell Gabriel what beautiful places there were in Scotland and beautiful scenery. Her son-in-law brought them every year to the lakes and they used to go fishing. Her son-in-law was a splendid fisher. One day he caught a beautiful big fish and the man in the hotel cooked it for their dinner.

Gabriel hardly heard what she said. Now that supper was coming near he began to think again about his speech and about the quotation. When he saw Freddy Malins coming across the room to visit his mother Gabriel left the chair free for him and retired into the embrasure of the window. The room had already cleared and from the back room came the clatter of plates and knives. Those who still remained in the drawing-room seemed tired of dancing and were conversing quietly in

136

little groups. Gabriel's warm trembling fingers tapped
the cold pane of the window. How cool it must be outside! How pleasant it would be to walk out alone,
first along by the river and then through the park!
The snow would be lying on the branches of the trees
and forming a bright cap on the top of the Wellington
Monument. How much more pleasant it would be there
than at the supper-table!

He ran over the headings of his speech: Irish hospitality, sad memories, the Three Graces, Paris, the
quotation from Browning. He repeated to himself a
phrase he had written in his review: "One feels that
one is listening to a thought-tormented music." Miss
Ivors had praised the review. Was she sincere? Had
she really any life of her own behind all her propa-
gandism? There had never been any ill-feeling between
them until that night. It unnerved him to think that
she would be at the supper-table, looking up at him
while he spoke with her critical quizzing eyes. Perhaps
she would not be sorry to see him fail in his speech.
An idea came into his mind and gave him courage. He
would say, alluding to Aunt Kate and Aunt Julia: "Ladies and Gentlemen, the generation which is now on the
wane among us may have had its faults but for my part I
think it had certain qualities of hospitality, of humour, of humanity, which the new and very serious and
hypereducated generation that is growing up around us
seems to me to lack." Very good: that was one for
Miss Ivors. What did he care that his aunts were only
two ignorant old women?

A murmur in the room attracted his attention. Mr.
Browne was advancing from the door, gallantly escorting
Aunt Julia, who leaned upon his arm, smiling and hanging her head. An irregular musketry of applause es-
corted her also as far as the piano and then, as Mary
Jane seated herself on the stool, and Aunt Julia, no
longer smiling, half turned so as to pitch her voice
fairly into the room, gradually ceased. Gabriel recognised the prelude. It was that of an old song of Aunt
Julia's--Arrayed for the Bridal. Her voice, strong and
clear in tone, attacked with great spirit the runs
which embellish the air and though she sang very rapidly she did not miss even the smallest of the grace
notes. To follow the voice, without looking at the
singer's face, was to feel and share the excitement of
swift and secure flight. Gabriel applauded loudly with
all the others at the close of the song and loud applause was borne in from the invisible supper-table.
It sounded so genuine that a little colour struggled

137

into Aunt Julia's face as she bent to replace in the music-stand the old leather-bound song-book that had her initials on the cover. Freddy Malins, who had listened with his head perched sideways to hear her better, was still applauding when everyone else had ceased and talking animatedly to his mother who nodded her head gravely and slowly in acquiescence. At last, when he could clap no more, he stood up suddenly and hurried across the room to Aunt Julia whose hand he seized and held in both his hands, shaking it when words failed him or the catch in his voice proved too much for him.

"I was just telling my mother," he said, "I never heard you sing so well, never. No, I never heard your voice so good as it is to-night. Now! Would you believe that now? That's the truth. Upon my word and honour that's the truth. I never heard your voice sound so fresh and so . . . so clear and fresh, never."

Aunt Julia smiled broadly and murmured something about compliments as she released her hand from his grasp. Mr. Browne extended his open hand towards her and said to those who were near him in the manner of a showman introducing a prodigy to an audience:

"Miss Julia Morkan, my latest discovery!"

He was laughing very heartily at this himself when Freddy Malins turned to him and said:

"Well, Browne, if you're serious you might make a worse discovery. All I can say is I never heard her sing half so well as long as I am coming here. And that's the honest truth."

"Neither did I," said Mr. Browne. "I think her voice has greatly improved."

Aunt Julia shrugged her shoulders and said with meek pride:

"Thirty years ago I hadn't a bad voice as voices go."

"I often told Julia," said Aunt Kate emphatically, "that she was simply thrown away in that choir. But she never would be said by me."

She turned as if to appeal to the good sense of the others against a refractory child while Aunt Julia gazed in front of her, a vague smile of reminiscence playing on her face.

"No," continued Aunt Kate, "she wouldn't be said or
led by anyone, slaving there in that choir night and
day, night and day. Six o'clock on Christmas morning!
And all for what?"

"Well, isn't it for the honour of God, Aunt Kate?"
asked Mary Jane, twisting round on the piano-stool and
smiling.

Aunt Kate turned fiercely on her niece and said:

"I know all about the honour of God, Mary Jane, but
I think it's not at all honourable for the pope to turn
out the women out of the choirs that have slaved there
all their lives and put little whipper-snappers of boys
over their heads. I suppose it is for the good of the
Church if the pope does it. But it's not just, Mary
Jane, and it's not right."

She had worked herself into a passion and would have
continued in defence of her sister for it was a sore
subject with her but Mary Jane, seeing that all the
dancers had come back, intervened pacifically:

"Now, Aunt Kate, you're giving scandal to Mr. Browne
who is of the other persuasion."

Aunt Kate turned to Mr. Browne, who was grinning at
this allusion to his religion, and said hastily:

"O, I don't question the pope's being right. I'm
only a stupid old woman and I wouldn't presume to do
such a thing. But there's such a thing as common
everyday politeness and gratitude. And if I were in
Julia's place I'd tell that Father Healey straight up
to his face . . ."

"And besides, Aunt Kate," said Mary Jane, "we really
are all hungry and when we are hungry we are all very
quarrelsome."

"And when we are thirsty we are also quarrelsome,"
added Mr. Browne.

"So that we had better go to supper," said Mary
Jane, "and finish the discussion afterwards."

On the landing outside the drawing-room Gabriel
found his wife and Mary Jane trying to persuade Miss

Ivors to stay for supper. But Miss Ivors, who had put on her hat and was buttoning her cloak, would not stay. She did not feel in the least hungry and she had already over-stayed her time.

"But only for ten minutes, Molly," said Mrs. Conroy. "That won't delay you."

"To take a pick itself," said Mary Jane, "after all your dancing."

"I really couldn't," said Miss Ivors.

"I am afraid you didn't enjoy yourself at all," said Mary Jane hopelessly.

"Ever so much, I assure you," said Miss Ivors, "but you really must let me run off now."

"But how can you get home?" asked Mrs. Conroy.

"O, it's only two steps up the quay."

Gabriel hesitated a moment and said:

"If you will allow me, Miss Ivors, I'll see you home if you are really obliged to go."

But Miss Ivors broke away from them.

"I won't hear of it," she cried. "For goodness' sake go in to your suppers and don't mind me. I'm quite well able to take care of myself."

"Well, you're the comical girl, Molly," said Mrs. Conroy frankly.

"Beannacht libh,"[7] cried Miss Ivors, with a laugh, as she ran down the staircase.

Mary Jane gazed after her, a moody puzzled expression on her face, while Mrs. Conroy leaned over the banisters to listen for the hall-door. Gabriel asked himself was he the cause of her abrupt departure. But she did not seem to be in ill humour: she had gone away laughing. He stared blankly down the staircase.

At the moment Aunt Kate came toddling out of the

7. Trans. "Blessings be with you."

supper-room, almost wringing her hands in despair.

"Where is Gabriel?" she cried. "Where on earth is Gabriel? There's everyone waiting in there, stage to let, and nobody to carve the goose!"

"Here I am, Aunt Kate!" cried Gabriel, with sudden animation, "ready to carve a flock of geese, if necessary."

A fat brown goose lay at one end of the table and at the other end, on a bed of creased paper strewn with sprigs of parsley, lay a great ham, stripped of its outer skin and peppered over with crust crumbs, a neat paper frill round its shin and beside this was a round of spiced beef. Between these rival ends ran parallel lines of side-dishes: two little minsters of jelly, red and yellow; a shallow dish full of blocks of blanc-mange and red jam, a large green leaf-shaped dish with a stalk-shaped handle, on which lay bunches of purple raisins and peeled almonds, a companion dish on which lay a solid rectangle of Smyrna figs, a dish of custard topped with grated nutmeg, a small bowl full of chocolates and sweets wrapped in gold and silver papers and a glass vase in which stood some tall celery stalks. In the centre of the table there stood, as sentries to a fruit-stand which upheld a pyramid of oranges and American apples, two squat old-fashioned decanters of cut glass, one containing port and the other dark sherry. On the closed square piano a pudding in a huge yellow dish lay in waiting and behind it were three squads of bottles of stout and ale and minerals, drawn up according to the colours of their uniforms, the first two black, with brown and red labels, the third and smallest squad white, with transverse green sashes.

Gabriel took his seat boldly at the head of the table and, having looked to the edge of the carver, plunged his fork firmly into the goose. He felt quite at ease now for he was an expert carver and liked nothing better than to find himself at the head of a well-laden table.

"Miss Furlong, what shall I send you?" he asked. "A wing or a slice of the breast?"

"Just a small slice of the breast."

"Miss Higgins, what for you?"

"O, anything at all, Mr. Conroy."

141

While Gabriel and Miss Daly exchanged plates of
goose and plates of ham and spiced beef Lily went from
guest to guest with a dish of hot floury potatoes wrapped in a white napkin. This was Mary Jane's idea and
she had also suggested apple sauce for the goose but
Aunt Kate had said that plain roast goose without any
apple sauce had always been good enough for her and she
hoped she might never eat worse. Mary Jane waited on
her pupils and saw that they got the best slices and
Aunt Kate and Aunt Julia opened and carried across from
the piano bottles of stout and ale for the gentlemen
and bottles of minerals for the ladies. There was a
great deal of confusion and laughter and noise, the
noise of orders and counter-orders, of knives and
forks, of corks and glass-stoppers. Gabriel began to
carve second helpings as soon as he had finished the
first round without serving himself. Everyone protest-
ed loudly so that he compromised by taking a long
draught of stout for he had found the carving hot work.
Mary Jane settled down quietly to her supper but Aunt
Kate and Aunt Julia were still toddling round the
table, walking on each other's heels, getting in each
other's way and giving each other unheeded orders. Mr.
Browne begged of them to sit down and eat their suppers
and so did Gabriel but they said there was time enough,
so that, at last, Freddy Malins stood up and, capturing
Aunt Kate, plumped her down on her chair amid general
laughter.

When everyone had been well served Gabriel said,
smiling:

"Now, if anyone wants a little more of what vulgar
people call stuffing let him or her speak."

A chorus of voices invited him to begin his own supper and Lily came forward with three potatoes which she
had reserved for him.

"Very well," said Gabriel amiably, as he took another preparatory draught, "kindly forget my existence,
ladies and gentlemen, for a few minutes."

He set to his supper and took no part in the conversation with which the table covered Lily's removal of
the plates. The subject of talk was the opera company
which was then at the Theatre Royal. Mr. Bartell
D'Arcy, the tenor, a dark-complexioned young man with
a smart moustache, praised very highly the leading con-
tralto of the company but Miss Furlong thought she had
a rather vulgar style of production. Freddy Malins

142

said there was a negro chieftain singing in the second
part of the Gaiety pantomime who had one of the finest
tenor voices he had ever heard.

"Have you heard him?" he asked Mr. Bartell D'Arcy
across the table.

"No," answered Mr. Bartell D'Arcy carelessly.

"Because," Freddy Malins explained, "now I'd be
curious to hear your opinion of him. I think he has a
grand voice."

"It takes Teddy to find out the really good things,"
said Mr. Browne familiarly to the table.

"And why couldn't he have a voice too?" asked Freddy
Malins sharply. "Is it because he's only a black?"

Nobody answered this question and Mary Jane led the
table back to the legitimate opera. One of her pupils
had given her a pass for Mignon. Of course it was very
fine, she said, but it made her think of poor Georgina
Burns. Mr. Browne could go back farther still, to the
old Italian companies that used to come to Dublin--
Tietjens, Ilma de Murzka, Campanini, the great Trebelli
Giuglini, Ravelli, Aramburo. Those were the days, he
said, when there was something like singing to be heard
in Dublin. He told too of how the top gallery of the
old Royal used to be packed night after night, of how
one night an Italian tenor had sung five encores to Let
me like a Soldier fall, introducing a high C every time
and of how the gallery boys would sometimes in their
enthusiasm unyoke the horses from the carriage of some
great prima donna and pull her themselves through the
streets to her hotel. Why did they never play the
grand old operas now, he asked, Dinorah, Lucrezia Bor-
gia? Because they could not get the voices to sing
them: that was why."

"O, well," said Mr. Bartell D'Arcy, "I presume there
are as good singers to-day as there were then."

"Where are they?" asked Mr. Browne defiantly.

"In London, Paris, Milan," said Mr. Bartell D'Arcy
warmly. "I suppose Caruso, for example, is quite as
good, if not better than any of the men you have mentioned."

"Maybe so," said Mr. Browne. "But I may tell you I
143

doubt it strongly."

"O, I'd give anything to hear Caruso sing," said
Mary Jane.

"For me," said Aunt Kate, who had been picking a
bone, "there was only one tenor.  To please me, I mean.
But I suppose none of you ever heard of him."

"Who was he, Miss Morkan?" asked Mr. Bartell D'Arcy
politely.

"His name," said Aunt Kate, "was Parkinson.  I heard
him when he was in his prime and I think he had then
the purest tenor voice that was ever put into a man's
throat."

"Strange," said Mr. Bartell D'Arcy.  "I never even
heard of him."

"Yes, yes, Miss Morkan is right," said Mr. Browne.
"I remember hearing of old Parkinson, but he's too far
back for me."

"A beautiful, pure, sweet, mellow English tenor,"
said Aunt Kate with enthusiasm.

Gabriel having finished, the huge pudding was trans-
ferred to the table.  The clatter of forks and spoons
began again.  Gabriel's wife served out spoonfuls of
the pudding and passed the plates down the table.  Mid-
way down they were held up by Mary Jane, who replenish-
ed them with respberry or orange jelly or with blanc-
mange and jam.  The pudding was of Aunt Julia's making
and she received praises for it from all quarters.  She
herself said that it was not quite brown enough.

"Well, I hope, Miss Morkan," said Mr. Browne, "that
I'm brown enough for you because, you know, I'm all
brown."

All the gentlemen, except Gabriel, ate some of the
pudding out of compliment to Aunt Julia.  As Gabriel
never ate sweets the celery had been left for him.
Freddy Malins also took a stalk of celery and ate it
with his pudding.  He had been told that celery was a
capital thing for the blood and he was just then under
doctor's care.  Mrs. Malins, who had been silent all
through the supper, said that her son was going down to
Mount Melleray in a week or so.  The table then spoke
of Mount Melleray, how bracing the air was down there,

144

how hospitable the monks were and how they never asked
for a penny-piece from their guests.

"And do you mean to say." asked Mr. Browne incredu-
lously, "that a chap can go down there and put up there
as if it were a hotel and live on the fat of the land
and then come away without paying anything?"

"O, most people give some donation to the monastery
when they leave," said Mary Jane.

"I wish we had an institution like that in our
Church," said Mr. Browne candidly.

He was astonished to hear that the monks never
spoke, got up at two in the morning and slept in their
coffins.  He asked what they did it for.

"That's the rule of the order," said Aunt Kate
firmly.

"Yes, but why?" asked Mr. Browne.

Aunt Kate repeated that it was the rule, that was
all.  Mr. Browne still seemed not to understand.
Freddy Malins explained to him, as best he could, that
the monks were trying to make up for the sins committed
by all the sinners in the outside world.  The explana-
tion was not very clear for Mr. Browne grinned and
said:

"I like that idea very much but wouldn't a comfortable spring bed do them as well as a coffin?"

"The coffin," said Mary Jane, "is to remind them of
their last end."

As the subject had grown lugubrious it was buried in
a silence of the table during which Mrs. Malins could
be heard saying to her neighbour in an indistinct undertone:

"They are very good men, the monks, very pious men."

The raisins and almonds and figs and apples and oranges and chocolates and sweets were now passed about
the table and Aunt Julia invited all the guests to have
either port or sherry.  At first Mr. Bartell D'Arcy refused to take either but one of his neighbours nudged
him and whispered something to him upon which he allowed his glass to be filled.  Gradually as the last

glasses were being filled the conversation ceased. A
pause followed, broken only by the noise of the wine
and by unsettlings of chairs. The Misses Morkan, all
three, looked down at the tablecloth. Someone coughed
once or twice and then a few gentlemen patted the table
gently as a signal for silence. The silence came and
Gabriel pushed back his chair and stood up.

The patting at once grew louder in encouragement and
then ceased altogether. Gabriel leaned his ten trembling fingers on the tablecloth and smiled nervously at
the company. Meeting a row of upturned faces he raised
his eyes to the chandelier. The piano was playing a
waltz tune and he could hear the skirts sweeping
against the drawing-room door. People, perhaps, were
standing in the snow on the quay outside, gazing up at
the lighted windows and listening to the waltz music.
The air was pure there. In the distance lay the park
where the trees were weighted with snow. The Wellington Monument wore a gleaming cap of snow that flashed
westward over the white field of Fifteen Acres.

He began:

"Ladies and Gentlemen,

"It has fallen to my lot this evening, as in years
past, to perform a very pleasing task but a task for
which I am afraid my poor powers as a speaker are all
too inadequate."

"No, no!" said Mr. Browne.

"But, however that may be, I can only ask you to-
night to take the will for the deed and to lend me your
attention for a few moments while I endeavour to express to you in words what my feelings are on this occasion.

"Ladies and Gentlemen, it is not the first time that
we have gathered together under this hospitable roof,
around this hospitable board. It is not the first time
that we have been the recipients--or perhaps, I had
better say, the victims--of the hospitality of certain
great ladies."

He made a circle in the air with his arm and paused.
Everyone laughed or smiled at Aunt Kate and Aunt Julia
and Mary Jane who all turned crimson with pleasure.
Gabriel went on more boldly:

146

"I feel more strongly with every recurring year that
our country has no tradition which does it so much hon-
or and which it should guard so jealously as that of
its hospitality. It is a tradition that is unique as
far as my experience goes (and I have visited not a few
places abroad) among the modern nations. Some would
say, perhaps, that with us it is rather a failing than
anything to be boasted of. But granted even that, it
is, to my mind, a princely failing, and one that I
trust will long be cultivated among us. Of one thing,
at least, I am sure. As long as this one roof shel-
ters the good ladies aforesaid--and I wish from my
heart it may do so for many and many a long year to
come--the tradition of genuine warm-hearted courteous
Irish hospitality, which our forefathers have handed
down to us and which we in turn must hand down to our
descendants, is still alive among us."

A hearty murmur of assent ran round the table. It
shot through Gabriel's mind that Miss Ivors was not
there and that she had gone away discourteously: and he
said with confidence in himself:

"Ladies and Gentlemen,

"A new generation is growing up in our midst, a
generation actuated by new ideas and new principles.
It is serious and enthusiastic for these new ideas and
its enthusiasm, even when it is misdirected, is, I believe, in the main sincere. But we are living in a
sceptical and, if I may use the phrase, a thought-
tormented age: and sometimes I fear that this new generation, educated or hypereducated as it is, will lack
those qualities of humanity, of hospitality, of kindly
humour which belonged to an older day. Listening to-
night to the names of all those great singers of the
past it seemed to me, I must confess, that we were
living in a less spacious age. Those days might, without exaggeration, be called spacious days: and if they
are gone beyond recall let us hope, at least, that in
gatherings such as this we shall still speak of them
with pride and affection, still cherish in our hearts
the memory of those dead and gone great ones whose fame
the world will not willingly let die."

"Hear, hear!" said Mr. Browne loudly.

"But yet," continued Gabriel, his voice falling into
a softer inflection, "there are always in gatherings
such as this sadder thoughts that will recur to our
minds: thoughts of the past, of youth, of changes, of

147

absent faces that we miss here to-night. Our path through life is strewn with many such sad memories: and were we to brood upon them always we could not find the heart to go on bravely with our work among the living. We have all of us living duties and living affections which claim, and rightly claim, our strenuous endeavours.

"Therefore, I will not linger on the past. I will not let any gloomy moralising intrude upon us here tonight. Here we are gathered together for a brief moment from the bustle and rush of our everyday routine. We are met here as friends, in the spirit of goodfellowship, as colleagues, also to a certain extent, in the true spirit of camaraderie, and as the guests of--what shall I call them?--the three Graces of the Dublin musical world."

The table burst into applause and laughter at this allusion. Aunt Julia vainly asked each of her neighbours in turn to tell her what Gabriel had said.

"He says we are the Three Graces, Aunt Julia," said Mary Jane.

Aunt Julia did not understand but she looked up, smiling, at Gabriel, who continued in the same vein:

"Ladies and Gentlemen,

"I will not attempt to play to-night the part that Paris played on another occasion.[8] I will not attempt to choose between them. The task would be an invidious one and one beyond my poor powers. For when I view them in turn, whether it be our chief hostess herself, whose good heart, whose too good heart, has become a byword with all who know her, or her sister, who seems to be gifted with perennial youth and whose singing must have been a surprise and a revelation to us all to-night, or, last but not least, when I consider our youngest hostess, talented, cheerful, hard-working and the best of nieces, I confess, Ladies and Gentlemen, that I do not know to which of them I should award the prize."

Gabriel glanced down at his aunts and, seeing the

8. A reference to the myth where Paris, son of Priam, King of Troy, was to judge who was the fairest of three goddesses: Hera, Athena, and Aphrodite.

large smile on Aunt Julia's face and the tears which
had risen to Aunt Kate's eyes, hastened to his close.
He raised his glass of port gallantly, while every member of the company fingered a glass expectantly, and
said loudly:

"Let us toast them all three together. Let us drink
to their health, wealth, long life, happiness and pros-
perity and may they long continue to hold the proud and
self-won position which they hold in their profession
and the position of honour and affection which they
hold in our hearts."

All the guests stood up, glass in hand, and turning
towards the three seated ladies, sang in unison, with
Mr. Browne as leader:

          "For they are jolly gay fellows,
           For they are jolly gay fellows,
           For they are jolly gay fellows,
           Which nobody can deny."

Aunt Kate was making frank use of her handkerchief
and even Aunt Julia seemed moved. Freddy Malins beat
time with his pudding-fork and the singers turned
towards one another, as if in melodious conference,
while they sang with emphasis:

          "Unless he tells a lie,
           Unless he tells a lie."

Then, turning once more towards their hostesses,
they sang:

          "For they are jolly gay fellows,
           For they are jolly gay fellows,
           For they are jolly gay fellows,
           Which nobody can deny."

The acclamation which followed was taken up beyond
the door of the supper-room by many of the other guests
and renewed time after time, Freddy Malins acting as
officer with his fork on high.

          .    .    .    .    .    .    .    .    .

The piercing morning air came into the hall where
they were standing so that Aunt Kate said:

"Close the door, somebody. Mrs. Malins will get her
death of cold."

"Browne is out there, Aunt Kate," said Mary Jane.

"Browne is everywhere," said Aunt Kate, lowering her voice.

Mary Jane laughed at her tone.

"Really," she said archly, "he is very attentive."

"He has been laid on here like the gas," said Aunt Kate in the same tone, "all during the Christmas."

She laughed herself this time good-humouredly and then added quickly:

"But tell him to come in, Mary Jane, and close the door. I hope to goodness he didn't hear me."

At the moment the hall-door was opened and Mr. Browne came in from the doorstep, laughing as if his heart would break. He was dressed in a long green overcoat with mock astrakhan cuffs and collar and wore on his head an oval fur cap. He pointed down the snow-covered quay from where the sound of shrill prolonged whistling was borne in.

"Teddy will have all the cabs in Dublin out," he said.

Gabriel advanced from the little pantry behind the office, struggling into his overcoat and, looking round the hall, said:

"Gretta not down yet?"

"She's getting on her things, Gabriel," said Aunt Kate.

"Who's playing up there?" asked Gabriel.

"Nobody. They're all gone."

"O no, Aunt Kate," said Mary Jane. "Bartell D'Arcy and Miss O'Callaghan aren't gone yet."

"Someone is fooling at the piano anyhow," said Gabriel.

Mary Jane glanced at Gabriel and Mr. Browne and said with a shiver:

"It makes me feel cold to look at you two gentlemen muffled up like that. I wouldn't like to face your journey home at this hour."

"I'd like nothing better this minute," said Mr. Browne stoutly, "than a rattling fine walk in the country or a fast drive with a good spanking goer between the shafts."

"We used to have a very good horse and trap[9] at home," said Aunt Julia sadly.

"The never-to-be-forgotten Johnny," said Mary Jane laughing.

Aunt Kate and Gabriel laughed too.

"Why, what was wonderful about Johnny?" asked Mr. Browne.

"The late lamented Patrick Morkan, our grandfather, that is," explained Gabriel, "commonly known in his later years as the old gentleman, was a glue-boiler."

"O, now, Gabriel," said Aunt Kate, laughing, "he had a starch mill."

"Well, glue or starch," said Gabriel, "the old gentleman had a horse by the name of Johnny. And Johnny used to work in the old gentleman's mill, walking round and round in order to drive the mill. That was all very well; but now comes the tragic part about Johnny. One fine day the old gentleman thought he'd like to drive out with the quality to a military review in the park."

"The Lord have mercy on his soul," said Aunt Kate compassionately.

"Amen," said Gabriel. "So the old gentleman, as I said, harnessed Johnny and put on his very best tall hat and his very best stock collar and drove out in grand style from his ancestral mansion somewhere near Back Lane, I think."

Everyone laughed, even Mrs. Malins, at Gabriel's manner and Aunt Kate said:

9. A light, usually two-wheeled, one-horse carriage with springs.

151

"O, now, Gabriel, he didn't live in Back Lane,
really. Only the mill was there."

"Out from the mansion of his forefathers," continued
Gabriel, "he drove with Johnny. And everything went on
beautifully until Johnny came in sight of King Billy's
statue: and whether he fell in love with the horse
King Billy sits on or whether he thought he was back
again in the mill, anyhow he began to walk round the
statue."

Gabriel paced in a circle round the hall in his goloshes amid the laughter of the others.

"Round and round he went," said Gabriel, "and the
old gentleman, who was a very pompous old gentleman,
was highly indignant. 'Go on, sir! What do you mean,
sir? Johnny! Johnny! Most extraordinary conduct!
Can't understand the horse!'"

The peals of laughter which followed Gabriel's imitation of the incident was interrupted by a resounding
knock at the hall door. Mary Jane ran to open it and
let in Freddy Malins. Freddy Malins, with his hat well
back on his head and his shoulders humped with cold,
was puffing and steaming after his exertions.

"I could only get one cab," he said.

"O, we'll find another along the quay," said
Gabriel.

"Yes," said Aunt Kate. "Better not keep Mrs. Malins
standing in the draught."

Mrs. Malins was helped down the front steps by her
son and Mr. Browne and, after many manoeuvres, hoisted
into the cab. Freddy Malins clambered in after her and
spent a long time settling her on the seat, Mr. Browne
helping him with advice. At last she was settled com-
fortably and Freddy Malins invited Mr. Browne into the
cab. There was a good deal of confused talk, and then
Mr. Browne got into the cab. The cabman settled his
rug over his knees, and bent down for the address. The
confusion grew greater and the cabman was directed dif-
ferently by Freddy Malins and Mr. Browne, each of whom
had his head out through a window of the cab. The dif-
ficulty was to know where to drop Mr. Browne along the
route, and Aunt Kate, Aunt Julia, and Mary Jane helped
the discussion from the doorstep with cross-directions
and contradictions and abundance of laughter. As for

152

Freddy Malins he was speechless with laughter. He
popped his head in and out of the window every moment
to the great danger of his hat, and told his mother
how the discussion was progressing, till at last Mr.
Browne shouted to the bewildered cabman above the din
of everybody's laughter:

"Do you know Trinity College?"

"Yes, sir," said the cabman.

"Well, drive bang up against Trinity College gates,"
said Mr. Browne, "and then we'll tell you where to go.
You understand now?"

"Yes, sir," said the cabman.

"Make like a bird for Trinity College."

"Right, sir," said the cabman.

The horse was whipped up and the cab rattled off
along the quay amid a chorus of laughter and adieus.

Gabriel had not gone to the door with the others.
He was in a dark part of the hall gazing up the staircase. A woman was standing near the top of the first
flight, in the shadow also. He could not see her face
but he could see the terra-cotta and salmon-pink panels
of her skirt which the shadow made appear black and
white. It was his wife. She was leaning on the banisters, listening to something. Gabriel was surprised
at her stillness and strained his ear to listen also.
But he could hear little save the noise of laughter and
dispute on the front steps, a few chords struck on the
piano and a few notes of a man's voice singing.

He stood still in the gloom of the hall, trying to
catch the air that the voice was singing and gazing up
at his wife. There was grace and mystery in her attitude as if she were a symbol of something. He asked
himself what is a woman standing on the stairs in the
shadow, listening to distant music, a symbol of. If he
were a painter he would paint her in that attitude.
Her blue felt hat would show off the bronze of her hair
against the darkness and the dark panels of her skirt
would show off the light ones. Distant Music he would
call the picture if he were a painter.

The hall-door was closed; and Aunt Kate, Aunt Julia
and Mary Jane came down the hall, still laughing.

153

"Well, isn't Freddy terrible?" said Mary Jane.
"He's really terrible."

Gabriel said nothing but pointed up the stairs
towards where his wife was standing. Now that the
hall-door was closed the voice and the piano could be
heard more clearly. Gabriel held up his hand for them
to be silent. The song seemed to be in the old Irish
tonality and the singer seemed uncertain both of his
words and of his voice. The voice, made plaintive by
distance and by the singer's hoarseness, faintly illuminated the cadence of the air with words expressing
grief:

> "O, the rain falls on my heavy locks
> And the dew wets my skin,
> My babe lies cold . . ."

"O," exclaimed Mary Jane. "It's Bartell D'Arcy
singing and he wouldn't sing all the night. O, I'll
get him to sing a song before he goes."

"O, do, Mary Jane," said Aunt Kate.

Mary Jane brushed past the others and ran to the
staircase, but before she reached it the singing stopped and the piano was closed abruptly.

"O, what a pity!" she cried. "Is he coming down,
Gretta?"

Gabriel heard his wife answer yes and saw her come
down towards them. A few steps behind her were Mr.
Bartell D'Arcy and Miss O'Callaghan.

"O, Mr. D'Arcy," cried Mary Jane, "it's downright
mean of you to break off like that when we were all in
raptures listening to you."

"I have been at him all the evening," said Miss
O'Callaghan, "and Mrs. Conroy, too, and he told us he
had a dreadful cold and couldn't sing."

"O, Mr. D'Arcy," said Aunt Kate, "now that was a
great fib to tell."

"Can't you see that I'm as hoarse as a crow?" said
Mr. D'Arcy roughly.

He went into the pantry hastily and put on his overcoat. The others, taken aback by his rude speech,

could find nothing to say. Aunt Kate wrinkled her
brows and made signs to the others to drop the subject.
Mr. D'Arcy stood swathing his neck carefully and frowning.

"It's the weather," said Aunt Julia, after a pause.

"Yes, everybody has colds," said Aunt Kate readily,
"everybody."

"They say," said Mary Jane, "we haven't had snow
like it for thirty years; and I read this morning in
the newspapers that the snow is general all over Ireland."

"I love the look of snow," said Aunt Julia sadly.

"So do I," said Miss O'Callaghan. "I think Christmas is never really Christmas unless we have the snow
on the ground."

"But poor Mr. D'Arcy doesn't like the snow," said
Aunt Kate, smiling.

Mr. D'Arcy came from the pantry, fully swathed and
buttoned, and in a repentant tone told them the history
of his cold. Everyone gave him advice and said it was
a great pity and urged him to be very careful of his
throat in the night air. Gabriel watched his wife, who
did not join in the conversation. She was standing
right under the dusty fanlight and the flame of the gas
lit up the rich bronze of her hair, which he had seen
her drying at the fire a few days before. She was in
the same attitude and seemed unaware of the talk about
her. At last she turned towards them and Gabriel saw
that there was colour on her cheeks and that her eyes
were shining. A sudden tide of joy went leaping out of
his heart.

"Mr. D'Arcy," she said, "what is the name of that
song you were singing?"

"It's called The Lass of Aughrim," said Mr. D'Arcy,
"but I couldn't remember it properly. Why? Do you
know it?"

"The Lass of Aughrim," she repeated. "I couldn't
think of the name."

"It's a very nice air," said Mary Jane. "I'm sorry
you were not in voice to-night."

155

"Now, Mary Jane," said Aunt Kate, "don't annoy Mr. D'Arcy. I won't have him annoyed."

Seeing that all were ready to start she shepherded them to the door, where good-night was said:

"Well, good-night, Aunt Kate, and thanks for the pleasant evening."

"Good-night, Gabriel. Good-night, Gretta!"

"Good-night, Aunt Kate, and thanks ever so much. Good-night, Aunt Julia."

"O, good-night, Gretta, I didn't see you."

"Good-night, Mr. D'Arcy. Good-night, Miss O'Callaghan."

"Good-night, Miss Morkan."

"Good-night, again."

"Good-night, all. Safe home."

"Good-night. Good night."

The morning was still dark. A dull, yellow light brooded over the houses and the river; and the sky seemed to be descending. It was slushy underfoot; and only streaks and patches of snow lay on the roofs, on the parapets of the quay and on the area railings. The lamps were still burning redly in the murky air and, across the river, the palace of the Four Courts[10] stood out menacingly against the heavy sky.

She was walking on before him with Mr. Bartell D'Arcy, her shoes in a brown parcel tucked under one arm and her hands holding her skirt up from the slush. She had no longer any grace of attitude, but Gabriel's eyes were still bright with happiness. The blood went bounding along his veins; and the thoughts went rioting

10. An architectural complex formed like a four-leafed shamrock about a central hall which was the center of juridical and political life in Dublin. After the Treaty of 1921 had been accepted a section of the Republican forces seized the Four Courts and mined it. It was destroyed, but re-built on the old lines.

through his brain, proud, joyful, tender, valorous.

She was walking on before him so lightly and so
erect that he longed to run after her noiselessly,
catch her by the shoulders and say something foolish
and affectionate into her ear. She seemed to him so
frail that he longed to defend her against something
and then to be alone with her. Moments of their secret
life together burst like stars upon his memory. A
heliotrope envelope was lying beside his breakfast-cup
and he was caressing it with his hand. Birds were
twittering in the ivy and the sunny web of the curtain
was shimmering along the floor: he could not eat for
happiness. They were standing on the crowded platform
and he was placing a ticket inside the warm palm of her
glove. He was standing with her in the cold, looking
in through a grated window at a man making bottles in
a roaring furnace. It was very cold. Her face, fragrant in the cold air, was quite close to his; and suddenly he called out to the man at the furnace:

"Is the fire hot, sir?"

But the man could not hear with the noise of the
furnace. It was just as well. He might have answered
rudely.

A wave of yet more tender joy escaped from his heart
and went coursing in warm flood along his arteries.
Like the tender fire of stars moments of their life together, that no one knew of or would ever know of,
broke upon and illumined his memory. He longed to recall to her those moments, to make her forget the years
of their dull existence together and remember only
their moments of ecstasy. For the years, he felt, had
not quenched his soul or hers. Their children, his
writing, her household cares had not quenched all their
souls' tender fire. In one letter that he had written
to her then he had said: "Why is it that words like
these seem to me so dull and cold? Is it because there
is no word tender enough to be your name?"

Like distant music these words that he had written
years before were borne towards him from the past. He
longed to be alone with her. When the others had gone
away, when he and she were in the room in the hotel,
then they would be alone together. He would call her
softly:

"Gretta!"

Perhaps she would not hear at once: she would be
undressing. Then something in his voice would strike
her. She would turn and look at him. . . .

At the corner of Winetavern Street they met a cab.
He was glad of its rattling noise as it saved him from
conversation. She was looking out of the window and
seemed tired. The others spoke only a few words,
pointing out some building or street. The horse gal-
loped along wearily under the murky morning sky, drag-
ging his old rattling box after his heels, and Gabriel
was again in a cab with her, galloping to catch the
boat, galloping to their honeymoon.

As the cab drove across O'Connell Bridge Miss O'Callaghan said:

"They say you never cross O'Connell Bridge without
seeing a white horse."

"I see a white man this time," said Gabriel.

"Where?" asked Mr. Bartell D'Arcy.

Gabriel pointed to the statue, on which lay patches
of snow. Then he nodded familiarly to it and waved his
hand.

"Good-night, Dan" he said gaily.

When the cab drew up before the hotel, Gabriel
jumped out and, in spite of Mr. Bartell D'Arcy's protest, paid the driver. He gave the man a shilling over
his fare. The man saluted and said:

"A prosperous New Year to you, sir."

"The same to you," said Gabriel cordially.

She leaned for a moment on his arm in getting out of
the cab and while standing at the curbstone, bidding
the others good-night. She leaned lightly on his arm,
as lightly as when she had danced with him a few hours
before. He had felt proud and happy then, happy that
she was his, proud of her grace and wifely carriage.
But now, after the kindling again of so many memories,
the first touch of her body, musical and strange and
perfumed, sent through him a keen pang of lust. Under
cover of her silence he pressed her arm closely to his
side; and, as they stood at the hotel door, he felt
that they had escaped from their lives and duties,

158

escaped from home and friends and run away together
with wild and radiant hearts to a new adventure.

An old man was dozing in a great hooded chair in the
hall. He lit a candle in the office and went before
them to the stairs. They followed him in silence,
their feet falling in soft thuds on the thickly car-
peted stairs. She mounted the stairs behind the porter, her head bowed in the ascent, her frail shouldiers
curved as with a burden, her skirt girt tightly about
her. He could have flung his arms about her hips and
held her still, for his arms were trembling with desire
to seize her and only the stress of his nails against
the palms of his hands held the wild impulse of his
body in check. The porter halted on the stairs to settle his guttering candle. They halted, too, on the
steps below him. In the silence Gabriel could hear the
falling of the molten wax into the tray and the thump-
ing of his own heart against his ribs.

The porter led them along a corridor and opened a
door. Then he set his unstable candle down on a
toilet-table and asked at what hour they were to be
called in the morning.

"Eight," said Gabriel.

The porter pointed to the tap of the electric light
and began a muttered apology, but Gabriel cut him
short.

"We don't want any light. We have light enough from
the street. And I say," he added, pointing to the
candle, "you might remove that handsome article, like a
good man."

The porter took up his candle again, but slowly, for
he was surprised by such a novel idea. Then he mumbled
good-night and went out. Gabriel shot the lock to.

A ghastly light from the street lamp lay in a long
shaft from one window to the door. Gabriel threw his
overcoat and hat on a couch and crossed the room towards the window. He looked down into the street in
order that his emotion might calm a little. Then he
turned and leaned against a chest of drawers with his
back to the light. She had taken off her hat and cloak
and was standing before a large swinging mirror, un-
hooking her waist. Gabriel paused for a few moments,
watching her, and then said:

159

"Gretta!"

She turned away from the mirror slowly and walked along the shaft of light towards him. Her face looked so serious and weary that the words would not pass Gabriel's lips. No, it was not the moment yet.

"You looked tired," he said.

"I am a little," she answered.

"You don't feel ill or weak?"

"No, tired: that's all."

She went on to the window and stood there, looking out. Gabriel waited again and then, fearing that diffidence was about to conquer him, he said abruptly:

"By the way, Gretta!"

"What is it?"

"You know that poor fellow Malins?" he said quickly.

"Yes. What about him?"

"Well, poor fellow, he's a decent sort of chap, after all," continued Gabriel in a false voice. "He gave me back that sovereign I lent him, and I didn't expect it, really. It's a pity he wouldn't keep away from that Browne, because he's not a bad fellow, really."

He was trembling now with annoyance. Why did she seem so abstracted? He did not know how he could begin. Was she annoyed, too, about something? If she would only turn to him or come to him of her own accord! To take her as she was would be brutal. No, he must see some ardour in her eyes first. He longed to be master of her strange mood.

"When did you lend him the pound?" she asked, after a pause.

Gabriel strove to restrain himself from breaking out into brutal language about the sottish Malins and his pound. He longed to cry to her from his soul, to crush her body against his, to overmaster her. But he said:

160

"O, at Christmas, when he opened that little Christmas-card shop in Henry Street."

He was in such a fever of rage and desire that he did not hear her come from the window. She stood before him for an instant, looking at him strangely. Then, suddenly raising herself on tiptoe and resting her hands lightly on his shoulders, she kissed him.

"You are a very generous person, Gabriel," she said.

Gabriel, trembling with delight at her sudden kiss and at the quaintness of her phrase, put his hands on her hair and began smoothing it back, scarcely touching it with his fingers. The washing had made it fine and brilliant. His heart was brimming over with happiness. Just when he was wishing for it she had come to him of her own accord. Perhaps her thoughts had been running with his. Perhaps she had felt the impetuous desire that was in him, and then the yielding mood had come upon her. Now that she had fallen to him so easily, he wondered why he had been so diffident.

He stood, holding her head between his hands. Then, slipping one arm swiftly about her body and drawing her towards him, he said softly:

"Gretta, dear, what are you thinking about?"

She did not answer nor yield wholly to his arm. He said again, softly:

"Tell me what it is, Gretta. I think I know what is the matter. Do I know?"

She did not answer at once. Then she said in an outburst of tears:

"O, I am thinking about that song, The Lass of Aughrim."

She broke loose from him and ran to the bed and, throwing her arms across the bed-rail, hid her face. Gabriel stood stock-still for a moment in astonishment and then followed her. As he passed in the way of the cheval-glass[11] he caught sight of himself in full length, his broad, well-filled shirt-front, the face whose expression always puzzled him when he saw it in

11. A full-length mirror swinging in a frame.

161

a mirror, and his glimmering gilt-rimmed eyeglasses.
He halted a few paces from her and said:

"What about the song?  Why does that make you cry?"

She raised her head from her arms and dried her eyes
with the back of her hand like a child.  A kinder note
than he had intended went into his voice.

"Why, Gretta?" he asked.

"I am thinking about a person long ago who used to
sing that song."

"And who was the person long ago?" asked Gabriel,
smiling.

"It was a person I used to know in Galway when I was
living with my grandmother," she said.

The smile passed away from Gabriel's face.  A dull
anger began to gather again at the back of his mind
and the dull fires of his lust began to glow angrily
in his veins.

"Someone you were in love with?" he asked ironically.

"It was a young boy I used to know," she answered,
"named Michael Furey.  He used to sing that song, The
Lass of Aughrim.  He was very delicate."

Gabriel was silent.  He did not wish her to think
that he was interested in this delicate boy.

"I can see him so plainly," she said, after a moment.  "Such eyes as he had:  big, dark eyes!  And
such an expression in them--an expression!"

"O, then, you are in love with him?" said Gabriel.

"I used to go out walking with him," she said, "when
I was in Galway."

A thought flew across Gabriel's mind.

"Perhaps that was why you wanted to go to Galway
with that Ivors girl?" he said coldly.

She looked at him and asked in surprise:

"What for?"

Her eyes made Gabriel feel awkward.  He shrugged his
shoulders and said:

"How do I know?  To see him, perhaps."

She looked away from him along the shaft of light
towards the window in silence.

"He is dead," she said at length.  "He died when he
was only seventeen.  Isn't it a terrible thing to die
so young as that?"

"What was he?" asked Gabriel, still ironically.

"He was in the gasworks," she said.

Gabriel felt humiliated by the failure of his irony
and by the evocation of this figure from the dead, a
boy in the gasworks.  While he had been full of memories of their secret life together, full of tenderness
and joy and desire, she had been comparing him in her
mind with another.  A shameful consciousness of his own
person assailed him.  He saw himself as a ludicrous
figure, acting as a pennyboy for his aunts, a nervous,
well-meaning sentimentalist, orating to vulgarians and
idealising his own clownish lusts, the pitiable fatuous
fellow he had caught a glimpse of in the mirror.  Instinctively he turned his back more to the light lest
she might see the shame that burned upon his forehead.

He tried to keep up his tone of cold interrogation,
but his voice when he spoke was humble and indifferent.

"I suppose you were in love with this Michael Furey,
Gretta," he said.

"I was great with him at that time," she said.

Her voice was veiled and sad.  Gabriel, feeling now
how vain it would be to try to lead her whither he had
purposed, caressed one of her hands, and said, also
sadly:

"And what did he die of so young, Gretta?  Consumption,[12] was it?"

12. Tuberculosis.

163

"I think he died for me," she answered.

A vague terror seized Gabriel at this answer, as if, at that hour when he had hoped to triumph, some impalpable and vindictive being was coming against him, gathering forces against him in its vague world. But he shook himself free of it with an effort of reason and continued to caress her hand. He did not question her again, for he felt that she would tell him of herself. Her hand was warm and moist: it did not respond to his touch, but he continued to caress it just as he had caressed her first letter to him that spring morning.

"It was in the winter," she said, "about the beginning of the winter when I was going to leave my grandmother's and come up here to the convent. And he was ill at the time in his lodgings in Galway and wouldn't be let out, and his people in Oughterard were written to. He was in decline, they said, or something like that. I never knew rightly."

She paused for a moment and sighed.

"Poor fellow," she said. "He was very fond of me and he was such a gentle boy. We used to go out together, walking, you know, Gabriel, like the way they do in the country. He was going to study singing only for his health. He had a very good voice, poor Michael Furey."

"Well; and then?" asked Gabriel.

"And then when it came to the time for me to leave Galway and come up to the convent he was much worse and I wouldn't be let see him so I wrote him a letter saying I was going up to Dublin and would be back in the summer, and hoping he would be better then."

She paused for a moment to get her voice under control, and then went on:

"Then the night before I left, I was in my grandmother's house in Nuns' Island, packing up, and I heard gravel thrown up against the window. The window was so wet I couldn't see, so I ran downstairs as I was and slipped out the back into the garden and there was the poor fellow at the end of the garden, shivering."

"And did you not tell him to go back?" asked

164

Gabriel.

"I implored of him to go home at once and told him
he would get his death in the rain. But he said he did
not want to live. I can see his eyes as well as well!
He was standing at the end of the wall where there was
a tree."

"And did he go home?" asked Gabriel.

"Yes, he went home. And when I was only a week in
the convent he died and he was buried in Oughterard,
where his people came from. O, the day I heard that,
that he was dead!"

She stopped, choking with sobs, and, overcome by
emotion, flung herself face downward on the bed, sob-
bing in the quilt. Gabriel held her hand for a moment
longer, irresolutely, and then, shy of intruding on her
grief, let it fall gently and walked quietly to the
window.

She was fast asleep.

Gabriel, leaning on his elbow, looked for a few moments unresentfully on her tangled hair and half-open
mouth, listening to her deep-drawn breath. So she had
had that romance in her life: a man had died for her
sake. It hardly pained him now to think how poor a
part he, her husband, had played in her life. He
watched her while she slept, as though he and she had
never lived together as man and wife. His curious eyes
rested long upon her face and on her hair: and, as he
thought of what she must have been then, in that time
of her first girlish beauty, a strange, friendly pity
for her entered his soul. He did not like to say even
to himself that her face was no longer beautiful, but
he knew that it was no longer the face for which
Michael Furey had braved death.

Perhaps she had not told him all the story. His
eyes moved to the chair over which she had thrown some
of her clothes. A petticoat string dangled to the
floor. One boot stood upright, its limp upper fallen
down: the fellow of it lay upon its side. He wondered
at his riot of emotions of an hour before. From what
had it proceeded? From his aunt's supper, from his own
foolish speech, from the wine and dancing, the merry-
making when saying good-night in the hall, the pleasure
of the walk along the river in the snow. Poor Aunt

165

Julia! She, too, would soon be a shade with the shade
of Patrick Morkan and his horse. He had caught that
haggard look upon her face for a moment when she was
singing Arrayed for the Bridal. Soon, perhaps, he
would be sitting in that same drawing-room, dressed in
black, his silk hat on his knees. The blinds would be
drawn down and Aunt Kate would be sitting beside him,
crying and blowing her nose and telling him how Julia
had died. He would cast about in his mind for some
words that might console her, and would find only lame
and useless ones. Yes, yes: that would happen very
soon.

The air of the room chilled his shoulders. He
stretched himself cautiously along under the sheets
and lay down beside his wife. One by one, they were
all becoming shades. Better pass boldly into that
other world, in the full glory of some passion, than
fade and wither dismally with age. He thought of how
she who lay beside him had locked in her heart for so
many years that image of her lover's eyes when he had
told her that he did not wish to live.

Generous tears filled Gabriel's eyes. He had never
felt like that himself towards any woman, but he knew
that such a feeling must be love. The tears gathered
more thickly in his eyes and in the partial darkness
he imagined he saw the form of a young man standing
under a dripping tree. Other forms were near. His
soul had approached that region where dwell the vast
hosts of the dead. He was conscious of, but could not
apprehend, their wayward and flickering existence. His
own identity was fading out into a grey impalpable
world: the solid world itself, which these dead had
one time reared and lived in, was dissolving and dwin-
dling.

A few light taps upon the pane made him turn to the
window. It had begun to snow again. He watched
sleepily the flakes, silver and dark, falling obliquely
against the lamplight. The time had come for him to
set out on his journey westward. Yes, the newspapers
were right, snow was general all over Ireland. It was
falling on every part of the dark central plain, on the
treeless hills, falling softly upon the Bog of Allen
and, farther westward, softly falling into the dark
mutinous Shannon waves. It was falling, too, upon
every part of the lonely churchyard on the hill where
Michael Furey lay buried. It lay thickly drifted on
the crooked crosses and headstones, on the spears of
the little gate, on the barren thorns. His soul

swooned slowly as he heard the snow falling faintly
through the universe and faintly falling, like the
descent of their last end, upon all the living and the
dead.

SPREADING THE NEWS

by Lady Gregory

Characters

| | |
|---|---|
| Bartley Fallon | Mrs. Tarpey |
| Mrs. Fallon | Mrs. Tully |
| Jack Smith | A Policeman |
| Shawn Early | (Jo Muldoon) |
| Tim Casey | A Removable |
| James Ryan | Magistrate |


SCENE: The outskirts of a Fair. An Apple Stall. MRS.
TARPEY sitting at it. MAGISTRATE and POLICEMAN enter.

MAGISTRATE. So that is the Fair Green. Cattle and
 sheep and mud. No system. What a repulsive sight!
POLICEMAN. That is so, indeed.
MAGISTRATE. I suppose there is a good deal of disorder
 in this place?
POLICEMAN. There is.
MAGISTRATE. Common assault.
POLICEMAN. It's common enough.
MAGISTRATE. Agrarian crime, no doubt?
POLICEMAN. That is so.
MAGISTRATE. Boycotting? Maiming of cattle? Firing
 into houses?
POLICEMAN. There was one time, and there might be
 again.
MAGISTRATE. That is bad. Does it go any farther than
 that?
POLICEMAN. Far enough, indeed.
MAGISTRATE. Homicide, then! This district has been
 shamefully neglected! I will change all that. When
 I was in the Andaman Islands,[1] my system never fail-
 ed. Yes, yes, I will change all that. What has that
 woman on her stall?
POLICEMAN. Apples mostly--and sweets.
MAGISTRATE. Just see if there are any unlicensed goods
 underneath--spirits or the like. We had evasions of
 the salt tax in the Andaman Islands.
POLICEMAN. (sniffing cautiously and upsetting a heap of
 apples). I see no spirits here--or salt.
MAGISTRATE (to MRS. TARPEY). Do you know this town
 well, my good woman?

1. British controlled islands in the Bay of Bengal.

169

MRS. TARPEY (holding out some apples). A penny the
half-dozen, your honour.
POLICEMAN (shouting). The gentleman is asking do you
know the town? He's the new magistrate!
MRS. TARPEY (rising and ducking). Do I know the town?
I do, to be sure.
MAGISTRATE (shouting). What is its chief business?
MRS. TARPEY. Business, is it? What business would the
people here have but to be minding one another's
business?
MAGISTRATE. I mean what trade have they?
MRS. TARPEY. Not a trade. No trade at all but to be
talking.
MAGISTRATE. I shall learn nothing here.

(JAMES RYAN comes in, pipe in mouth. Seeing MAGISTRATE
he retreats quickly, taking pipe from mouth.)

MAGISTRATE. The smoke from that man's pipe had a
greenish look; he may be growing unlicensed tobacco
at home. I wish I had brought my telescope to this
district. Come to the post-office, I will telegraph
for it. I found it very useful in the Andaman Islands.

(MAGISTRATE and POLICEMAN go out left.)

MRS. TARPY. Bad luck to Jo muldoon, knocking my apples this way and that way. (Begins arranging them.)
Showing off he was to the new magistrate.

(Enter BARTLEY FALLON and MRS. FALLON.)

BARTLEY. Indeed it's a poor country and a scarce
country to be living in. But I'm thinking if I went
to America it's long ago the day I'd be dead!

MRS. FALLON. So you might indeed. (She puts her basket on a barrel and begins putting parcels in it,
taking them from under her cloak.)

BARTLEY. And it's a great expense for a poor man to be
buried in America.
MRS. FALLON. Never fear, Bartley Fallon, but I'll give
you a good burying the day you'll die.
BARTLEY. Maybe it's yourself will be buried in the
graveyard of Cloonmara before me, Mary Fallon, and I
myself that will be dying unbeknownst some night, and
no one a-near me. And the cat itself may be gone
straying through the country, and the mice squealing
over the quilt.

170

MRS. FALLON. Leave off talking of dying. It might be twenty years you'll be living yet.

BARTLEY (with a deep sigh). I'm thinking if I'll be living at the end of twenty years, it's a very old man I'll be then!

MRS. TARPEY (turns and sees them). Good morrow, Bartley Fallon; good morrow, Mrs. Fallon. Well, Bartley, you'll find no cause for complaining today; they are all saying it was a good fair.

BARTLEY (raising his voice). It was not a good fair, Mrs. Tarpey. It was a scattered sort of a fair. If we didn't expect more, we got less. That's the way with me always; whatever I have to sell goes down and whatever I have to buy goes up. If there's ever any misfortune coming to this world, it's on myself it pitches, like a flock of crows on seed potatoes.

MRS. FALLON. Leave off talking of misfortunes, and listen to Jack Smith that is coming the way, and he singing.

(Voice of JACK SMITH heard singing):
 I thought, my first love,
  There'd be but one house between you and me,
 And I thought I would find
  Yourself coaxing my child on your knee.
 Over the tide
  I would leap with the leap of a swan,
 Till I came to the side
  Of the wife of the red-haired man!

(JACK SMITH comes in; he is a red-haired man, and is carrying a hayfork.)

MRS. TARPEY. That should be a good song if I had my hearing.

MRS. FALLON (shouting). It's "The Red-haired Man's Wife."

MRS. TARPEY. I know it well. That's the song that has a skin² on it! (She turns her back to them and goes on arranging her apples.)

MRS. FALLON. Where's herself, Jack Smith?

JACK SMITH. She was delayed with her washing, bleaching the clothes on the hedge she is, and she daren't leave them, with all the tinkers that do be passing to the fair. It isn't to the fair I came myself, but up to the Five Acre Meadow I'm going, where I have a contract for the hay. We'll get a share of it into

2. Meaning a thin covering or film that obscures, that hides something beneath.

tramps today. (He lays down hayfork and lights his
pipe.)
BARTLEY. You will not get it into tramps today. The
rain will be down on it by evening, and on myself
too. It's seldom I ever started on a journey but the
rain would come down on me before I'd find any place
of shelter.
JACK SMITH. If it didn't itself, Bartley, it is my
belief you would carry a leaky pail on your head in
place of a hat, the way you'd not be without some
cause for complaining.

(A voice heard, "Go on, now, go on out o' that. Go on
I say.")

JACK SMITH. Look at that young mare of Pat Ryan's that
is backing into Shaughnessy's bullocks with the dint
of the crowd! Don't be daunted, Pat, I'll give you
a hand with her. (He goes out, leaving his hayfork.)
MRS. FALLON. It's time for ourselves to be going home.
I have all I bought put in the basket. Look at
there, Jack Smith's hayfork he left after him! He'll
be wanting it. (Calls) Jack Smith! Jack Smith!--
He's gone through the crowd--hurry after him, Bartley, he'll be wanting it.
BARTLEY. I'll do that. This is no safe place to be
leaving it. (He takes up fork awkwardly and upsets
the basket.) Look at that now! If there is any basket in the fair upset, it must be our own basket!
(He goes out to right.)
MRS. FALLON. Get out of that! It is your own fault,
it is. Talk of misfortunes and misfortunes will
come. Glory be! Look at my new egg-cups rolling in
every part--and my two pound of sugar with the paper
broke--
MRS. TARPEY (turning from stall). God help us, Mrs.
Fallon, what happened to your basket?
MRS. FALLON. It's himself that knocked it down, bad
manners to him. (Putting things up.) My grand sugar
that's destroyed, and he'll not drink his tea without
it. I had best go back to the shop for more, much
good may it do him!

(Enter TIM CASEY.)

TIM CASEY. Where is Bartley Fallon, Mrs. Fallon! I
want a word with him before he'll leave the fair. I
was afraid he might have gone home by this, for he's
a temperate man.
MRS. FALLON. I wish he did go home! It'd be best for
me if he went home straight from the fair green, or

172

if he never came with me at all!  Where is he, is it?
He's gone up the road (jerks elbow) following Jack
Smith with a hayfork.  (She goes out to left.)
TIM CASEY.  Following Jack Smith with a hayfork!  Did
ever any one hear the like of that.  (Shouts)  Did
you hear that news, Mrs. Tarpey?
MRS. TARPEY.  I heard no news at all.
TIM CASEY.  Some dispute I suppose it was that rose
between Jack Smith and Bartley Fallon, and it seems
Jack made off, and Bartley is following him with a
hayfork!
MRS. TARPEY.  Is he now?  Well, that was quick work!
It's not ten minutes since the two of them were here,
Bartley going home and Jack going to the Five Acre
Meadow; and I had my apples to settle up, that Jo
Muldoon of the police had scattered, and when I looked round again Jack Smith was gone, and Bartley Fallon was gone, and Mrs. Fallon's basket upset, and
all in it strewed upon the ground--the tea here--the
two pound of sugar there--the egg-cups there--Look,
now, what a great hardship the deafness puts upon me,
that I didn't hear the commincement of the fight!
Wait till I tell James Ryan that I see below; he is
a neighbour of Bartley's, it would be a pity if he
wouldn't hear the news!

(She goes out.  Enter SHAWN EARLY and MRS. TULLY.)

TIM CASEY.  Listen, Shawn Early!  Listen, Mrs. Tully,
to the news!  Jack Smith and Bartley Fallon had a
falling out, and Jack knocked Mrs. Fallon's basket
into the road, and Bartley made an attack on him with
a hayfork, and away with Jack, and Bartley after him.
Look at the sugar here yet on the road!
SHAWN EARLY.  Do you tell me so?  Well, that's a queer
thing, and Bartley Fallon so quiet a man!
MRS. TULLY.  I wouldn't wonder at all.  I would never
think well of a man that would have that sort of a
mouldering look.  It's likely he has overtaken Jack
by this.

(Enter JAMES RYAN and MRS. TARPEY.)

JAMES RYAN.  That is great news Mrs. Tarpey was telling
me!  I suppose that's what brought the police and the
magistrate up this way.  I was wondering to see them
in it a while ago.
SHAWN EARLY.  The police after them?  Bartley Fallon
must have injured Jack so.  They wouldn't meddle in
a fight that was only for show!
MRS. TULLY.  Why wouldn't he injure him?  There was

173

many a man killed with no more of a weapon than a
hayfork.
JAMES RYAN. Wait till I run north as far as Kelly's
bar to spread the news! (He goes out.)
TIM CASEY. I'll go tell Jack Smith's first cousin that
is standing there south of the church after selling
his lambs. (Goes out.)
MRS. TULLY. I'll go telling a few of the neighbours I
see beyond to the west. (Goes out.)
SHAWN EARLY. I'll give word of it beyond at the east
of the green. (Is going out when MRS. TARPEY seizes
hold of him.)
MRS. TARPEY. Stop a minute, Shawn Early, and tell me
did you see red Jack Smith's wife, Kitty Keary, in
any place?
SHAWN EARLY. I did. At her own house she was, drying
clothes on the hedge as I passed.
MRS. TARPEY. What did you say she was doing?
SHAWN EARLY (breaking away). Laying out a sheet on the
hedge. (He goes.)
MRS. TARPEY. Laying out a sheet for the dead! The
Lord have mercy on us! Jack Smith dead, and his wife
laying out a sheet for his burying! (Calls out) Why
didn't you tell me that before, Shawn Early? Isn't
the deafness the great hardship? Half the world
might be dead without me knowing of it or getting
word of it at all! (She sits down and rocks herself.)
O my poor Jack Smith! To be going to his work so
nice and so hearty, and to be left stretched on the
ground in the full light of the day!

(Enter TIM CASEY.)

TIM CASEY. What is it, Mrs. Tarpey? What happened
since?
MRS. TARPEY. O my poor Jack Smith!
TIM CASEY. Did Bartley overtake him?
MRS. TARPEY. O the poor man!
TIM CASEY. Is it killed he is?
MRS. TARPEY. Stretched in the Five Acre Meadow!
TIM CASEY. The Lord have mercy on us! Is that a fact?
MRS. TARPEY. Without the rites of the Church or a
ha'porth!3
TIM CASEY. Who was telling you?
MRS. TARPEY. And the wife laying out a sheet for his
corpse. (Sits up and wipes her eyes.) I suppose
they'll wake him the same as another?


3. Halfpennyworth.

174

(Enter MRS. TULLY, SHAWN EARLY, and JAMES RYAN.)

MRS. TULLY. There is great talk about this work in
  every quarter of the fair.
MRS. TARPEY. Ochone![4] cold and dead. And myself maybe
  the last he was speaking to!
JAMES RYAN. The Lord save us! Is it dead he is?
TIM CASEY. Dead surely, and his wife getting provision
  for the wake.
SHAWN EARLY. Well, now, hadn't Bartley Fallon great
  venom in him?
MRS. TULLY. You may be sure he had some cause. Why
  would he have made an end of him if he had not? (To
  MRS. TARPEY, raising her voice.) What was it rose
  the dispute at all, Mrs. Tarpey?
MRS. TARPEY. Not a one of me knows. The last I saw
  of them, Jack Smith was standing there, and Bartley
  Fallon was standing there, quiet and easy, and he
  listening to "The Red-haired Man's Wife."
MRS. TULLY. Do you hear that, Tim Casey? Do you hear
  that, Shawn Early and James Ryan? Bartley Fallon was
  here this morning listening to red Jack Smith's wife,
  Kitty Keary that was! Listening to her and whispering with her! It was she started the fight so!
SHAWN EARLY. She must have followed him from her own
  house. It is likely some person roused him.
TIM CASEY. I never knew, before, Bartley Fallon was
  great with Jack Smith's wife.
MRS. TULLY. How would you know it? Sure it's not in
  the streets they would be calling it. If Mrs. Fallon
  didn't know of it, and if I that have the next house
  to them didn't know of it, and if Jack Smith himself
  didn't know of it, it is not likely you would know of
  it, Tim Casey.
SHAWN EARLY. Let Bartley Fallon take charge of her
  from this out so, and let him provide for her. It is
  little pity she will get from any person in this
  parish.
TIM CASEY. How can he take charge of her? Sure he
  has a wife of his own. Sure you don't think he'd
  turn souper[5] and marry her in a Protestant church?
JAMES RYAN. It would be easy for him to marry her if
  he brought her to America.
SHAWN EARLY. With or without Kitty Keary, believe me
  it is for America he's making at this minute. I saw
  the new magistrate and Jo Muldoon of the police going

4. Trans. Alas.
5. In Ireland, a Protestant clergyman seeking to make
  proselytes by means of dispensing soup in charity.

175

into the post-office as I came up--there was hurry on
them--you may be sure it was to telegraph they went,
the way he'll be stopped in the docks at Queenstown!
MRS. TULLY. It's likely Kitty Keary is gone with him,
and not minding a sheet or a wake at all. The poor
man, to be deserted by his own wife, and the breath
hardly gone out yet from his body that is lying
bloody in the field!

(Enter MRS. FALLON.)

MRS. FALLON. What is it the whole of the town is talking about? And what is it you yourselves are talking
about? Is it about my man Bartley Fallon you are
talking? Is it lies about him you are telling, saying that he went killing Jack Smith? My grief that
ever he came into this place at all!
JAMES RYAN. Be easy now, Mrs. Fallon. Sure there is
no one at all in the whole fair but is sorry for you!
MRS. FALLON. Sorry for me, is it? Why would any one
be sorry for me? Let you be sorry for yourselves,
and that there may be shame on you for ever and at
the day of judgment, for the words you are saying and
the lies you are telling to take away the character
of my poor man, and to take the good name off of him,
and to drive him to destruction! That is what you
are doing!
SHAWN EARLY. Take comfort now, Mrs. Fallon. The police are not so smart as they think. Sure he might
give them the slip yet, the same as Lynchehaun.
MRS. TULLY. If they do get him, and if they do put a
rope around his neck, there is no one can say he does
not deserve it!
MRS. FALLON. Is that what you are saying, Bridget Tully, and is that what you think? I tell you it's too
much talk you have, making yourself out to be such a
great one, and to be running down every respectable
person! A rope, is it? It isn't much of a rope was
needed to tie up your own furniture the day you came
into Martin Tully's house, and you never bringing as
much as a blanket, or a penny, or a suit of clothes
with you and I myself bringing seventy pounds and two
feather beds. And now you are stiffer than a woman
would have a hundred pounds! It is too much talk the
whole of you have. A rope, is it? I tell you the
whole of this town is full of liars and schemers that
would hang you up for half a glass of whisky. (Turning to go.) People they are you wouldn't believe as
much as daylight from without you'd get up to have a
look at it yourself. Killing Jack Smith indeed!
Where are you at all, Bartley, till I bring you out

of this? My nice quiet little man? My decent comrade! He that is as kind and as harmless as an innocent beast of the field! He'll be doing no harm at
all if he'll shed the blood of some of you after this
day's work! That much would be no harm at all.
(Calls out.) Bartley! Bartley Fallon! Where are
you? (Going out.) Did any one see Bartley Fallon?

(All turn to look after her.)

JAMES RYAN. It is hard for her to believe any such a
thing. God help her!

(Enter BARTLEY FALLON from right, carrying hayfork.)

BARTLEY. It is what I often said to myself, if there
is ever any misfortune coming to this world it is on
myself it is sure to come!

(All turn round and face him.)

BARTLEY. To be going about with this fork and to find
no one to take it, and no place to leave it down, and
I wanting to be gone out of this--Is that you, Shawn
Early? (Holds out fork.) It's well I met you. You
have no call to be leaving the fair for a while the
way I have, and how can I go till I'm rid of this
fork? Will you take it and keep it until such time
as Jack Smith--
SHAWN EARLY (backing). I will not take it, Bartley
Fallon, I'm very thankful to you!
BARTLEY (turning to apple stall). Look at it now, Mrs.
Tarpey, it was here I got it; let me thrust it in
under the stall. It will lie there safe enough, and
no one will take notice of it until such time as
Jack Smith--
MRS. TARPEY. Take your fork out of that! Is it to
put trouble on me and to destroy me you want, putting
it there for the police to be rooting it out maybe?
(Thrusts him back.)
BARTLEY. That is a very unneighbourly thing for you to
do, Mrs. Tarpey. Hadn't I enough care on me with
that fork before this, running up and down with it
like the swinging of a clock, and afeard to lay it
down in any place! I wish I never touched it or med-
dled with it at all!
JAMES RYAN. It is a pity, indeed, you ever did.
BARTLEY. Will you yourself take it, James Ryan? You
were always a neighbourly man.
JAMES RYAN (backing). There is many a thing I would
do for you, Bartley Fallon, but I won't do that!

177

SHAWN EARLY. I tell you there is no man will give you
    any help or any encouragement for this day's work.
    If it was something agrarian now--
BARTLEY. If no one at all will take it, maybe it's
    best to give it up to the police.
TIM CASEY. There'd be a welcome for it with them
    surely!  (Laughter.)
MRS. Tully. And it is to the police Kitty Keary her-
    self will be brought.
MRS. TARPEY (rocking to and fro). I wonder now who
    will take the expense of the wake for poor Jack
    Smith?
BARTLEY. The wake for Jack Smith!
TIM CASEY. Why wouldn't he get a wake as well as
    another? Would you begrudge him that much?
BARTLEY. Red Jack Smith dead! Who was telling you?
SHAWN EARLY. The whole town knows of it by this.
BARTLEY. Do they say what way did he die?
JAMES RYAN. You don't know that yourself, I suppose,
    Bartley Fallon? You don't know he was followed and
    that he was laid dead with the stab of a hayfork?
BARTLEY. The stab of a hayfork!
SHAWN EARLY. You don't know, I suppose, that the body
    was found in the Five Acre Meadow!
BARTLEY. The Five Acre Meadow!
TIM CASEY. It is likely you don't know that the police
    are after the man that did it?
BARTLEY. The man that did it?
MRS. TULLY. You don't know, maybe, that he was made
    away with for the sake of Kitty Keary, his wife?
BARTLEY. Kitty Keary, his wife!  (Sits down bewil-
    dered.)
MRS. TULLY. And what have you to say now, Bartley
    Fallon?
BARTLEY. (crossing himself). I to bring that fork
    here, and to find that news before me! It is much if
    I can ever stir from this place at all, or reach as
    far as the road!
TIM CASEY. Look, boys, at the new magistrate, and Jo
    Muldoon along with him! It's best for us to quit
    this.
SHAWN EARLY. That is so. It is best not to be mixed
    in this business at all.
JAMES RYAN. Bad as he is, I wouldn't like to be an
    informer against any man.

(All hurry away except MRS. TARPEY, who remains behind
    her stall. Enter MAGISTRATE and POLICEMAN.)

MAGISTRATE. I knew the district was in a bad state,
    but I did not expect to be confronted with a murder

178

at the first fair I came to.
POLICEMAN. I am sure you did not, indeed.
MAGISTRATE. It was well I had not gone home. I caught
a few words here and there that roused my suspicions.
POLICEMAN. So they would, too.
MAGISTRATE. You heard the same story from everyone you
asked?
POLICEMAN. The same story--or if it was not altogether
the same, anyway it was no less than the first story.
MAGISTRATE. What is that man doing? He is sitting
alone with a hayfork. He has a guilty look. The
murder was done with a hayfork!
POLICEMAN (in a whisper). That's the very man they say
did the act; Bartley Fallon himself!
MAGISTRATE. He must have found escape difficult--he is
trying to brazen it out. A convict in the Andaman
Islands tried the same game, but he could not escape
my system! Stand aside--Don't go far--Have the handcuffs ready. (He walks up to BARTLEY, folds his
arms, and stands before him.) Here, my man, do you
know anything of John Smith?
BARTLEY. Of John Smith! Who is he, now?
POLICEMAN. Jack Smith, sir--Red Jack Smith!
MAGISTRATE (coming a step nearer and tapping him on the
shoulder). Where is Jack Smith?
BARTLEY (with a deep sigh, and shaking his head slowly). Where is he, indeed?
MAGISTRATE. What have you to tell?
BARTLEY. It is where he was this morning, standing in
this spot, singing his share of songs--no, but lighting his pipe--scraping a match on the sole of his
shoe--
MAGISTRATE. I ask you, for the third time, where is
he?
BARTLEY. I wouldn't like to say that. It is a great
mystery, and it is hard to say of any man, did he
earn hatred or love.
MAGISTRATE. Tell me all you know.
BARTLEY. All that I know--Well, there are the three
estates; there is Limbo, and there is Purgatory, and
there is--
MAGISTRATE. Nonsense! This is trifling! Get to the
point.
BARTLEY. Maybe you don't hold with the clergy so?
That is the teaching of the clergy. Maybe you hold
with the old people. It is what they do be saying,
that the shadow goes wandering, and the soul is
tired, and the body is taking a rest--The shadow!
(Starts up.) I was nearly sure I saw Jack Smith not
ten minutes ago at the corner of the forge, and I
lost him again--Was it his ghost I saw, do you think?

MAGISTRATE (to POLICEMAN). Conscience-struck! He will confess all now!

BARTLEY. His ghost to come before me! It is likely it was on account of the fork! I do have it and he to have no way to defend himself the time he met with his death!

MAGISTRATE (to POLICEMAN). I must note down his words. (Takes out notebook.) (To BARTLEY): I warn you that your words are being noted.

BARTLEY. If I had ha' run faster in the beginning, this terror would not be on me at the latter end! Maybe he will cast it up against me at the day of judgment--I wouldn't wonder at all at that.

MAGISTRATE (writing). At the day of judgment--

BARTLEY. It was soon for his ghost to appear to me-- is it coming after me always by day it will be, and stripping the clothes off in the night time?-- I wouldn't wonder at all at that, being as I am an un- fortunate man!

MAGISTRATE (sternly). Tell me this truly. What was the motive of this crime?

BARTLEY. The motive, is it?

MAGISTRATE. Yes, the motive; the cause.

BARTLEY. I'd sooner not say that.

MAGISTRATE. You had better tell me truly. Was it money?

BARTLEY. Not at all! What did poor Jack Smith ever have in his pockets unless it might be his hands that would be in them?

MAGISTRATE. Any dispute about land?

BARTLEY (indignantly). Not at all! He never was a grabber or grabbed from any one!

MAGISTRATE. You will find it better for you if you tell me at once.

BARTLEY. I tell you I wouldn't for the whole world wish to say what it was--it is a thing I would not like to be talking about.

MAGISTRATE. There is no use in hiding it. It will be discovered in the end.

BARTLEY. Well, I suppose it will, seeing that mostly everybody knows it before. Whisper here now. I will tell no lie; where would be the use? (Puts his hand to his mouth, and MAGISTRATE stoops.) Don't be put- ting the blame on the parish, for such a thing was never done in the parish before--it was done for the sake of Kitty Keary, Jack Smith's wife.

MAGISTRATE (to POLICEMAN). Put on the handcuffs. We have been saved some trouble. I knew he would con- fess if taken in the right way.

(POLICEMAN puts on handcuffs.)

180

BARTLEY. Handcuffs now! Glory be! I always said, if
there was ever any misfortune coming to this place it
was on myself it would fall. I to be in handcuffs!
There's no wonder at all in that.

(Enter MRS. FALLON, followed by the rest. She is looking back at them as she speaks.)

MRS. FALLON. Telling lies the whole of the people of
this town are; telling lies, telling lies as fast as
a dog will trot! Speaking against my poor respectable man! Saying he made an end of Jack Smith! My
decent comrade! There is no better man and no kinder
man in the whole of the five parishes! It's little
annoyance he ever gave to any one! (Turns and sees
him.) What in the earthly world do I see before me?
Bartley Fallon in charge of the police! Handcuffs on
him! O Bartley, what did you do at all at all?
BARTLEY. O Mary, there has a great misfortune come
upon me! It is what I always said, that if there is
ever any misfortune--
MRS. FALLON. What did he do at all, or is it bewitched
I am?
MAGISTRATE. This man has been arrested on a charge of
murder.
MRS. FALLON. Whose charge is that? Don't believe
them! They are all liars in this place! Give me
back my man!
MAGISTRATE. It is natural that you should take his
part, but you have no cause of complaint against your
neighbours. He has been arrested for the murder of
John Smith, on his own confession.
MRS. FALLON. The saints of heaven protect us! And
what did he want killing Jack Smith?
MAGISTRATE. It is best you should know all. He did it
on account of a love affair with the murdered man's
wife.
MRS. FALLON (sitting down). With Jack Smith's wife!
With Kitty Keary!--Ochone, the traitor!
THE CROWD. A great shame, indeed. He is a traitor,
indeed.
MRS. TULLY. To America he was bringing her, Mrs.
Fallon.
BARTLEY. What are you saying, Mary? I tell you--
MRS. FALLON. Don't say a word! I won't listen to any
word you'll say! (Stops her ears.) O, isn't he the
treacherous villain? Ochone go deo![6]

6. Trans. Alas, forever.

181

BARTLEY. Be quiet till I speak! Listen to what I say!
MRS. FALLON. Sitting beside me on the ass car coming
   to the town, so quiet and so respectable, and treachery like that in his heart!
BARTLEY. Is it your wits you have lost or is it I myself that have lost my wits?
MRS. FALLON. And it's hard I earned you, slaving,
   slaving--and you grumbling, and sighing, and coughing, and discontented, and the priest wore out
   anointing you, with all the times you threatened to
   die!
BARTLEY. Let you be quiet till I tell you!
MRS. FALLON. You to bring such a disgrace into the
   parish. A thing that was never heard of before!
BARTLEY. Will you shut your mouth and hear me speaking?
MRS. FALLON. And if it was for any sort of a fine
   handsome woman, but for a little fistful of a woman
   like Kitty Keary, that's not four feet high hardly,
   and not three teeth in her head unless she got new
   ones! May God reward you, Bartley Fallon, for the
   black treachery in your heart and the wickedness in
   your mind, and the red blood of poor Jack Smith that
   is wet upon your hand!

(Voice of JACK SMITH heard singing):
   The sea shall be dry.
   The earth under mourning and ban!
   Then loud shall he cry
   For the wife of the red-haired man!

BARTLEY. It's Jack Smith's voice--I never knew a ghost
   to sing before--It is after myself and the fork he is
   coming! (Goes back. Enter JACK SMITH.) Let one of
   you give him the fork and I will be clear of him now
   and for eternity!
MRS. TARPEY. The Lord have mercy on us! Red Jack
   Smith! The man that was going to be waked!
JAMES RYAN. Is it back from the grave you are come?
SHAWN EARLY. Is it alive you are, or is it dead you
   are?
TIM CASEY. Is it yourself at all that's in it?
MRS. TULLY. Is it letting on you were to be dead?
MRS. FALLON. Dead or alive, let you stop Kitty Keary,
   your wife, from bringing my man away with her to
   America!
JACK SMITH. It is what I think, the wits are gone
   astray on the whole of you. What would my wife want
   bringing Bartley Fallon to America?
MRS. FALLON. To leave yourself, and to get quit of you
   she wants, Jack Smith, and to bring him away from

182

myself. That's what the two of them had settled to-
gether.
JACK SMITH. I'll break the head of any man that says
    that! Who is it says it? (To TIM CASEY.) Was it
    you said it? (To SHAWN EARLY.) Was it you?
ALL TOGETHER (backing and shaking their heads). It
    wasn't I said it!
JACK SMITH. Tell me the name of any man that said it!
ALL TOGETHER (pointing to BARTLEY). It was him that
    said it!
JACK SMITH. Let me at him till I break his head!

(BARTLEY backs in terror. Neighbours hold JACK SMITH
    back.)

JACK SMITH (trying to free himself). Let me at him!
    Isn't he the pleasant sort of a scarecrow for any
    woman to be crossing the ocean with! It's back from
    the docks of New York he'd be turned (trying to rush
    at him again), with a lie in his mouth and treachery
    in his heart, and another man's wife by his side, and
    he passing her off as his own! Let me at him can't
    you. (Makes another rush, but is held back.)
MAGISTRATE (pointing to JACK SMITH). Policeman, put
    the handcuffs on this man. I see it all now. A case
    of false impersonation, a conspiracy to defeat the
    ends of justice. There was a case in the Andaman
    Islands, a murderer of the Mopsa tribe, a religious
    enthusiast--
POLICEMAN. So he might be, too.
MAGISTRATE. We must take both these men to the scene
    of the murder. We must confront them with the body
    of the real Jack Smith.
JACK SMITH. I'll break the head of any man that will
    find my dead body!
MAGISTRATE. I'll call more help from the barracks.
    (Blows POLICEMAN'S whistle.)
BARTLEY. It is what I am thinking, if myself and Jack
    Smith are put together in the one cell for the night,
    the handcuffs will be taken off him, and his hands
    will be free, and murder will be done that time
    surely!
MAGISTRATE. Come on! (They turn to the right.)

183

CATHLEEN NI HOULIHAN[1]

by William Butler Yeats

Persons in the Play

Peter Gillane
Michael Gillane, his son,
  going to be married
Patrick Gillane, a lad of
  twelve, Michael's brother

Bridget Gillane, Peter's
  wife
Delia Cahel, engaged to
  Michael
The Poor Old Woman
Neighbours

Interior of a cottage close to Killala, in 1798.
BRIDGET is standing at a table undoing a parcel. PETER
is sitting at one side of the fire, PATRICK at the
other.

PETER. What is the sound I hear?
PATRICK. I don't hear anything. (He listens.) I hear
  it now. It's like cheering. (He goes to the window
  and looks out.) I wonder what they are cheering
  about. I don't see anybody.
PETER. It might be a hurling.[2]
PATRICK. There's no hurling to-day. It must be down
  in the town the cheering is.
BRIDGET. I suppose the boys must be having some sport
  of their own. Come over here, Peter, and look at
  Michael's wedding clothes.
PETER (shifts his chair to table). Those are grand
  clothes, indeed.
BRIDGET. You hadn't clothes like that when you married
  me, and no coat to put on of a Sunday more than any
  other day.
PETER. That is true, indeed. We never thought a son
  of our own would be wearing a suit of that sort for
  his wedding, or have so good a place to bring a wife
  to.
PATRICK (who is still at the window). There's an old
  woman coming down the road. I don't know is it here
  she is coming.
BRIDGET. It will be a neighbour coming to hear about
  Michael's wedding. Can you see who it is?
PATRICK. I think it is a stranger, but she's not
  coming to the house. She's turned into the gap that

1. An allegorical name for Ireland.
2. A game resembling field hockey in Ireland.

185

goes down where Maurteen and his sons are shearing
sheep. (He turns towards BRIDGET.) Do you remember
what Winny of the Cross-Roads was saying the other
night about the strange woman that goes through the
country whatever time there's war or trouble coming?
BRIDGET. Don't be bothering us about Winny's talk, but
go and open the door for your brother. I hear
him coming up the path.
PETER. I hope he has brought Delia's fortune with him
safe, for fear the people might go back on the bargain and I after making it. Trouble enough I had
making it.

(PATRICK opens the door and MICHAEL comes in.)

BRIDGET. What kept you, Michael? We were looking out
for you this long time.
MICHAEL. I went round by the priest's house to bid him
be ready to marry us to-morrow.
BRIDGET. Did he say anything?
MICHAEL. He said it was a very nice match, and that he
was never better pleased to marry any two in his par-
ish than myself and Delia Cahel.
PETER. Have you got the fortune, Michael?
MICHAEL. Here it is.

(MICHAEL puts bag on table and goes over and leans
against chimney-jamb. BRIDGET, who has been all this
time examining the clothes, pulling the seams and
trying the lining of the pockets, etc., puts the
clothes on the dresser.)

PETER (getting up and taking the bag in his hand and
turning out the money). Yes, I made the bargain well
for you, Michael. Old John Cahel would sooner have
kept a share of this a while longer. 'Let me keep
the half of it until the first boy is born,' says he.
'You will not,' says I. 'Whether there is or is not
a boy, the whole hundred pounds must be in Michael's
hands before he brings your daughter to the house.'
The wife spoke to him then, and he gave in at the
end.
BRIDGET. You seem well pleased to be handling the
money, Peter.
PETER. Indeed, I wish I had had the luck to get a
hundred pounds, or twenty pounds itself, with the
wife I married.
BRIDGET. Well, if I didn't bring much I didn't get
much. What had you the day I married you but a flock
of hens and you feeding them, and a few lambs and you
driving them to the market at Ballina? (She is vexed
186

and bangs a jug on the dresser.) If I brought no
fortune I worked it out in my bones, laying down the
baby, Michael that is standing there now, on a stook
of straw, while I dug the potatoes, and never asking
big dresses or anything but to be working.
PETER. That is true, indeed. (He pats her arm.)
BRIDGET. Leave me alone now till I ready the house for
the woman that is to come into it.
PETER. You are the best woman in Ireland, but money is
good, too. (He begins handling the money again and
sits down.) I never thought to see so much money
within my four walls. We can do great things now we
have it. We can take the ten acres of land we have
the chance of since Jamsie Dempsey died, and stock
it. We will go to the fair at Ballina to buy the
stock. Did Delia ask any of the money for her own
use, Michael?
MICHAEL. She did not, indeed. She did not seem to
take much notice of it, or to look at it at all.
BRIDGET. That's no wonder. Why would she look at it
when she had yourself to look at, a fine, strong
young man? It is proud she must be to get you; a
good steady boy that will make use of the money, and
not be running through it or spending it on drink
like another.
PETER. It's likely Michael himself was not thinking
much of the fortune either, but of what sort the girl
was to look at.
MICHAEL (coming over towards the table). Well, you
would like a nice comely girl to be beside you, and
to go walking with you. The fortune only lasts for a
while, but the woman will be there always.
PATRICK (turning round from the window). They are
cheering again down in the town. Maybe they are
landing horses from Enniscrone. They do be cheering
when the horses take the water well.
MICHAEL. There are no horses in it. Where would they
be going and no fair at hand? Go down to the town,
Patrick, and see what is going on.
PATRICK (opens the door to go out, but stops for a moment on the threshold). Will Delia remember, do you
think, to bring the greyhound pup she promised me
when she would be coming to the house?
MICHAEL. She will surely. (Patrick goes out, leaving
the door open.)
PETER. It will be Patrick's turn next to be looking
for a fortune, but he won't find it so easy to get it
and he with no place of his own.
BRIDGET. I do be thinking sometimes, now things are
going so well with us, and the Cahels such a good
back to us in the district, and Delia's own uncle a

187

priest, we might be put in the way of making Patrick
a priest some day, and he so good at his books.
PETER. Time enough, time enough. You have always your
head full of plans, Bridget.
BRIDGET. We will be well able to give him learning,
and not to send him tramping the country like a poor
scholar that lives on charity.
MICHAEL. They're not done cheering yet.

(He goes over to the door and stands there for a moment, putting up his hand to shade his eyes.)

BRIDGET. Do you see anything?
MICHAEL. I see an old woman coming up the path.
BRIDGET. Who is it, I wonder? It must bê the strange
woman Patrick saw a while ago.
MICHAEL. I don't think it's one of the neighbours anyway, but she has her cloak over her face.
BRIDGET. It might be some poor woman heard we were
making ready for the wedding and came to look for her
share.
PATER. I may as well put the money out of sight. There
is no use leaving it out for every stranger to look
at.

(He goes over to a large box in the corner, opens it
and puts the bag in and fumbles at the lock.)

MICHAEL. There she is, father! (An OLD WOMAN passes
the window slowly. She looks at MICHAEL as she
passes.) I'd sooner a stranger not to come to the
house the night before my wedding.
BRIDGET. Open the door, Michael; don't keep the poor
woman waiting.

(The OLD WOMAN comes in. MICHAEL stands aside to make
way for her.)

OLD WOMAN. God save all here!
PETER. God save you kindly!
OLD WOMAN. You have good shelter here.
PETER. You are welcome to whatever shelter we have.
BRIDGET. Sit down there by the fire and welcome.
OLD WOMAN (warming her hands). There is a hard wind
outside.

(MICHAEL watches her curiously from the door. PETER
comes over to the table.)

PETER. Have you travelled far to-day?

188

OLD WOMAN. I have travelled far, very far; there are
    few have travelled so far as myself, and there's many
    a one that doesn't make me welcome. There was one
    that had strong sons I thought were friends of mine,
    but they were shearing their sheep, and they wouldn't
    listen to me.
PETER. It's a pity indeed for any person to have no
    place of their own.
OLD WOMAN. That's true for you indeed, and it's long
    I'm on the roads since I first went wandering.
BRIDGET. It is a wonder you are not worn out with so
    much wandering.
OLD WOMAN. Sometimes my feet are tired and my hands
    are quiet, but there is no quiet in my heart. When
    the people see me quiet, they think old age has come
    on me and that all the stir has gone out of me. But
    when the trouble is on me I must be talking to my
    friends.
BRIDGET. What was it put you wandering?
OLD WOMAN. Too many strangers in the house.
BRIDGET. Indeed you look as if you'd had your share of
    trouble.
OLD WOMAN. I have had trouble indeed.
BRIDGET. What was it put the trouble on you?
OLD WOMAN. My land that was taken from me.
PETER. Was it much land they took from you?
OLD WOMAN. My four beautiful green fields.
PETER (aside to BRIDGET). Do you think could she be
    the widow Casey that was put out of her holding at
    Kilglass a while ago?
BRIDGET. She is not. I saw the widow Casey one time
    at the market in Ballina, a stout fresh woman.
PETER (to OLD WOMAN). Did you hear a noise of cheering,
    and you coming up the hill?
OLD WOMAN. I thought I heard the noise I used to hear
    when my friends came to visit me.

(She begins singing half to herself.)
        I will go cry with the woman,
        For yellow-haired Donough is dead,
        With a hempen rope for a neckcloth,
        And a white cloth on his head,----

MICHAEL (coming from the door). What is it that you
    are singing, ma'am?
OLD WOMAN. Singing I am about a man I knew one time,
    yellow-haired Donough that was hanged in Galway.

(She goes on singing, much louder.)
        I am come to cry with you, woman,
        My hair is unwound and unbound;
189

```
I remember him ploughing his field,
Turning up the red side of the ground,
And building his barn on the hill
With the good mortared stone;
O! we'd have pulled down the gallows
Had it happened in Enniscrone!
```

MICHAEL. What was it brought him to his death?
OLD WOMAN. He died for love of me: many a man has
died for love of me.
PETER (aside to BRIDGET). Her trouble has put her wits
astray.
MICHAEL. Is it long since that song was made? Is it
long since he got his death?
OLD WOMAN. Not long, not long. But there were others
that died for love of me a long time ago.
MICHAEL. Were they neighbours of your own, ma'am?
OLD WOMAN. Come here beside me and I'll tell you about
them. (MICHAEL sits down beside her on the hearth.)
There was a red man of the O'Donnells from the north,
and a man of the O'Sullivans from the south, and
there was one Brian that lost his life at Clontarf by
the sea, and there were a great many in the west,
some that died hundreds of years ago, and there are
some that will die to-morrow.
MICHAEL. Is it in the west that men will die to-morrow?
OLD WOMAN. Come nearer, nearer to me.
BRIDGET. Is she right, do you think? Or is she a
woman from beyond the world?
PETER. She doesn't know well what she's talking about,
with the want and the trouble she has gone through.
BRIDGET. The poor thing, we should treat her well.
PETER. Give her a drink of milk and a bit of the oaten
cake.
BRIDGET. Maybe we should give her something along with
that, to bring her on her way. A few pence or a
shilling itself, and we with so much money in the
house.
PETER. Indeed I'd not begrudge it to her if we had it
to spare, but if we go running through what we have,
we'll soon have to break the hundred pounds, and that
would be a pity.
BRIDGET. Shame on you, Peter. Give her the shilling
and your blessing with it, or our own luck will go
from us.

(PETER goes to the box and takes out a shilling.)

BRIDGET (to the OLD WOMAN). Will you have a drink of
milk, ma'am?
OLD WOMAN. It is not food or drink that I want.

PETER (offering the shilling). Here is something for you.
OLD WOMAN. This is not what I want. It is not silver I want.
PETER. What is it you would be asking for?
OLD WOMAN. If anyone would give me help he must give me himself, he must give me all.

(PETER goes over to the table staring at the shilling in his hand in a bewildered way, and stands whispering to BRIDGET.)

MICHAEL. Have you no one to care you in your age, ma'am?
OLD WOMAN. I have not. With all the lovers that brought me their love I never set out the bed for any.
MICHAEL. Are you lonely going the roads, ma'am?
OLD WOMAN. I have my thoughts and I have my hopes.
MICHAEL. What hopes have you to hold to?
OLD WOMAN. The hope of getting my beautiful fields back again; the hope of putting the strangers out of my house.
MICHAEL. What way will you do that, ma'am?
OLD WOMAN. I have good friends that will help me. They are gathering to help me now. I am not afraid. If they are put down to-day they will get the upper hand to-morrow. (She gets up.) I must be going to meet my friends. They are coming to help me and I must be there to welcome them. I must call the neighbours together to welcome them.
MICHAEL. I will go with you.
BRIDGET. It is not her friends you have to go and welcome, Michael; it is the girl coming into the house you have to welcome. You have plenty to do; it is food and drink you have to bring to the house. The woman that is coming home is not coming with empty hands; you would not have an empty house before her. (To the OLD WOMAN.) Maybe you don't know, ma'am, that my son is going to be married to-morrow.
OLD WOMAN. It is not a man going to his marriage that I look to for help.
PETER (to BRIDGET). Who is she, do you think, at all?
BRIDGET. You did not tell us your name yet, ma'am.
OLD WOMAN. Some call me the Poor Old Woman, and there are some that call me Cathleen, the daughter of Houlihan.
PETER. I think I knew some one of that name, once. Who was it, I wonder? It must have been some one I knew when I was a boy. No, no; I remember, I heard it in a song.
OLD WOMAN (who is standing in the doorway). They are

191

wondering that there were songs made for me; there
have been many songs made for me. I heard one on the
wind this morning. (Sings)

> Do not make a great keening
> When the graves have been dug to-morrow.
> Do not call the white-scarfed riders
> To the burying that shall be to-morrow.
> Do not spread food to call strangers
> To the wakes that shall be to-morrow;
> Do not give money for prayers
> For the dead that shall die to-morrow. . . .

They will have no need of prayers, they will have no
need of prayers.

MICHAEL. I do not know what that song means, but tell
me something I can do for you.

PETER. Come over to me, Michael.

MICHAEL. Hush, father, listen to her.

OLD WOMAN. It is a hard service they take that help
me. Many that are red-cheeked now will be pale-
cheeked; many that have been free to walk the hills
and the bogs and the rushes will be sent to walk hard
streets in far countries; many a good plan will be
broken; many that have gathered money will not stay
to spend it; many a child will be born and there will
be no father at its christening to give it a name.
They that have red cheeks will have pale cheeks for
my sake, and for all that, they will think they are
well paid.

(She goes out; her voice is heard outside singing.)

> They shall be remembered for ever,
> They shall be alive for ever,
> They shall be speaking for ever,
> The people shall hear them for ever.

BRIDGET (to PETER). Look at him, Peter; he has the
look of a man that has got the touch. (Raising her
voice.) Look here, Michael, at the wedding clothes.
Such grand clothes as these are! You have a right
to fit them on now; it would be a pity to-morrow if
they did not fit. The boys would be laughing at
you. Take them, Michael, and go into the room and
fit them on. (She puts them on his arm.)

MICHAEL. What wedding are you talking of? What
clothes will I be wearing to-morrow?

BRIDGET. These are the clothes you are going to wear
when you marry Delia Cahel to-morrow.

MICHAEL. I had forgotten that.

192

(He looks at the clothes and turns towards the inner
room, but stops at the sound of cheering outside.)

PETER.   There is the shouting come to our own door.
What is it has happened?

(NEIGHBOURS come crowding in, PATRICK and DELIA with
them.)

PATRICK.   There are ships in the Bay; the French are
landing at Killala![3]

(PETER takes his pipe from his mouth and his hat off,
and stands up.  The clothes slip from MICHAEL'S arm.)

DELIA.   Michael!  (He takes no notice.)  Michael!  (He
turns towards her.)  Why do you look at me like a
stranger?

(She drops his arm.  BRIDGET goes over towards her.)

PATRICK.   The boys are all hurrying down the hillside
to join the French.
DELIA.   Michael won't be going to join the French.
BRIDGET (to PETER).   Tell him not to go, Peter.
PETER.   It's no use.  He doesn't hear a word we're
saying.
BRIDGET.   Try and coax him over to the fire.
DELIA.   Michael, Michael!  You won't leave me!  You
won't join the French, and we going to be married!

(She puts her arms about him, he turns towards her as
if about to yield.)

                OLD WOMAN'S voice outside.
            They shall be speaking for ever,
            The people shall hear them for ever.

(MICHAEL breaks away from DELIA, stands for a second at
the door, then rushes out, following the OLD WOMAN'S
voice.  BRIDGET takes DELIA, who is crying silently,
into her arms.)

PETER (to PATRICK, laying a hand on his arm).   Did you
see an old woman going down the path?


3. The United Irishmen, a secret society founded in
1791 in Belfast, was responsible, under the leadership of Wolfe Tone, for two abortive attempts to
invade Ireland from France in 1798.

PATRICK.  I did not, but I saw a young girl, and she
    had the walk of a queen.

RIDERS TO THE SEA

by John Millington Synge

Characters

Maurya, an old woman        Nora, a younger daughter
Bartley, her son            Men and Women
Cathleen, her daughter

SCENE: An Island off the West of Ireland.

(Cottage kitchen, with nets, oil-skins, spinningwheel,
  some new boards standing by the wall, etc. CATHLEEN,
  a girl of about twenty, finishes kneading cake, and
  puts it down in the pot oven by the fire; then wipes
  her hands, and begins to spin at the wheel. NORA, a
  young girl, puts her head in at the door.)

NORA (in a low voice). Where is she?
CATHLEEN. She's lying down, God help her, and may be
  sleeping, if she's able.

(NORA comes in softly, and takes a bundle from under
  her shawl.)

CATHLEEN (spinning the wheel rapidly). What is it you
  have?
NORA. The young priest is after bringing them. It's
  a shirt and a plain stocking were got off a drowned
  man in Donegal.

(CATHLEEN stops her wheel with a sudden movement, and
  leans out to listen.)

NORA. We're to find out if it's Michael's they are,
  some time herself will be down looking by the sea.
CATHLEEN. How would they be Michael's, Nora? How
  would he go the length of that way to the far north?
NORA. The young priest says he's known the like of it.
  "If it's Michael's they are," says he, "you can tell
  herself he's got a clean burial by the grace of God,
  and if they're not his, let no one say a word about
  them, for she'll be getting her death," says he,
  "with crying and lamenting."

(The door which NORA half closed is blown open by a
  gust of wind.)

CATHLEEN (looking out anxiously). Did you ask him

195

would he stop Bartley going this day with the horses
to the Galway fair?

NORA. "I won't stop him," says he, "but let you not
be afraid. Herself does be saying prayers half
through the night, and the Almighty God won't leave
her destitute," says he, "with no son living."

CATHLEEN. Is the sea bad by the white rocks, Nora?

NORA. Middling bad, God help us. There's a great
roaring in the west, and it's worse it'll be getting
when the tide's turned to the wind. (She goes over
to the table with the bundle.) Shall I open it now?

CATHLEEN. Maybe she'd wake up on us, and come in before we'd done. (Coming to the table.) It's a long
time we'll be, and the two of us crying.

NORA (goes to the inner door and listens). She's
moving about on the bed. She'll be coming in a
minute.

CATHLEEN. Give me the ladder, and I'll put them up in
the turf-loft, the way she won't know of them at all,
and maybe when the tide turns she'll be going down
to see would he be floating from the east.

(They put the ladder against the gable of the chimney;
CATHLEEN goes up a few steps and hides the bundle in
the turf-loft. MAURYA comes from the inner room.)

MAURYA (looking up at CATHLEEN and speaking queru-
lously). Isn't it turf enough you have for this day
and evening?

CATHLEEN. There's a cake baking at the fire for a
short space (throwing down the turf) and Bartley will
want it when the tide turns if he goes to Connemara.

(NORA picks up the turf and puts it round the pot-oven.)

MAURYA (sitting down on a stool at the fire). He won't
go this day with the wind rising from the south and
west. He won't go this day, for the young priest
will stop him surely.

NORA. He'll not stop him, mother, and I heard Eamon
Simon and Stephen Pheety and Colum Shawn saying he
would go.

MAURYA. Where is he itself?

NORA. He went down to see would there be another boat
sailing in the week, and I'm thinking it won't be
long till he's here now, for the tide's turning at
the green head, and the hooker's[1] tacking from the

1. A kind of fishing boat with one mast, used on the
coasts of England and Ireland.

east.

CATHLEEN. I hear some one passing the big stones.

NORA (looking out). He's coming now, and he in a
hurry.

BARTLEY (comes in and looks round the room. Speaking
sadly and quietly). Where is the bit of new rope,
Cathleen, was bought in Connemara?

CATHLEEN (coming down). Give it to him, Nora; it's on
a nail by the white boards. I hung it up this morning, for the pig with the black feet was eating it.

NORA (giving him a rope). Is that it, Bartley?

MAURYA. You'd do right to leave that rope, Bartley,
hanging by the board. (BARTLEY takes the rope.) It
will be wanting in this place, I'm telling you, if
Michael is washed up tomorrow morning, or the next
morning, or any morning in the week, for it's a deep
grave we'll make him by the grace of God.

BARTLEY (beginning to work with the rope). I've no
halter the way I can ride down on the mare, and I
must go now quickly. This is the one boat going for
two weeks or beyond it, and the fair will be a good
fair for horses ⊥ heard them saying below.

MAURYA. It's a hard thing they'll be saying below if
the body is washed up and there's no man in it to
make the coffin, and I after giving a big price for
the finest white boards you'd find in Connemara.
(She looks round at the boards.)

BARTLEY. How would it be washed up, and we after looking each day for nine days, and a strong wind blowing
a while back from the west and south?

MAURYA. If it wasn't found itself, that wind is raising the sea, and there was a star up against the
moon, and it rising in the night. If it was a hundred horses, or a thousand horses you had itself,
what is the price of a thousand horses against a son
where there is one son only?

BARTLEY (working at the halter, to CATHLEEN). Let you
go down each day, and see the sheep aren't jumping in
on the rye, and if the jobber comes you can sell the
pig with the black feet if there is a good price
going.

MAURYA. How would the like of her get a good price for
a pig?

BARTLEY (to CATHLEEN). If the west wind holds with the
last bit of the moon let you and Nora get up weed
enough for another cock for the kelp.[2] It's hard
set we'll be from this day with no one in it but one

2. Meaning: to gather enough kelp to make into a
small conical pile.

197

man to work.

MAURYA. It's hard set we'll be surely the day you're drownd'd with the rest. What way will I live and the girls with me, and I an old woman looking for the grave?

(BARTLEY lays down the halter, takes off his old coat, and puts on a newer one of the same flannel.)

BARTLEY (to NORA). Is she coming to the pier?

NORA (looking out). She's passing the green head and letting fall her sails.

BARTLEY (getting his purse and tobacco). I'll have half an hour to go down, and you'll see me coming again in two days, or in three days, or maybe in four days if the wind is bad.

MAURYA (turning round to the fire, and putting her shawl over her head). Isn't it a hard and cruel man won't hear a word from an old woman, and she holding him from the sea?

CATHLEEN. It's the life of a young man to be going on the sea, and who would listen to an old woman with one thing and she saying it over?

BARTLEY (taking the halter). I must go now quickly. I'll ride down on the red mare, and the gray pony'll run behind me. . . . The blessing of God on you. (He goes out.)

MAURYA (crying out as he is in the door). He's gone now, God spare us, and we'll not see him again. He's gone now, and when the black night is falling I'll have no son left me in the world.

CATHLEEN. Why wouldn't you give him your blessing and he looking round in the door? Isn't it sorrow enough is on every one in this house without your sending him out with an unlucky word behind him, and a hard word in his ear?

(MAURYA takes up the tongs and begins raking the fire aimlessly without looking round.)

NORA (turning towards her). You're taking away the turf from the cake.

CATHLEEN (crying out). The Son of God forgive us, Nora, we're forgetting his bit of bread. (She comes over to the fire.)

NORA. And it's destroyed he'll be going till dark night, and he after eating nothing since the sun went up.

CATHLEEN (turning the cake out of the oven). It's destroyed he'll be, surely. There's no sense left on any person in a house where an old woman will be talking forever.

(MAURYA sways herself on her stool.)

CATHLEEN (cutting off some of the bread and rolling it
   in a cloth; to MAURYA). Let you go down now to the
   spring well and give him this and he passing. You'll
   see him then and the dark word will be broken, and
   you can say "God speed you," the way he'll be easy
   in his mind.
MAURYA (taking the bread). Will I be in it as soon as
   himself?
CATHLEEN. If you go now quickly.
MAURYA (standing up unsteadily). It's hard set I am to
   walk.
CATHLEEN (looking at her anxiously). Give her the
   stick, Nora, or maybe she'll slip on the big stones.
NORA. What stick?
CATHLEEN. The stick Michael brought from Connemara.
MAURYA (taking a stick NORA gives her). In the big
   world the old people do be leaving things after them
   for their sons and children, but in this place it is
   the young men do be leaving things behind for them
   that do be old.

(She goes out slowly. NORA goes over to the ladder.)

CATHLEEN. Wait, Nora, maybe she'd turn back quickly.
   She's that sorry, God help her, you wouldn't know
   the thing she'd do.
NORA. Is she gone round by the bush?
CATHLEEN (looking out). She's gone now. Throw it
   down quickly, for the Lord knows when she'll be out
   of it again.
NORA (getting the bundle from the loft). The young
   priest said he'd be passing tomorrow, and we might
   go down and speak to him below if it's Michael's they
   are surely.
CATHLEEN (taking the bundle). Did he say what way they
   were found?
NORA (coming down). "There were two men," says he,
   "and they rowing round with poteen³ before the cocks
   crowed, and the oar of one of them caught the body,
   and they passing the black cliffs of the north."
CATHLEEN (trying to open the bundle). Give me a knife,
   Nora, the string's perished with the salt water, and
   there's a black knot on it you wouldn't loosen in a
   week.

3. Illicit whiskey.
                           199

NORA (giving her a knife). I've heard tell it was a
   long way to Donegal.
CATHLEEN (cutting the string). It is surely. There
   was a man in here a while ago--the man sold us that
   knife--and he said if you set off walking from the
   rocks beyond, it would be seven days you'd be in
   Donegal.
NORA.  And what time would a man take, and he floating?

(CATHLEEN opens the bundle and takes out a shirt and a
   bit of a stocking. They look at them eagerly.)

CATHLEEN (in a low voice). The Lord spare us, Nora!
   isn't it a queer hard thing to say if it's his they
   are surely?
NORA.  I'll get his shirt off the hook the way we can
   put the one flannel on the other. (She looks through
   some clothes hanging in the corner.) It's not with
   them, Cathleen, and where will it be?
CATHLEEN.  I'm thinking Bartley put it on him in the
   morning, for his own shirt was heavy with the salt in
   it. (Pointing to the corner.) There's a bit of a
   sleeve was of the same stuff. Give me that and it
   will do.

(NORA brings it to her and they compare the flannel.)

CATHLEEN.  It's the same stuff, Nora; but if it is itself aren't there great rolls of it in the shops of
   Galway, and isn't it many another man may have a
   shirt of it as well as Michael himself?
NORA (who has taken up the stocking and counted the
   stitches, crying out). It's Michael, Cathleen, it's
   Michael; God spare his soul, and what will herself
   say when she hears this story, and Bartley on the sea?
CATHLEEN (taking the stocking). It's a plain stocking.
NORA.  It's the second one of the third pair I knitted,
   and I put up three score stitches, and I dropped four
   of them.
CATHLEEN (counts the stitches). It's that number is in
   it. (Crying out.) Ah, Nora, isn't it a bitter thing
   to think of him floating that way to the far north,
   and no one to keen[4] him but the black hags that do be
   flying on the sea?
NORA (swinging herself round, and throwing out her arms
   on the clothes). And isn't it a pitiful thing when

4. A lamentation or dirge for the dead, uttered in a
   loud wailing voice; sometimes, a wordless cry or
   wail.

there is nothing left of a man who was a great rower
and fisher, but a bit of an old shirt and a plain
stocking?

CATHLEEN (after an instant). Tell me is herself coming,
Nora? I hear a little sound on the path.

NORA (looking out). She is, Cathleen. She's coming up
to the door.

CATHLEEN. Put these things away before she'll come in.
Maybe it's easier she'll be after giving her blessing
to Bartley, and we won't let on we've heard anything
the time he's on the sea.

NORA (helping CATHLEEN to close the bundle). We'll put
them here in the corner.

(They put them into a hole in the chimney corner.
CATHLEEN goes back to the spinning-wheel.)

NORA. Will she see it was crying I was?

CATHLEEN. Keep your back to the door the way the
light'll not be on you.

(NORA sits down at the chimney corner, with her back
to the door. MAURYA comes in very slowly, without
looking at the girls, and goes over to her stool at
the other side of the fire. The cloth with the bread
is still in her hand. The girls look at each other,
and NORA points to the bundle of bread.)

CATHLEEN (after spinning for a moment). You didn't
give him his bit of bread?

(MAURYA begins to keen softly, without turning round.)

CATHLEEN. Did you see him riding down?

(MAURYA goes on keening.)

CATHLEEN (a little impatiently). God forgive you;
isn't it a better thing to raise your voice and tell
what you seen, than to be making lamentation for a
thing that's done? Did you see Bartley, I'm saying
to you.

MAURYA (with a weak voice). My heart's broken from
this day.

CATHLEEN (as before). Did you see Bartley?

MAURYA. I seen the fearfulest thing.

CATHLEEN (leaves her wheel and looks out). God forgive
you; he's riding the mare now over the green head,
and the gray pony behind him.

MAURYA (starts, so that her shawl falls back from her
head and shows her white tossed hair. With a

201

frightened voice). The gray pony behind him.
CATHLEEN (coming to the fire). What is it ails you,
   at all?
MAURYA (speaking very slowly). I've seen the fearfulest thing any person has seen, since the day Bride
   Dara seen the dead man with the child in his arms.
CATHLEEN and NORA. Uah. (They crouch down in front of
   the old woman at the fire.)
NORA. Tell us what it is you seen.
MAURYA. I went down to the spring well, and I stood
   there saying a prayer to myself. Then Bartley came
   along, and he riding on the red mare with the gray
   pony behind him. (She puts up her hands, as if to
   hide something from her eyes.) The Son of God spare
   us, Nora!
CATHLEEN. What is it you seen?
MAURYA. I seen Michael himself.
CATHLEEN (speaking softly). You did not, mother; it
   wasn't Michael you seen, for his body is after being
   found in the far north, and he's got a clean burial
   by the grace of God.
MAURYA (a little defiantly). I'm after seeing him this
   day, and he riding and galloping. Bartley came first
   on the red mare; and I tried to say "God speed you,"
   but something choked the words in my throat. He went
   by quickly; and "the blessing of God on you," says
   he, and I could say nothing. I looked up then, and
   I crying, at the gray pony, and there was Michael
   upon it--with fine clothes on him, and new shoes on
   his feet.
CATHLEEN (begins to keen). It's destroyed we are from
   this day. It's destroyed, surely.
NORA. Didn't the young priest say the Almighty God
   wouldn't leave her destitute with no son living?
MAURYA (in a low voice, but clearly). It's little the
   like of him knows of the sea. . . . Bartley will be
   lost now, and let you call in Eamon and make me a
   good coffin out of the white boards, for I won't live
   after them. I've had a husband, and a husband's
   father, and six sons in this house--six fine men,
   though it was a hard birth I had with every one of
   them and they coming to the world--and some of them
   were found and some of them were not found, but
   they're gone now the lot of them. . . . There were
   Stephen, and Shawn, were lost in the great wind, and
   found after in the Bay of Gregory of the Golden
   Mouth, and carried up the two of them on the one
   plank, and in by that door. (She pauses for a moment,
   the girls start as if they heard something through
   the door that is half open behind them.)
NORA (in a whisper). Did you hear that, Cathleen? Did

you hear a noise in the northeast?
CATHLEEN (in a whisper). There's some one after crying
   out by the seashore.
MAURYA (continues without hearing anything). There was
   Sheamus and his father, and his own father again,
   were lost in a dark night, and not a stick or sign
   was seen of them when the sun went up. There was
   Patch after was drowned out of a curragh5 that turned
   over. I was sitting here with Bartley, and he a
   baby, lying on my two knees, and I seen two women,
   and three women, and four women coming in, and they
   crossing themselves, and not saying a word. I looked
   out then, and there were men coming after them, and
   they holding a thing in the half of a red sail, and
   water dripping out of it--it was a dry day, Nora--
   and leaving a track to the door.

(She pauses again with her hand stretched out towards
   the door. It opens softly and old women begin to
   come in, crossing themselves on the threshold, and
   kneeling down in front of the stage with red petticoats over their heads.)

MAURYA (half in a dream, to CATHLEEN). Is it Patch,
   or Michael, or what is it at all?
CATHLEEN. Michael is after being found in the far
   north, and when he is found there how could he be
   here in this place?
MAURYA. There does be a power of young men floating
   round in the sea, and what way would they know if it
   was Michael they had, or another man like him, for
   when a man is nine days in the sea, and the wind
   blowing, it's hard set his own mother would be to
   say what man was it.
CATHLEEN. It's Michael, God spare him, for they're
   after sending us a bit of his clothes from the far
   north.

(She reaches out and hands MAURYA the clothes that belonged to Michael. MAURYA stands up slowly and takes
   them in her hands. NORA looks out.)

NORA. They're carrying a thing among them and there's
   water dripping out of it and leaving a track by the
   big stones.
CATHLEEN (in a whisper to the women who have come in).
   Is it Bartley it is?


5. A wicker boat covered formerly with hides but now
   with tarred canvas.

203

ONE OF THE WOMEN. It is surely, God rest his soul.

(Two younger women come in and pull out the table.
Then men carry in the body of BARTLEY, laid on a
plank, with a bit of a sail over it, and lay it on
the table.)

CATHLEEN (to the women, as they are doing so). What
way was he drowned?
ONE OF THE WOMEN. The gray pony knocked him into the
sea, and he was washed out where there is a great
surf on the white rocks.

(MAURYA has gone over and knelt down at the head of the
table. The women are keening softly and swaying
themselves with a slow movement. CATHLEEN and NORA
kneel at the other end of the table. The men kneel
near the door.)

MAURYA (raising her head and speaking as if she did not
see the people around her). They're all gone now,
and there isn't anything more the sea can do to me...
I'll have no call now to be up crying and praying
when the wind breaks from the south, and you can hear
the surf is in the east, and the surf is in the west,
making a great stir with the two noises, and they
hitting one on the other. I'll have no call now to
be going down and getting Holy Water in the dark
nights after Samhain,[6] and I won't care what way the
sea is when the other women will be keening. (To
NORA.) Give me the Holy Water, Nora, there's a small
sup still on the dresser.

(NORA gives it to her.)

MAURYA (drops Michael's clothes across Bartley's feet,
and sprinkles the Holy Water over him). It isn't
that I haven't prayed for you, Bartley, to the Almighty God. It isn't that I haven't said prayers in
the dark night till you wouldn't know what I'd be
saying; but it's a great rest I'll have now, and it's
time surely. It's a great rest I'll have now, and
great sleeping in the long nights after Samhain, if
it's only a bit of wet flour we do have to eat, and
maybe a fish that would be stinking. (She kneels
down again, crossing herself, and saying prayers

6. November 1st, the beginning of the Celtic winter
   half year and also a feast of the dead that was
   observed with many religious harvest rites.

204

under her breath.)

CATHLEEN (to AN OLD MAN). Maybe yourself and Eamon would make a coffin when the sun rises. We have fine white boards herself bought, God help her, thinking Michael would be found, and I have a new cake you can eat while you'll be working.

THE OLD MAN (looking at the boards). Are there nails with them?

CATHLEEN. There are not, Colum; we didn't think of the nails.

ANOTHER MAN. It's a great wonder she wouldn't think of the nails, and all the coffins she's seen made already.

CATHLEEN. It's getting old she is, and broken.

(MAURYA stands up again very slowly and spreads out the pieces of Michael's clothes beside the body, sprinkling them with the last of the Holy Water.)

NORA (in a whisper to CATHLEEN). She's quiet now and easy; but the day Michael was drowned you could hear her crying out from this to the spring well. It's fonder she was of Michael, and would any one have thought that?

CATHLEEN (slowly and clearly). An old woman will be soon tired with anything she will do, and isn't it nine days herself is after crying and keening, and making great sorrow in the house?

MAURYA (puts the empty cup mouth downwards on the table, and lays her hands together on Bartley's feet). They're all together this time, and the end is come. May the Almighty God have mercy on Bartley's soul, and on Michael's soul, and on the souls of Sheamus and Patch, and Stephen and Shawn; (bending her head) and may He have mercy on my soul, Nora, and on the soul of every one is left living in the world.

(She pauses, and the keen rises a little more loudly from the women, then sinks away.)

MAURYA (continuing). Michael has a clean burial in the far north, by the grace of the Almighty God. Bartley will have a fine coffin out of the white boards, and a deep grave surely. What more can we want than that? No man at all can be living forever, and we must be satisfied. (She kneels down again and the curtain falls slowly.)

205

THE PLOUGH AND THE STARS[1]

A Tragedy in Four Acts

  by Sean O'Casey

          To the Gay Laugh of my Mother
            at the Gate of the Grave


            Characters in the Play

Jack Clitheroe (a bricklayer), Commandant in the Irish
  Citizen Army
Nora Clitheroe, his wife
Peter Flynn (a labourer), Nora's uncle
The Young Covey (a fitter), Clitheroe's cousin
Bessie Burgess (a street fruit-vendor)
Mrs. Gogan (a charwoman)
Mollser, her consumptive child
Fluther Good (a carpenter)
Lieut. Langon (a Civil Servant), of the Irish
  Volunteers
Capt. Brennan (a chicken butcher), of the Irish Citizen
  Army
Corporal Stoddart, of the Wiltshires
Sergeant Tinley, of the Wiltshires
Rosie Redmond, a daughter of "the Digs"[2]
A Bar-tender
A Woman
The Figure in the Window

Act.  I.--The living-room of the Clitheroe flat in a
           Dublin tenement.
Act.  II.--A public-house, outside of which a meeting
           is being held.
Act. III.--The street outside the Clitheroe tenement.
Act.  IV.--The room of Bessie Burgess.


1. The title of the play is taken from the flag of the
  Irish Citizen Army. O'Casey described the flag in
  Drums under the Windows, the third of his autobiog-
  raphical volumes: "There it was--the most beautiful
  flag among the flags of the world's nations; a rich,
  deep poplin field of blue; across its whole length
  and breadth stretched the formalized shape of a
  plough, a golden-brown colour, seamed with a rusty
  red, while through all glittered the gorgeous group
  of stars, enriching and ennobling the northern skies."
2. A poor section of Dublin.

[Jack and Nora Clitheroe, Peter Flynn, The Young Covey, Bessie Burgess, Mrs. Gogan, Mollser, and Fluther Good are Residents in the Tenement.]

Time.--Acts I and II, November 1915; Acts III and IV, Easter Week, 1916. A few days elapse between Acts III and IV.

## Act I

The home of the Clitheroes. It consists of the front and back drawing-rooms in a fine old Georgian house, struggling for its life against the assaults of time, and the more savage assaults of the tenants. The room shown is the back drawing-room,wide, spacious, and lofty. At back is the entrance to the front drawing-room. The space, originally occupied by folding doors, is now draped with casement cloth of a dark purple, decorated with a design in reddish-purple and cream. One of the curtains is pulled aside, giving a glimpse of front drawing-room, at the end of which can be seen the wide, lofty windows looking out into the street. The room directly in front of the audience is furnished in a way that suggests an attempt towards a finer expression of domestic life. The large fireplace on right is of wood, painted to look like marble (the original has been taken away by the landlord). On the mantelshelf are two candlesticks of dark carved wood. Between them is a small clock. Over the clock is hanging a calendar which displays a picture of "The Sleeping Venus". In the centre of the breast of the chimney hangs a picture of Robert Emmet.[3] On the right of the entrance to the front drawing-room is a copy of "The Gleaners", on the opposite side a copy of "The Angelus". Underneath "The Gleaners" is a chest of drawers on which stands a green bowl filled with scarlet dahlias and white chrysanthemums. Near to the fireplace is a settee which at night forms a double bed for Clitheroe and Nora. Underneath "The Angelus" are a number of shelves containing saucepans and a frying-pan. Under these is a table on which are various articles of delf ware. Near the end of the room, opposite to the fireplace is a gate-legged table, covered with a cloth. On top of the table a huge cavalry sword is lying. To the right is a door which leads to a lobby from which the staircase leads to the hall. The floor is covered with a dark green linoleun. The room is dim except where it is illuminated from the glow of the fire.

3. Irish insurrectionist, 1858-1934.

208

Through the window of the room at back can be seen the
flaring of the flame of a gasolene lamp giving light to
workmen repairing the street.  Occasionally can be
heard the clang of crowbars striking the setts.[4]
Fluther Good is repairing the lock of door, Right.  A
claw-hammer is on a chair beside him, and he has a
screw-driver in his hand.  He is a man of forty years
of age, rarely surrendering to thoughts of anxiety,
fond of his "oil" but determined to conquer the habit
before he dies.  He is square-jawed and harshly fea-
tured; under the left eye is a scar, and his nose is
bent from a smashing blow received in a fistic battle
long ago.  He is bald, save for a few peeping tufts of
reddish hair around his ears; and his upper lip is hidden by a scrubby red moustache, embroidered here and
there with a grey hair.  He is dressed in a seedy black
suit, cotton shirt with a soft collar, and wears a very
respectable little black bow.  On his head is a faded
jerry hat, which, when he is excited, he has a habit of
knocking farther back on his head, in a series of taps.
In an argument he usually fills with sound and fury
generally signifying a row.  He is in his shirt-sleeves
at present, and wears a soiled white apron, from a
pocket in which sticks a carpenter's two-foot rule.  He
has just finished the job of putting on a new lock,and,
filled with satisfaction, he is opening and shutting
the door, enjoying the completion of a work well done.
Sitting at the fire, airing a white shirt, is Peter
Flynn.  He is a little, thin bit of a man, with a face
shaped like a lozenge; on his cheeks and under his chin
is a straggling wiry beard of a dirty-white and lemon
hue.  His face invariably wears a look of animated anguish, mixed with irritated defiance, as if everybody
was at war with him, and he at war with everybody.  He
is cocking his head in a way that suggests resentment
at the presence of Fluther, who pays no attention to
him, apparently, but is really furtively watching him.
Peter is clad in a singlet, white whipcord knee-
breeches, and is in his stocking-feet.
   A voice is heard speaking outside of door, Left (it
is that of Mrs. Gogan).

MRS. GOGAN (outside).  Who are you lookin' for, sir?
   Who?  Mrs. Clitheroe? . . . Oh, excuse me.  Oh ay, up
   this way.  She's out, I think:  I seen her goin'. Oh,
   you've somethin' for her; oh, excuse me.  You're from
   Arnott's. . . . I see. . . . You've a parcel for her.
   . . . Righto. . . . I'll take it. . . . I'll give it

4. Stone paving blocks.

209

to her the minute she comes in. . . . It'll be quite
safe. . . . Oh, sign that. . . . Excuse me. . . .
Where? . . . Here? . . . No, there; righto. Am I to
put Maggie or Mrs.? What is it? You dunno? Oh, excuse me.

(MRS. GOGAN opens the door and comes in. She is a
doleful-looking little woman of forty, insinuating
manner and sallow complexion. She is fidgety and
nervous, terribly talkative, has a habit of taking
up things that may be near her and fiddling with
them while she is speaking. Her heart is aflame with
curiosity, and a fly could not come into nor go out
of the house without her knowing. She has a draper's
parcel in her hand, the knot of the twine tying it is
untied. PETER, more resentful of this intrusion than
of FLUTHER'S presence, gets up from the chair, and
without looking around, his head carried at an angry
cock, marches into the room at back.)

MRS. GOGAN (removing the paper and opening the cardboard box it contains). I wondher what's that now?
   A hat! (She takes out a hat, black, with decorations
   in red and gold.) God, she's goin' to th' divil
   lately for style! That hat, now, cost more than a
   penny. Such notions of upperosity she's gettin'.
   (Putting the hat on her head) Oh, swank, what! (She
   replaces it in parcel.)
FLUTHER. She's a pretty little Judy, all the same.
MRS. GOGAN. Ah, she is, an' she isn't. There's prettiness an' prettiness in it. I'm always sayin' that
   her skirts are a little too short for a married woman. An' to see her, sometimes of an evenin', in her
   glad-neck gown would make a body's blood run cold.
   I do be ashamed of me life before her husband. An'
   th' way she thries to be polite, with her "Good morning, Mrs. Gogan," when she's goin' down, an' her
   "Good evenin', Mrs. Gogan," when she's comin' up.
   But there's politeness an' politeness in it.
FLUTHER. They seem to get on well together, all th'
   same.
MRS. GOGAN. Ah, they do, an' they don't. The pair o'
   them used to be like two turtle doves always billin'
   an' cooin'. You couldn't come into th' room but
   you'd feel, instinctive like, that they'd just been
   afther kissin' an' cuddlin' each other. . . . It often made me shiver, for, afther all, there's kissin'
   an' cuddlin' in it. But I'm thinkin' he's beginnin'
   to take things more quietly; the mysthery of havin' a
   woman's a mysthery no longer. . . . She dhresses herself to keep him with her, but it's no use--afther a

210

month or two, th' wondher of a woman wears off.

FLUTHER. I dunno, I dunno. Not wishin' to say anything derogatory, I think it's all a question of location: when a man finds th' wondher of one woman beginnin' to die, it's usually beginnin' to live in another.

MRS. GOGAN. She's always grumblin' about havin' to live in a tenement house. "I wouldn't like to spend me last hour in one, let alone live me life in a tenement," says she. "Vaults," says she, "that are hidin' th' dead, instead of homes that are sheltherin' th' livin'." "Many a good one," says I, "was reared in a tenement house." Oh, you know, she's a well-up little lassie, too; able to make a shillin' go where another would have to spend a pound. She's wipin' th' eyes of th' Covey⁵ an' poor oul' Pether—everybody knows that—screwin' every penny she can out o' them, in ordher to turn th' place into a babby-house. An' she has th' life frightened out o' them; washin' their face, combin' their hair, wipin' their feet, brushin' their clothes, thrimmin' their nails, cleanin' their teeth—God Almighty, you'd think th' poor men were undhergoin' penal servitude.

FLUTHER (with an exclamation of disgust). A-a-ah, that's goin' beyond th' beyonds in a tenement house. That's a little bit too derogatory.

(PETER enters from room, Back, head elevated and resentful fire in his eyes; he is still in his singlet and trousers, but is now wearing a pair of unlaced boots—possibly to be decent in the presence of MRS. GOGAN. He places the white shirt, which he has carried in on his arm, on the back of a chair near the fire, and, going over to the chest of drawers, he opens drawer after drawer, looking for something; as he fails to find it he closes each drawer with a snap; he pulls out pieces of linen neatly folded, and bundles them back again any way.)

PETER (in accents of anguish). Well, God Almighty, give me patience! (He returns to room, Back, giving the shirt a vicious turn as he passes.)

MRS. GOGAN. I wondher what he is foostherin'⁶ for now?

FLUTHER. He's adornin' himself for th' meeting to-night. (Pulling a handbill from his pocket and reading) "Great Demonstration an' torchlight procession around

---

5. A nickname for Jack Clitheroe's cousin; in Dublin slang the word "covey" means a "smart aleck".
6. Hurrying.

211

places in th' city sacred to th' memory of Irish
Patriots, to be concluded by a meetin', at which
will be taken an oath of fealty to th' Irish Republic. Formation in Parnell Square at eight o'clock."
Well, they can hold it for Fluther. I'm up th'
pole; no more dhrink for Fluther. It's three days
now since I touched a dhrop, an' I feel a new man
already.

MRS. GOGAN. Isn't oul' Peter a funny-lookin' little
man? . . . Like somethin' you'd pick off a Christmas
Tree. . . . When he's dhressed up in his canonicals,
you'd wondher where he'd been got. God forgive me,
when I see him in them, I always think he must ha'
had a Mormon for a father! He an' th' Covey can't
abide each other; th' pair o' them is always at it,
thryin' to best each other. There'll be blood
dhrawn one o' these days.

FLUTHER. How is it that Clitheroe himself, now, doesn't
have anythin' to do with th' Citizen Army? A couple
o' months ago, an' you'd hardly ever see him without
his gun, an' th' Red Hand o' Liberty Hall[7] in his
hat.

MRS. GOGAN. Just because he wasn't made a Captain of.
He wasn't goin' to be in anything where he couldn't
be conspishuous. He was so cocksure o' being made
one that he bought a Sam Browne belt,[8] an' was always puttin' it on an' standin' at th' door showing
it off, till th' man came an' put out th' street
lamps on him. God, I think he used to bring it to
bed with him! But I'm tellin' you herself was de-
lighted that that cock didn't crow, for she's like
a clockin' hen if he leaves her sight for a minute.

(While she is talking, she takes up book after book
from the table, looks into each of them in a near-
sighted way, and then leaves them back. She now
lifts up the sword, and proceeds to examine it.)

MRS. GOGAN. Be th' look of it, this must ha' been a
general's sword. . . . All th' gold lace an' th'
fine figaries on it. . . . Sure it's twiced too big
for him.


7. Liberty Hall was the headquarters of the Irish
   Citizen Army.
8. After General Sir Samuel James Browne (1824-1901),
   a British army officer. A leather waist belt supported by a light strap passing over the right
   shoulder.

FLUTHER.  A-ah; it's a baby's rattle he ought to have,
an' he as he is with thoughts tossin' in his head of
what may happen to him on th' day of judgement.

(PETER has entered, and seeing MRS. GOGAN with the
sword, goes over to her, pulls it resentfully out of
her hands, and marches into the room, Back, without
speaking.)

MRS. GOGAN (as PETER whips the sword).  Oh, excuse me!
. . . (To FLUTHER) Isn't he th' surly oul' rascal!
FLUTHER.  Take no notice of him. . . . You'd think he
was dumb, but when you get his goat, or he has a few
jars up,[9] he's vice versa.  (He coughs.)
MRS. GOGAN (she has now sidled over as far as the shirt
hanging on the chair).  Oh, you've got a cold on
you, Fluther.
FLUTHER (carelessly).  Ah, it's only a little one.
MRS. GOGAN.  You'd want to be careful, all th' same.  I
knew a woman, a big lump of a woman, red-faced an'
round-bodied, a little awkward on her feet; you'd
think, to look at her, she could put out her two
arms an' lift a two-storied house on th' top of her
head; got a ticklin' in her throat, an' a little
cough, an' the' next mornin' she had a little
catchin' in her chest, an' they had just time to wet
her lips with a little rum, an' off she went.  (She
begins to look at and handle the shirt.)
FLUTHER (a little nervously).  It's only a little cold
I have; there's nothing derogatory wrong with me.
MRS. GOGAN.  I dunno; there's many a man this minute
lowerin' a pint, thinkin' of a woman, or pickin' out
a winner, or doin' work as you're doin', while th'
hearse dhrawn be th' horses with the black plumes is
dhrivin' up to his own hall door, an' a voice that
he doesn't hear is muttherin' in his ear, "Earth to
earth, an' ashes t' ashes, an' dust to dust."
FLUTHER (faintly).  A man in th' pink o' health should
have a holy horror of allowin' thoughts o' death to
be festherin' in his mind, for--(with a frightened
cough) be God, I think I'm afther gettin' a little
catch in me chest that time--it's a creepy thing to
be thinkin' about.
MRS. GOGAN.  It is, an' it isn't; it's both bad an'
good. . . . It always gives meself a kind o' thress-
passin' joy to feel meself movin' along in a mourn-
in' coach, an' me thinkin' that, maybe, th' next
funeral'll be me own, an' glad, in a quiet way, that

9. i.e. Been drinking.

this is somebody else's.

FLUTHER. An' a curious kind of a gaspin' for breath--I hope there's nothin' derogatory wrong with me.

MRS. GOGAN (examining the shirt). Frills on it, like a woman's petticoat.

FLUTHER. Suddenly gettin' hot, an' then, just as suddenly, gettin' cold.

MRS. GOGAN (holding out the shirt towards FLUTHER). How would you like to be wearin' this Lord Mayor's nightdhress, Fluther?

FLUTHER (vehemently). Blast you an' your nightshirt! Is a man fermentin' with fear to stick th' showin' off to him of a thing that looks like a shinin' shroud?

MRS. GOGAN. Oh, excuse me!

(PETER has again entered, and he pulls the shirt from the hands of MRS. GOGAN, replacing it on the chair. He returns to room.)

PETER (as he goes out). Well, God Almighty, give me patience!

MRS. GOGAN (to PETER). Oh, excuse me!

(There is heard a cheer from the men working outside on the street, followed by the clang of tools being thrown down, then silence. The glare of the gasolene light diminishes and finally goes out.)

MRS. GOGAN (running into the back room to look out of the window). What's the men repairin' th' streets cheerin' for?

FLUTHER (sitting down weakly on a chair). You can't sneeze but that oul' one wants to know th' why an' th' wherefore. . . . I feel as dizzy as bedamned! I hope I didn't give up th' beer too suddenly.

(THE COVEY comes in by door, Right. He is about twenty-five, tall, thin, with lines on his face that form a perpetual protest against life as he conceives it to be. Heavy seams fall from each side of nose, down around his lips, as if they were suspenders keeping his mouth from falling. He speaks in a slow, wailing drawl; more rapidly when he is excited. He is dressed in dungarees, and is wearing a vividly red tie. He flings his cap with a gesture of disgust on the table, and begins to take off his overalls.)

MRS. GOGAN (to THE COVEY, as she runs back into the room). What's after happenin', Covey?

THE COVEY (with contempt). Th' job's stopped. They've

214

been mobilized to march in th' demonstration to-
night undher th' Plough an' th' Stars. Didn't you
hear them cheerin', th' mugs! They have to renew
their political baptismal vows to be faithful in
seculo seculorum.[10]

FLUTHER (forgetting his fear in his indignation).
There's no reason to bring religion into it. I
think we ought to have as great a regard for religion as we can, so as to keep it out of as many
things as possible.

THE COVEY (pausing in the taking off of his dungarees).
Oh, you're one o' the boys that climb into religion
as high as a short Mass on Sunday mornin's? I suppose you'll be singin' songs o' Sion an' songs o'
Tara at th' meetin', too.

FLUTHER. We're all Irishmen, anyhow; aren't we?

THE COVEY (with hand outstretched, and in a professional tone). Look here, comrade, there's no such thing
as an Irishman, or an Englishman, or a German or a
Turk; we're all only human bein's. Scientifically
speakin', it's all a question of the accidental
gatherin' together of mollycewels an' atoms.

(PETER comes in with a collar in his hand. He goes over
to mirror, Left, and proceeds to try to put it on.)

FLUTHER. Mollycewels an' atoms! D'ye think I'm goin'
to listen to you thryin' to juggle Fluther's mind
with complicated cunundhrums of mollycewels an'
atoms?

THE COVEY (rather loudly). There's nothing complicated
in it. There's no fear o' th' Church tellin' you
that mollycewels is a stickin' together of millions
of atoms o' sodium, carbon, potassium o' iodide,
etcetera, that, accordin' to th' way they're mixed,
make a flower, a fish, a star that you see shinin'
in th' sky, or a man with a big brain like me, or a
man with a little brain like you!

FLUTHER (more loudly still). There's no necessity to
be raisin' your voice; shoutin's no manifestin'
forth of a growin' mind.

PETER (struggling with his collar). God, give me patience with this thing. . . . She makes these col-
lars as stiff with starch as a shinin' band o' solid
steel! She does it purposely to thry an' twart me.
If I can't get it on th' singlet, how, in th' Name
o' God, am I goin' to get it on th' shirt?

10. From--per omnia saecula saeculorum; meaning: for
    all times and all times; or, forever and forever.

215

THE COVEY (loudly). There's no use o' arguin' with
you; it's education you want, comrade.
FLUTHER. The Covey an' God made th' world, I suppose,
wha'?
THE COVEY. When I hear some men talkin' I'm inclined
to disbelieve that th' world's eight-hundhred million
years old, for it's not long since th' fathers o'
some o' them crawled out o' th' sheltherin' slime o'
the sea.
MRS. GOGAN (from room at back). There, they're afther
formin' fours, an' now they're goin' to march away.
FLUTHER (scornfully). Mollycewels! (He begins to un-
tie his apron.) What about Adam an' Eve?
THE COVEY. Well, what about them?
FLUTHER (fiercely). What about them, you?
THE COVEY. Adam an' Eve! Is that as far as you've
got? Are you still thinkin' there was nobody in th'
world before Adam an' Eve? (Loudly) Did you ever
hear, man, of th' skeleton of th' man o' Java[11]?
PETER (casting the collar from him). Blast it, blast
it, blast it.
FLUTHER (viciously folding his apron). Ah, you're not
goin' to be let tap your rubbidge o' thoughts into
th' mind o' Fluther.
THE COVEY. You're afraid to listen to th' thruth!
FLUTHER. Who's afraid?
THE COVEY. You are!
FLUTHER. G'way, you wurum!
THE COVEY. Who's a worum?
FLUTHER. You are, or you wouldn't talk th' way you're
talkin'.
THE COVEY. Th' oul, ignorant savage leppin' up in
you, when science shows you that th' head of your god
is an empty one. Well, I hope you're enjoyin' th'
blessin' o' havin' to live be th' sweat of your brow.
FLUTHER. You'll be kickin' an' yellin' for th' priest
yet, me boyo. I'm not goin' to stand silent an'
simple listenin' to a thick like you makin' a mad-
denin' mockery o' God Almighty. It 'ud be a nice
derogatory thing on me conscience, an' me dyin', to
look back in rememberin' shame of talkin' to a word-
weavin' little ignorant yahoo of a red flag Socialist!


11. A genus of two species, erectus and robustus, regarded as primitive forms of extinct man, known
from skulls of five individuals, more or less frag-
mentary, found (a single skull-cap in 1891, ad-
ditional fragments 1936-37) in Trinil, Java, hence
called Java Man.

MRS. GOGAN (she has returned to the front room, and has
    wandered around looking at things in general, and is
    now in front of the fireplace looking at the picture
    hanging over it). For God's sake, Fluther, dhrop it;
    there's always th' makin's of a row in th' mention of
    religion. . . (Looking at picture) God bless us, it's
    a naked woman!
FLUTHER (coming over to look at it). What's undher it?
    (Reading) "Georgina: The Sleepin' Venus". Oh, that's
    a terrible picture; oh, that's a shockin' picture!
    Oh, th' one that got that taken, she must have been
    a prime lassie!
PETER (who also has come over to look, laughing, with
    his body bent at the waist, and his head slightly
    tilted back). Hee, hee, hee, hee, hee!
FLUTHER (indignantly, to PETER). What are you hee,
    hee-in' for? That's a nice thing to be hee, hee-in'
    at. Where's your morality, man?
MRS. GOGAN. God forgive us, it's not right to be
    lookin' at it.
FLUTHER. It's nearly a derogatory thing to be in th'
    room where it is.
MRS. GOGAN (giggling hysterically). I couldn't stop
    any longer in th' same room with three men, afther
    lookin' at it! (She goes out.)

(THE COVEY, who has divested himself of his dungarees,
    throws them with a contemptuous motion on top of
    PETER'S white shirt.)

PETER (plaintively). Where are you throwin' them?
    Are you thryin' to twart an' torment me again?
THE COVEY. Who's thryin' to twart you?
PETER (flinging the dungarees violently on the floor).
    You're not goin' to make me lose me temper, me young
    Covey.
THE COVEY (flinging the white shirt on the floor). If
    you're Nora's pet, aself, you're not goin' to get
    your way in everything.
PETER (plaintively, with his eyes looking up at the
    ceiling). I'll say nothin'. . . . I'll leave you to
    th' day when th' all-pitiful, all-merciful, all-
    lovin' God'll be handin' you to th' angels to be
    rievin' an' roastin' you, tearin' an' tormentin'
    you, burnin' an' blastin' you!
THE COVEY. Aren't you th' little malignant oul'
    bastard, you lemon-whiskered oul' swine!

(PETER runs to the sword, draws it, and makes for THE
    COVEY, who dodges him around the table; PETER has no
    intention of striking, but THE COVEY wants to take

217

no chances.)

THE COVEY (dodging). Fluther, hold him, there. It's
a nice thing to have a lunatic like this lashin'
around with a lethal weapon!

(THE COVEY darts out of the room, Right, slamming the
door in the face of PETER.)

PETER (battering and pulling at the door). Lemme out,
lemme out; isn't it a poor thing for a man who
wouldn't say a word against his greatest enemy to
have to listen to that Covey's twartin' animosities,
shovin' poor, patient people into a lashin' out of
curses that darken his soul with th' shadow of th'
wrath of th' last day!
FLUTHER. Why d'ye take notice of him? If he seen you
didn't, he'd say nothin' derogatory.
PETER. I'll make him stop his laughin' an' leering,
jibin' an' jeering' an' scarifyin' people with his
corner-boy insinuations!. . . He's always thryin' to
rouse me: if it's not a song, it's a whistle; if it
isn't a whistle, it's a cough. But you can taunt an'
taunt--I'm laughin' at you; he, hee, hee, hee, hee,
heee!
THE COVEY (singing through the keyhole):
   Dear harp o' me counthry, in darkness I found thee,
   The dark chain of silence had hung o'er thee long--
PETER (frantically). Jasus, d'ye hear that? D'ye
hear him soundin' forth his divil-souled song o'
provocation?
THE COVEY (singing as before):
   When proudly, me own island harp, I unbound thee,
   An' gave all thy chords to light, freedom an' song!
PETER (battering at door). When I get out I'll do for
you, I'll do for you, I'll do for you!
THE COVEY (through the keyhole). Cuckoo-oo!

(NORA enters by door, Right. She is a young woman of
   twenty-two, alert, swift, full of nervous energy,
   and a little anxious to get on in the world. The
   firm lines of her face are considerably opposed by a
   soft, amorous mouth and gentle eyes. When her firm-
   ness fails her, she persuades with her feminine
   charm. She is dressed in a tailor-made costume, and
   wears around her neck a silver fox fur.)

NORA (running in and pushing PETER away from the door).
   Oh, can I not turn me back but th' two o' yous are
   at it like a pair o' fightin' cocks! Uncle Peter.
   . . . Uncle Peter . . . UNCLE PETER!

218

PETER (vociferously). Oh, Uncle Peter, Uncle Peter be
damned! D'ye think I'm goin' to give a free pass to
th' young Covey to turn me whole life into a Holy
Manual o' penances an' martyrdoms?
THE COVEY (angrily rushing into the room). If you
won't exercise some sort o' conthrol over that Uncle
Peter o' yours, there'll be a funeral, an' it won't
be me that'll be in th' hearse!
NORA (between PETER and THE COVEY, to THE COVEY). Are
yous always goin' to be tearin' down th' little bit
of respectability that a body's thryin' to build up?
Am I always goin' to be havin' to nurse yous into th'
hardy habit o' thryin' to keep up a little bit of
appearance?
THE COVEY. Why weren't you here to see th' way he run
at me with th' sword?
PETER. What did you call me a lemon-whiskered oul'
swine for?
NORA. If th' two o' yous don't thry to make a generous
altheration in your goin's on, an' keep on thryin' t'
inaugurate th' customs o' th' rest o' th' house into
this place, yous can flit into other lodgin's where
your bowsey battlin' 'ill meet, maybe, with an encore.
PETER (to NORA). Would you like to be called a lemon-
whiskered oul' swine?
NORA. If you attempt to wag that sword of yours at
anybody again, it'll have to be taken off you an' put
in a safe place away from babies that don't know th'
danger o' them things.
PETER (at entrance to room, Back). Well, I'm not goin'
to let anybody call me a lemon-whiskered oul' swine.
(He goes in.)
FLUTHER (trying the door). Openin' an' shuttin' now
with a well-mannered motion, like a door of a select
bar in a high-class pub.
NORA (to THE COVEY, as she lays table for tea). An',
once for all, Willie, you'll have to thry to deliver
yourself from th' desire of provokin' oul' Pether
into a wild forgetfulness of what's proper an' allow-
able in a respectable home.
THE COVEY. Well, let him mind his own business, then.
Yestherday, I caught him hee-hee-in' out of him an'
he readin' bits out of Jenersky's Thesis on th'
Origin, Development, an' Consolidation of th' Evolutionary Idea of th' Proletariat.
NORA. Now, let it end at that, for God's sake; Jack'll
be in any minute, an' I'm not goin' to have th' quiet
of his evenin' tossed about in an everlastin' uproar
between you an' Uncle Pether. (To FLUTHER) Well,
did you manage to settle th' lock, yet, Mr. Good?
FLUTHER (opening and shutting door). It's betther than

a new one, now, Mrs. Clitheroe; it's almost ready to
open and shut of its own accord.
NORA (giving him a coin). You're a whole man. How
many pints will that get you?
FLUTHER (seriously). Ne'er a one at all, Mrs. Clitheroe, for Fluther's on th' wather waggon now. You
could stan' where you're stannin' chantin', "Have a
glass o' malt, Fluther; Fluther, have a glass o'
malt," till th' bells would be ringin' th' ould year
out an' th' New Year in, an' you'd have as much
chance o' movin' Fluther as a tune on a tin whistle
would move a deaf man an' he dead.

(As NORA is opening and shutting door, MRS. BESSIE
BURGESS appears at it. She is a woman of forty,
vigorously built. Her face is a dogged one, hardened
by toil, and a little coarsened by drink. She looks
scornfully and viciously at NORA for a few moments
before she speaks.)

BESSIE. Puttin' a new lock on her door . . . afraid
her poor neighbours ud break through an' steal. . . .
(In a loud tone) Maybe, now, they're a damn sight
more honest than your ladyship . . . checkin' th'
children playin' on th' stairs . . . gettin' on th!
nerves of your ladyship. . . . Complainin' about
Bessie Burgess singin' her hymns at night, when she
has a few up. . . . (She comes in half-way on the
threshold, and screams) Bessie Burgess 'll sing
whenever she damn well likes!

(NORA tries to shut door, but BESSIE violently shoves
it in, and, gripping NORA by the shoulders, shakes
her.)

BESSIE. You little over-dressed throllope, you, for
one pin I'd paste th' white face o' you!
NORA (frightened). Fluther, Fluther!
FLUTHER (running over and breaking the hold of BESSIE
from NORA). Now, now, Bessie, Bessie, leave poor
Mrs. Clitheroe alone; she'd do no one any harm, an'
minds no one's business but her own.
BESSIE. Why is she always thryin' to speak proud
things, an' lookin' like a mighty one in th' congre-
gation o' th' people!

(NORA sinks frightened on to the couch as JACK
CLITHEROE enters. He is a tall, well-made fellow of
twenty-five. His face has none of the strength of
NORA'S. It is a face in which is the desire for
authority, without the power to attain it.)

CLITHEROE (excitedly). What's up? what's afther hap-
    penin'?
FLUTHER. Nothin', Jack. Nothin'. It's all over now.
    Come on, Bessie, come on.
CLITHEROE (to NORA). What's wrong, Nora? Did she say
    anything to you?
NORA. She was bargin' out of her, an' I only told her
    to g'up ower o' that to her own place; an' before I
    knew where I was, she flew at me like a tiger, an'
    thried to guzzle me!
CLITHEROE (going to door and speaking to BESSIE). Get
    up to your own place, Mrs. Burgess, and don't you be
    interferin' with my wife, or it'll be th' worse for
    you. . . . Go on, go on!
BESSIE (as CLITHEROE is pushing her out). Mind who
    you're pushin', now. . . . I attend me place o' wor-
    ship, anyhow . . . not like some o' them that go to
    neither church, chapel nor meetin'-house. . . . If me
    son was home from th' threnches he'd see me righted.

(BESSIE and FLUTHER depart, and CLITHEROE closes the
    door.)

CLITHEROE (going over to NORA, and putting his arm
    round her). There, don't mind that old bitch, Nora,
    darling; I'll soon put a stop to her interferin'.
NORA. Some day or another, when I'm here be meself,
    she'll come in an' do somethin' desperate.
CLITHEROE (kissing her). Oh, sorra fear of her doin'
    anythin' desperate. I'll talk to her to-morrow when
    she's sober. A taste o' me mind that'll shock her
    into the sensibility of behavin' herself!

(NORA gets up and settles the table. She sees the
    dungarees on the floor and stands looking at them,
    then she turns to THE COVEY, who is reading Jener-
    sky's "Thesis" at the fire.)

NORA. Willie, is that th' place for your dungarees?
THE COVEY (getting up and lifting them from the floor).
    Ah, they won't do th' floor any harm, will they? (He
    carries them into room, Back.)
NORA (calling). Uncle Peter, now, Uncle Peter; tea's
    ready.

(PETER and THE COVEY come in from room, Back; they all
    sit down to tea. PETER is in full dress of the
    Foresters[12]: green coat, gold braided; white

12. A patriotic Irish organization to which Peter be-
    longs.

221

breeches, top boots, frilled shirt. He carries the slouch hat, with the white ostrich plume, and the sword in his hands. They eat for a few moments in silence, THE COVEY furtively looking at PETER with scorn in his eyes. PETER knows it and is fidgety.)

THE COVEY (provokingly). Another cut o' bread, Uncle Peter?

(PETER maintains a dignified silence.)

CLITHEROE. It's sure to be a great meetin' to-night. We ought to go, Nora.
NORA (decisively). I won't go, Jack; you can go if you wish.

(A pause.)

THE COVEY. D'ye want th' sugar, Uncle Peter?
PETER (explosively). Now, are you goin' to start your thryin' an' your twartin' again?
NORA. Now, Uncle Peter, you musn't be so touchy; Willie has only assed you if you wanted th' sugar.
PETER. He doesn't care a damn whether I want th' sugar or no. He's only thryin' to twart me!
NORA (angrily, to THE COVEY). Can't you let him alone, Willie? If he wants the sugar, let him stretch his hand out an' get it himself!
THE COVEY (to PETER). Now, if you want the sugar, you can stretch out your hand and get it yourself!
CLITHEROE. To-night is th' first chance that Brennan has got of showing himself off since they made a Captain of him—why, God only knows. It'll be a treat to see him swankin' it at th' head of the Citizen Army carryin' th' flag of the Plough an' th' Stars. . . . (Looking roguishly at NORA) He was sweet on you, once, Nora?
NORA. He may have been. . . . I never liked him. I always thought he was a bit of a thick.
THE COVEY. They're bringin' nice disgrace on that banner now.
CLITHEROE (remonstratively). How are they bringin' disgrace on it?
THE COVEY (snappily). Because it's a Labour flag, an' was never meant for politics. . . . What does th' design of th' field plough, bearin' on it th' stars of th' heavenly plough, mean, if it's not Communism? It's a flag that should only be used when we're buildin' th' barricades to fight for a Workers' Republic!
PETER (with a puff of derision). P-phuh.

THE COVEY (angrily). What are you phuhin' out o' you
    for? Your mind is th' mind of a mummy. (Rising) I
    betther go an' get a good place to have a look at
    Ireland's warriors passin' by. (He goes into room,
    Left, and returns with his cap.)
NORA (to THE COVEY). Oh, Willie, brush your clothes
    before you go.
THE COVEY. Oh, they'll do well enough.
NORA. Go an' brush them; th' brush is in th' drawer
    there.

(THE COVEY goes to the drawer, muttering, gets the
    brush, and starts to brush his clothes.)

THE COVEY (singing at PETER, as he does so):
    Oh, where's th' slave so lowly,
    Condemn'd to chains unholy,
    Who, could he burst his bonds at first,
    Would pine beneath them slowly?

    We tread th' land that . . . bore us,
    Th' green flag glitters . . . o'er us,
    Th' friends we've tried are by our side,
    An' th' foe we hate . . . before us!

PETER (leaping to his feet in a whirl of rage). Now,
    I'm telling you, me young Covey, once for all, that
    I'll not stick any longer these tittherin' taunts of
    yours, rovin' around to sing your slights an' sland-
    ers, reddenin' th' mind of a man to th' thinkin'
    an' sayin' of things that sicken his soul with sin!
    (Hysterically; lifting up a cup to fling at The
    COVEY) Be God, I'll--
CLITHEROE (catching his arm). Now then, none o' that,
    none o' that!
NORA. Uncle Pether, Uncle Pether, UNCLE PETHER!
THE COVEY (at the door, about to go out). Isn't that
    th' malignant oul' varmint! Lookin' like th' il-
    legitimate son of an illegitimate child of a corporal
    in th' Mexican army! (He goes out.)
PETER (plaintively). He's afther leavin' me now in
    such a state of agitation that I won't be able to do
    meself justice when I'm marchin' to th' meetin'.
NORA (jumping up). Oh, for God's sake, here, buckle
    your sword on, and go to your meetin', so that we'll
    have at least one hour of peace! (She proceeds to
    belt on the sword.)
CLITHEROE (irritably). For God's sake hurry him up ou'
    o' this, Nora.
PATER. Are yous all goin' to thry to start to twart
    me now?

223

NORA (putting on his plumed hat). S-s-sh. Now, your
hat's on, your house is thatched; off you pop! (She
gently pushes him from her.)
PETER (going, and turning as he reaches the door).
Now, if that young Covey--
NORA. Go on, go on. (He goes.)

(CLITHEROE sits down in the lounge, lights a cigarette,
and looks thoughtfully into the fire. NORA takes the
things from the table, placing them on the chest of
drawers. There is a pause, then she swiftly comes
over to him and sits beside him.)

NORA (softly). A penny for them, Jack!
CLITHEROE. Me? Oh, I was thinkin' of nothing.
NORA. You were thinkin' of th' . . . meetin' . . .
Jack. When we were courtin' an' I wanted you to go,
you'd say, "Oh, to hell with meetin's," an' that you
felt lonely in cheerin' crowds when I was absent.
An' we weren't a month married when you began that
you couldn't keep away from them.
CLITHEROE. Oh, that's enough about th' meetin'. It
looks as if you wanted me to go, th' way you're
talkin'. You were always at me to give up th' Citizen Army, an' I gave it up; surely that ought to
satisfy you.
NORA. Ay, you gave it up--because you got th' sulks
when they didn't make a Captain of you. It wasn't
for my sake, Jack.
CLITHEROE. For your sake or no, you're benefitin' by
it, aren't you? I didn't forget this was your birthday, did I? (He puts his arms around her) And you
liked your new hat; didn't you, didn't you? (He
kisses her rapidly several times.)
NORA (panting). Jack, Jack; please, Jack! I thought
you were tired of that sort of thing long ago.
CLITHEROE. Well, you're finding out now that I amn't
tired of it yet, anyhow. Mrs. Clitheroe doesn't want
to be kissed, sure she doesn't? (He kisses her
again) Little, little red-lipped Nora!
NORA (coquettishly removing his arm from around her).
Oh, yes, your little, little red-lipped Nora's a
sweet little girl when th' fit seizes you; but your
little, little red-lipped Nora has to clean your
boots every mornin', all the same.
CLITHEROE (with a movement of irritation). Oh, well,
if we're goin' to be snotty!

(A pause.)

NORA. It's lookin' like as if it was you that was

224

goin' to be . . . snotty! Bridlin' up with bittherness, th' minute a body attempts t' open her mouth.
CLITHEROE. Is it any wondher, turnin' a tendher sayin' into a meanin' o' malice an' spite!
NORA. It's hard for a body to be always keepin' her mind bent on makin' thoughts that'll be no longer than th' length of your own satisfaction.

(A pause.)

NORA (standing up). If we're goin' to dhribble th' time away sittin' here like a pair o' cranky mummies, I'd be as well sewin' or doin' something about th' place.

(She looks appealingly at him for a few moments; he doesn't speak. She swiftly sits down beside him, and puts her arm around his neck.)

NORA (imploringly). Ah, Jack, don't be so cross!
CLITHEROE (doggedly). Cross? I'm not cross; I'm not a bit cross. It was yourself started it.
NORA (coaxingly). I didn't mean to say anything out o' the way. You take a body up too quickly, Jack. (In an ordinary tone as if nothing of an angry nature had been said) You didn't offer me me evenin' allowance yet.

(CLITHEROE silently takes out a cigarette for her and himself and lights both.)

NORA (trying to make conversation). How quiet th' house is now; they must be all out.
CLITHEROE (rather shortly). I suppose so.
NORA (rising from the seat). I'm longin' to show you me new hat, to see what you think of it. Would you like to see it?
CLITHEROE. Ah, I don't mind.

(NORA suppresses a sharp reply, hesitates for a moment, then gets the hat, puts it on, and stands before CLITHEROE.)

NORA. Well, how does Mr. Clitheroe like me new hat?
CLITHEROE. It suits you, Nora, it does right enough.

(He stands up, puts his hand beneath her chin, and tilts her head up. She looks at him roguishly. He bends down and kisses her.)

NORA. Here, sit down, an' don't let me hear another

225

cross word out of you for th' rest o' the night.
(They sit down.)
CLITHEROE (with his arms around her). Little, little,
red-lipped Nora!
NORA (with a coaxing movement of her body towards him).
Jack!
CLITHEROE (tightening his arms around her). Well?
NORA. You haven't sung me a song since our honeymoon.
Sing me one now, do . . . please, Jack!
CLITHEROE. What song? "Since Maggie Went Away"?
NORA. Ah, no, Jack, not that; it's too sad. "When You
said You Loved Me."

(Clearing his throat, CLITHEROE thinks for a moment,
and then begins to sing. NORA, putting an arm around
him, nestles her head on his breast and listens de-
lightedly.)

CLITHEROE (singing verses following to the air of "When
You and I were Young, Maggie"):

Th' violets were scenting th' woods, Nora,
  Displaying their charm to th' bee,
When I first said I lov'd only you, Nora,
An' you said you lov'd only me!

Th' chestnut blooms gleam'd through th' glade, Nora,
  A robin sang loud from a tree,
When I first said I lov'd only you, Nora,
An' you said you lov'd only me!

Th' golden-rob'd daffodils shone, Nora,
  An' danc'd in th' breeze on th' lea,
When I first said I lov'd only you, Nora,
An' you said you lov'd only me!

Th' trees, birds, an' bees sang a song, Nora,
  Of happier transports to be,
When I first said I lov'd only you, Nora,
An' you said you lov'd only me!

(NORA kisses him.)

(A knock is heard at the door, Right; a pause as they
  listen. NORA clings closely to CLITHEROE. Another
  knock, more imperative than the first.)

CLITHEROE. I wonder who can that be, now?
NORA (a little nervous). Take no notice of it, Jack;
  they'll go away in a minute.

(Another knock, followed by a voice.)

VOICE. Commandant Clitheroe, Commandant Clitheroe, are you there? A message from General Jim Connolly.

CLITHEROE. Damn it, it's Captain Brennan.

NORA (anxiously). Don't mind him, don't mind, Jack. Don't break our happiness. . . . Pretend we're not in. Let us forget everything to-night but our two selves!

CLITHEROE (reassuringly). Don't be alarmed, darling; I'll just see what he wants, an' send him about his business.

NORA (tremulously). No, no. Please, Jack; don't open it. Please, for your own little Nora's sake!

CLITHEROE (rising to open the door). Now don't be silly, Nora.

(CLITHEROE opens door, and admits a young man in the full uniform of the Irish Citizen Army--green suit; slouch green hat caught up at one side by a small Red Hand badge; Sam Browne belt, with a revolver in the holster. He carries a letter in his hand. When he comes in he smartly salutes CLITHEROE. The young man is CAPTAIN BRENNAN.)

CAPT. BRENNAN (giving the letter to CLITHEROE). A dispatch from General Connolly.

CLITHEROE (reading. While he is doing so, BRENNAN'S eyes are fixed on NORA, who droops as she sits on the lounge). "Commandant Clitheroe is to take command of the eighth battalion of the I.C.A. which will assemble to proceed to the meeting at nine o'clock. He is to see that all units are provided with full equipment; two days' rations and fifty rounds of ammunition. At two o'clock A.M. the army will leave Liberty Hall for a reconnaissance attack on Dublin Castle. --Com.-Gen. Connolly."

CLITHEROE. I don't understand this. Why does General Connolly call me Commandant?

CAPT. BRENNAN. Th' Staff appointed you Commandant, and th' General agreed with their selection.

CLITHEROE. When did this happen?

CAPT. BRENNAN. A fortnight ago.

CLITHEROE. How is it word was never sent to me?

CAPT. BRENNAN. Word was sent to you. . . . I meself brought it.

CLITHEROE. Who did you give it to, then?

CAPT. BRENNAN (after a pause). I think I gave it to Mrs. Clitheroe, there.

CLITHEROE. Nora, d'ye hear that? (NORA makes no answer.)

227

CLITHEROE (there is a note of hardness in his voice).
Nora . . . Captain Brennan says he brought a letter
to me from General Connolly, and that he gave it to
you. . . . Where is it? What did you do with it?
NORA (running over to him, and pleadingly putting her
arms around him). Jack, please, Jack, don't go out
to-night an' I'll tell you; I'll explain everything.
. . . Send him away, an' stay with your own little
red-lipp'd Nora.
CLITHEROE (removing her arms from around him). None o'
this nonsense, now; I want to know what you did with
th' letter? (Nora goes slowly to the lounge and sits
down.)
CLITHEROE (angrily). Why didn't you give me th' letter? What did you do with it? . . . (He shakes her
by the shoulder) What did you do with th' letter?
NORA (flaming up). I burned it, I burned it! That's
what I did with it! Is General Connolly an' th'
Citizen Army goin' to be your only care? Is your
home goin' to be only a place to rest in? Am I goin'
to be only somethin' to provide merry-making at night
for you? Your vanity'll be th' ruin of you an' me
yet. . . . That's what's movin' you: because they've
made an officer of you, you'll make a glorious cause
of what you're doin', while your little red-lipp'd
Nora can go on sittin' here, makin' a companion of
th' loneliness of th' night!
CLITHEROE (fiercely). You burned it, did you? (He
grips her arm) Well, me good lady--
NORA. Let go--you're hurtin' me!
CLITHEROE. You deserve to be hurt. . . . Any letter
that comes to me for th' future, take care that I get
it. . . . D'ye hear--take care that I get it!

(He goes to the chest of drawers and takes out a Sam
Browne belt, which he puts on, and then puts a revolver in the holster. He puts on his hat, and looks
towards NORA. While this dialogue is proceeding, and
while CLITHEROE prepares himself, BRENNAN softly
whistles "The Soldiers' Song".

CLITHEROE (at door, about to go out). You needn't wait
up for me; if I'm in at all, it won't be before six
in th' morning.
NORA (bitterly). I don't care if you never come back!
CLITHEROE (to CAPT. BRENNAN). Come along, Ned.

(They go out; there is a pause. NORA pulls the new
hat from her head and with a bitter movement flings
it to the other end of the room. There is a gentle
knock at door, Right, which opens, and MOLLSER comes

228

into the room. She is about fifteen, but looks to be
only about ten, for the ravages of consumption have
shrivelled her up. She is pitifully worn, walks feebly,
and frequently coughs. She goes over to NORA.)

MOLLSER (to NORA). Mother's gone to th' meetin', an' I
was feeling terrible lonely, so I come down to see if
you'd let me sit with you, thinkin' you mightn't be
goin' yourself. . . . I do be terrible afraid I'll
die sometime when I'm be meself. . . . I often envy
you, Mrs. Clitheroe, seein' th' health you have, an'
th' lovely place you have here, an' wondherin' if I'll
ever be sthrong enough to be keepin' a home together
for a man. Oh, this must be some more o' the Dublin
Fusiliers flyin' off to the front.

(Just before MOLLSER ceases to speak, there is heard in
the distance the music of a brass band playing a regiment to the boat on the way to the front. The tune
that is being played is "It's a Long Way to Tipperary"; as the band comes to the chorus, the regiment is swinging into the street by Nora's house, and
the voices of the soldiers can be heard lustily singing the chorus of the song.)

It's a long way to Tipperary, it's a long way to go;
It's a long way to Tipperary, to th' sweetest girl I
    know!
Goodbye Piccadilly, farewell Leicester Square.
It's a long, long way to Tipperary, but my heart's
    right there!

(NORA and MOLLSER remain silently listening. As the
chorus ends and the music is faint in the distance
again, BESSIE BURGESS appears at door, Right, which
MOLLSER has left open.)

BESSIE (speaking in towards the room). There's th' men
marchin' out into th' dhread dimness o' danger, while
th' lice is crawlin' about feedin' on th' fatness o'
the land! But yous'll not escape from th' arrow that
flieth be night, or th' sickness that wasteth be day.
. . . An' ladyship an' all, as some o' them may be,
they'll be scattered abroad, like th' dust in th'
darkness!

(BESSIE goes away; NORA steals over and quietly shuts
the door. She comes back to the lounge and wearily
throws herself on it beside MOLLSER.)

MOLLSER (after a pause and a cough). Is there anybody

goin', Mrs. Clitheroe, with a titther o' sense?

CURTAIN


Act II

A commodious public-house at the corner of the street
in which the meeting is being addressed from Platform
No. I. It is the south corner of the public-house that
is visible to the audience. The counter, beginning at
Back about one-fourth of the width of the space shown,
comes across two-thirds of the length of the stage, and,
taking a circular sweep, passes out of sight to Left.
On the counter are beer-pulls, glasses, and a carafe.
The other three-fourths of the Back is occupied by a
tall, wide, two-paned window. Beside this window at
the Right is a small, box-like, panelled snug.[13] Next
to the snug is a double swing door, the entrance to
that particular end of the house. Farther on is a shelf
on which customers may rest their drinks. Underneath
the windows is a cushioned seat. Behind the counter at
Back can be seen the shelves running the whole length
of the counter. On these shelves can be seen the end
(or the beginning) of rows of bottles. The Barman is
seen wiping the part of the counter which is in view.
Rosie is standing at the counter toying with what remains of a half of whisky in a wine-glass. She is a
sturdy, well-shaped girl of twenty; pretty, and pert in
manner. She is wearing a cream blouse, with an obviously suggestive glad neck; a grey tweed dress, brown
stockings and shoes. The blouse and most of the dress
are hidden by a black shawl. She has no hat, and in
her hair is jauntily set a cheap, glittering, jewelled
ornament. It is an hour later.

BARMAN (wiping counter). Nothin' much doin' in your
    line to-night, Rosie?
ROSIE. Curse o' God on th' haporth, hardly, Tom. There
    isn't much notice taken of a pretty petticoat of a
    night like this. . . . They're all in a holy mood.
    Th' solemn-lookin' dials on th' whole o' them an' they
    marchin' to th' meetin'. You'd think they were th'
    glorious company of th' saints, an' th' noble army of
    martyrs thrampin' through th' sthreets of paradise.
    They're all thinkin' of higher things than a girl's

13. A small private room in an inn or public house.
                230

garthers. . . . It's a tremendous meetin'; four plat-
forms they have--there's one o' them just outside opposite th' window.
BARMAN.  Oh, ay; sure when th' speaker comes (motioning
with his hand) to th' near end, here, you can see him
plain, an' hear nearly everythin' he's a spoutin' out
of him.
ROSIE.  It's no joke thryin' to make up fifty-five
shillin's a week for your keep an' laundhry, an' then
taxin' you a quid for your own room if you bring home
a friend for th' night. . . . If I could only put by
a couple of quid for a swankier outfit, everythin' in
th' garden ud look lovely--
BARMAN.  Whisht, till we hear what he's sayin'.

(Through the window is silhouetted the figure of a tall
man who is speaking to the crowd.  The BARMAN and
ROSIE look out of the window and listen.)

THE VOICE OF THE MAN.  It is a glorious thing to see
arms in the hands of Irishmen.  We must accustom ourselves to the thought of arms, we must accustom ourselves to the sight of arms, we must accustom ourselves to the use of arms. . . . Bloodshed is a
cleansing and sanctifying thing, and the nation that
regards it as the final horror has lost its manhood.
. . . There are many things more horrible than bloodshed, and slavery is one of them![14]

(The figure moves away towards the Right, and is lost
to sight and hearing.)

ROSIE.  It's th' sacred thruth, mind you, what that
man's afther sayin'.
BARMAN.  If I was only a little younger, I'd be plungin'
mad into th' middle of it!
ROSIE (who is still looking out of the window).  Oh,
here's the two gems runnin' over again for their oil!

(PETER and FLUTHER enter tumultously.  They are hot,
and full and hasty with the things they have seen and
heard.  Emotion is bubbling up in them, so that when
they drink, and when they speak, they drink and speak
with the fullness of emotional passion.  PETER leads
the way to the counter.)

14. This speech, with slight changes, comes from Padraic H. Pearse's "The Coming Revolution," which was
first published in November, 1913.

231

PETER (splutteringly to BARMAN). Two halves . . . (To
   FLUTHER). A meetin' like this always makes me feel
   as if I could dhrink Loch Erinn dhry!
FLUTHER. You couldn't feel any way else at a time like
   this when th' spirit of a man is pulsin' to be out
   fightin' for th' thruth with his feet thremblin' on
   th' way, maybe to th' gallows, an' his ears tinglin'
   with th' faint, far-away sound of burstin' rifle-
   shots that'll maybe whip th' last little shock o'
   life out of him that's left lingerin' in his body!
PETER. I felt a burnin' lump in me throat when I heard
   th' band playin' "The Soldiers' Song", rememberin'
   last hearin' it marchin' in military formation, with
   th' people starin' on both sides at us, carryin' with
   us th' pride an' resolution o' Dublin to th' grave of
   Wolfe Tone.[15]
FLUTHER. Get th' Dublin men goin' an' they'll go on
   full force for anything that's thryin' to bar them
   away from what they're wantin', where th' slim
   thinkin' counthry boyo ud limp away from th' first
   faintest touch of compromization!
PETER (hurriedly to the BARMAN). Two more, Tom! . . .
   (To FLUTHER) Th' memory of all th' things that was
   done, an' all th' things that was suffered be th'
   people, was boomin' in me brain. . . . Every nerve in
   me body was quiverin' to do somethin' desperate!
FLUTHER. Jammed as I was in th' crowd, I listened to
   th' speeches pattherin' on th' people's head, like
   rain fallin' on th' corn; every derogatory thought
   went out o' me mind, an' I said to meself, "You can
   die now, Fluther, for you've seen th' shadow-dhreams
   of th' past leppin' to life in th' bodies of livin'
   men that show, if we were without a titther o' courage for centuries, we're vice versa now!" Looka
   here. (He stretches out his arm under PETER'S face
   and rolls up his sleeve.) The blood was BOILIN' in
   me veins!

(The silhouette of the tall figure again moves into the
   frame of the window speaking to the people.)

PETER (unaware, in his enthusiasm, of the speaker's appearance, to FLUTHER). I was burnin' to dhraw me
   sword, an' wave an' wave it over me--
FLUTHER (overwhelming PETER). Will you stop your
   blatherin' for a minute, man, an' let us hear what
   he's sayin'!
VOICE OF THE MAN. Comrade soldiers of the Irish

15. Irish revolutionist, 1763-1798.

232

Volunteers and of the Citizen Army, we rejoice in
this terrible war.  The old heart of the earth needed
to be warmed with the red wine of the battlefields.
. . . Such august homage was never offered to God as
this:  the homage of millions of lives given gladly
for love of country.  And we must be ready to pour
out the same red wine in  the same glorious sacrifice,
for without shedding of blood there is no redemption!

(The figure moves out of sight and hearing.)

FLUTHER (gulping down the drink that remains in his
  glass, and rushing out).  Come on, man; this is too
  good to be missed!

(PETER finishes his drink less rapidly, and as he is
  going out wiping his mouth with the back of his hand
  he runs into THE COVEY coming in.  He immediately
  erects his body like a young cock, and with his chin
  thrust forward, and a look of venomous dignity on his
  face, he marches out.)

THE COVEY (at counter).  Give us a glass o' malt, for
  God's sake, till I stimulate meself from th' shock o'
  seein' th' sight that's afther goin' out!
ROSIE (all business, coming over to the counter, and
  standing near THE COVEY).  Another one for me, Tommy;
  (to the BARMAN) th' young gentleman's ordherin' it in
  th' corner of his eye.

(The BARMAN brings the drink for THE COVEY, and leaves
  it on the counter.  ROSIE whips it up.)

BARMAN.  Ay, houl' on there, houl' on there, Rosie!
ROSIE (to the BARMAN).  What are you houldin' on out o'
  you for?  Didn't you hear th' young gentleman say
  that he couldn't refuse anything to a nice little
  bird?  (To THE COVEY)  Isn't that right, Jiggs?  (THE
  COVEY says nothing.)  Didn't I know, Tommy, it would
  be all right?  It takes Rosie to size a young man up,
  an' tell th' thoughts that are thremblin' in his
  mind.  Isn't that right, Jiggs?

(THE COVEY stirs uneasily, moves a little farther away,
  and pulls his cap over his eyes.)

ROSIE (moving after him).  Great meetin' that's gettin'
  held outside.  Well, it's up to us all, anyway, to
  fight for our freedom.
THE COVEY (to BARMAN).  Two more, please.  (To ROSIE)
  Freedom!  What's th' use o' freedom, if it's not

233

            economic freedom!
ROSIE (emphasizing with extended arm and moving finger).
    I used them very words just before you come in. "A
    lot of thricksters," says I, "that wouldn't know what
    freedom was if they got it from their mother." . . .
    (To BARMAN) Didn't I, Tommy?
BARMAN.  I disremember.
ROSIE.  No, you don't disremember.  Remember you said,
    yourself, it was all "only a flash in th' pan."
    Well, "flash in th' pan, or no flash in th' pan,"
    says I, "they're not goin' to get Rosie Redmond,"
    says I, "to fight for freedom that wouldn't be worth
    winnin' in a raffle!"
THE COVEY.  There's only one freedom for th' workin'
    man:  conthrol o' th' means o' production, rates of
    exchange, an' th' means of disthribution.  (Tapping
    Rosie on the shoulder) Look here, comrade, I'll leave
    here to-morrow night for you a copy of Jenersky's
    Thesis on the Origin, Development, an' Consolidation
    of the Evolutionary Idea of the Proletariat.)
ROSIE (throwing off her shawl on to the counter, and
    showing an exemplified glad neck, which reveals a
    good deal of a white bosom).  If y'ass Rosie, it's
    heartbreakin' to see a young fella thinkin' of any-
    thing, or admirin' anything, but silk thransparent
    stockin's showin' off the shape of a little lassie's
    legs!

(THE COVEY, frightened, moves a little away.)

ROSIE (following on).  Out in th' park in th' shade of
    a warm summery evenin', with your little darlin'
    bridie to be, kissin' and cuddlin' (she tries to put
    her arm around his neck), kissin' and cuddlin', ay?
THE COVEY (frightened).  Ay, what are you doin'?  None
    o' that, now; none o' that.  I've something else to
    do besides shinannickin' afther Judies!

(He turns away, but ROSIE follows, keeping face to face
    with him.)

ROSIE.  Oh, little duckey, oh, shy little duckey! Never
    held a mot's[16] hand, an' wouldn't know how to tittle
    a little Judy!  (She clips him under the chin.)
    Tittle him undher th' chin, tittle him undher th'
    chin!
THE COVEY (breaking away and running out).  Ay, go on,
    now; I don't want to have any meddlin' with a lassie


16. A harlot.
                        234

like you!

ROSIE (enraged). Jasus, it's in a monasthery some of us
ought to be, spendin' our holidays kneelin' on our
adorers, tellin' our beads, an' knockin' hell out of
our buzzums!

THE COVEY (outside). Cuckoo-oo!

(PETER and FLUTHER come in again, followed by MRS.
GOGAN, carrying a baby in her arms. They go over to
the counter.)

PETER (with plaintive anger). It's terrible that young
Covey can't let me pass without proddin' at me! Did
you hear him murmurin' "cuckoo" when we were passin'?

FLUTHER (irritably). I wouldn't be everlastin' cockin'
me ear to hear every little whisper that was floatin'
around about me! It's my rule never to lose me temper till it would be dethrimental to keep it. There's
nothin' derogatory in th' use o' th' word "cuckoo",
is there?

PETER (tearfully). It's not th' word; it's th' way he
says it; he never says it straight out, but murmurs
it with curious quiverin' ripples, like variations
on a flute!

FLUTHER. Ah, what odds if he gave it with variations
on a thrombone! (To MRS. GOGAN) What's yours goin'
to be, ma'am?

MRS. GOGAN. Ah, a half o' malt, Fluther.

FLUTHER (to BARMAN). Three halves, Tommy.

(The BARMAN brings the drinks.)

MRS. GOGAN (drinking). The Foresthers' is a gorgeous
dhress! I don't think I've seen nicer, mind you, in
a pantomime. . . . Th' loveliest part of th' dhress,
I think, is th' osthrichess plume. . . . When yous
are goin' along, an' I see them wavin' an' nodding
an' waggin', I seem to be lookin' at each of yous
hangin' at th' end of a rope, your eyes bulgin' an'
your legs twistin' an jerkin', gaspin' an' gaspin'
for breath while yous are thryin' to die for Ireland!

FLUTHER. If any o' them is hangin' at the end of a
rope, it won't be for Ireland!

PATER. Are you goin' to start th' young Covey's game
o' proddin' an' twartin' a man? There's not many
that's talkin' can say that for twenty-five years he
never missed a pilgrimage to Bodenstown!

FLUTHER. You're always blowin' about goin' to Bodenstown. D'ye think no one but yourself ever went to
Bodenstown?

PETER (plaintively). I'm not blowin' about it; but

235

there's not a year that I go there but I pluck a leaf
off Tone's grave, an' this very day me prayer-book is
nearly full of them.

FLUTHER (scornfully). Then Fluther has a vice versa
opinion of them that put ivy leaves into their prayer-
books, scabbin' it on th' clergy, an' thryin' to out-
do th' haloes o' th' saints be lookin' as if he was
wearin' around his head a glittherin' aroree boree
allis! (Fiercely) Sure, I don't care a damn if you
slep' in Bodenstown! You can take your breakfast,
dinner, an' tea on th' grave in Bodenstown, if you
like, for Fluther!

MRS. GOGAN. Oh, don't start a fight, boys, for God's
sake; I was only sayin' what a nice costume it is--
nicer than th' kilts, for, God forgive me, I always
think th' kilts is hardly decent.

FLUTHER. Ah, sure, when you'd look at him, you'd
wondher whether th' man was makin' fun o' th' costume, or th' costume was makin' fun o' the man!

BARMAN. Now, then, thry to speak asy, will yous? We
don't want no shoutin' here.

(THE COVEY followed by BESSIE BURGESS comes in. They
go over to the opposite end of the counter, and direct their gaze on the other group.)

THE COVEY (to BARMAN). Two glasses o' malt.

PETER. There he is, now; I knew he wouldn't be long
till he folleyed me in.

BESSIE (speaking to THE COVEY, but really at the other
party). I can't for th' life o' me undherstand how
they can call themselves Catholics, when they won't
lift a finger to help poor little Catholic Belgium.

MRS. GOGAN (raising her voice). What about poor little
Catholic Ireland?

BESSIE (over to MRS. GOGAN). You mind your own business, ma'am, an' stupefy your foolishness be gettin'
dhrunk.

PETER (anxiously). Take no notice of her; pay no attention to her. She's just tormentin' herself
towards havin' a row with somebody.

BESSIE. There's a storm of anger tossin' in me heart,
thinkin' of all th' poor Tommies, an' with them me
own son, dhrenched in water an' soaked in blood,
gropin' their way to a shattherin' death, in a shower
o' shells! Young men with th' sunny lust o' life
beamin' in them, layin' down their white bodies,
shredded into torn an' bloody pieces, on th' althar
that God Himself has built for th' sacrifice of
heroes!

MRS. GOGAN. Isn't it a nice thing to have to be

listenin' to a lassie an' hangin' our heads in a dead
silence, knowin' that some persons think more of a
ball of malt than they do of th' blessed saints.
FLUTHER. Whisht; she's always dangerous an' derogatory
when she's well oiled. Th' safest way to hindher her
from havin' any enjoyment out of her spite, is to dip
our thoughts into the fact of her bein' a female person that has moved out of th' sight of ordinary sensible people.
BESSIE. To look at some o' th' women that's knockin'
about, now, is a thing to make a body sigh. . . A
woman on her own, dhrinkin' with a bevy o' men, is
hardly an example to her sex. . . . . A woman dhrinkin'
with a woman is one thing, an' a woman dhrinkin' with
herself is still a woman--flappers may be put in
another category altogether--but a middle-aged married woman makin' herself th' centre of a circle of
men is as a woman that is loud an' stubborn, whose
feet abideth not in her own house.
THE COVEY (to BESSIE). When I think of all th' problems in front o' th' workers, it makes me sick to be
lookin' at oul' codgers goin' about dhressed up like
green-accoutred figures gone asthray out of a toy-
shop!
PETER. Gracious God, give me patience to be listenin'
to that blasted young Covey proddin' at me from over
at th' other end of th' shop!
MRS. GOGAN (dipping her finger in the whisky, and
moistening with it the lips of her baby). Cissie
Gogan's a woman livin' for nigh on twenty-five years
in her own room, an' beyond biddin' th' time o' day
to her neighbours, never yet as much as nodded her
head in th' direction of other people's business,
while she knows some as are never content unless
they're standin' senthry over other people's doin's!

(BESSIE is about to reply, when the tall, dark figure
is again silhouetted against the window, and the
voice of the speaker is heard speaking passionately.)

VOICE OF SPEAKER. The last sixteen months have been
the most glorious in the history of Europe. Heroism
has come back to the earth. War is a terrible thing,
but war is not an evil thing. People in Ireland
dread war because they do not know it. Ireland has
not known the exhilaration of war for over a hundred
years. When war comes to Ireland she must welcome

237

it as she would welcome the Angel of God![17]

(The figure passes out of sight and hearing.)

THE COVEY (towards all present). Dope, dope. There's
only one war worth havin': th' war for th' economic
emancipation of th' proletariat.

BESSIE. They may crow away out o' them; but it ud be
fitther for some o' them to mend their ways, an'
cease from havin' scouts out watchin' for th' comin'
of th' Saint Vincent de Paul man, for fear they'd be
nailed lowerin' a pint of beer, mockin' th' man with
an angel face, shinin' with th' glamour of deceit an'
lies!

MRS. GOGAN. An' a certain lassie standin' stiff behind
her own door with her ears cocked listenin' to what's
being said, stuffed till she's sthrained with envy of
a neighbour thryin' for a few little things that may
be got be hard sthrivin' to keep up to th' letther
an' th' law, an' th' practices of th' Church!

PETER (to MRS. GOGAN). If I was you, Mrs. Gogan, I'd
parry her jabbin' remarks be a powerful silence
that'll keep her tantalizin' words from penethratin'
into your feelin's. It's always betther to leave
these people to th' vengeance o' God!

BESSIE. Bessie Burgess doesn't put up to know much,
never havin' a swaggerin' mind, thanks be to God, but
goin' on packin' up knowledge accordin' to her conscience: precept upon precept, line upon line; here
here a little, an' there a little. But (with a passionate swing of her shawl), thanks be to Christ, she
knows when she was got, where she was got, an' how
she was got; while there's some she knows, decoratin'
their finger with a well-polished weddin' ring, would
be hard put to it if they were assed to show their
weddin' lines!

MRS. GOGAN (plunging out into the centre of the floor
in a wild tempest of hysterical rage). Y' oul' rip
of a blasted liar, me weddin' ring's been well earned
be twenty years be th' side o' me husband, now takin'
his rest in heaven, married to me be Father Dempsey,
in th' Chapel o' Saint Jude's, in th' Christmas Week
of eighteen hundhred an' ninety-five; an' any kid,
livin' or dead, that Jinnie Gogan's had since, was
got between th' bordhers of th' Ten Commandments!
. . . An' that's more than some o' you can say that

17. These lines are taken from a speech delivered by
P. H. Pearse entitled "Peace and the Gael," which
was published in December, 1915.

are kep' from th' dhread o' desthruction be a few
drowsy virtues, that th' first whisper of temptation
lulls into a sleep, that'll know one sin from another
only on th' day of their last anointin', an' that use
th' innocent light o' th' shinin' stars to dip into
th' sins of a night's diversion!
BESSIE (jumping out to face MRS. GOGAN, and bringing
the palms of her hands together in sharp claps to
emphasize her remarks). Liar to you, too, ma'am,
y' oul' hardened thresspasser on other people's good
nature, wizenin' up your soul in th' arts o' dodg-
eries, till every dhrop of respectability in a female
is dhried up in her, lookin' at your ready-made
manoeuverin' with th' menkind!
BARMAN. Here, there; here, there; speak asy there. No
rowin' here, no rowin' here, now.
FLUTHER (trying to calm MRS. GOGAN). Now, Jinnie, Jinnie, it's a derogatory thing to be smirchin' a night
like this with a row; it's rompin' with th' feelin's
of hope we ought to be, instead o' being vice versa! [18]
PETER (trying to quiet BESSIE). I'm terribly dawny, [18]
Mrs. Burgess, an' a fight leaves me weak for a long
time aftherwards. . . . Please, Mrs. Burgess, before
there's damage done, thry to have a little respect
for yourself.
BESSIE (with a push of her hand that sends PETER tot-
tering to the end of the shop). G'way, you little
sermonizing, little yella-faced, little consequential,
little pudgy, little bum, you!
MRS. GOGAN (screaming). Fluther, leggo! I'm not goin'
to keep an unresistin' silence, an' her scattherin'
her festherin' words in me face, stirrin' up every
dhrop of decency in a respectable female, with her
restless rally o' lies that would make a saint say
his prayer backwards!
BESSIE (shouting). Ah, everybody knows well that th'
best charity that can be shown to you is to hide th'
thruth as much as our thrue worship of God Almighty
will allow us!
MRS. GOGAN (frantically). Here, houl' th' kid, one o'
yous; houl' th' kid for a minute! There's nothin'
for it but to show this lassie a lesson or two. . . .
(To PETER) Here, houl' th' kid, you. (Before PETER
is aware of it, she places the infant in his arms.)
MRS. GOGAN (to BESSIE, standing before her in a fighting attitude). Come on, now, me loyal lassie, dyin'
with grief for little Catholic Belgium! When Jinnie
Gogan's done with you, you'll have a little leisure

18. Wretched; miserable; in poor health; puny; small.

lyin' down to think an' pray for your king an'
counthry!

BARMAN (coming from behind the counter, getting between
the women, and proceeding to push them towards the
door). Here, now, since yous can't have a little
friendly argument quietly, you'll get out o' this
place in quick time. Go on, an' settle your differences somewhere else--I don't want to have another
endorsement on me license.

PETER (anxiously, over to MRS. GOGAN). Here, take your
kid back, ower this. How nicely I was picked, now,
for it to be plumped into me arms!

THE COVEY. She knew who she was givin' it to, maybe.

PETER (hotly to THE COVEY). Now, I'm givin' you fair
warnin', me young Covey, to quit firin' your jibes
an' jeers at me. . . . For one o' these days, I'll
run out in front o' God Almighty an' take your sacred
life!

BARMAN (pushing BESSIE out after MRS. GOGAN). Go on,
now; out you go.

BESSIE (as she goes out). If you think, me lassie,
that Bessie Burgess has an untidy conscience, she'll
soon show you to th' differ!

PETER (leaving the baby down on the floor). Ay, be
Jasus, wait there, till I give her back her youngster!
(He runs to the door.) Ay, there, ay! (He comes
back.) There, she's afther goin' without her kid.
What are we goin' to do with it, now?

THE COVEY. What are we goin' to do with it? Bring it
outside an' show everybody what you're afther findin'!

PETER (in a panic to Fluther). Pick it up, you,
Fluther, an' run afther her with it, will you?

FLUTHER. What d'ye take Fluther for? You must think
Fluther's a right gom.[19] D'ye think Fluther's like
yourself, destitute of a titther of undherstandin'?

BARMAN (imperatively to PETER). Take it up, man, an'
run our afther her with it, before she's gone too
far. You're not goin' to leave th' bloody thing
here, are you?

PETER (plaintively, as he lifts up the baby). Well,
God Almighty, give me patience with all th' scorners,
tormentors, an' twarters that are always an' ever
thryin' to goad me into prayin' for their blindin'
an' blastin' an' burnin' in th' world to come!

(He goes out.)


19. A shortened version of gommul, gommeril, or
gommula; all meaning a simple-minded fellow, a
half fool.

240

FLUTHER. God, it's a relief to get rid o' that crowd.
Women is terrible when they start to fight. There's
no holdin' them back. (To THE COVEY) Are you goin'
to have anything?
THE COVEY. Ah, I don't mind if I have another half.
FLUTHER (to BARMAN). Two more, Tommy, me son.

(The BARMAN gets the drinks.)

FLUTHER. You know, there's no conthrollin' a woman
when she loses her head.

(ROSIE enters and goes over to the counter on the side
nearest to Fluther.)

ROSIE (to BARMAN). Divil a use o' havin' a thrim little
leg on a night like this; things was never worse.
. . . Give us a half till to-morrow, Tom, duckey.
BARMAN (coldly). No more to-night, Rosie; you owe me
for three already.
ROSIE (combatively). You'll be paid, won't you?
BARMAN. I hope so.
ROSIE. You hope so! Is that th' way with you, now?
FLUTHER (to BARMAN). Give her one; it'll be all right.
ROSIE (clapping Fluther on the back). Oul' sport!
FLUTHER. Th' meetin' should be soon over, now.
THE COVEY. Th' sooner th' betther. It's all a lot o'
blasted nonsense, comrade.
FLUTHER. Oh, I wouldn't say it was all nonsense.
Afther all, Fluther can remember th' time, an' him
only a dawny chiselur, bein' taught at his mother's
knee to be faithful to th' Shan Van Vok[20]!
THE COVEY. That's all dope, comrade; th' sort o' thing
that workers are fed on be th' Boorzwawzee.
FLUTHER (a little sharply). What's all dope? Though
I'm sayin' it that shouldn't: (catching his cheek
with his hand, and pulling down the flesh from the
eye) d'ye see that mark there, undher me eye? . . .
(Thrusting his head forward towards ROSIE) Feel that
dint in th' middle o' me nut!
ROSIE (rubbing Fluther's head, and winking at THE
COVEY). My God, there's a holla!
FLUTHER (putting on his hat with quiet pride). A skelp
from a bobby's baton at a Labour meetin' in th'
Phoenix Park!
THE COVEY. He must ha' hitten you in mistake. I don't
know what you ever done for th' Labour movement.


20. The Poor Old Woman;--an allegorical name for
Ireland.

241

FLUTHER (loudly). D'ye not? Maybe, then, I done as
    much, an' know as much about th' Labour movement as
    th' chancers[21] that are blowin' about it!
BARMAN. Speak easy, Fluther, thry to speak easy.
THE COVEY. There's no necessity to get excited about
    it comrade.
FLUTHER (more loudly). Excited? Who's gettin' excited?
    There's no one gettin' excited! It would take some-
    thing more than a thing like you to flutther a feather
    o' Fluther. Blatherin', an', when all is said, you
    know as much as th' rest in th' wind up!
THE COVEY. Well, let us put it to th' test, then, an'
    see what you know about th' Labour movement: what's
    the mechanism of exchange?
FLUTHER (roaring, because he feels he is beaten). How
    th' hell do I know what it is? There's nothin' about
    that in th' rules of our Thrades Union!
BARMAN. For God's sake, thry to speak easy, Fluther.
THE COVEY. What does Karl Marx say about th' Relation
    of Value to th' Cost o' Production?
FLUTHER (angrily). What th' hell do I care what he
    says? I'm Irishman enough not to lose me head be
    follyin' foreigners!
BARMAN. Speak easy, Fluther.
THE COVEY. It's only waste o' time talkin' to you,
    comrade.
FLUTHER. Don't be comradin' me, mate. I'd be on me
    last legs if I wanted you for a comrade.
ROSIE (to THE COVEY). It seems a highly rediculous
    thing to hear a thing that's only an inch or two away
    from a kid, swingin' heavy words about he doesn't
    know th' meanin' of, an' uppishly thrying to down a
    man like Misther Fluther here, that's well flavoured
    in th' knowledge of th' world he's livin' in.
THE COVEY (savagely to ROSIE). Nobody's askin' you to
    be buttin' in with your prate. . . . I have you well
    taped, me lassie. . . . Just you keep your opinions
    for your own place. . . . It'll be a long time before
    th' Covey takes any insthructions or reprimandin'
    from a prostitute!
ROSIE (wild with humiliation). You louse, you louse,
    you! . . . You're no man. . . . You're no man . . .
    I'm a woman, anyhow, an' if I'm a prostitute aself,
    I have me feelin's. . . . Thryin' to put his arm
    around me a minute ago, an' givin' me th' glad eye,
    th' little wrigglin' lump o' desolation turns on me
    now, because he saw there was nothin' doin'. . . .
    You louse, you! If I was a man, or you were a woman,

21. Liars.

242

I'd bate th' puss o' you!

BARMAN. Ay, Rosie, ay! You'll have to shut your
mouth altogether, if you can't learn to speak easy!

FLUTHER (to ROSIE). Houl' on there, Rosie; houl' on
there. There's no necessity to flutther yourself
when you're with Fluther. . . . Any lady that's in
th' company of Fluther is goin' to get a fair hunt.
. . . This is outside your province. . . . I'm not
goin' to let you demean yourself be talkin' to a
tittherin' chancer. . . . Leave this to Fluther--this
is a man's job. (To THE COVEY) Now, if you've anything to say, say it to Fluther, an', let me tell
you, you're not goin' to be pass-remarkable to any
lady in my company.

THE COVEY. Sure I don't care if you were runnin' all
night afther your Mary o' th' Curlin' Hair, but, when
you start tellin' luscious lies about what you done
for th' Labour movement, it's nearly time to show
y' up!

FLUTHER (fiercely). Is it you show Fluther up? G'way,
man, I'd beat two o' you before me breakfast!

THE COVEY (contemptuously). Tell us where you bury
your dead, will you?

FLUTHER (with his face stuck into the face of THE
COVEY). Sing a little less on th' high note, or,
when I'm done with you, you'll put a Christianable
consthruction on things, I'm tellin' you!

THE COVEY. You're a big fella, you are.

FLUTHER (tapping THE COVEY threateningly on the shoulder). Now, you're temptin' Providence when you're
temptin' Fluther!

THE COVEY (losing his temper, and bawling). Easy with
them hands, there, easy with them hands! You're
startin' to take a little risk when you commence to
paw the Covey!

(FLUTHER suddenly springs into the middle of the shop,
flings his hat into the corner, whips off his coat,
and begins to paw the air.)

FLUTHER (roaring at the top of his voice). Come on,
come on, you lowser; put your mits up now, if there's
a man's blood in you! Be God, in a few minutes you'll
see some snots flyin' around, I'm telling you. . . .
When Fluther's done with you, you'll have a vice versa
opinion of him! Come on, now, come on!

BARMAN (running from behind the counter and catching
hold of THE COVEY). Here, out you go, me little
bowsey. Because you got a couple o' halves you think
you can act as you like. (He pushes THE COVEY to the
door) Fluther's a friend o' mine, an' I'll not have

him insulted.

THE COVEY (struggling with the BARMAN). Ay, leggo, leggo there; fair hunt, give a man a fair hunt! One minute with him is all I ask; one minute alone with him, while you're runnin' for th' priest an' th' doctor.

FLUTHER (to the BARMAN). Let him go, let him go, Tom: let him open th' door to sudden death if he wants to!

BARMAN (to THE COVEY). Go on, out you go an' do th' bowsey somewhere else. (He pushes THE COVEY out and comes back.)

ROSIE (getting FLUTHER'S hat as he is putting on his coat). Be God, you put th' fear o' God in his heart that time! I thought you'd have to be dug out of him. . . . Th' way you lepped out without any of your fancy side-steppin'! "Men like Fluther," say I to meself, "is gettin' scarce nowadays."

FLUTHER (with proud complacency). I wasn't goin' to let meself be malignified by a chancer. . . . He got a little bit too derogatory for Fluther. . . . Be God, to think of a cur like that comin' to talk to a man like me!

ROSIE (fixing on his hat). Did j'ever!

FLUTHER. He's lucky he got off safe. I hit a man last week, Rosie, an' he's fallin' yet!

ROSIE. Sure, you'd ha' broken him in two if you'd ha' hitten him one clatther!

FLUTHER (amorously, putting his arm around ROSIE). Come on into th' snug, me little darlin', an' we'll have a few dhrinks before I see you home.

ROSIE. Oh, Fluther, I'm afraid you're a terrible man for th' women.

(They go into the snug as CLITHEROE, CAPTAIN BRENNAN, and LIEUT. LANGON of the Irish Volunteers enter hurriedly. CAPTAIN BRENNAN carries the banner of The Plough and the Stars, and LIEUT. LANGON a green, white, and orange Tri-colour. They are in a state of emotional excitement. Their faces are flushed and their eyes sparkle; they speak rapidly, as if unaware of the meaning of what they said. They have been mesmerized by the fervency of the speeches.)

CLITHEROE (almost pantingly). Three glasses o' port!

(The BARMAN brings the drinks.)

CAPT. BRENNAN. We won't have long to wait now.

LIEUT. LANGON. Th' time is rotten ripe for revolution.

CLITHEROE. You have a mother, Langon.

LIEUT. LANGON. Ireland is greater than a mother.

CAPT. BRENNAN. You have a wife, Clitheroe.
CLITHEROE. Ireland is greater than a wife.
LIEUT. LANGON. Th' time for Ireland's battle is now--
th' place for Ireland's battle is here.

(The tall, dark figure again is silhouetted against the
window. The three men pause and listen.)

VOICE OF THE MAN. Our foes are strong, but strong as
they are, they cannot undo the miracles of God, who
ripens in the heart of young men the seeds sown by
the young men of a former generation. They think
they have pacified Ireland; think they have foreseen
everything; think they have provided against everything; but the fools, the fools, the fools!--they
have left us our Fenian dead, and, while Ireland
holds these graves, Ireland, unfree, shall never be
at peace![22]
CAPT. BRENNAN (catching up The Plough and the Stars).
Imprisonment for th' Independence of Ireland!
LIEUT. LANGON (catching up the Tri-colour). Wounds for
th' Independence of Ireland!
CLITHEROE. Death for th' Independence of Ireland!
THE THREE (together). So help us God!

(They drink. A bugle blows the Assembly. They hurry
out. A pause. FLUTHER and ROSIE come out of the
snug; ROSIE is linking FLUTHER, who is a little drunk.
Both are in a merry mood.)

ROSIE. Come on home, ower o' that, man. Are you
afraid or what? Are you goin' to come home, or are
you not?
FLUTHER. Of course I'm goin' home. What ud ail me
that I wouldn't go?
ROSIE (lovingly). Come on, then, oul' sport.
OFFICER'S VOICE (giving command outside). Irish Volun-
teers, by th' right, quick march!
ROSIE (putting her arm round FLUTHER and singing):
I once had a lover, a tailor, but he could do nothin'
for me,
An' then I fell in with a sailor as strong an' as
wild as th' sea.
We cuddled an' kissed with devotion, till th' night
from th' mornin' had fled;
An' there, to our joy, a bright bouncin' boy
Was dancin' a jig in th' bed!

22. These lines are from a delivery made by P.H. Pearse
at the graveside of O'Donovan Rossa, an Irish rebel.

245

Dancin' a jig in th' bed, an' bawlin' for butther an'
    bread.
An' there, to our joy, a bright bouncin' boy
Was dancin' a jig in th' bed!

(They go out with their arms round each other.)

CLITHEROE'S VOICE (in command outside). Dublin, Bat-
    talion of the Irish Citizen Army, by th' right, quick
    march!


                        CURTAIN



                        Act III

The corner house in a street of tenements; it is the
home of the Clitheroes. The house is a long, gaunt,
five-story tenement; its brick front is chipped and
scarred with age and neglect. The wide and heavy hall
door, flanked by two pillars, has a look of having been
charred by a fire in the distant past. The door lurches
a little to one side, disjointed by the continual and
reckless banging when it is being closed by most of the
residents. The diamond-paned fanlight is destitute of
a single pane, the framework alone remaining. The windows, except the two looking into the front parlour
(Clitheroe's room), are grimy, and are draped with
fluttering and soiled fragments of lace curtains. The
front parlour windows are hung with rich, comparatively,
casement cloth. Five stone steps lead from the door to
the path on the street. Branching on each side are
railings to prevent people from falling into the area.
At the left corner of the house runs a narrow lane, bi-
secting the street, and connecting it with another of
the same kind. At the corner of the lane is a street
lamp.

As the house is revealed, Mrs. Gogan is seen helping
Mollser to a chair, which stands on the path beside
the railings, at the left side of the steps. She then
wraps a shawl around Mollser's shoulders. It is some
months later.

MRS. GOGAN (arranging shawl around MOLLSER). Th' sun'll
    do you all th' good in th' world. A few more weeks
    o' this weather, an' there's no knowin' how well
    you'll be. . . . Are you comfy, now?

                        246

MOLLSER (weakly and wearily). Yis, ma; I'm all right.
MRS. GOGAN. How are you feelin'?
MOLLSER. Betther, ma, betther. If th' horrible sinkin'
feelin' ud go, I'd be all right.
MRS. GOGAN. Ah, I wouldn't put much pass on that. Your
stomach maybe's out of ordher. . . . Is th' poor
breathin' any betther, d'ye think?
MOLLSER. Yis, yis, ma; a lot betther.
MRS. GOGAN. Well, that's somethin' anyhow. . . . With
th' help o' God, you'll be on th' mend from this out.
. . . D'your legs feel any sthronger undher you, d'ye
think?
MOLLSER (irritably). I can't tell, ma. I think so.
. . . A little.
MRS. GOGAN. Well, a little aself is somethin'. . . .
I thought I heard you coughin' a little more than
usual last night. . . . D'ye think you were?
MOLLSER. I wasn't, ma, I wasn't.
MRS. GOGAN. I thought I heard you, for I was kep'
awake all night with th' shootin'. An' thinkin' o'
that madman, Fluther, runnin' about through th' night
lookin' for Nora Clitheroe to bring her back when he
heard she'd gone to folly her husband, an' in dhread
any minute he might come staggerin' in covered with
bandages, splashed all over with th' red of his own
blood, an' givin' us barely time to bring th' priest
to hear th' last whisper of his final confession, as
his soul was passin' through th' dark doorway o'
death into th' way o' th' wondherin dead. . . . You
don't feel cold, do you?
MOLLSER. No, ma; I'm all right.
MRS. GOGAN. Keep your chest well covered, for that's
th' delicate spot in you . . . if there's any danger,
I'll whip you in again. . . . (Looking up the street)
Oh, here's th' Covey an' oul' Pether hurryin' along.
God Almighty, sthrange things is happenin' when them
two is pullin' together.

(THE COVEY and PETER come in, breathless and excited.)

MRS. GOGAN (to the two men). Were yous far up th'town?
Did yous see any sign o' Fluther or Nora? How is
things lookin'? I hear they're blazin' away out o'
th' G.P.O.[23] That th' Tommies[24] is sthretched in
heaps around Nelson's Pillar an' th' Parnell Statue,
an' that th' pavin' sets in O'Connell Street is
nearly covered be pools o' blood.


23. General Post Office.
24. British soldiers.

PETER. We seen no sign o' Nora or Fluther anywhere.
MRS. GOGAN. We should ha' held her back be main force
   from goin' to look for her husband. . . . God knows
   what's happened to her--I'm always seein' her
   stretched on her back in some hospital, moanin' with
   th' pain of a bullet in her vitals, an' nuns thryin'
   to get her to take a last look at th' crucifix!
THE COVEY. We can do nothin'. You can't stick your
   nose into O'Connell Street, an' Tyler's is on fire.
PETER. An' we seen th' Lancers[25]--
THE COVEY (interrupting). Throttin' along, heads in
   th' air; spurs an' sabres jinglin', an' lances quiverin', an' lookin' as if they were assin' themselves,
   "Where's these blighters, till we get a prod at them?"
   when there was a volley from th' Post Office that
   stretched half o' them, an' sent th' rest gallopin'
   away wondherin' how far they'd have to go before
   they'd feel safe.
PETER (rubbing his hands). "Damn it," says I to meself, "this looks like business!"
THE COVEY. An' then out comes General Pearse[26] an' his
   staff, an' standin' in th' middle o' th' street, he
   reads th' Proclamation.
MRS. GOGAN. What proclamation?
PETER. Declarin' an Irish Republic.
MRS. GOGAN. Go to God!
PETER. The gunboat Helga's shellin' Liberty Hall, an'
   I hear the people livin' on th' quays had to crawl
   on their bellies to Mass with th' bullets that were
   flyin' around from Boland's Mills.
MRS. GOGAN. God bless us, what's goin' to be th' end
   of it all!
BESSIE (looking out of the top window). Maybe yous are
   satisfied now; maybe yous are satisfied now. Go on
   an' get guns if yous are men--Johnny get your gun,
   get your gun, get your gun! Yous are all nicely
   shanghaied[27] now; th' boyo hasn't a sword on his
   thigh now! Oh, yous are all nicely shanghaied now!
MRS. GOGAN (warningly to PETER and THE COVEY).
   S-s-sh, don't answer her. She's th' right oul'


25. Light cavalry soldiers; especially a regiment officially called Lancers.
26. Patrick Henry Pearse--Irish poet and political
   leader who was executed--1879-1916.
27. Literally: Drugged, intoxicated, or rendered in-
   sensible and shipped as a sailor; hence, to bring
   by combined deceit and coercion.

248

Orange[28] bitch!  She's been chantin' "Rule, Brittan-
nia" all th' mornin'.
PETER.  I hope Fluther hasn't met with any accident,
he's such a wild card.
MRS. GOGAN.  God grant it; but last night I dreamt I
seen gettin' carried into th' house a sthretcher with
a figure lyin' on it, stiff an' still, dhressed in
th' habit of Saint Francis.  An, then, I heard th'
murmurs of a crowd no one could see sayin' th' litany
for th' dead; an' then it got so dark that nothin'
was seen but th' white face of th' corpse, gleamin'
like a white wather-lily floatin' on th' top of a
dark lake.  Then a tiny whisper thrickled into me
ear, sayin' "Isn't the face very like th' face o'
Fluther?" an' then, with a thremblin' flutther, th'
dead lips opened, an', although I couldn't hear, I
knew they were sayin', "Poor oul' Fluther, afther
havin' handed in his gun at last, his shakin' soul
moored in th' place where th' wicked are at rest an'
th' weary cease from throublin'."
PETER (who has put on a pair of spectacles, and has been
looking down the street).  Here they are, be God,
here they are; just afther turnin' th' corner--Nora
an' Fluther!
THE COVEY.  She must be wounded or something--he seems
to be carryin' her.

(FLUTHER and NORA enter.  FLUTHER has his arm around
her and is half leading, half carrying her in.  Her
eyes are dim and hollow, her face pale and strained-
looking; her hair is tossed, and her clothes are
dusty.)

MRS. GOGAN (running over to them).  God bless us, is it
wounded y'are, Mrs. Clitheroe, or what?
FLUTHER.  Ah, she's all right, Mrs. Gogan; only worn
out from thravellin' an' want o' sleep.  A night's
rest, now, an' she'll be as fit as a fiddle.  Bring
her in, an' make her lie down.
MRS. GOGAN (to NORA).  Did you hear e'er a whisper o'
Mr. Clitheroe?
NORA (wearily).  I could find him nowhere, Mrs. Gogan.


28. A reference to a secret society organized in the
    north of Ireland in 1795, the professed objects of
    which are the defense of the reigning sovereign of
    Great Britain, the support of the Protestant reli-
    gion, the maintainence of the laws of the Kingdom,
    etc.;--so called in honor of William, Prince of
    Orange, who became William III of England.

249

None o' them would tell me where he was. They told
me I shamed my husband an' th' women of Ireland be
carryin' on as I was. . . . They said th' women must
learn to be brave an' cease to be cowardly. . . . Me
who risked more for love than they would risk for
hate. . . . (Raising her voice in hysterical protest)
My Jack will be killed, my Jack will be killed!. . .
He is to be butchered as a sacrifice to th' dead!
BESSIE (from upper window). Yous are all nicely shanghaied now! Sorra mend th' lasses that have been
kissin' an' cuddlin' their boys into th' sheddin' of
blood! . . . Fillin' their minds with fairy tales
that had no beginnin', but, please God, 'll have a
bloody quick endin'! . . . Stabbin' in th' back th'
men that are dyin' in th' threnches for them! It's
a bad thing for any one that thries to jilt th' Ten
Commandments, for judgements are prepared for scorners an' sthripes for th' back o' fools! (Going away
from window as she sings:)
    Rule, Britannia, Britannia rules th' waves,
    Britons never, never, never shall be slaves!
FLUTHER (with a roar up at the window). Y'ignorant
oul' throllope, you!
MRS. GOGAN (to NORA). He'll come home safe enough to
you, you'll find, Mrs. Clitheroe; afther all, there's
a power o' women that's handed over sons an' husbands
to take a runnin' risk in th' fight they're wagin'.
NORA. I can't help thinkin' every shot fired'll be
fired at Jack, an' every shot fired at Jack'll be
fired at me. What do I care for th' others? I can
think only of me own self. . . . An' there's no woman
gives a son or a husband to be killed--if they say
it, they're lyin', lyin', against God, Nature, an'
against themselves! . . . One blasted hussy at a barricade told me to go home an' not be thryin' to dis-
hearten th' men. . . . That I wasn't worthy to bear a
son to a man that was out fightin' for freedom. . . .
I clawed at her, an' smashed her in th' face till we
were separated. . . . I was pushed down th' street,
an' I cursed them--cursed the rebel ruffians an'
Volunteers that had dhragged me ravin' mad into th'
sthreets to seek me husband!
PETER. You'll have to have patience, Nora. We all
have to put up with twarthers an' tormentors in this
world.
THE COVEY. If they were fightin' for anything worth
while, I wouldn't mind.
FLUTHER (to NORA). Nothin' derogatory'll happen to Mr.
Clitheroe. You'll find, now, in th' finish up it'll
be vice versa.
NORA. Oh, I know that wherever he is, he's thinkin' of

wantin' to be with me.  I know he's longin' to be
passin' his hand through me hair, to be caressin' me
neck, to fondle me hand an' to feel me kisses clingin'
to his mouth. . . . An' he stands wherever he is because he's brave?  (Vehemently) No, but because he's
a coward, a coward, a coward!
MRS. GOGAN.  Oh, they're not cowards anyway.
NORA (with denunciatory anger).  I tell you they're
afraid to say they're afraid! . . . Oh, I saw it, I
saw it, Mrs. Gogan. . . . At th' barricade in North
King Street I saw fear glowin' in all their eyes. . .
An' in th' middle o' th' sthreet was somethin' hud-
dled up in a horrible tangled heap. . . . His face
was jammed again th' stones, an' his arm was twisted
round his back. . . . An' every twist of his body was
a cry against th' terrible thing that had happened to
him. . . . An' I saw they were afraid to look at it.
. . . An' some o' them laughed at me, but th' laugh
was a frightened one. . . . An' some o' them shouted
at me, but th' shout had in it th' shiver o' fear.
. . . I tell you they were afraid, afraid, afraid!
MRS. GOGAN (leading her towards the house).  Come on
in, dear.  If you'd been a little longer together,
th' wrench asundher wouldn't have been so sharp.
NORA.  Th' agony I'm in since he left me has thrust
away every rough thing he done, an' every unkind word
he spoke; only th' blossoms that grew out of our
lives are before me now; shakin' their colours before
me face, an' breathin' their sweet scent on every
thought springin' up in me mind, till, sometimes, Mrs.
Gogan, sometimes I think I'm goin' mad!
MRS. GOGAN.  You'll be a lot betther when you have a
little lie down.
NORA (turning towards FLUTHER as she is going in). I
don't know what I'd have done, only for Fluther.  I'd
have been lyin' in th' streets, only for him. . . .
(As she goes in) They have dhriven away th' little
happiness life had to spare for me.  He has gone from
me for ever, for ever. . . . Oh, Jack, Jack, Jack!

(She is led in by MRS. GOGAN as BESSIE comes out with a
shawl around her shoulders.  She passes by them with
her head in the air.  When they have gone in, she
gives a mug of milk to MOLLSER silently.)

FLUTHER.  Which of yous has th' tossers[29]?
THE COVEY.  I have.
BESSIE (as she is passing them to go down the street).

29. Pennies used in pitch and toss.

251

You an' your Leadhers an' their sham-battle soldiers
has landed a body in a nice way, havin' to go an' fer-
ret out a bit o' bread God knows where. . . . Why
aren't yous in th' G.P.O. if yous are men? It's paler
an! paler yous are gettin'. . . . A lot o' vipers,
that's what th' Irish people is! (She goes out.)
FLUTHER. Never mind her. . . . (To THE COVEY) Make a
start an' keep us from th' sin o' idleness. (To
MOLLSER) Well, how are you to-day, Mollser, oul' son?
What are you dhrinkin', milk?
MOLLSER. Grand, Fluther, grand, thanks. Yis, milk.
FLUTHER. You couldn't get a betther thing down you.
. . . This turn-up has done one good thing, anyhow;
you can't get dhrink anywhere, an' if it lasts a week,
I'll be so used to it that I won't think of a pint.
THE COVEY (who has taken from his pocket two worn coins
and a thin strip of wood about four inches long).
What's th' bettin'?
PETER. Heads, a juice.30
FLUTHER. Harps, a tanner.31

(THE COVEY places the coins on the strip of wood, and
flips them up into the air. As they jingle on the
ground the distant boom of a big gun is heard. They
stand for a moment listening.)

FLUTHER. What th' hell's that?
THE COVEY. It's like th' boom of a big gun!
FLUTHER. Surely to God they're not goin' to use artil-
lery on us?
THE COVEY (scornfully). Not goin'! (Vehemently)
Wouldn't they use anything on us, man.
FLUTHER. Aw, holy Christ, that's not playin' th' game!
PETER (plaintively). What would happen if a shell
landed here now?
THE COVEY (ironically). You'd be off to heaven in a
fiery chariot.
PETER. In spite of all th' warnin's that's ringin'
around us, are you goin' to start your pickin' at me
again?
FLUTHER. Go on, toss them again, toss them again. . . .
Harps, a tanner.
PETER. Heads, a juice.

(THE COVEY tosses the coins.)

FLUTHER (as the coins fall). Let them roll, let them

30. A drink.
31. A sixpence.

252

roll.  Heads, be God!

(BESSIE runs in excitedly.  She has a new hat on her
head, a fox fur round her neck over her shawl, three
umbrellas under her right arm, and a box of biscuits
under her left.  She speaks rapidly and breathlessly.)

BESSIE.  They're breakin' into th' shops, they're
breakin' into th' shops!  Smashin' th' windows, bat-
therin' in th' doors, an' whippin' away everything!
An' th' Volunteers is firin' on them.  I seen two men
an' a lassie pushin' a piano down th' sthreet, an'
th' sweat rollin' off them thryin' to get it up on
th' pavement; an' an oul' wan that must ha' been
seventy lookin' as if she'd dhrop every minute with
th' dint o' heart beatin', thryin' to pull a big
double bed out of a broken shop-window!  I was goin'
to wait till I dhressed meself from th' skin out.
MOLLSER (to BESSIE, as she is going in).  Help me in,
Bessie; I'm feelin' curious.

(BESSIE leaves the looted things in the house, and,
rapidly returning, helps MOLLSER in.)

THE COVEY.  Th' selfishness of that one--she waited
till she got all she could carry before she'd come to
tell anyone!
FLUTHER (running over to the door of the house and
shouting in to BESSIE).  Ay, Bessie, did you hear of
e'er a pub gettin' a shake up?
BESSIE (inside).  I didn't hear o' none.
FLUTHER (in a burst of enthusiasm).  Well, you're goin'
to hear of one soon!
THE COVEY.  Come on, man, an' don't be wastin' time.
PETER (to them as they are about to run off).  Ay, ay,
are you goin' to leave me here?
FLUTHER.  Are you goin' to leave yourself here?
PETER (anxiously).  Didn't yous hear her sayin' they
were firin' on them?
THE COVEY and FLUTHER (together).  Well?
PETER.  Supposin' I happened to be potted?
FLUTHER.  We'd give you a Christian burial, anyhow.
THE COVEY (ironically).  Dhressed up in your regiment-
als.
PETER (to THE COVEY, passionately).  May th' all-lovin'
God give you a hot knock one o' these days, me young
Covey, tuthorin' Fluther up now to be tiltin' at me,
an' crossin' me with his mockeries an' jibin'!

(A fashionably dressed, middle-aged, stout woman comes
hurriedly in, and makes for the group.  She is almost

253

fainting with fear.)

THE WOMAN. For Gawd's sake, will one of you kind men
show any safe way for me to get to Wrathmines? . . .
I was foolish enough to visit a friend, thinking the
howl thing was a joke, and now I cawn't get a car or
a tram to take me home--isn't it awful?
FLUTHER. I'm afraid, ma'am, one way is as safe as
another.
WOMAN. And what am I gowing to do? Oh, isn't this
awful? . . . I'm so different from others. . . . The
mowment I hear a shot, my legs give way under me--I
cawn't stir, I'm paralysed--isn't it awful?
FLUTHER (moving away). It's a derogatory way to be,
right enough, ma'am.
WOMAN (catching FLUTHER'S coat). Creeping along the
street there, with my head down and my eyes half
shut, a bullet whizzed past within an inch of my
nowse. . . . I had to lean against the wall for a
long time, gasping for breath--I nearly passed away--
it was awful! . . . I wonder, would you kind men come
some of the way and see me safe?
FLUTHER. I have to go away, ma'am, to thry an' save a
few things from th' burnin' buildin's.
THE COVEY. Come on, then, or there won't be anything
left to save.

(THE COVEY and FLUTHER hurry away.)

WOMAN (to PETER). Wasn't it an awful thing for me to
leave my friend's house? Wasn't it an idiotic thing
to do? . . . I haven't the slightest idea where I am.
. . . You have a kind face, sir. Could you possibly
come and pilot me in the direction of Wrathmines?
PETER (indignantly). D'ye think I'm goin' to risk me
life throttin' in front of you? An' maybe get a
bullet that would gimme a game leg or something that
would leave me a jibe an' a jeer to Fluther an' th'
young Covey for th' rest of me days! (With an indignant toss of his head he walks into the house.)
THE WOMAN (going out). I know I'll fall down in a dead
faint if I hear another shot go off anyway near me--
isn't it awful!

(MRS. GOGAN comes out of the house pushing a pram before her. As she enters the street, BESSIE rushes
out, follows MRS. GOGAN, and catches hold of the
pram, stopping MRS. GOGAN'S progress.)

BESSIE. Here, where are you goin' with that? How
quick you were, me lady, to clap your eyes on th'

254

pram. . . . Maybe you don't know that Mrs. Sullivan, before she went to spend Easther with her people in Dunboyne, gave me sthrict injunctions to give an accasional look to see if it was still standin' where it was left in th' corner of th' lobby.

MRS. GOGAN. That remark of yours, Mrs. Bessie Burgess, requires a little considheration, seein' that th' pram was left on our lobby, an' not on yours; a foot or two a little to th' left of th' jamb of me own room door; nor is it needful to mention th' name of th' person that gave a squint to see if it was there th' first thing in th' mornin', an' th' last thing in th' stillness o' th' night; never failin' to realize that her eyes couldn't be goin' wrong, be sthretchin' out her arm an' runnin' her hand over th' pram, to make sure that th' sight was no deception! Moreover, somethin's tellin' me that th' runnin' hurry of an inthrest you're takin' in it now is a sudden ambition to use th' pram for a purpose that a loyal woman of law an' ordher would stagger away from!

(She gives the pram a sudden push that pulls BESSIE forward.)

BESSIE (still holding the pram). There's not as much as one body in th' house that doesn't know that it wasn't Bessie Burgess that was always shakin' her voice complainin' about people leavin' bassinettes in th' way of them that, week in an' week out, had to pay their rent, an' always had to find a regular accommodation for her own furniture in her own room. . . . An' as for law an' ordher, puttin' aside th' harp an' shamrock[32], Bessie Burgess'll have as much respect as she wants for th' lion an' unicorn[33]!

PETER (appearing at the door). I think I'll go with th' pair of yous an' see th' fun. A fella might as well chance it, anyhow.

MRS. GOGAN (taking no notice of PETER, and pushing the pram on another step). Take your rovin' lumps o' hands from pattin' the bassinette, if you please, ma'am; an', steppin' from th' threshold of good manners, let me tell you, Mrs. Burgess, that it's a fat wondher to Jennie Gogan that a lady-like singer o' hymns like yourself would lower her thoughts from sky-thinkin' to sthretch out her arm in a sly-seekin'

32. Traditional symbols that appeared on various flags of Ireland, either separately or together, before the present tri-color National Flag.
33. Creatures on the Royal Arms of England.

way to pinch anything dhriven asthray in th' confusion of th' battle our boys is makin' for th' freedom of their counthry!
PETER (laughing and rubbing his hands together). Hee,
hee, hee, hee, hee! I'll go with th' pair o' yous
an' give yous a hand.
MRS. GOGAN (with a rapid turn of her head as she shoves
the pram forward). Get up in th' prambulator an'
we'll wheel you down.
BESSIE (to MRS. GOGAN). Poverty an' hardship has sent
Bessie Burgess to abide with sthrange company, but
she always knew them she had to live with from back-
side to breakfast time; an' she can tell them, always
havin' had a Christian kinch on her conscience, that
a passion for thievin' an' pinchin' would find her
soul a foreign place to live in, an' that her present
intention is quite th' lofty-hearted one of pickin'
up anything shaken up an' scatthered about in th'
loose confusion of a general plundher!

(By this time they have disappeared from view. PETER
is following, when the boom of a big gun in the distance brings him to a quick halt.)

PETER. God Almighty, that's th' big gun again! God
forbid any harm would happen to them, but sorra mind
I'd mind if they met with a dhrop in their mad en-
deyvours to plundher an' desthroy.

(He looks down the street for a moment, then runs to
the hall door of the house, which is open, and shuts
it with a vicious pull; he then goes to the chair in
which MOLLSER had sat, sits down, takes out his pipe,
lights it and begins to smoke with his head carried
at a haughty angle. THE COVEY comes staggering in
with a ten-stone sack of flour on his back. On the
top of the sack is a ham. He goes over to the door,
pushes it with his head, and finds he can't open it;
he turns slightly in the direction of PETER.)

THE COVEY (to PETER). Who shut th' door? . . . (He
kicks at it) Here, come on an' open it, will you?
This isn't a mot's hand-bag I've got on me back.
PETER. Now, me young Covey, d'ye think I'm goin' to be
your lackey?
THE COVEY (angrily). Will you open th' door, y'oul--
PETER (shouting). Don't be assin' me to open any door,
don't be assin' me to open any door for you. . . .
Makin' a shame an' a sin o' th' cause that good men
are fightin' for. . . . Oh, God forgive th' people
that, instead o' burnishin' th' work th' boys is doin'

256

to-day with quiet honesty an' patience, is revilin'
their sacrifices with a riot of lootin' an' roguery!
THE COVEY. Isn't your own eyes leppin' out o' your
head with envy that you haven't th' guts to ketch a
few o' th' things that God is givin' to His chosen
people? . . . Y'oul' hypocrite, if everyone was blind
you'd steal a cross off an ass's back!
PETER (very calmly). You're not going to make me lose
me temper; you can go on with your proddin' as long
as you like; goad an' goad an' goad away; hee, hee,
hee! I'll not lose me temper.

(Somebody opens door and THE COVEY goes in.)

THE COVEY (inside mockingly). Cuckoo-oo!
PETER (running to the door and shouting in a blaze of
passion as he follows THE COVEY in). You lean, long,
lanky lath of a lowsey bastard. . . . (Following him
in) Lowsey bastard, lowsey bastard!

(BESSIE and MRS. GOGAN enter, the pride of a great joy
illuminating their faces. BESSIE is pushing the
pram, which is filled with clothes and boots; on the
top of the boots and clothes is a fancy table, which
MRS. GOGAN is holding on with her left hand, while
with her right hand she holds a chair on the top of
her head. They are heard talking to each other before they enter.)

MRS. GOGAN (outside). I don't remember ever havin'
seen such lovely pairs as them, (they appear) with
th' pointed toes an' th' cuban heels.
BESSIE. They'll go grand with th' dhresses we're
afther liftin', when we've stitched a sthray bit o'
silk to lift th' bodices up a little bit higher, so
as to shake th' shame out o' them, an' make them fit
for women that hasn't lost themselves in th' naked-
ness o' th' times.

(They fussily carry in the chair, the table, and some
of the other goods. They return to bring in the
rest.)

PETER (at door, sourly to MRS. GOGAN). Ay, you. Mollser looks as if she was goin' to faint, an' your
youngster is roarin' in convulsions in her lap.
MRS. GOGAN (snappily). She's never any other way but
faintin'!

(She goes to go in with some things in her arms, when
a shot from a rifle rings out. She and BESSIE make

a bolt for the door, which PETER, in a panic, tries to shut before they have got inside.)

MRS. GOGAN. Ay, ay, ay, you cowardly oul' fool, what are you thryin' to shut th' door on us for?

(They retreat tumultuously inside. A pause; then CAPTAIN BRENNAN comes in supporting LIEUTENANT LANGON, whose arm is around BRENNAN'S neck. LANGON'S face, which is ghastly white, is momentarily convulsed with spasms of agony. He is in a state of collapse, and BRENNAN is almost carrying him. After a few moments CLITHEROE, pale, and in a state of calm nervousness, follows, looking back in the direction from which he came, a rifle, held at the ready, in his hands.)

CAPT. BRENNAN (savagely to CLITHEROE). Why did you fire over their heads? Why didn't you fire to kill?
CLITHEROE. No, no, Bill; bad as they are they're Irish men an' women.
CAPT. BRENNAN (savagely). Irish be damned! Attackin' an' mobbin' th' men that are riskin' their lives for them. If these slum lice gather at our heels again, plug one o' them, or I'll soon shock them with a shot or two meself!
LIEUT. LANGON (moaningly). My God, is there ne'er an ambulance knockin' around anywhere? . . . Th' stomach is ripped out o' me; I feel it--o-o-oh, Christ!
CAPT. BRENNAN. Keep th' heart up, Jim; we'll soon get help, now.

(NORA rushes wildly out of the house and flings her arms round the neck of CLITHEROE with a fierce and joyous insistence. Her hair is down, her face is haggard, but her eyes are agleam with the light of happy relief.)

NORA. Jack, Jack, Jack; God be thanked. . . be thanked. . . . He has been kind and merciful to His poor handmaiden. . . . My Jack, my own Jack, that I thought was lost is found, that I thought was dead is alive again! . . . Oh, God be praised for ever, evermore! . . . My poor Jack. . . . Kiss me, kiss me, Jack, kiss your own Nora!
CLITHEROE (kissing her, and speaking brokenly). My Nora; my little, beautiful Nora, I wish to God I'd never left you.
NORA. Ir doesn't matter--not now, not now, Jack. It will make us dearer than ever to each other. . . . Kiss me, kiss me again.
CLITHEROE. Now, for God's sake, Nora, don't make a

scene.

NORA. I won't, I won't; I promise, I promise, Jack; honest to God. I'll be silent an' brave to bear th' joy of feelin' you safe in my arms again. . . . It's hard to force away th' tears of happiness at th' end of an awful agony.

BESSIE (from the upper window). Th' Minsthrel Boys aren't feelin' very comfortable now. Th' big guns has knocked all th' harps out of their hands. General Clitheroe'd rather be unlacin' his wife's bodice than standin' at a barricade . . . An' th' professor of chicken-butcherin' there, finds he's up against somethin' a little tougher even than his own chickens, an' that's sayin' a lot!

CAPT. BRENNAN (up to BESSIE). Shut up, y' oul' hag!

BESSIE (down to BRENNAN). Choke th' chicken, choke th' chicken, choke th' chicken!

LIEUT. LANGON. For God's sake, Bill, bring me some place where me wound'll be looked afther. . . . Am I to die before anything is done to save me?

CAPT. BRENNAN (to CLITHEROE). Come on, Jack. We've got to get help for Jim, here--have you no thought for his pain an' danger?

BESSIE. Choke th' chicken, choke th' chicken, choke th' chicken!

CLITHEROE (to NORA). Loosen me, darling, let me go.

NORA (clinging to him). No, no, no, I'll not let you go! Come on, come up to our home, Jack, my sweetheart, my lover, my husband, an' we'll forget th' last few terrible days! . . . I look tired now, but a few hours of happy rest in your arms will bring back th' bloom of freshness again, an' you will be glad, you will be glad, glad . . . glad!

LIEUT. LANGON. Oh, if I'd kep' down only a little longer, I mightn't ha' been hit! Everyone else escapin', an' me gettin' me belly ripped asundher!. . . I couldn't scream, couldn't even scream. . . . D'ye think I'm really badly wounded, Bill? Me clothes seem to be all soakin' wet. . . . It's blood . . . My God, it must be me own blood!

CAPT. BRENNAN (to CLITHEROE). Go on, Jack, bid her good-bye with another kiss, an' be done with it! D'ye want Langon to die in me arms while you're dallyin' with your Nora?

CLITHEROE (to NORA). I must go, I must go, Nora. I'm sorry we met at all. . . . It couldn't be helped-- all other ways were blocked be th' British. . . .Let me go, can't you, Nora? D'ye want me to be unthrue to me comrades?

NORA. No, I won't let you go. . . . I want you to be thrue to me, Jack. . . . I'm your dearest comrade;

I'm your thruest comrade. . . . They only want th'
comfort of havin' you in th' same danger as themselves. . . . Oh, Jack, I can't let you go!
CLITHEROE. You must, Nora, you must.
NORA. All last night at th' barricades I sought you,
Jack. . . . I didn't think of th' danger--I could
only think of you. . . . I asked for you everywhere.
. . . Some o' them laughed. . . . I was pushed away,
but I shoved back. . . . Some o' them even sthruck
me. . . . an' I screamed an' screamed your name!
CLITHEROE (in fear her action would give him future
shame). What possessed you to make a show of yourself, like that? . . . What way d'ye think I'll feel
when I'm told my wife was bawlin' for me at th' barricades? What are you more than any other woman?
NORA. No more, maybe; but you are more to me than any
other man, Jack. . . . I didn't mean any harm, hon-
estly, Jack. . . . I couldn't help it. . . . I
shouldn't have told you. . . . My love for you made
me mad with terror.
CLITHEROE (angrily). They'll say now that I sent you
out th' way I'd have an excuse to bring you home.
. . . Are you goin' to turn all th' risks I'm taking
into a laugh?
LIEUT. LANGON. Let me lie down, let me lie down, Bill;
th' pain would be easier, maybe, lying down. . . .
Oh, God, have mercy on me!
CAPT. BRENNAN (to LANGON). A few steps more, Jim, a
few steps more; thry to stick it for a few steps more.
LIEUT. LANGON. Oh, I can't, I can't, I can't!
CAPT. BRENNAN (to CLITHEROE). Are you comin', man, or
are you goin' to make an arrangement for another
honeymoon? . . . If you want to act th' renegade, say
so, an' we'll be off!
BESSIE (from above). Runnin' from th' Tommies--choke
th' chicken. Runnin' from th' Tommies--choke th'
chicken!
CLITHEROE (savagely to BRENNAN). Damn you, man, who
wants to act th' renegade? (To NORA) Here, let go
your hold; let go, I say!
NORA (clinging to CLITHEROE, and indicating BRENNAN).
Look, Jack, look at th' anger in his face; look at
th' fear glintin' in his eyes. . . . He himself's
afraid, afraid, afraid! . . . He wants you to go th'
way he'll have th' chance of death sthrikin' you an'
missin' him! . . . Turn round an' look at him, Jack,
look at him, look at him! . . . His very soul is
cold . . . shiverin' with th' thought of what may
happen to him. . . . It is his fear that is thryin'
to frighten you from recognizin' th' same fear that
is in your own heart!

CLITHEROE (struggling to release himself from NORA).
    Damn you, woman, will you let me go!
CAPT. BRENNAN (fiercely, to CLITHEROE). Why are you
    beggin' her to let you go? Are you afraid of her, or
    what? Break her hold on you, man, or go up, an' sit
    on her lap!

(CLITHEROE trying roughly to break her hold.)

NORA (imploringly). Oh, Jack. . . . Jack. . . .Jack!
LIEUT. LANGON (agonisingly). Brennan, a priest; I'm
    dyin', I think, I'm dyin!
CLITHEROE (to NORA). If you won't do it quietly, I'll
    have to make you! (To BRENNAN) Here, hold this gun,
    you, for a minute. (He hands the gun to BRENNAN.)
NORA (pitifully). Please, Jack. . . . You're hurting
    me, Jack. . . . Honestly. . . . Oh, you're hurting
    . . . me! . . . I won't, I won't, I won't! . . . Oh,
    Jack, I gave you everything you asked of me. . . .
    Don't fling me from you, now!

(He roughly loosens her grip, and pushes her away from
    him. NORA sinks to the ground and lies there.)

NORA (weakly). Ah, Jack. . . . Jack. . . . Jack!
CLITHEROE (taking the gun back from BRENNAN). Come on,
    come on.

(They go out. BESSIE looks at NORA lying on the street,
    for a few moments, then, leaving the window, she comes
    out, runs over to NORA, lifts her up in her arms, and
    carries her swiftly into the house. A short pause,
    then down the street is heard a wild, drunken yell;
    it comes nearer, and FLUTHER enters, frenzied, wild-
    eyed, mad, roaring drunk. In his arms is an earthen
    half-gallon jar of whisky; streaming from one of the
    pockets of his coat is the arm of a new tunic shirt;
    on his head is a woman's vivid blue hat with gold
    lacing, all of which he has looted.)

FLUTHER (singing in a frenzy):
    Fluther's a jolly good fella! . . . Fluther's a jolly
        good fella!
    Up th' rebels! . . . That nobody can deny!
    (He beats on the door.) Get us a mug or a jug, or
    somethin', some o' yous, one o' yous, will yous, be-
    fore I lay one o' yous out! . . . (Looking down the
    street) Bang an' fire away for all Fluther cares.
    . . . (Banging at door) Come down an' open th' door,
    some of yous, one o' yous, will yous, before I lay
    some o' yous out! . . . Th' whole city can topple

home to hell, for Fluther!

(Inside the house is heard a scream from NORA, followed
by a moan.)

FLUTHER (singing furiously):
   That nobody can deny, that nobody can deny,
   For Fluther's a jolly good fella, Fluther's a jolly
      good fella,
   Fluther's a jolly good fella. . . Up th' rebels! That
   nobody can deny!

(His frantic movements cause him to spill some of the
whisky out of the jar.)

   Blast you, Fluther, don't be spillin' th' precious
   liquor!  (He kicks at the door.)  Ay, give us a mug
   or a jug, or somethin', one o' yous, some o' yous,
   will yous, before I lay one o' yous out!

(The door suddenly opens, and BESSIE, coming out, grips
him by the collar.)

BESSIE (indignantly).  You bowsey, come in ower o' that.
   . . . I'll thrim your thricks o' dhrunken dancin' for
   you, an' none of us knowin' how soon we'll bump into
   a world we were never in before!
FLUTHER (as she is pulling him in).  Ay, th' jar, th'
   jar, th' jar!

(A short pause, then again is heard a scream of pain
from NORA.  The door opens and MRS. GOGAN and BESSIE
are seen standing at it.)

BESSIE.  Fluther would go, only he's too dhrunk. . . .
   Oh, God, isn't it a pity he's so dhrunk!  We'll have
   to thry to get a docthor somewhere.
MRS. GOGAN.  I'd be afraid to go. . . . Besides, Mollser's terrible bad.  I don't think you'll get a
   docthor to come.  It's hardly any use goin'.
BESSIE (determinedly).  I'll risk it. . . . Give her a
   little of Fluther's whisky. . . . It's th' fright
   that's brought it on her so soon. . . . Go on back to
   her, you.

(MRS. GOGAN goes in, and BESSIE softly closes the door.
She is moving forward, when the sound of some rifle
shots, and the tok, tok, tok of a distant machine-
gun bring her to a sudden halt.  She hesitates for a
moment, then she tightens her shawl round her, as if
it were a shield, then she firmly and swiftly goes

262

out.)

BESSIE (as she goes out).   Oh, God, be Thou my help in
    time o' throuble.   An' shelter me safely in th'
    shadow of Thy wings!


CURTAIN



Act IV

The living-room of Bessie Burgess.  It is one of two
small attic rooms (the other, used as a bedroom, is to
the Left), the ceiling slopes up towards the back,
giving to the apartment a look of compressed confine-
ment.  In the centre of the ceiling is a small skylight.
There is an unmistakable air of poverty bordering on
destitution.  The paper on the walls is torn and soiled,
particularly near the fire where the cooking is done,
and near the washstand where the washing is done.  The
fireplace is to the Left.  A small armchair near fire.
One small window at Back.  A pane of this window is
starred by the entrance of a bullet.  Under the window
to the Right is an oak coffin standing on two kitchen
chairs.  Near the coffin is a home-manufactured stool,
on which are two lighted candles.  Beside the window
is a worn-out dresser on which is a small quantity of
delf.  Tattered remains of cheap lace curtains drape
the window.  Standing near the window on Left is a
brass standard-lamp with a fancy shade; hanging on the
wall near the same window is a vividly crimson silk
dress, both of which have been looted.  A door on Left
leading to the bedroom.  Another opposite giving a way
to the rest of the house.  To the Left of this door a
common washstand.  A tin kettle, very black, and an old
saucepan inside the fender.  There is no light in the
room but that given from the two candles and the fire.
The dusk has well fallen, and the glare of the burning
buildings in the town can be seen through the window,
in the distant sky.  The Covey and Fluther have been
playing cards, sitting on the floor by the light of the
candles on the stool near the coffin.  When the curtain
rises the Covey is shuffling the cards, Peter is sitting
in a stiff, dignified way beside him, and Fluther is
kneeling beside the window, cautiously looking out.
It is a few days later.

263

FLUTHER (furtively peeping out of the window). Give
them a good shuffling. . . . Th' sky's gettin' reddher an' reddher. . . . You'd think it was afire.
. . . Half o' th' city must be burnin'.
THE COVEY. If I was you, Fluther, I'd keep away from
that window. . . . It's dangerous, an' besides, if
they see you, you'll only bring a nose on th' house.
PETER. Yes, an' he knows we had to leave our own place
th' way they were riddlin' it with machine-gun fire.
. . . He'll keep on pimpin' an' pimpin' there, till
we have to fly out o' this place too.
FLUTHER (ironically) If they make any attack here,
we'll send you out in your green an' glory uniform,
shakin' your sword over your head, an' they'll fly
before you as th' Danes flew before Brian Boru[34]!
THE COVEY (placing the cards on the floor, after shuffling them). Come on, an' cut.

(FLUTHER comes over, sits on floor, and cuts the cards.)

THE COVEY (having dealt the cards). Spuds up again.

(NORA moans feebly in room on Left.)

FLUTHER. There, she's at it again. She's been quiet
for a long time, all th' same.
THE COVEY. She was quiet before, sure, an' she broke
out again worse than ever. . . . What was led that
time?
PETER. Thray o' Hearts, Thray o' Hearts, Thray o'
Hearts.
FLUTHER. It's damned hard lines to think of her dead-
born kiddie lyin' there in th' arms o' poor little
Mollser. Mollser snuffed it sudden too, after all.
THE COVEY. Sure she never got any care. How could
she get it, an' th' mother out day an' night lookin'
for work, an' her consumptive husband leavin' her
with a baby to be born before he died!
VOICES in a lilting chant to the Left in a distant
street. Red Cr . . . oss, Red Cr . . . oss! . . .
Ambu . . . lance, Ambu . . . lance!
THE COVEY (to FLUTHER). Your deal, Fluther.
FLUTHER (shuffling and dealing the cards). It'll take
a lot out o' Nora--if she'll ever be th' same.
THE COVEY. Th' docthor thinks she'll never be th'
same; thinks she'll be a little touched here. (He
touches his forehead.) She's ramblin' a lot; thinkin' she's out in th' counthry with Jack; or gettin'

34. King of Ireland (1002-1014).

264

his dinner ready for him before he comes home; or
yellin' for her kiddie. All that, though, might be
th' chloroform she got. . . . I don't know what we'd
have done only for oul' Bessie: up with her for th'
past three nights, hand runnin'.
FLUTHER. I always knew there was never anything really
derogatory wrong with poor oul' Bessie. (To PETER,
who is taking a trick) Ay, houl' on, there, don't be
so damn quick--that's my thrick.
PETER. What's your thrick? It's my thrick, man.
FLUTHER (loudly). How is it your thrick?
PETER (answering as loudly). Didn't I lead th' deuce!
FLUTHER. You must be gettin' blind, man; don't you
see th' ace?
BESSIE (appearing at door of room, Left; in a tense
whisper). D'ye want to waken her again on me, when
she's just gone asleep? If she wakes will yous come
an' mind her? If I hear a whisper out o' one o' yous
again, I'll . . . gut yous!
THE COVEY (in a whisper). S-s-s-h. She can hear anything above a whisper.
PETER (looking up at the ceiling). Th' gentle an'
merciful God'll give th' pair o' yous a scawldin' an'
a scarifyin' one o' these days!

(FLUTHER takes a bottle of whisky from his pocket, and
takes a drink.)

THE COVEY (to FLUTHER). Why don't you spread that out,
man, an' thry to keep a sup for to-morrow?
FLUTHER. Spread it out? Keep a sup for to-morrow?
How th' hell does a fella know there'll be any to-
morrow? If I'm goin' to be whipped away, let me be
whipped away when it's empty, an' not when it's half
full! (To BESSIE, who has seated herself in an armchair at the fire) How is she, now, Bessie?
BESSIE. I left her sleeping quietly. When I'm listenin' to her babblin', I think she'll never be much
betther than she is. Her eyes have a hauntin' way of
lookin' in instead of lookin' out, as if her mind had
been lost alive in madly minglin' memories of th'
past. . . . (Sleepily) Crushin' her thoughts . . .to-
gether . . . in a fierce . . . an' fanciful . . .
(she nods her head and starts wakefully) idea that
dead things are livin', an' livin' things are dead.
. . . (With a start) Was that a scream I heard her
give? (Reassured) Blessed God, I think I hear her
screamin' every minute! An' it's only there with me
that I'm able to keep awake.
THE COVEY. She'll sleep, maybe, for a long time, now.
Ten there.

FLUTHER. Ten here. If she gets a long sleep, she
    might be all right. Peter's th' lone five.
THE COVEY. Whisht! I think I hear somebody movin'
    below. Whoever it is, he's comin' up.

(A pause. Then the door opens and CAPTAIN BRENNAN
    comes into the room. He has changed his uniform for
    a suit of civvies. His eyes droop with the heaviness
    of exhaustion; his face is pallid and drawn. His
    clothes are dusty and stained here and there with mud.
    He leans heavily on the back of a chair as he stands.)

CAPT. BRENNAN. Mrs. Clitheroe; where's Mrs. Clitheroe?
    I was told I'd find her here.
BESSIE. What d'ye want with Mrs. Clitheroe?
CAPT. BRENNAN. I've a message, a last message for her
    from her husband.
BESSIE. Killed! He's not killed, is he!
CAPT. BRENNAN (sinking stiffly and painfully on to a
    chair). In th' Imperial Hotel; we fought till th'
    place was in flames. He was shot through th' arm,
    an' then through th' lung. . . . I could do nothin'
    for him--only watch his breath comin' an' goin' in
    quick, jerky gasps, an' a tiny sthream o' blood
    thricklin' out of his mouth, down over his lower
    lip. . . . I said a prayer for th' dyin', an' twined
    his Rosary beads around his fingers. . . . Then I had
    to leave him to save meself. . . . (He shows some
    holes in his coat) Look at th' way a machine-gun tore
    at me coat, as I belted out o' th' buildin' an'
    darted across th' sthreet for shelter. . . . An' then,
    I seen The Plough an' th' Stars fallin' like a shot
    as th' roof crashed in, an' where I'd left poor Jack
    was nothin' but a leppin' spout o' flame!
BESSIE (with partly repressed vehemence). Ay, you left
    him! You twined his Rosary beads round his fingers,
    an' then you run like a hare to get out o' danger!
CAPT. BRENNAN. I took me chance as well as him. . . .
    He took it like a man. His last whisper was to "Tell
    Nora to be brave; that I'm ready to meet my God, an'
    that I'm proud to die for Ireland." An' when our
    General heard it he said that "Commandant Clitheroe's
    end was a gleam of glory." Mrs. Clitheroe's grief
    will be a joy when she realizes that she has had a
    hero for a husband.
BESSIE. If you only seen her, you'd know to th' differ.

(NORA appears at door, Left. She is clad only in her
    nightdress; her hair, uncared for some days, is hang-
    ing in disorder over her shoulders. Her pale face
    looks paler still because of a vivid red spot on the

tip of each cheek. Her eyes are glimmering with the
light of incipient insanity; her hands are nervously
fiddling with her nightgown. She halts at the door
for a moment, looks vacantly around the room, and
then comes slowly in. The rest do not notice her
till she speaks.

NORA (in a quiet and monotonous tone). No . . . Not
   there, Jack. . . . I can feel comfortable only in our
   own familiar place beneath th' bramble tree. . . . We
   must be walking for a long time; I feel very, very
   tired. . . . Have we to go farther, or have we passed
   it by? (Passing her hand across her eyes) Curious
   mist on my eyes. . . . Why don't you hold my hand,
   Jack. . . . (Excitedly) No, no, Jack, it's not. Can't
   you see it's a goldfinch. Look at th' black-satiny
   wings with th' gold bars, an' th' splash of crimson
   on its head. . . . (Wearily) Something ails me, something ails me. . . . Don't kiss me like that; you
   take my breath away, Jack. . . . Why do you frown at
   me? . . . You're going away, and (frightened) I can't
   follow you. Something's keeping me from moving. . . .
   (Crying out) Jack, Jack, Jack!
BESSIE (who has gone over and caught NORA'S arm). Now,
   Mrs. Clitheroe, you're a terrible woman to get up out
   of bed. . . . You'll get cold if you stay here in
   them clothes.
NORA. Cold? I'm feelin' very cold; it's chilly out
   here in th' counthry. . . . (Looking around frightened) What place is this? Where am I?
BESSIE (coaxingly). You're all right, Nora; you're
   with friends, an' in a safe place. Don't you know
   your uncle an' your cousin, an' poor oul' Fluther?
PETER (about to go over to NORA). Nora, darlin', now--
FLUTHER (pulling him back). Now, leave her to Bessie,
   man. A crowd'll only make her worse.
NORA (thoughtfully). There is something I want to remember, an' I can't. (With agony) I can't, I can't,
   I can't! My head, my head! (Suddenly breaking from
   BESSIE, and running over to the men, and gripping
   FLUTHER by the shoulders) Where is it? Where's my
   baby? Tell me where you've put it, where've you
   hidden it? My baby, my baby; I want my baby! My
   head, my poor head. . . . Oh, I can't tell what is
   wrong with me. (Screaming) Give him to me, give me
   my husband!
BESSIE. Blessin' o' God on us, isn't this pitiful!
NORA (struggling with BESSIE). I won't go away for
   you; I won't. Not till you give me back my husband.
   (Screaming) Murderers, that's what yous are; murderers, murderers!

BESSIE. S-s-sh. We'll bring Mr. Clitheroe back to
    you, if you'll only lie down an' stop quiet. . . .
    (Trying to lead her in) Come on, now, Nora, an' I'll
    sing something to you.
NORA. I feel as if my life was thryin' to force its
    way out of my body. . . . I can hardly breathe . . .
    I'm frightened, I'm frightened, I'm frightened! For
    God's sake, don't leave me, Bessie. Hold my hand,
    put your arms around me!
FLUTHER (to BRENNAN). Now you can see th' way she is,
    man.
PETER. An' what way would she be if she heard Jack had
    gone west?
THE COVEY (to PETER). Shut up, you, man!
BESSIE (to NORA). We'll have to be brave, an' let
    patience clip away th' heaviness of th' slow-movin'
    hours, rememberin' that sorrow may endure for th'
    night, but joy cometh in th' mornin'. . . . Come on
    in, an' I'll sing to you, an' you'll rest quietly.
NORA (stopping suddenly on her way to the room). Jack
    an' me are goin' out somewhere this evenin'. Where
    I can't tell. Isn't it curious I can't remember.
    . . . Maura, Maura, Jack, if th' baby's a girl; any
    name you like, if th' baby's a boy! . . . He's there.
    (Screaming) He's there, an' they won't give him back
    to me!
BESSIE. S-ss-s-h, darlin', s-ssh. I won't sing to
    you, if you're not quiet.
NORA (nervously holding BESSIE). Hold my hand, hold
    my hand, an' sing to me, sing to me!
BESSIE. Come in an' lie down, an' I'll sing to you.
NORA (vehemently). Sing to me, sing to me; sing, sing!
BESSIE (singing as she leads NORA into room):
    Lead, kindly light, amid th' encircling gloom,
        Lead Thou me on.
    Th' night is dark an' I am far from home,
        Lead Thou me on.
    Keep Thou my feet, I do not ask to see
    Th' distant scene--one step enough for me.

    So long that Thou hast blessed me, sure Thou still
        Wilt lead me on;

(They go in.)

BESSIE (singing in room):

    O'er moor an' fen, o'er crag an' torrent, till
        Th' night is gone.
    An' in th' morn those angel faces smile
    That I have lov'd long since, an' lost awhile!

THE COVEY (to BRENNAN). Now that you've seen how bad
she is, an' that we daren't tell her what has happened till she's betther, you'd best be slippin' back to
where you come from.
CAPT. BRENNAN. There's no chance o' slippin' back now,
for th' military are everywhere: a fly couldn't get
through. I'd never have got here, only I managed to
change me uniform for what I'm wearin'. . . . I'll
have to take me chance, an' thry to lie low here for
a while.
THE COVEY (frightened). There's no place here to lie
low. Th' Tommies'll be hoppin' in here, any minute!
PETER (aghast). An' then we'd all be shanghaied!
THE COVEY. Be God, there's enough afther happenin' to
us!
FLUTHER (warningly, as he listens). Whisht, whisht,
th' whole o' yous. I think I heard th' clang of a
rifle butt on th' floor of th' hall below. (All
alertness.) Here, come on with th' cards again.
I'll deal.

(He shuffles and deals the cards to all.)

FLUTHER. Clubs up. (To BRENNAN) Thry to keep your
hands from shakin', man. You lead, Peter. (As PETER
throws out a card) Four o' Hearts led.

(The door opens and CORPORAL STODDART of the Wiltshires
enters in full war kit; steel helmet, rifle and bayo-
net, and trench tool. He looks round the room. A
pause and a palpable silence.)

FLUTHER (breaking the silence). Two tens an' a five.
CORPORAL STODDART. 'Ello. (Indicating the coffin)
This the stiff?
THE COVEY. Yis.
CORPORAL STODDART. Who's gowing with it? Ownly one
allowed to gow with it, you know.
THE COVEY. I dunno.
CORPORAL STODDART. You dunnow?
THE COVEY. I dunno.
BESSIE (coming into the room). She's afther slippin'
off to sleep again, thanks be to God. I'm hardly
able to keep me own eyes open. (To the soldier) Oh,
are yous goin' to take away poor little Mollser?
CORPORAL STODDART. Ay; 'oo's agowing with 'er?
BESSIE. Oh, th' poor mother, o' course. God help her,
it's a terrible blow to her!
FLUTHER. A terrible blow? Sure, she's in her element
now, woman, mixin' earth to earth, an' ashes t'ashes
an' dust to dust, an' revellin' in plumes an'hearses,

269

last days an' judgements!

BESSIE (falling into chair by the fire). God bless us! I'm jaded!

CORPORAL STODDART. Was she plugged?

THE COVEY. Ah, no; died o' consumption.

CORPORAL STODDART. Ow, is that all? Thought she might 've been plugged.

THE COVEY. Is that all? Isn't it enough? D'ye know, comrade, that more die o' consumption than are killed in th' wars? An' it's all because of th' system we're livin' undher?

CORPORAL STODDART. Ow, I know. I'm a Sowcialist moi-self, but I 'as to do my dooty.

THE COVEY (ironically). Dooty! Th' only dooty of a Socialist is th' emancipation of th' workers.

CORPORAL STODDART. Ow, a man's a man, an 'e 'as to foight for 'is country, 'asn't 'e?

FLUTHER (aggressively). You're not fighting for your counthry here, are you?

PETER (anxiously, to FLUTHER). Ay, ay, Fluther, none o' that, none o' that!

THE COVEY. Fight for your counthry! Did y'ever read, comrade, Jenersky's <u>Thesis</u> on <u>the</u> <u>Origin</u>, <u>Develop</u>-<u>ment</u>, <u>an' Consolidation of th' Evolutionary Idea of the Proletariat</u>?

CORPORAL STODDART. Ow, cheese it, Paddy, cheese it!

BESSIE (sleepily). How is things in th' town, Tommy?

CORPORAL STODDART. Ow, I fink it's nearly hover. We've got 'em surrounded, and we're clowsing in on the bloighters. Ow, it was only a little bit of a dawg-foight.

(The sharp ping of the sniper's rifle is heard, fol-lowed by a squeal of pain.)

VOICES to the Left in a chant. Red Cr . . . oss, Red Cr . . . oss! Ambu . . . lance, Ambu . . . lance!

CORPORAL STODDART (excitedly). Christ, that's another of our men 'it by that blawsted sniper! 'E's knock-abaht 'ere, somewheres. Gawd, when we gets th' bloighter, we'll give 'im the cold steel, we will. We'll jab the belly aht of 'im, we will!

(MRS. GOGAN comes in tearfully, and a little proud of the importance of being directly connected with death.)

MRS. GOGAN (to FLUTHER). I'll never forget what you done for me, Fluther, goin' around at th' risk of your life settlin' everything with th' undhertaker an' th' cemetery people. When all me own were afraid

270

to put their noses out, you plunged like a good one
through hummin' bullets, an' they knockin' fire out
o' th' road, tinklin' through th' frightened windows,
an' splashin' themselves to pieces on th' walls! An'
you'll find, that Mollser, in th' happy place she's
gone to, won't forget to whisper, now an' again, th'
name o' Fluther.
CORPORAL STODDART. Git it aht, mother, git it aht.
BESSIE (from the chair). It's excusin' me you'll be,
Mrs. Gogan, for not stannin' up, seein' I'm shaky on
me feet for want of a little sleep, an' not desirin'
to show any disrespect to poor little Mollser.
FLUTHER. Sure, we all know, Bessie, that it's vice
versa with you.
MRS. GOGAN (to BESSIE). Indeed, it's meself that has
well chronicled, Mrs. Burgess, all your gentle hurryin's to me little Mollser, when she was alive, bringin' her somethin' to dhrink, or somethin' t'eat, an'
never passin' her without liftin' up her heart with
a delicate word o' kindness.
CORPORAL STODDART (impatiently, but kindly). Git it
aht, git it aht, mother.

(THE COVEY, FLUTHER, BRENNAN, and PETER carry out the
coffin, followed by MRS. GOGAN.)

CORPORAL STODDART (to BESSIE, who is almost asleep).
'Ow many men is in this 'ere 'ouse? (No answer.
Loudly) 'Ow many men is in this 'ere 'ouse?
BESSIE (waking with a start). God, I was nearly asleep!
. . . How many men? Didn't you see them?
CORPORAL STODDART. Are they all that are in the 'ouse?
BESSIE. Oh, there's none higher up, but there may be
more lower down. Why?
CORPORAL STODDART. All men in the district 'as to be
rounded up. Somebody's giving 'elp to the snipers,
and we 'as to take precautions. If I 'ad my woy, I'd
make 'em all join hup, and do their bit! But I suppowse they and you are all Shinners[35].
BESSIE (who has been sinking into sleep, waking up to
a sleepy vehemence). Bessie Burgess is no Shinner,
an' never had no thruck with anything spotted be th'
fingers o' th' Fenians; but always made it her business to harness herself for Church whenever she knew

35. A reference to members of the Sinn Fein. The Sinn
    Fein was established by Arthur Griffith in 1905,
    and advocated the organization of an Irish govern-
    ment completely independent of the British Parlia-
    ment.

that God Save the King was goin' to be sung at t'end
of th' service; whose only son went to th' front in
th' first contingent of the Dublin Fusiliers, an'
that's on his way home carryin' s shatthered arm that
he got fightin' for his King an' counthry!

(Her head sinks slowly forward again. PETER comes into
the room; his body is stiffened and his face is wearing a comically indignant look. He walks to and fro
at the back of the room, evidently repressing a violent desire to speak angrily. He is followed in by
FLUTHER, THE COVEY, and BRENNAN, who slinks into an
obscure corner of the room, nervous of notice.)

FLUTHER (after an embarrassing pause). Th' air in th'
    sthreet outside's shakin' with the firin' o' rifles
    an' machine-guns. It must be a hot shop in th' mid-
    dle o' th' scrap.
CORPORAL STODDART. We're pumping lead in on 'em from
    every side, now; they'll soon be shoving up th' white
    flag.
PETER (with a shout). I'm tellin' you either o' yous
    two lowsers 'ud make a betther hearse-man than Peter;
    proddin' an' pokin' at me an' I helpin' to carry out
    a corpse!
FLUTHER. It wasn't a very derogatory thing for th'
    Covey to say that you'd make a fancy hearse-man, was
    it?
PETER (furiously). A pair o' redjesthered bowseys
    pondherin' from mornin' till night on how they'll get
    a chance to break a gap through th' quiet nature of a
    man that's always endeavourin' to chase out of him
    any sthray thought of venom against his fella-man!
THE COVEY. Oh, shut it, shut it, shut it!
PETER. As long as I'm a livin' man, responsible for
    me thoughts, words, an' deeds to th' Man above, I'll
    feel meself instituted to fight again' th' sliddher-
    in' ways of a pair o' picaroons, whisperin', con-
    currin', concoctin', an' conspirin' together to
    rendher me unconscious of th' life I'm thryin' to
    live!
CORPORAL STODDART (dumbfounded). What's wrong, Daddy;
    wot 'ave they done to you?
PETER (savagely to the CORPORAL). You mind your own
    business! What's it got to do with you, what's wrong
    with me?
BESSIE (in a sleepy murmur). Will yous thry to con-
    throl yourselves into quietness? Yous'll waken her
    . . . up . . . on . . . me . . . again. (She sleeps.)
FLUTHER. Come on, boys, to th' cards again, an' never
    mind him.

CORPORAL STODDART. No use of you gowing to start
cawds; you'll be gowing out of 'ere, soon as Ser-
geant comes.
FLUTHER. Goin' out o' here? An' why're we goin' out
o' here?
CORPORAL STODDART. All men in district to be rounded
up, and 'eld in till the scrap is hover.
FLUTHER. An' where're we goin' to be held in?
CORPORAL STODDART. They're putting 'em in a church.
THE COVEY. A church?
FLUTHER. What sort of a church? Is it a Protestan'
Church?
CORPORAL STODDART. I dunnow; I suppowse so.
FLUTHER (dismayed). Be God, it'll be a nice thing to
be stuck all night in a Protestan' Church!
CORPORAL STODDART. Bring the cawds; you moight get a
chance of a goime.
FLUTHER. Ah, no, that wouldn't do. . . . I wondher?
(After a moment's thought) Ah, I don't think we'd be
doin' anything derogatory be playin' cards in a Pro-
testan' Church.
CORPORAL STODDART. If I was you I'd bring a little
snack with me; you moight be glad of it before the
mawning. (Sings):
        I do loike a snoice mince poy,
        I do loike a snoice mince poy!

(The snap of the sniper's rifle rings out again, followed simultaneously by a scream of pain. CORPORAL
STODDART goes pale, and brings his rifle to the
ready, listening.)

VOICES chanting to the Right. Red Cr . . . ss, Red
Cro . . . ss! Ambu . . . lance, Ambu . . . lance!

(SERGEANT TINLEY comes rapidly in, pale, agitated, and
fiercely angry.)

CORPORAL STODDART (to SERGEANT). One of hour men 'it,
Sergeant?
SERGEANT TINLEY. Private Taylor; got 'it roight
through the chest, 'e did; an 'ole in front of 'im
as 'ow you could put your fist through, and 'arf 'is
back blown awoy! Dum-dum bullets they're using.
Gang of Hassassins potting at us from behind roofs.
That's not playing the goime: why down't they come
into the owpen and foight fair!
FLUTHER (unable to stand the slight). Fight fair! A
few hundhred scrawls o' chaps with a couple o' guns
an' Rosary beads, again' a hundhred thousand thrained
men with horse, fut, an' artillery . . . an' he wants

273

us to fight fair! (To SERGEANT) D'ye want us to come
out in our skins an' throw stones?
SERGEANT TINLEY (to CORPORAL). Are these four all that
are 'ere?
CORPORAL STODDART. Four; that's all, Sergeant.
SERGEANT TINLEY (vindictively). Come on, then; get the
blighters aht. (To the men) 'Ere, 'op it aht! Aht
into the streets with you, and if a snoiper sends
another of our men west, you gow with 'im! (He
catches FLUTHER by the shoulder) Gow on, git aht!
FLUTHER. Eh, who are you chuckin', eh?
SERGEANT TINLEY (roughly). Gow on, git aht, you
blighter.
FLUTHER. Who are you callin' a blighter to, eh? I'm a
Dublin man, born an' bred in th' city, see?
SERGEANT TINLEY. I down't care if you were Broin
Buroo; git aht, git aht.
FLUTHER (halting as he is going out). Jasus, you an'
your guns! Leave them down, an' I'd beat th' two o'
yous without sweatin'!

(PETER, BRENNAN, THE COVEY, and FLUTHER, followed by
the soldiers, go out. BESSIE is sleeping heavily on
the chair by the fire. After a pause, NORA appears
at door, Left, in her nightdress. Remaining at door
for a few moments she looks vaguely around the room.
She then comes in quietly, goes over to the fire,
pokes it, and puts the kettle on. She thinks for a
few moments, pressing her hand to her forehead. She
looks questioningly at the fire, and then at the
press at back. She goes to the press, opens it,
takes out a soiled cloth and spreads it on the table.
She then places things for tea on the table.)

NORA. I imagine th' room looks very odd somehow. . . .
I was nearly forgetting Jack's tea. . . . Ah, I think
I'll have everything done before he gets in. . . .
(She lilts gently, as she arranges the table.)

Th' violets were scenting th' woods, Nora,
  Displaying their charms to th' bee,
When I first said I lov'd only you, Nora,
An' you said you lov'd only me.

Th' chestnut blooms gleam'd through th' glade, Nora,
  A robin sang loud from a tree,
When I first said I lov'd only you, Nora,
An' you said you lov'd only me.

(She pauses suddenly, and glances round the room.)

NORA (doubtfully). I can't help feelin' this room very
   strange. . . . What is it? . . . What is it? . . . I
   must think. . . . I must thry to remember. . . .
VOICES chanting in a distant street. Ambu . . . lance,
   Ambu . . . lance! Red Cro . . . ss, Red Cro . . .ss!
NORA (startled and listening for a moment, then resuming
   the arrangement of the table):

   Trees, birds, an' bees sang a song, Nora,
    Of happier transports to be,
   When I first said I lov'd only you, Nora,
    An' you said you lov'd only me.

(A burst of rifle fire is heard in a street near by,
   followed by the rapid rok, tok, tok of a machine-gun.)

NORA (staring in front of her and screaming). Jack,
   Jack, Jack! My baby, my baby, my baby!
BESSIE (waking with a start). You divil, are you
   afther gettin' out o' bed again!

(She rises and runs towards NORA, who rushes to the
   window, which she frantically opens.)

NORA (at window, screaming). Jack, Jack, for God's
   sake, come to me!
SOLDIERS (outside, shouting). Git away, git away from
   that window, there!
BESSIE (seizing hold of NORA). Come away, come away,
   woman, from that window!
NORA (struggling with BESSIE). Where is it; where have
   you hidden it? Oh, Jack, Jack, where are you?
BESSIE (imploringly). Mrs. Clitheroe, for God's sake,
   come away!
NORA (fiercely). I won't; he's below. Let . . . me
   . . . go! You're thryin' to keep me from me husband.
   I'll follow him. Jack, Jack, come to your Nora!
BESSIE. Hus-s-sh, Nora, Nora! He'll be here in a
   minute. I'll bring him to you, if you'll only be
   quiet--honest to God, I will.

(With a great effort BESSIE pushes NORA away from the
   window, the force used causing her to stagger against
   it herself. Two rifle shots ring out in quick succession. BESSIE jerks her body convulsively; stands
   stiffly for a moment, a look of agonized astonishment
   on her face, then she staggers forward, leaning
   heavily on the table with her hands.)

BESSIE (with an arrested scream of fear and pain).
   Merciful God, I'm shot, I'm shot, I'm shot! . . .

Th' life's pourin' out o' me! (To NORA) I've got
this through . . . through you . . . through you, you
bitch, you! . . . O God, have mercy on me! . . . (To
NORA) You wouldn't stop quiet, no, you wouldn't, you
wouldn't, blast you! Look at what I'm after gettin',
look at what I'm after gettin' . . . I'm bleedin' to
death, an' no one's here to stop th' flowin' blood!
(Calling) Mrs. Gogan, Mrs. Gogan! Fluther, Fluther,
for God's sake, somebody, a doctor, a doctor!

(She staggers frightened towards the door, to seek for
    aid, but, weakening half-way across the room, she
    sinks to her knees, and bending forward, supports
    herself with her hands resting on the floor. NORA is
    standing rigidly with her back to the wall opposite,
    her trembling hands held out a little from the sides
    of her body, her lips quivering, her breast heaving,
    staring wildly at the figure of BESSIE.)

NORA (in a breathless whisper). Jack, I'm frightened.
    . . . I'm frightened, Jack. . . . Oh, Jack, where are
    you?
BESSIE (moaningly). This is what's after comin' on
    me for nursin' you day an' night. . . . I was a fool,
    a fool, a fool! Get me a dhrink o' wather, you jade,
    will you? There's a fire burnin' in me blood!
    (Pleadingly) Nora, Nora, dear, for God's sake, run
    out an' get Mrs. Gogan, or Fluther, or somebody to
    bring a doctor, quick, quick, quick! (As NORA does
    not stir) Blast you, stir yourself, before I'm gone!
NORA. Oh, Jack, Jack, where are you?
BESSIE (in a whispered moan). Jesus Christ, me sight's
    goin'! It's all dark, dark! Nora, hold me hand!

(BESSIE'S body lists over and she sinks into a prostrate
    position on the floor.)

BESSIE. I'm dyin', I'm dyin' . . . I feel it. . . . Oh
    God, oh God! (She feebly sings)

    I do believe, I will believe
        That Jesus died for me;
    That on th' cross He shed His blood,
        From sin to set me free. . . .

    I do believe . . . I will believe
        . . . Jesus died . . . me;
    . . . th' cross He shed . . . blood,
        From sin . . . free.

(She ceases singing, and lies stretched out, still and

276

very rigid. A pause. Then MRS. GOGAN runs hastily in.)

MRS. GOGAN (quivering with fright). Blessed be God, what's afther happenin'? (To NORA) What's wrong, child, what's wrong? (She sees BESSIE, runs to her and bends over the body) Bessie, Bessie! (She shakes the body) Mrs. Burgess, Mrs. Burgess! (She feels BESSIE'S forehead) My God, she's as cold as death. They're afther murderin' th' poor inoffensive woman!

(SERGEANT TINLEY and CORPORAL STODDART enter agitatedly, their rifles at the ready.)

SERGEANT TINLEY (excitedly). This is the 'ouse. That's the window!
NORA (pressing back against the wall). Hide it, hide it; cover it up, cover it up!
SERGEANT TINLEY (going over to the body). 'Ere, what's this? Who's this? (Looking at BESSIE) Oh Gawd, we've plugged one of the women of the 'ouse.
CORPORAL STODDART. Whoy the 'ell did she gow to the window? Is she dead?
SERGEANT TINLEY. Oh, dead as bedamned. Well, we couldn't afford to toike any chawnces.
NORA (screaming). Hide it, hide it; don't let me see it! Take me away, take me away, Mrs. Gogan!

(MRS. GOGAN runs into room, Left, and runs out again with a sheet which she spreads over the body of BESSIE.)

MRS. GOGAN (as she spreads the sheet). Oh, God help her, th' poor woman, she's stiffenin' out as hard as she can! Her face has written on it th' shock o' sudden agony, an' her hands is whitenin' into th' smooth shininess of wax.
NORA (whimperingly). Take me away, take me away; don't leave me here to be lookin' an' lookin' at it!
MRS. GOGAN (going over to NORA and putting her arm around her). Come on with me, dear, an' you can doss36 in poor Mollser's bed, till we gather some neighbours to come an' give th' last friendly touches to Bessie in th' lonely layin' of her out.

(MRS. GOGAN and NORA go slowly out.)

CORPORAL STODDART (who has been looking around, to

36. Sleep.

SERGEANT TINLEY). Tea here, Sergeant. Wot abaht a
cup of scald?
SERGEANT TINLEY. Pour it aht, Stoddart, pour it aht.
I could scoff hanything just now.

(CORPORAL STODDART pours out two cups of tea, and the
two soldiers begin to drink. In the distance is
heard a bitter burst of rifle and machine-gun fire,
interspersed with the boom, boom of artillery. The
glare in the sky seen through the window flares into
a fuller and a deeper red.)

SERGEANT TINLEY. There gows the general attack on the
Powst Office.
VOICES in a distant street. Ambu . . . lance, Ambu .
. . lance! Red Cro . . . ss, Red Cro . . . ss!

(The voices of soldiers at a barricade outside the
house are heard singing:

They were summoned from the 'illside,
They were called in from the glen,
And the country found 'em ready
At the stirring call for men.
Let not tears add to their 'ardship,
As the soldiers pass along,
And although our 'eart is breaking,
Make it sing this cheery song.

SERGEANT TINLEY and CORPORAL STODDART (joining in the
chorus, as they sip the tea):

Keep the 'owme fires burning,
While your 'earts are yearning;
Though your lads are far away
They dream of 'owme;
There's a silver loining
Through the dark cloud shoining,
Turn the dark cloud inside out,
Till the boys come 'owme!

CURTAIN

JOHN KELLS INGRAM

The Memory of the Dead

Who fears to speak of Ninety-eight?[1]
Who blushes at the name?
When cowards mock the patriot's fate,
Who hangs his head for shame?
He's all a knave, or half a slave,
Who slights his country thus;
But a true man, like you, man,
Will fill your glass with us.

We drink the memory of the brave,
The faithful and the few;
Some lie far off beyond the wave,
Some sleep in Ireland, too;
All, all are gone; but still lives on
The fame of those who died;
All true men, like you, men,
Remember them with pride.

Some on the shores of distant lands
Their weary hearts have laid,
And by the stranger's heedless hands
Their lonely graves were made;
But though their clay be far away
Beyond the Atlantic foam,
In true men, like you, men,
Their spirit's still at home.

The dust of some is Irish earth,
Among their own they rest,
And the same land that gave them birth
Has caught them to her breast;
And we will pray that from their clay
Full many a race may start
Of true men, like you, men,
To act as brave a part.

They rose in dark and evil days
To right their native land;
They kindled here a living blaze
That nothing shall withstand.
Alas! that might can vanquish right--

1. The French sent aid to Wolfe Tone and his fellow
   rebels in 1798. Ireland was hopelessly divided by
   conflicting ideologies, and the rebellion was
   easily crushed.

They fell and passed away;
But true men, like you, men,
Are plenty here to-day.

Then here's their memory--may it be
For us a guiding light,
To cheer our strife for liberty,
And teach us to unite--
Through good and ill, be Ireland's still,
Though sad as theirs your fate,
And true men be you, men,
Like those of Ninety-eight.


A. E.

Carrowmore[1]

It's a lonely road through bogland to the
    lake at Carrowmore,
And a sleeper there lies dreaming where the
    water laps the shore;
Though the moth-wings of the twilight in
    their purples are unfurled,
Yet his sleep is filled with music by the
    masters of the world.

There's a hand is white as silver that is
    fondling with his hair:
There are glimmering feet of sunshine that
    are dancing by him there:
And half-open lips of faery that were dyed a
    faery red
In their revels where the Hazel Tree[2] its holy
    clusters shed.

"Come away," the red lips whisper, "all the
    world is weary now;
'Tis the twilight of the ages and it's time to
    quit the plough.
Oh, the very sunlight's weary ere it lightens
    up the dew,

1. A lake in Sligo county.
2. Hazels of wisdom grew above Connla's well. The
leaves, blossoms, and nuts fell into the water,
where they were eaten by salmon--the salmon of
knowledge of other tales. The Hazel tree is
associated with knowledge in early myths.

280

And its gold is changed and faded before it
      falls to you.

"Though your colleen's heart be tender, a
      tenderer heart is near.
What's the starlight in her glances when the
      stars are shining clear?
Who would kiss the fading shadow when the
      flower-face glows above?
'Tis the beauty of all Beauty that is calling
      for your love."

Oh, the great gates of the mountain have
      opened once again,
And the sound of song and dancing falls
      upon the ears of men,
And the Land of Youth lies gleaming, flushed
      with rainbow light and mirth,
And the old enchantment lingers in the
      honey-heart of earth.


   The Nuts of Knowledge

A cabin on the mountain side hid in a grassy
      nook
Where door and windows open wide that
      friendly stars may look.
The rabbit shy can patter in, the winds may
      enter free,
Who throng around the mountain throne in
      living ecstasy.

And when the sun sets dimmed in eve and
      purple fills the air,
I think the sacred Hazel Tree is dropping
      berries there
From starry fruitage waved aloft where
      Connla's Well[1] o'erflows;
For sure the enchanted waters run through
      every wind that blows.

I think when night towers up aloft and shakes
      the trembling dew,
How every high and lonely thought that
      thrills my being through


1. In the Land under waves; drinking from this well
   would bring about the inspiration for wisdom, although this knowledge was taboo even to some members of the divine land.
                    281

Is but a ruddy berry dropped down through
     the purple air,
And from the magic tree of life the fruit falls
     everywhere.


A New Theme

I fain would leave the tender songs
     I sang to you of old,
Thinking the oft-sung beauty wrongs
     The magic never told.

And touch no more the thoughts, the moods,
     That win the easy praise;
But venture in the untrodden woods
     To carve the future ways.

Though far or strange or cold appear
     The shadowy things I tell,
Within the heart the hidden seer
     Knows and remembers well.

I think that in the coming time
     The hearts and hopes of men
The mountain tops of life shall climb,
     The gods return again.

I strive to blow the magic horn;
     It feebly murmureth;
Arise on some enchanted morn,
     Poet, with God's own breath!

And sound the horn I cannot blow,
     And by the secret name
Each exile of the heart will know
     Kindle the magic flame.


In Connemara[1]

With eyes all untroubled she laughs as she
     passes,
   Bending beneath the creel with the seaweed
     brown,
Till evening with pearl dew dims the shining
     grasses

1. The western part of County Galway; a mountainous
   district.

282

And night lit with dreamlight enfolds the
    sleepy town.

Then she will wander, her heart all a
      laughter,
  Tracking the dream star that lights the
      purple gloom.
She follows the proud and golden races after,
  As high as theirs her spirit, as high will be
      her doom.


## Tragedy

A man went forth one day at eve:
The long day's toil for him was done:
The eye that scanned the page could leave
Its task until to-morrow's sun.

Upon the threshold where he stood
Flared on his tired eyes the sight,
Where host on host the multitude
Burned fiercely in the dusky night.

The starry lights at play--at play--
The giant children of the blue,
Heaped scorn upon his trembling clay
And with their laughter pierced him through.

They seemed to say in scorn of him
"The power we have was once in thee.
King, is thy spirit grown so dim,
That thou art slave and we are free?"

As out of him the power--the power--
The free--the fearless, whirled in play,
He knew himself that bitter hour
The close of all his royal day.

And from the stars' exultant dance
Within the fiery furnace glow,
Exile of all the vast expanse,
He turned him homeward sick and slow.


## Momentary

The sweetest song was ever sung
  May soothe you but a little while:
The gayest music ever rung
  Shall yield you but a fleeting smile.

The well I digged you soon shall pass:
    You may but rest with me an hour:
Yet drink, I offer you the glass,
    A moment of sustaining power,

And give to you, if it be gain,
    Whether in pleasure or annoy,
To see one elemental pain,
    One light of everlasting joy.


## Exiles

The gods have taken alien shapes upon them
Wild peasants driving swine
In a strange country. Through the swarthy faces
The starry faces shine.

Under grey tattered skies they strain and reel
    there:
Yet cannot all disguise
The majesty of fallen gods, the beauty,
The fire beneath their eyes.

They huddle at night within low clay-built
    cabins;
And, to themselves unknown,
They carry with them diadem and sceptre
And move from throne to throne.


## J. M. SYNGE

### The Passing of the Shee[1]
    (After looking at one of A. E.'s pictures)

Adieu, sweet Angus, Maeve and Fand,
Ye plumed yet skinny Shee,
That poets played with hand in hand
To learn their ecstasy.

We'll search in Red Dan Sally's ditch,
And drink in Tubber fair,
Or poach with Red Dan Philly's bitch
The badger and the hare.


1. A fairy, or fairies.

Beg-Innish

    Bring Kateen-Beag and Maurya Jude
    To dance in Beg-Innish,
    And when the lads (they're in Dunquin)
    Have sold their crabs and fish,
    Wave fawney shawls and call them in,
    And call the little girls who spin,
    And seven weavers from Dunquin,
    To dance in Beg-Innish.

    I'll play you jigs, and Maurice Kean,
    Where nets are laid to dry,
    I've silken strings would draw a dance
    From girls are lame or shy;
    Four strings I've brought from Spain and France
    To make your long men skip and prance,
    Till stars look out to see the dance
    Where nets are laid to dry.

    We'll have no priest or peeler in
    To dance at Beg-Innish;
    But we'll have drink from M'riarty Jim
    Rowed round while gannets fish,
    A keg with porter to the brim,
    That every lad may have his whim,
    Till we up with sails with M'riarty Jim
    And sail from Beg-Innish.


OLIVER ST. JOHN GOGARTY

To the Maids Not to Walk in the Wind

    When the wind blows, walk not abroad,
    For, Maids, you may not know
    The mad, quaint thoughts which incommode
    Me when the winds do blow.

    What though the tresses of the treen
    In doubled beauty move,
    With silver added to their green,
    They were not made for Love.

    But when your clothes reveal your thighs
    And surge around your knees,
    Until from foam you seem to rise,
    As Venus from the seas . . .

```
Though ye are fair, it is not fair!
Unless you will be kind,
Till I am dead, and changed to AIR,
O walk not in the wind!
```

Ringsend[1]
(After reading Tolstoi)

```
        I will live in Ringsend
        With a red-headed whore,
        And the fan-light gone in
        Where it lights the hall-door;
        And listen each night
        For her querulous shout,
        As at last she streels in
        And the pubs empty out.
        To soothe that wild breast
        With my old-fangled songs,
        Till she feels it redressed
        From inordinate wrongs,
        Imagined, outrageous,
        Preposterous wrongs,
        Till peace at last comes,
        Shall be all I will do,
        Where the little lamp blooms
        Like a rose in the stew;
        And up the back-garden
        The sound comes to me
        Of the lapsing, unsoilable,
        Whispering sea.
```

Death May Be Very Gentle

```
    Death may be very gentle after all:
    He turns his face away from arrogant knights
    Who fling themselves against him in their fights;
    But to the loveliest he loves to call.
    And he has with him those whose ways were mild
    And beautiful; and many a little child.
```

1. In Londonderry County, a little ways in from the sea.

## Golden Stockings

Golden stockings you had on
In the meadow where you ran;
And your little knees together
Bobbed like pippins in the weather,
When the breezes rush and fight
For those dimples of delight,
And they dance from the pursuit
And the leaf looks like the fruit.

I have many a sight in mind
That would last if I were blind;
Many verses I could write
That would bring me many a sight.
Now I only see but one,
See you running in the sun,
And the gold-dust coming up
From the trampled buttercup.


## THOMAS MACDONAGH

### The Man Upright

I once spent an evening in a village
Where the people are all taken up with tillage,
Or do some business in a small way
Among themselves, and all the day
Go crooked, doubled to half their size,
Both working and loafing, with their eyes
Stuck in the ground or in a board,--
For some of them tailor, and some of them hoard
Pence in a till in their little shops,
And some of them shoe-soles--they get the tops
Ready-made from England, and they die cobblers--
All bent up double, a village of hobblers
And slouchers and squatters, whether they straggle
Up and down, or bend to haggle
Over a counter, or bend at a plough,
Or to dig with a spade, or to milk a cow,
Or to shove the goose-iron[1] stiffly along
The stuff on the sleeve-board, or lace the fong
In the boot on the last, or to draw the wax-end
Tight cross-ways--and so to make or to mend
What will soon be worn out by the crooked people.


1. A tailor's smoothing iron, the handle being shaped
   like a goose's neck.

The only thing straight in the place was the steeple,
I thought at first.  I was wrong in that;
For there past the window at which I sat
Watching the crooked little men
Go slouching, and with the gait of a hen
An odd little woman go pattering past,
And the cobbler crouching over his last
In his window opposite, and next door
The tailor squatting inside on the floor--
While I watched them, as I have said before,
And thought that only the steeple was straight,
There came a man of a different gait--
A man who neither slouched nor pattered,
But planted his steps as if each step mattered;
Yet walked down the middle of the street
Not like a policeman on his beat,
But like a man with nothing to do
Except walk straight upright like me and you.


John-John

        I dreamt last night of you, John-John,
            And thought you called to me;
        And when I woke this morning, John,
            Yourself I hoped to see;
        But I was all alone, John-John,
            Though still I heard your call:
        I put my boots and bonnet on,
            And took my Sunday shawl,
        And went, full sure to find you, John,
                        To Nenagh fair.

        The fair was just the same as then,
            Five years ago to-day,
        When first you left the thimble men
            And came with me away;
        For there again were thimble men
            And shooting galleries,
        And card-trick men and Maggie men
            Of all sorts and degrees--
        But not a sight of you, John-John,
                        Was anywhere.

        I turned my face to home again,
            And called myself a fool
        To think you'd leave the thimble men
            And live again by rule,
        And go to Mass and keep the fast
            And till the little patch:

                        288

My wish to have you home was past
   Before I raised the latch
And pushed the door and saw you, John,
            Sitting down there.

How cool you came in here, begad,
   As if you owned the place!
But rest yourself there now, my lad,
   'Tis good to see your face;
My dream is out, and now by it
   I think I know my mind:
At six o'clock this house you'll quit,
   And leave no grief behind;--
But until six o'clock, John-John,
            My bit you'll share.

The neighbours' shame of me began
   When first I brought you in.
To wed and keep a tinker man
   They thought a kind of sin;
But now this three year since you're gone
   'Tis pity me they do,
And that I'd rather have, John-John,
   Than that they'd pity you.
Pity for me and you, John-John,
            I could not bear.

Oh, you're my husband right enough,
   But what's the good of that?
You know you never were the stuff
   To be the cottage cat,
To watch the fire and hear me lock
   The door and put out Shep--
But there now, it is six o'clock
   And time for you to step.
God bless and keep you far, John-John!
            And that's my prayer.


The Yellow Bittern
 (From the Irish of Cathal Buidhe Mac Giolla Ghunna)

The yellow bittern that never broke out
   In a drinking bout, might as well have drunk;
His bones are thrown on a naked stone
   Where he lived alone like a hermit monk.
O yellow bittern! I pity your lot,
   Though they say that a sot like myself is curst--
I was sober a while, but I'll drink and be wise
   For I fear I should die in the end of thirst.

289

It's not for the common birds that I'd mourn,
    The black-bird, the corn-crake, or the crane,
But for the bittern that's shy and apart
    And drinks in the marsh from the lone bog-drain.
Oh! if I had known you were near your death,
    While my breath held out I'd have run to you,
Till a splash from the Lake of the Son of the Bird
    Your soul would have stirred and waked anew.

My darling told me to drink no more
    Or my life would be o'er in a little short while;
But I told her 'tis drink gives me health and
        strength
    And will lengthen my road by many a mile.
You see how the bird of the long smooth neck
    Could get his death from the thirst at last--
Come, son of my soul, and drain your cup,
    You'll get no sup when your life is past.

In a wintering island by Constantine's halls
    A bittern calls from a wineless place,
And tells me that hither he cannot come
    Till the summer is here and the sunny days.
When he crosses the stream there and wings o'er
        the sea
    Then a fear comes to me he may fail in his flight--
Well, the milk and the ale are drunk every drop,
    And a dram won't stop our thirst this night.


JOSEPH CAMPBELL

  Chesspieces

        It was a time of trouble--executions,
        Dearth, searches, nightly firing, balked escapes--
        And I sat silent, while my cellmate figured
        Ruy Lopez' Gambit[1] from the Praxis.[2] Silence
        Best fitted with our mood: we seldom spoke.
        'I have a thought,' he said, tilting his stool.
        'We prisoners are so many pieces taken,
        Swept from the board, only used again
        When a new game is started.' 'There's that hope,'

1. A chess opening in which the first player voluntarily
   gives up a pawn or a piece, or several successively,
   for an advantage in position.
2. An example or form of exercise, or a collection of
   such examples, for practice.

I said, 'the hope of being used again.
Some day of strength, when ploughs are out in March,
The Dogs of Fionn[3] will slip their iron chains,
And, heedless of torn wounds and failing wind,
Will run the old grey Wolf[4] to death at last.'
He smiled, 'I like the image. My fat Kings
And painted Queens, and purple-cassocked Bishops
Are tame, indeed, beside your angry Dogs!'


Ad Limina[1]

The ewes and lambs, loving the far hillplaces,
Cropping by choice the succulent tops of heather,
Drinking the pure water of cloudborn lochlands,
Resting under erratics[2] fostered with Abel--
Come to my haggard gate, my very doorstep.

The birds of freest will and strongest wingbeat,
Sad curlew, garrulous stonechat, hawk and coaltit,
Haunting lone bog or scalp[3] or broken ruin,
Poising the rough thrust of air's excesses--
Come to my haggard gate, my very doorstep.

The trout in the river, below the hanging marllot,[4]
Swift, with ancestral fear of hook and shadow,
The elvers of cold drain and slough, remembering
The warm tangles of Caribbee and Sargasso--
Come to my haggard gate, my very doorstep.

Even the stoats and rats, who know a possessor
Of the rare sixth sense, the bardic insight,
Match, and more, for their devilish perversions,
And the deer, shyest of shy at autumn rutting--


3. Fionn was an early heroic mythic figure who was a
   leader of the Feinn. Fionn's hounds, Bran and
   Sgeolan, were nephews of his, for Illan married
   Fionn's wife's sister Tuirrean, whom his fairy mis-
   tress transformed into a wolf-hound which gave birth
   to those famous dogs.
4. A reference to England.
1. Short for ad limina apostolorum, to the tombs of the
   apostles (Peter and Paul);--designating a periodic
   official visit of a bishop to the Holy See.
2. Geol. Erratic boulders or blocks of rock, trans-
   ported from their original resting places, especially by ice.
3. A mountain cap.
4. A clayish deposit.

291

Come to my haggard gate, my very doorstep.

Am I not a lucky man, trusted, Franciscan,
That these spacious things gentle or hostile,
Following God's urge, denying their nature,
Harbingers of high thoughts and fathers of poems--
Come to my haggard gate, my very doorstep.


SEUMAS O'SULLIVAN

The Others

From our hidden places
By a secret path,
We come in the moonlight
To the edge of the green rath.[1]

There the night through
We take our pleasure,
Dancing to such a measure
As earth never knew.

To song and dance
And lilt without a name,
So sweetly breathed
'Twould put a bird to shame.

And many a young maiden
Is there, of mortal birth,
Her young eyes laden
With dreams of earth.

And many a youth entranced
Moves slowly in the wildered round,
His brave lost feet enchanted
In the rhythm of elfin sound.

Music so forest wild
And piercing sweet, would bring
Silence on blackbirds singing
Their best in the ear of Spring.

And now they pause in their dancing
And look with troubled eyes,


1. Belonging to or characteristic of the early portion
   of the day, season, year, etc.; as the rath green
   of spring.

292

Earth's straying children
With sudden memory wise.

They pause, and their eyes in the moonlight
With faery wisdom cold,
Grow dim and a thought goes fluttering
In hearts no longer old.

And then the dream forsakes them
And sighing, they turn anew
As the whispering music takes them
To the dance of the elfin crew.

Oh, many a thrush and a blackbird
Would fall to the dewy ground
And pine away in silence
For envy of such a sound.

So the night through
In our sad pleasure,
We dance to many a measure
That earth never knew.


Nelson Street

There is hardly a mouthful of air
In the room where the breakfast is set,
For the blind is still down tho' it's late,
And the curtains are redolent yet
Of tobacco smoke, stale from last night.
There's the little bronze teapot, and there
The rashers and eggs on a plate,
And the sleepy canary, a hen,
Starts faintly her chirruping tweet,
And I know could she speak she would say:
'Hullo there--what's wrong with the light?
Draw the blind up, let's look at the day.'
I see that it's Monday again,
For the man with the organ is there;
Every Monday he comes to the street
(Lest I, or the bird there, should miss
Our count of monotonous days)
With his reed-organ, wheezy and sweet,
And stands by the window and plays
'There's a Land that is Fairer than This.'

293

A Piper

A PIPER in the street today,
Set up, and tuned, and started to play,
And away, away, away on the tide
Of his music we started; on every side
Doors and windows were opened wide,
And men left down their work and came,
And women with petticoats coloured like flame,
And little bare feet that were blue with cold,
Went dancing back to the age of gold,
And all the world went gay, went gay,
For half an hour in the street today.


The Land War

Sorrow is over the fields,
The fields that never can know
The joy that the harvest yields
When the corn stands row on row.

But alien the cattle feed
Where many a furrow lies,
For the furrows remember the seed,
And the men have a dream in their eyes.

Not so did the strong men dream
E'er the fathers of these were born,
And the sons have remembered their deeds
As the fields have remembered the corn.


PADRAIC COLUM

An Old Man Said

An old man said, 'I saw
The chief of the things that are gone;
A stag with head held high,
A doe, and a fawn;

'And they were the deer of Ireland
That scorned to breed within bound:
The last; they left no race
Tame on a pleasure-ground.

'A stag with his hide all rough
With the dew, and a doe and a fawn;

294

Nearby, on their track on the mountain,
I watched them, two and one,

'Down to the Shannon going--
Did its waters cease to flow,
When they passed, they that carried the swiftness,
And the pride of long ago?

'The last of the troop that had heard
Finn's[1] and Oscar's[2] cry;
A doe and a fawn, and before
A stag with head held high!'


A Drover

To Meath of the pastures,
From wet hills by the sea,
Through Leitrim and Longford,
Go my cattle and me.

I hear in the darkness
Their slipping and breathing--
I name them the by-ways
They're to pass without heeding;

Then the wet, winding roads,
Brown bogs with black water,
And my thoughts on white ships
And the King o' Spain's daughter.

O farmer, strong farmer!
You can spend at the fair,
But your face you must turn
To your crops and your care;

And soldiers, red soldiers!
You've seen many lands,
But you walk two by two,
And by captain's commands!

O the smell of the beasts,
The wet wind in the morn,

1. A great leader of the _fiana_, Finn MacCumail.  The
   Fenian cycle is a great collection of stories which
   deals with bands of semi-nomadic warriors who are
   known as the _fiana_.
2. Oscar was the son of Oisin who, in turn, was the
   son of Finn.

And the proud and hard earth
Never broken for corn!

And the crowds at the fair,
The herds loosened and blind,
Loud words and dark faces,
And the wild blood behind!

(O strong men with your best
I would strive breast to breast,
I could quiet your herds,
With my words, with my words!)

I will bring you, my kine,
Where there's grass to the knee,
But you'll think of scant croppings
Harsh with salt of the sea.

## The Burial of St. Brendan[1]

On the third day from this (Saint Brendan said)
I will be where no wind that filled a sail
Has ever been, and it blew high or low:
For from this home-creek, from this body's close
I shall put forth: make ready, you, to go
With what remains to Cluan Hy-many,
For there my resurrection I'd have be.

But you will know how hard they'll strive to hold
This body o' me, and hold it for the place
Where I was bred, they say, and born and reared.
For they would have my resurrection here,
So that my sanctity might be matter shared
By every mother's child the tribeland polled
Who lived and died and mixed into the mould.

So you will have to use all canniness
To bring this body to its burial
When in your hands I leave what goes in clay;
The wagon that our goods are carried in--
Have it yoked up between the night and day,
And when the breath is from my body gone,
Bear body out, the wagon lay it on;

1. A sixth century Irish abbot, founder of the schools
   of Ardfert and Clonfert, in Ireland, apostle to the
   Orkneys and the isles of Scotland, and a patron
   saint of sailors.

And cover it with gear that's taken hence--
'The goods of Brendan is what's here,' you'll say
To those who'll halt you; they will pass you then:
Tinkers and tailors, soldiers, farmers, smiths,
You'll leave beside their doors--all those thwart men
For whom my virtue was a legacy
That they would profit in, each a degree--

As though it were indeed some chalice, staff,
Crozier or casket, that they might come to,
And show to those who chanced upon the way,
And have, not knowing how the work was done
In scrolls and figures and in bright inlay:
Whence came the gold and silver that they prize,
The blue enamels and the turquoises!

I, Brendan, had a name came from the sea--
I was the first who sailed the outer main,
And past all forelands and all fastnesses!
I passed the voiceless anchorites, their isles,
Saw the ice-palaces upon the seas,
Mentioned Christ's name to men cut off from men,
Heard the whales snort, and saw the Kraken![2]

And on a wide-branched, green and glistening tree
Beheld the birds that had been angels erst:
Between the earth and heaven 'twas theirs to wing:
Fallen from High they were, but they had still
Music of Heaven's Court: I heard them sing:
Even now that island of the unbeached coast
I see, and hear the white, resplendent host!

For this they'd have my burial in this place,
Their hillside, and my resurrection be
Out of the mould that they with me would share.
But I have chosen Cluan for my ground--
A happy place! Some grace came to me there:
And you, as you go towards it, to men say,
Should any ask you on that long highway:

'Brendan is here, who had great saints for friends:
Ita,[3] who reared him on a mother's knee,

2. A fabulous Scandinavian sea monster.
3. In The Martyrology of Angus the Culdee, a collection
of poems constituting a calendar of saints' days by
a monk named Angus (ninth or tenth century), there
is a poem on St. Ita, who is reputed to have nursed
the infant Jesus in a vision.

Enda,[4] who from his fastness blessed his sail:
Then Brighid,[5] she had the flaming heart,
And Colum-cille,[6] prime of all the Gael;
Gildas of Britain,[7] wisest child of light.'
And saying this, drive through the falling night.


JAMES STEPHENS

   To the Four Courts, Please

       The driver rubbed at his nettly chin
       With a huge loose forefinger, crooked and black;
       And his wobbly violet lips sucked in,
       And puffed out again and hung down slack:
       A black fang shone through his lop-sided smile,
       In his little pouched eye flickered years of guile.

       And the horse, poor beast! It was ribbed and forked;
       And its ears hung down, and its eyes were old;
       And its knees were knuckly; and, as we talked,
       It swung the stiff neck that could scarcely hold
       Its big skinny head up--then I stepped in,
       And the driver climbed to his seat with a grin.

       God help the horse, and the driver, too!
       And the people and beasts who have never a friend!
       For the driver easily might have been you,
       And the horse be me by a different end!
       And nobody knows how their days will cease!
       And the poor, when they're old, have little of peace!


4. Founder of a monastic school in the Aran Isles. The
   remains of the churches and cells of Enda and his
   followers make the Isles of Aran the most holy
   spots within the bounds of Britain's insular empire.
5. Irish Christian abbess (c. 452-524), known to her
   devoted countrymen as "the Mary of the Gael." She
   ranks with St. Patrick and St. Columkille.
6. One of the greatest of Irish saints:  also, Columkille.
7. An ecclesiastical author of Britain. About 548 he
   wrote in Latin the Destruction and Conquest of
   Britain, an invective against his own countrymen
   and their kings.

298

A Glass of Beer

The lanky hank of a she in the inn over there
Nearly killed me for asking the loan of a glass of
    beer;
May the devil grip the whey-faced slut by the hair,
And beat bad manners out of her skin for a year.

That parboiled ape, with the toughest jaw you will
    see
On virtue's path, and a voice that would rasp the
    dead,
Came roaring and raging the minute she looked at me,
And threw me out of the house on the back of my head!

If I asked her master he'd give me a cask a day;
But she, with the beer at hand, not a gill would
    arrange!
May she marry a ghost and bear him a kitten, and
    may
The High King of Glory permit her to get the mange.


Nora Criona

I have looked him round and looked him through,
Know everything that he will do

In such a case, and such a case;
And when a frown comes on his face

I dream of it, and when a smile
I trace its sources in a while.

He cannot do a thing but I
Peep to find the reason why;

For I love him, and I seek,
Every evening in the week,

To peep behind his frowning eye
With little query, little pry,

And make him, if a woman can,
Happier than any man.

-Yesterday he gripped her tight
And cut her throat.  And serve her right!


299

O Bruadair[1]
(From the Irish of O Bruadair)

I will sing no more songs: the pride of my country
    I sang
Through forty long years of good rhyme, without
    any avail;
And no one cared even as much as the half of a hang
For the song or the singer, so here is the end to
    the tale.

If a person should think I complain and have not
    got the cause,
Let him bring his eyes here and take a good look at
    my hand,
Let him say if a goose-quill has calloused this
    poor pair of paws
Or the spade that I grip on and dig with out there
    in the land?

When the great ones were safe and renowned and were
    rooted and tough,
Though my mind went to them and took joy in the
    fortune of those,
And pride in their pride and their fame, they gave
    little enough,
Not as much as two boots for my feet, or an old
    suit of clothes.

I ask of the Craftsman that fashioned the fly and
    the bird,
Of the Champion whose passion will lift me from
    death in a time,
Of the Spirit that melts icy hearts with the wind
    of a word,
That my people be worthy, and get better singing
    than mine.

I had hoped to live decent, when Ireland was quit
    of her care,
As a bailiff or steward perhaps in a house of
    degree,

1. O Bruadair, Dáibhí--An Irish poet whose life covered
most of the seventeenth century. He used the archa-
ic language of the classical schools, and his poetry
records the complete overthrow of his country
through the Confederate wars (1642-1649), the Crom-
wellian massacres, and the reigns of Charles II and
James II.

But the end of the tale is, old brogues and old
      britches to wear,
So I'll sing no more songs for the men that care
      nothing for me.


FREDERICK ROBERT HIGGINS

  A Tinker's Woman

        I'll throw no sorrowful hair at her--
            No tears for you, MacDara,
        For pride of beauty takes no slur
            When fierce of limb, MacDara;
        You thought my body's shine grew dusk
        Beside that girl you took at Lusk--
        Yet who but a fool would pluck the husk
            And leave the fruit to wither.

        You now forget when from the gorse
            I saw you swim sea water,
        Stark naked I flashed on a tinker's horse
            Down to the morning water
        And into green seas I took my ride
        Barebacked, horse-swimming I reached your side,
        Then who but a fool would rob the tide
            And throw away the salmon.

        Ah, now I know you wrongly thought
            You loved me then, MacDara,
        While peeled to the waist for me you fought
            Some mountainy fellow, MacDara,
        For there on wet grass and stript to my teeth
        I seemed as a sword of light at your feet--
        Yet who but a fool would keep the sheath
            And leave the sword unhandled.

        So now I'll throw no curse before
            Your lean ways with young women,
        For I'm too ripe in the old sun's lore
            To envy slips of women;
        Then keep the girlish slip who went
        To whet your taste, last night in my tent,
        For who but a fool would look for scent
            Along a budless bramble.


                        301

Father and Son

Only last week, walking the hushed fields
Of our most lovely Meath, now thinned by November,
I came to where the road from Laracor leads
To the Boyne river--that seemed more lake than river,
Stretched in uneasy light and stript of reeds.

And walking longside an old weir
Of my people's, where nothing stirs--only the
        shadowed
Leaden flight of a heron up the lean air--
I went unmanly with grief, knowing how my father,
Happy though captive in years, walked last with me
        there.

Yes, happy in Meath with me for a day
He walked, taking stock of herds hid in their own
        breathing;
And naming colts, gusty as wind, once steered by his
        hand
Lightnings winked in the eyes that were half shy in
        greeting
Old friends--the wild blades, when he gallivanted
        the land.

For that proud, wayward man now my heart breaks--
Breaks for that man whose mind was a secret eyrie,
Whose kind hand was sole signet of his race,
Who curbed me, scorned my green ways, yet increas-
        ingly loved me
Till Death drew its grey blind down his face.

And yet I am pleased that even my reckless ways
Are living shades of his rich calms and passions--
Witnesses for him and for those faint namesakes
With whom now he is one, under yew branches,
Yes, one in a graven silence no bird breaks.


To My Blackthorn Stick

When sap ebbed low and your green days were over--
Hedging a gap to rugged land,
Bare skinned and straight you were; and there I
        broke you
To champion my right hand.

302

Well shod in bronze and lithe with hillside breeding,
Yet, like a snarl, you dogged my side,
Mailed in your tridents and flaunting out the
      fierceness
That bristled through your hide.

So armed as one, have we not shared each journey
On noiseless path or road of stone;
O exiled brother of the flowering sloe tree,
Your past ways are my own.

Lonesome, like me, and song-bred on Mount Nephin,[1]
You, also, found that in your might
You broke in bloom before the time of leafing
And shocked a world with light.

But you grew shy,--eyed through by glowering
      twilights--
Sharing the still of night's grey brew,
Secret and shy, while things unseen were sighing
Their grass tunes under you.

Manured with earth's own sweat you stretched in
      saplings;
Seasoned, you cored your fruit with stone;
Then stript in fight, your strength came out of
      wrestling
All winds by winter blown.

I took that strength; my axe blow was your trumpet,
You rose from earth, god-cleaned and strong;
And here, as in green days you were the perch,
You're now the prop of song.


FRANK O'CONNOR

  Prayer for the Speedy End of Three Great Misfortunes
  (From the Irish)

      There be three things seeking my death,
          All at my heels run wild--
      Hang them, oh God, all three!--
          Devil, maggot and child.

      So much does each of them crave
          The morsel that falls to his share

1. A mountain in Mayo county.

He cares not a thraneen[1] what
   Falls to the other pair.

If the devil, that crafty man,
   Can capture my sprightly soul,
My money may go to my children,
   My flesh to the worm in the hole.

My children think more of the money
   That falls to them when I die,
Than a soul that they could not spend,
   A body that none would buy.

And how would the maggots fare
   On a soul too thin to eat
And money too tough to chew?
   They must have my body for meat.

Christ, speared by a fool that was blind,
   Christ, nailed to a naked tree,
Since these three are waiting my end,
   Hang them, oh Christ, all three!


A Grey Eye Weeping
   'Having gone with a poem to Sir Valentine Brown and
gotten from him nothing but denial, rejection and
flat refusal, the poet made these lines extempore.'

That my old mournful heart was pierced in this black
      doom,
That foreign devils have made our land a tomb,
That the sun that was Munster's glory has gone down,
Has made me travel to seek you, Valentine Brown.

That royal Cashel[2] is bare of house and guest,
That Brian's[3] turreted home is the otter's nest,
That the kings of the land have neither land nor
      crown,
Has made me travel to seek you, Valentine Brown.

That the wild deer wanders afar, that it perishes
      now,
That alien ravens croak on the topmost bough,


1. Variation of traneen--a blade of grass; a trifle;
   a bit.
2. Seat of the ancient Kings of Munster.
3. A reference to Brian Boru.

304

That fish are no more in stream or streamlet lit by
    the sun,
Has made me travel to seek you, Valentine Brown.

Dernish away in the west--and her master banned;
Hamburg the refuge of him that has lost his land;
Two old grey eyes that weep; great verse that lacks
    renown,
Have made me travel to seek you, Valentine Brown.
          (From the Irish of Egan O'Rahilly.[4])

'DERMOT O'BYRNE' (ARNOLD BAX)

 A Dublin Ballad - 1916

    O WRITE it up above your hearth
    And troll it out to sun and moon,
    To all true Irishmen on earth
    Arrest and death come late or soon.

    Some boy-o whistled Ninety-eight
    One Sunday night in College Green,
    And such a broth of love and hate
    Was stirred ere Monday morn was late
    As Dublin town had never seen.

    And god-like forces shocked and shook
    Through Irish hearts that lively day,
    And hope it seemed no ill could brook.
    Christ! for that liberty they took
    There was the ancient deuce to pay!

    The deuce in all his bravery,
    His girth and gall grown no whit less,
    He swarmed in from the fatal sea
    With pomp of huge artillery
    And brass and copper haughtiness.

    He cracked up all the town with guns
    That roared loud psalms to fire and death,
    And houses hailed down granite tons
    To smash our wounded underneath.

    And when at last the golden bell
    Of liberty was silenced--then
    He learned to shoot extremely well
    At unarmed Irish gentlemen!

4. Irish poet (1670-1726)

Ah, where were Michael and gold Moll
And Seumas and my drowsy self?
Why did fate blot us from the scroll?
Why were we left upon the shelf,

Fooling with trifles in the dark
When the light struck so wild and hard?
Sure our hearts were as good a mark
For Tommies up before the lark
At rifle practice in the yard!

Well, the last fire is trodden down,
Our dead are rotting fast in lime,
We all can sneak back into town,
Stravague[1] about as in old time,

And stare at gaps of grey and blue
Where Lower Mount Street used to be,
And where flies hum round muck we knew
For Abbey Street and Eden Quay.

And when the devil's made us wise
Each in his own peculiar hell,
With desert hearts and drunken eyes
We're free to sentimentalize
By corners where the martyrs fell.


JAMES JOYCE

Tilly[2]

He travels after a winter sun,
Urging the cattle along a cold red road,
Calling to them, a voice they know,
He drives his beasts above Cabra.

The voice tells them home is warm.
They moo and make brute music with their hoofs.
He drives them with a flowering branch before him,
Smoke pluming their foreheads.


1. To roam about idly.
2. The word "tilly" refers to the number thirteen in a
baker's dozen. In Joyce's collection of poems
<u>Pomes Penyeach</u>, there were thirteen poems, instead
of twelve. The book sold for a shilling.

Boor, bond of the herd,
Tonight stretch full by the fire!
I bleed by the black stream
For my torn bough!


She Weeps Over Rahoon[1]

Rain on Rahoon falls softly, softly falling,
Where my dark lover lies.
Sad is his voice that calls me, sadly calling,
At grey moonrise.

Love, hear thou
How soft, how sad his voice is ever calling,
Ever unanswered and the dark rain falling,
Then as now.

Dark too our hearts, O love, shall lie and cold
As his sad heart has lain
Under the moongrey nettles, the black mould
And muttering rain.


Ecce Puer[2]

Of the dark past
A child is born
With joy and grief
My heart is torn

Calm in his cradle
The living lies.
May love and mercy
Unclose his eyes!


1. Nora Joyce, James Joyce's wife, had had an early
   sweetheart by the name of Michael Bodkin. Joyce
   tried to reveal what he believed to be his wife's
   thoughts of her early love in this poem. Michael
   Bodkin was buried at Oughterard, but Joyce changed
   the location to Rahoon, the Galway cemetery. (cf.
   passage in "The Dead" between Gabriel and Gretta.)
2. Mrs. George Joyce, the wife of Joyce's son George
   (Giorgio), gave birth to a son on February 15, 1932.
   Joyce wrote the poem, "Ecce Puer" (Behold the Boy),
   on the same day.

WILLIAM BUTLER YEATS

The Stolen Child

Where dips the rocky highland
Of Sleuth Wood in the lake,
There lies a leafy island
Where flapping herons wake
The drowsy water-rats;
There we've hid our faery vats,
Full of berries
And of reddest stolen cherries.
Come away, O human child!
To the waters and the wild
With a faery, hand in hand,
For the world's more full of weeping than
    you can understand.

Where the wave of moonlight glosses
The dim grey sands with light,
Far off by furthest Rosses[1]
We foot it all the night,
Weaving olden dances,
Mingling hands and mingling glances
Till the moon has taken flight;
To and fro we leap
And chase the frothy bubbles,
While the world is full of troubles
And is anxious in its sleep.
Come away, O human child!
To the waters and the wild
With a faery, hand in hand,
For the world's more full of weeping than
    you can understand.

Where the wandering water gushes
From  the hills above Glen-Car,
In pools among the rushes
That scarce could bathe a star,
We seek for slumbering trout
And whispering in their ears
Give them unquiet dreams;
Leaning softly out
From ferns that drop their tears
Over the young streams.
Come away, O human child!

1. A geographical reference to Rosses Bay or Rosses
   Point in the northern part of Ireland, County
   Donegal.

308

To the waters and the wild
With a faery, hand in hand,
For the world's more full of weeping than
    you can understand.

Away with us he's going,
The solemn-eyed:
He'll hear no more the lowing
Of the calves on the warm hillside
Or the kettle on the hob
Sing peace into his breast,
Or see the brown mice bob
Round and round the oatmeal-chest.
For he comes, the human child,
To the waters and the wild
With a faery, hand in hand,
From a world more full of weeping than
    he can understand.


The Lake Isle of Innisfree[1]

I will arise and go now, and go to Innisfree,
And a small cabin build there, of clay and wattles
    made:
Nine bean-rows will I have there, a hive for the
    honey-bee,
And live alone in the bee-loud glade.

And I shall have some peace there, for peace comes
    dropping slow,
Dropping from the veils of the morning to where
    the cricket sings;
There midnight's all a glimmer, and noon a purple
    glow,
And evening full of linnet's wings.

I will arise and go now, for always night and day
I hear lake water lapping with low sounds by the
    shore;
While I stand on the roadway or on the pavements
    grey,
I hear it in the deep heart's core.


1. In Sligo County, one of the largest lakes is Lough
   Gill.  In Lough Gill is the island Innisfree, which
   is 5 miles long and 1 1/2 miles wide.

309

## To Ireland in the Coming Times

Know, that I would accounted be
True brother of a company
That sang, to sweeten Ireland's wrong,
Ballad and story, rann[1] and song;
Nor be I any less of them,
Because the red-rose-bordered hem
Of her, whose history began
Before God made the angelic clan,
Trails all about the written page.
When Time began to rant and rage
The measure of her flying feet
Made Ireland's heart begin to beat;
And Time bade all his candles flare
To light a measure here and there;
And may the thoughts of Ireland brood
Upon a measured quietude.

Nor may I less be counted one
With Davis,[2] Mangan,[3] Ferguson,[4]
Because, to him who ponders well,
My rhymes more than their rhyming tell
Of things discovered in the deep,
Where only body's laid asleep.
For the elemental creatures go
About my table to and fro,
That hurry from unmeasured mind
To rant and rage in flood and wind;
Yet he who treads in measured ways
May surely barter gaze for gaze.
Man ever journeys on with them
After the red-rose-bordered hem.
Ah, faeries, dancing under the moon,
A Druid land, a Druid tune!

While still I may, I write for you
The love I lived, the dream I knew.
From our birthday, until we die,
Is but the winking of an eye;
And we, our singing and our love,
What measurer Time has lit above,
And all benighted things that go
About my table to and fro,

1. A verse; strain; stanza.
2. Thomas Osborne Davis.  Irish politician and poet
   (1814-1845).
3. James Clarence Mangan.  Irish poet (1803-1849).
4. Samuel Ferguson.  Irish poet (1810-1886).

Are passing on to where may be,
In truth's consuming ecstasy,
No place for love and dream at all;
For God goes by with white footfall.
I cast my heart into my rhymes,
That you, in the dim coming times,
May know how my heart went with them
After the red-rose-bordered hem.[5]

The Host of the Air[1]

O'Driscoll drove with a song
The wild duck and the drake
From the tall and the tufted reeds
Of the drear Hart Lake.

And he saw how the reeds grew dark
At the coming of night-tide,
And dreamed of the long dim hair
Of Bridget his bride.

He heard while he sang and dreamed
A piper piping away,
And never was piping so sad,
And never was piping so gay.

And he saw young men and young girls
Who danced on a level place,
And Bridget his bride among them,
With a sad and a gay face.

The dancers crowded about him,
And many a sweet thing said,

5. The red rose symbolized for Yeats the realization
that what is idealized involves as much human suffering as does ordinary life. It is a part of
Yeats' romanticism that persisted throughout his
career.
1. The theme is of a mortal woman who leaves her husband to join the Sidhe. Yeats was attracted to the
theme because of his relations with Maud Gonne. In
his Autobiographies he writes: "I could not tell
why Maud Gonne had turned from me unless she had
done so from some vague desire for some impossible
life, for some unwearying excitement like that of
the heroine in my play." (A reference to The Land
of Heart's Desire).

311

And a young man brought him red wine
And a young girl white bread.

But Bridget drew him by the sleeve,
Away from the merry bands,
To old men playing at cards
With a twinkling of ancient hands.

The bread and the wine had a doom,
For these were the host of the air;
He sat and played in a dream
Of her long dim hair.

He played with the merry old men
And thought not of evil chance,
Until one bore Bridget his bride
Away from the merry dance.

He bore her away in his arms,
The handsomest young man there,
And his neck and his breast and his arms
Were drowned in her long dim hair.

O'Driscoll scattered the cards
And out of his dream awoke:
Old men and young men and young girls
Were gone like a drifting smoke;

But he heard high up in the air
A piper piping away,
And never was piping so sad,
And never was piping so gay.


## The Song of Wandering Aengus[1]

I went out to the hazel wood,
Because a fire was in my head,
And cut and peeled a hazel wand,
And hooked a berry to a thread;
And when white moths were on the wing,
And moth-like stars were flickering out,
I dropped the berry in a stream
And caught a little silver trout.


1. In Celtic religion, the Irish Eros, god of love,
youth, and beauty.

312

When I had laid it on the floor
I went to blow the fire aflame,
But something rustled on the floor,
And some one called me by my name:
It had become a glimmering girl
With apple blossom in her hair
Who called me by my name and ran
And faded through the brightening air.

Though I am old with wandering
Through hollow lands and hilly lands,
I will find out where she has gone,
And kiss her lips and take her hands;
And walk among long dappled grass,
And pluck till time and times are done
The silver apples of the moon,
The golden apples of the sun.

Adam's Curse

We sat together at one summer's end,
That beautiful mild woman,[1] your close friend,
And you[2] and I, and talked of poetry.
I said, 'A line will take us hours maybe;
Yet if it does not seem a moment's thought,
Our stitching and unstitching has been naught.

Better go down upon your marrow-bones
And scrub a kitchen pavement, or break stones
Like an old pauper, in all kinds of weather;
For to articulate sweet sounds together
Is to work harder than all these, and yet
Be thought an idler by the noisy set
Of bankers, schoolmasters, and clergymen
The martyrs call the world.'

                              And thereupon
That beautiful mild woman for whose sake
There's many a one shall find out all heartache
On finding that her voice is sweet and low
Replied, 'To be born woman is to know--
Although they do not talk of it at school--
That we must labour to be beautiful.'


1. Kathleen, the sister of Maud Gonne.
2. Maud Gonne.

313

I said, 'It's certain there is no fine thing
Since Adam's fall but needs much labouring.
There have been lovers who thought love should be
So much compounded of high courtesy
That they would sigh and quote with learned looks
Precedents out of beautiful old books;
Yet now it seems an idle trade enough.'

We sat grown quiet at the name of love;
We saw the last embers of daylight die,
And in the trembling blue-green of the sky
A moon, worn as if it had been a shell
Washed by time's waters as they rose and fell
About the stars and broke in days and years.

I had a thought for no one's but your ears:
That you were beautiful, and that I strove
To love you in the old high way of love;
That it had all seemed happy, and yet we'd grown
As weary-hearted as that hollow moon.

## No Second Troy

Why should I blame her[1] that she filled my days
With misery, or that she would of late
Have taught to ignorant men most violent ways,
Or hurled the little streets upon the great,
Had they but courage equal to desire?
What could have made her peaceful with a mind
That nobleness made simple as a fire,
With beauty like a tightened bow, a kind
That is not natural in an age like this,
Being high and solitary and most stern?
Why, what could she have done, being what she is?
Was there another Troy for her to burn?

## September 1913

What need you, being come to sense,
But fumble in a greasy till
And add the halfpence to the pence
And prayer to shivering prayer, until
You have dried the marrow from the bone;
For men were born to pray and save:
Romantic Ireland's dead and gone

1. Maud Gonne.

314

It's with O'Leary[1] in the grave.

Yet they were of a different kind,
The names that stilled your childish play,
They have gone about the world like wind,
But little time had they to pray
For whom the hangman's rope was spun,
And what, God help us, could they save?
Romantic Ireland's dead and gone,
It's with O'Leary in the grave.

Was it for this the wild geese spread
The grey wing upon every tide;
For this that all that blood was shed,
For this Edward Fitzgerald[2] died,
And Robert Emmet and Wolfe Tone,
All that delirium of the brave?
Romantic Ireland's dead and gone,
It's with O'Leary in the grave.

Yet could we turn the years again,
And call those exiles as they were
In all their loneliness and pain,
You'd cry, 'Some woman's yellow hair
Has maddened every mother's son':
They weighed so lightly what they gave.
But let them be, they're dead and gone,
They're with O'Leary in the grave.


The Magi

Now as at all times I can see in the mind's eye,
In their stiff, painted clothes, the pale unsatis-
    fied ones
Appear and disappear in the blue depth of the sky
With all their ancient faces like rain-beaten stones,
And all their helms of silver hovering side by side,
And all their eyes still fixed, hoping to find once
    more,
Being by Calvary's turbulence unsatisfied,
The uncontrollable mystery on the bestial floor.


1. John O'Leary (1830-1907): Fenian leader who was
   imprisoned 1865-1870 and then sent into exile for
   fifteen years.
2. Lord Edward Fitzgerald. Irish revolutionist (1763-
   1798).

The Fisherman

Although I can see him still,
The freckled man who goes
To a grey place on a hill
In grey Connemara clothes
At dawn to cast his flies
It's long since I began
To call up to the eyes
This wise and simple man.
All day I'd looked in the face
What I had hoped 'twould be
To write for my own race
And the reality;
The living men that I hate,
The dead man that I loved,
The craven man in his seat,
The insolent unreproved,
And no knave brought to book
Who has won a drunken cheer,
The witty man and his joke
Aimed at the commonest ear,
The clever man who cries
The catch-cries of the clown,
The beating down of the wise
And great Art beaten down.

Maybe a twelvemonth since
Suddenly I began,
In scorn of this audience,
Imagining a man,
And his sun-freckled face,
And grey Connemara cloth,
Climbing up to a place
Where stone is dark under froth,
And the down-turn of his wrist
When the flies drop in the stream;
A man who does not exist,
A man who is but a dream;
And cried, 'Before I am old
I shall have written him one
Poem maybe as cold
And passionate as the dawn.'

Two Songs of a Fool

> A speckled cat and a tame hare
> Eat at my hearthstone
> And sleep there;
> And both look up to me alone
> For learning and defence
> As I look up to Providence.
>
> I start out of my sleep to think
> Some day I may forget
> Their food and drink;
> Or, the house door left unshut,
> The hare may run till it's found
> The horn's sweet note and the tooth of the
>      hound.
>
> I bear a burden that might well try
> Men that do all by rule,
> And what can I
> That am a wandering-witted fool
> But pray to God that He ease
> My great responsibilities?

II

> I slept on my three-legged stool by the fire,
> The speckled cat slept on my knee;
> We never thought to enquire
> Where the brown hare might be,
> And whether the door were shut.
> Who knows how she drank the wind
> Stretched up on two legs from the mat,
> Before she had settled her mind
> To drum with her heel and to leap?
> Had I but awakened from sleep
> And called her name, she had heard,
> It may be, and had not stirred,
> That now, it may be, has found
> The horn's sweet note and the tooth of the
>      hound.

317

# Easter, 1916[1]

I have met them at close of day
Coming with vivid faces
From counter or desk among grey
Eighteenth-century houses.
I have passed with a nod of the head
Or polite meaningless words,
Or have lingered awhile and said
Polite meaningless words,
And thought before I had done
Of a mocking tale or a gibe
To please a companion
Around the fire at the club,
Being certain that they and I
But lived where motley is worn:
All changed, changed utterly:
A terrible beauty is born.

That woman's[2] days were spent
In ignorant good-will,
Her nights in argument
Until her voice grew shrill.
What voice more sweet than hers
When, young and beautiful,
She rode to harriers?
This man[3] had kept a school
And rode our winged horse;
This other[4] his helper and friend
Was coming into his force;
He might have won fame in the end,
So sensitive his nature seemed,
So daring and sweet his thought.

1. The Sinn Fein was a body of extreme Irish Nationalists which opposed the establishment of the Irish
Free State; the political party of the extreme Re-
publicans. On Easter 1916 the Sinn Fein, expectant
of German aid, attempted to seize Dublin by force
and declared Ireland a republic. The British navy,
however, cut off German support and the rebellion
collapsed. Many of the leaders were arrested and
subsequently shot.
2. Countess Constance Marciewicz, née Gore-Booth.
3. Patrick Pearse (1879-1916): Author, teacher, com-
mander-in-chief of Irish forces in Easter Rebellion.
He was executed after surrender.
4. Thomas MacDonagh (1878-1916): Poet executed for
participation in Easter Rebellion.

This other man[5] I had dreamed
A drunken, vainglorious lout.
He had done most bitter wrong
To some who are near my heart,
Yet I number him in the song;
He, too, has resigned his part
In the casual comedy;
He, too, has been changed in his turn,
Transformed utterly:
A terrible beauty is born.

Hearts with one purpose alone
Through summer and winter seem
Enchanted to a stone
To trouble the living stream.
The horse that comes from the road,
The rider, the birds that range
From cloud to tumbling cloud,
Minute by minute they change;
A shadow of cloud on the stream
Changes minute by minute;
A horse-hoof slides on the brim,
And a horse plashes within it;
The long-legged moor-hens dive,
And hens to moor-cocks call;
Minute by minute they live:
The stone's in the midst of all.

Too long a sacrifice
Can make a stone of the heart.
O when may it suffice?
That is Heaven's part, our part
To murmur name upon name,
As a mother names her child
When sleep at last has come
On limbs that had run wild.
What is it but nightfall?
No, no, not night but death;
Was it needless death after all?
For England may keep faith
For all that is done and said.
We know their dream; enough
To know they dreamed and are dead;
And what if excess of love
Bewildered them till they died?

5. Major John MacBride (d. 1916): Executed for his part
in Easter Rebellion.  Maud Gonne married MacBride
in 1903, and separated from him in 1905.

I write it out in a verse--
MacDonagh and MacBride
And Connolly[6] and Pearse
Now and in time to be,
Wherever green is worn,
Are changed, changed utterly:
A terrible beauty is born.

September 25, 1916

## The Second Coming

Turning and turning in the widening gyre
The falcon cannot hear the falconer;
Things fall apart; the centre cannot hold;
Mere anarchy is loosed upon the world,
The blood-dimmed tide is loosed, and everywhere
The ceremony of innocence is drowned;
The best lack all conviction, while the worst
Are full of passionate intensity.

Surely some revelation is at hand;
Surely the Second Coming is at hand.
The Second Coming! Hardly are those words out
When a vast image out of Spiritus Mundi[1]
Troubles my sight: somewhere in sands of the desert
A shape with lion body and the head of a man,
A gaze blank and pitiless as the sun,
Is moving its slow thighs, while all about it
Reel shadows of the indignant desert birds.
The darkness drops again; but now I know
That twenty centuries of stony sleep
Were vexed to nightmare by a rocking cradle,
And what rough beast, its hour come round at last,
Slouches towards Bethlehem to be born?

## Sailing to Byzantium

### I

That is no country for old men. The young
In one another's arms, birds in the trees,

6. James Connolly (1870-1916):  Marxian commander-in-
   chief of Easter Rebellion.  He was executed for his
   part in the uprising.
1. Spiritus mundi=anima mundi: the soul, life, or vital
   or natural force of the world; the organizing essence, principle, or activity of the physical universe.

--Those dying generations--at their song,
The salmon-falls, the mackerel-crowded seas,
Fish, flesh, or fowl, commend all summer long
Whatever is begotten, born, and dies.
Caught in that sensual music all neglect
Monuments of unageing intellect.

## II

An aged man is but a paltry thing,
A tattered coat upon a stick, unless
Soul clap its hands and sing, and louder sing
For every tatter in its mortal dress,
Nor is there singing school but studying
Monuments of its own magnificence;
And therefore I have sailed the seas and come
To the holy city of Byzantium.

## III

O sages standing in God's holy fire
As in the gold mosaic of a wall,
Come from the holy fire, perne[1] in a gyre,
And be the singing-masters of my soul.
Consume my heart away; sick with desire
And fastened to a dying animal
It knows not what it is; and gather me
Into the artifice of eternity.

## IV

Once out of nature I shall never take
My bodily form from any natural thing,
But such a form as Grecian goldsmiths make
Of hammered gold and gold enamelling
To keep a drowsy Emperor awake;
Or set upon a golden bough to sing
To lords and ladies of Byzantium
Of what is past, or passing, or to come.

1. Reference to a spiralling motion. Perne, (or pirn)
   is literally a spool, reel, or bobbin on which something is wound. Yeats associated the spinning
   motion with the spinning of fate.

Two Songs from a Play

### I

I saw a staring virgin[1] stand
Where holy Dionysus died,
And tear the heart out of his side,
And lay the heart upon her hand
And bear that beating heart away;
And then did all the Muses sing
Of Magnus Annus[2] at the spring,
As though God's death were but a play.

Another Troy must rise and set,
Another lineage feed the crow,
Another Argo's[3] painted prow
Drive to a flashier bauble yet.
The Roman Empire stood appalled:
It dropped the reins of peace and war
When that fierce virgin and her Star[4]
Out of the fabulous darkness called.

### II

In pity for man's darkening thought
He walked that room and issued thence
In Galilean turbulence;
The Babylonian starlight brought
A fabulous, formless darkness in;
Odour of blood when Christ was slain
Made all Platonic tolerance vain
And vain all Doric discipline.

Everything that man esteems
Endures a moment or a day.
Love's pleasure drives his love away,

1. Athena.
2. Great Year.
3. The name of the ship in which the Argonauts sailed
   with Jason in search of the Golden Fleece.
4. The work at this point involves an astrological ana-
   logue by way of Virgil's Fourth Eclogue. Virgil
   prophesies the return of Astraea and her Age of Gold,
   a prophecy long assimilated with Christian tradition
   as the great pagan foretelling of the Christ. At
   the time of divine death and rebirth, a full moon in
   March, the moon stands next to Virgo, which bears
   the star Spica. So Athena, Astraea, Virgo, and Mary
   form a series, with Dionysus and Christ, the beating
   star or heart, as another.

The painter's brush consumes his dreams;
The herald's cry, the soldier's tread
Exhaust his glory and his might:
Whatever flames upon the night
Man's own resinous heart has fed.

## Byzantium

The unpurged images of day recede;
The Emperor's drunken soldiery are abed;
Night resonance recedes, night-walkers' song
After great cathedral[1] gong;
A starlit or a moonlit dome disdains
All that man is,
All mere complexities,
The fury and the mire of human veins.[2]

Before me floats an image, man or shade,
Shade more than man, more image than a shade;
For Hades' bobbin bound in mummy-cloth
May unwind the winding path;
A mouth that has no moisture and no breath
Breathless mouths may summon;
I hail the superhuman;
I call it death-in-life and life-in-death.[3]

Miracle, bird or golden handiwork,
More miracle than bird or handiwork,
Planted on the star-lit golden bough,
Can like the cocks of Hades crow,
Or, by the moon embittered, scorn aloud
In glory of changeless metal
Common bird or petal
And all complexities of mire or blood.[4]

1. Saint Sophia, a famous Christian church in Constantinople, noted for its great central dome. The church was converted into a mosque in 1453.
2. The first three stanzas present three images between the human and superhuman. The first stanza presents the dome of the cathedral rising above human complexities, and transcending them through disdain.
3. The second stanza presents a ghostly image linking the living speaker in the poem to life beyond death.
4. The third stanza relates in its imagery to that found in the last stanza of "Sailing to Byzantium".

At midnight on the Emperor's pavement flit
Flames that no faggot feeds, nor steel has lit,
Nor storm disturbs, flames begotten of flame,
Where blood-begotten spirits come
And all complexities of fury leave,
Dying into a dance,
An agony of trance,
An agony of flame that cannot singe a sleeve.[5]

Astraddle on the dolphin's[6] mire and blood,
Spirit after spirit! The smithies break the flood,
The golden smithies of the Emperor!
Marbles of the dancing floor
Break bitter furies of complexity,
Those images that yet
Fresh images beget,
That dolphin-torn, that gong-tormented sea.[7]


After Long Silence

Speech after long silence; it is right,
All other lovers being estranged or dead,
Unfriendly lamplight hid under its shade,
The curtains drawn upon unfriendly night,
That we descant and yet again descant
Upon the supreme theme of Art and Song:
Bodily decrepitude is wisdom; young
We loved each other and were ignorant.


Crazy Jane Talks with the Bishop

I met the Bishop on the road
And much said he and I.
'Those breasts are flat and fallen now,
Those veins must soon be dry;
Live in a heavenly mansion,
Not in some foul sty.'


5. The fourth stanza symbolically puts before the
   reader the midnight moment of aesthetic transforma-
   tion.
6. Traditionally, the dolphin is depicted as carrying
   the dead on its back to the Isles of the Blessed.
7. The fifth stanza presents the notion of the endless
   life of the body and the emotional context out of
   which the transcendent images of art derive.

'Fair and foul are near of kin,
And fair needs foul,' I cried.
'My friends are gone, but that's a truth
Nor grave nor bed denied,
Learned in bodily lowliness
And in the heart's pride.

'A woman can be proud and stiff
When on love intent;
But Love has pitched his mansion in
The place of excrement;
For nothing can be sole or whole
That has not been rent.'


Crazy Jane on the Mountain

I am tired of cursing the Bishop,
(Said Crazy Jane)
Nine books or nine hats
Would not make him a man.
I have found something worse
To meditate on.
A King had some beautiful cousins,
But where are they gone?
Battered to death in a cellar,
And he stuck to his throne.
Last night I lay on the mountain,
(Said Crazy Jane)
There in a two-horsed carriage
That on two wheels ran
Great-bladdered Emer[1] sat,
Her violent man
Cuchulain sat at her side;
Thereupon,
Propped upon my two knees,
I kissed a stone;
I lay stretched out in the dirt
And I cried tears down.


'I am of Ireland'

'I AM of Ireland,
And the Holy Land of Ireland,
And time runs on,' cried she.


1. Wife of Cuchulain and personification of ideal
womanhood.

'Come out of charity,
Come dance with me in Ireland.'[1]

One man, one man alone
In that outlandish gear,
One solitary man
Of all that rambled there
Had turned his stately head.
"That is a long way off,
And time runs on,' he said,
'And the night grows rough.'

'I am of Ireland,
And the Holy Land of Ireland,
And time runs on,' cried she.
'Come out of charity
And dance with me in Ireland.'

'The fiddlers are all thumbs,
Or the fiddle-string accursed,
The drums and the kettledrums
And the trumpets all are burst,
And the trombone,' cried he,
'The trumpet and trombone,'
And cocked a malicious eye,
'But time runs on, runs on.'

'I am of Ireland,
And the Holy Land of Ireland,
And time runs on,' cried she.
'Come out of charity
And dance with me in Ireland.'


Lapis Lazuli
(For Harry Clifton)

I have heard that hysterical women say
They are sick of the palette and fiddle-bow,
Of poets that are always gay,
For everybody knows or else should know
That if nothing drastic is done
Aeroplane and Zeppelin will come out,


1. The words of the refrain, with the exception of the
   third line, are essentially the same as those of a
   fourteenth century lyric from which it is taken.


326

Pitch like King Billy[1] bomb-balls in
Until the town lie beaten flat.

All perform their tragic play,
There struts Hamlet, there is Lear,
That's Ophelia, that Cordelia;
Yet they, should the last scene be there,
The great stage curtain about to drop,
If worthy their prominent part in the play,
Do not break up their lines to weep.
They know that Hamlet and Lear are gay;
Gaiety transfiguring all that dread.
All men have aimed at, found and lost;
Black out; Heaven blazing into the head:
Tragedy wrought to its uttermost.
Though Hamlet rambles and Lear rages,
And all the drop-scenes drop at once
Upon a hundred thousand stages,
It cannot grow by an inch or an ounce.

On their own feet they came, or on shipboard,
Camel-back, horse-back, ass-back, mule-back,
Old civilisations put to the sword.
Then they and their wisdom went to rack:
No handiwork of Callimachus,[2]
Who handled marble as if it were bronze,
Made draperies that seemed to rise
When sea-wind swept the corner, stands;
His long lamp-chimney shaped like the stem
Of a slender palm, stood but a day;
All things fall and are built again,
And those that build them again are gay.

Two Chinamen, behind them a third,
Are carved in lapis lazuli,
Over them flies a long-legged bird,
A symbol of longevity;
The third, doubtless a serving-man,
Carries a musical instrument.

Every discoloration of the stone,
Every accidental crack or dent,
Seems a water-course or an avalanche,

1. King William III (William of Orange), who defeated
   the army of King James II at the Battle of Boyne
   in 1690.
2. Greek sculptor, of late 5th century B.C.; reputed
   inventor of the Corinthian column, and first to use
   the running drill in carving folds in drapery, etc.

Or lofty slope where it still snows
Though doubtless plum or cherry-branch
Sweetens the little half-way house
Those Chinamen climb towards, and I
Delight to imagine them seated there;
There, on the mountain and the sky,
On all the tragic scene they stare.
One asks for mournful melodies;
Accomplished fingers begin to play.
Their eyes mid many wrinkles, their eyes,
Their ancient, glittering eyes, are gay.

The Circus Animals' Desertion

I

I sought a theme and sought for it in vain,
I sought it daily for six weeks or so.
Maybe at last, being but a broken man,
I must be satisfied with my heart, although
Winter and summer till old age began
My circus animals were all on show,
Those stilted boys,[1] that burnished chariot,
Lion and woman and the Lord knows what.

II

What can I but enumerate old themes?
First that sea-rider Oisin led by the nose
Through three enchanted islands, allegorical dreams,
Vain gaiety, vain battle, vain repose,
Themes of the embittered heart, or so it seems,
That might adorn old songs or courtly shows;
But what cared I that set him on to ride,
I, starved for the bosom of his faery bride?

And then a counter-truth filled out its play,
The Countess Cathleen[2] was the name I gave it;
She, pity-crazed, had given her soul away,
But masterful Heaven had intervened to save it.
I thought my dear[3] must her own soul destroy,
So did fanaticism and hate enslave it,
And this brought forth a dream and soon enough
This dream itself had all my thought and love.

1. Figures out of the Celtic legendary past, such as
   Oisin and Fergus; also involves Yeats' poem, The
   Wanderings of Oisin.
2. A play by Yeats written for Maud Gonne.
3. Maud Gonne.

328

And when the Fool and Blind Man[4] stole the bread
Cuchulain fought the ungovernable sea;
Heart-mysteries there, and yet when all is said
It was the dream itself enchanted me:
Character isolated by a deed
To engross the present and dominate memory.
Players and painted stage took all my love,
And not those things that they were emblems of.

### III

Those masterful images because complete
Grew in pure mind, but out of what began?
A mound of refuse or the sweepings of a street,
Old kettles, old bottles, and a broken can,
Old iron, old bones, old rags, that raving slut
Who keeps the till. Now that my ladder's gone,
I must lie down where all the ladders start,
In the foul rag-and-bone shop of the heart.


Under Ben Bulben[1]

### I

Swear by what the sages spoke
Round the Mareotic Lake[2]
That the Witch of Atlas[3] knew,
Spoke and set the cocks a-crow.

Swear by those horsemen, by those women
Complexion and form prove superhuman,
That pale, long-visaged company
That air in immortality
Completeness of their passions won;
Now they ride the wintry dawn
Where Ben Bulben sets the scene.

Here's the gist of what they mean.


4. Two characters out of the play On Baile's Strand,
   by Yeats.
1. A mountain in Sligo County.
2. A salt lagoon south of Alexandria, Egypt.
3. A mythological narrative by P. B. Shelley written
   in 1820; the Witch of Atlas symbolizes the beauty
   of wisdom.

## II

Many times man lives and dies
Between his two eternities,
That of race and that of soul,
And ancient Ireland knew it all.
Whether man die in his bed
Or the rifle knocks him dead,
A brief parting from those dear
Is the worst man has to fear.
Though grave-diggers' toil is long,
Sharp their spades, their muscles strong,
They but thrust their buried men
Back in the human mind again.

## III

You that Mitchel's[4] prayer have heard,
'Send war in our time, O Lord!'
Know that when all words are said
And a man is fighting mad,
Something drops from eyes long blind,
He completes his partial mind,
For an instant stands at ease,
Laughs aloud, his heart at peace.
Even the wisest man grows tense
With some sort of violence
Before he can accomplish fate,
Know his work or choose his mate.

## IV

Poet and sculptor, do the work,
Nor let the modish painter shirk
What his great forefathers did,
Bring the soul of man to God.
Make him fill the cradles right.

Measurement began our might:
Forms a stark Egyptian thought,
Forms that gentler Phidias wrought.
Michael Angelo left a proof
On the Sistine Chapel roof,
Where but half-awakened Adam
Can disturb globe-trotting Madam
Till her bowels are in heat,
Proof that there's a purpose set

4. John Mitchel (1815-1875?): Founder of United Irishmen.

Before the secret working mind:
Profane perfection of mankind.

Quattrocento[5] put in paint
On backgrounds for a God or Saint
Gardens where a soul's at ease;
Where everything that meets the eye,
Flowers and grass and cloudless sky,
Resemble forms that are or seem
When sleepers wake and yet still dream,
And when it's vanished still declare,
With only bed and bedstead there,
That heavens had opened.
                Gyres run on;
When that greater dream had gone
Calvert[6] and Wilson,[7] Blake[8] and Claude,[9]
Prepared a rest for the people of God,
Palmer's[10] phrase, but after that
Confusion fell upon our thought.

V

Irish poets, learn your trade,
Sing whatever is well made,
Scorn the sort now growing up
All out of shape from toe to top,
Their unremembering hearts and heads
Base-born products of base beds.
Sing the peasantry, and then
Hard-riding country gentlemen,
The holiness of monks, and after
Porter-drinkers' randy laughter;
Sing the lords and ladies gay
That were beaten into the clay
Through seven heroic centuries;
Cast your mind on other days
That we in coming days may be
Still the indomitable Irishry.

5. The fifteenth century when applied to Italian art
   or literature.
6. Denis Calvert (1540-1619):  Flemish painter who was
   the founder of the Bolognese school.
7. Richard Wilson (1714-1782):  Landscape painter.
8. William Blake (1757-1827):  English poet.
9. Claude Lorraine (1600-1682):  Landscape painter.
10. Samuel Palmer (1805-1881):  English painter and
    etcher.

Under bare Ben Bulben's head
In Drumcliff churchyard Yeats is laid.
An ancestor was rector there
Long years ago, a church stands near,
By the road an ancient cross.
No marble, no conventional phrase;
On limestone quarried near the spot
By his command these words are cut:

> Cast a cold eye
> On life, on death.
> Horseman, pass by!

September 4, 1938